THE ISTHMUS ROUTE

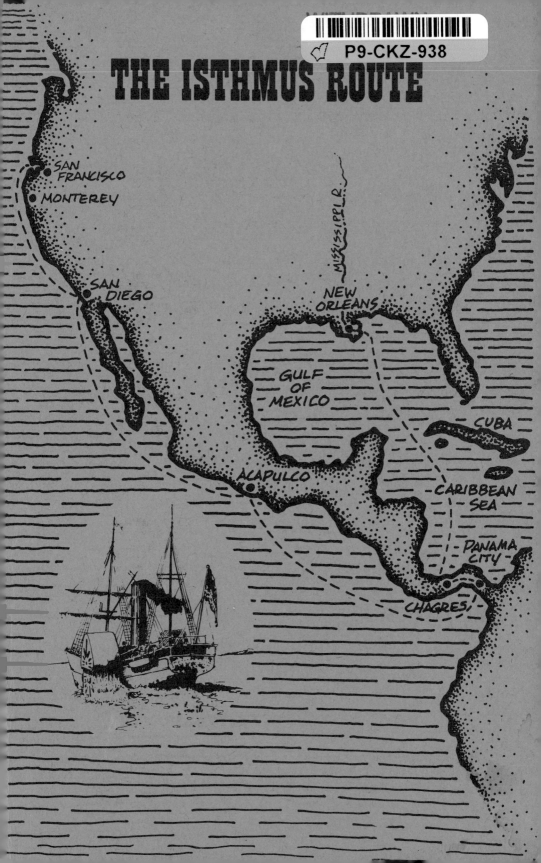

················ # The Argonauts

The Argonauts

* *

Yvonne Schoell

* *

PRENTICE-HALL, INC.
Englewood Cliffs, New Jersey

The Argonauts by Yvonne Schoell
Copyright © 1972 by Yvonne Schoell
Copyright under International and Pan American
Copyright Conventions
Printed in the United States of America *T*
Prentice-Hall International, Inc., London
Prentice-Hall of Australia, Pty. Ltd., North Sydney
Prentice-Hall of Canada, Ltd., Toronto
Prentice-Hall of India Private Ltd., New Delhi
Prentice-Hall of Japan, Inc., Tokyo

Library of Congress Cataloging in Publication Data

Schoell, Yvonne, date
  The Argonauts.

    1. California—History—1846-1850—Fiction.
I. Title.
PZ4.S362Ar [PS3569.C5234] 813′.5′4 72-4486
ISBN 0-13-045872-4

To my husband

EDWIN SCHOELL

*Whose willing help was
and always has been there*

I would like to thank Editor Nancy M. Roodenburg for her unflagging enthusiasm and invaluable assistance in preparing the manuscript for publication

The California Emigrant
to
"Oh, Susannah"
(Jonathan Nichols' version)

Like Argonauts of ancient times,
I'll leave this modern Greece,
I'm bound to California mines,
To find the golden fleece.
For who would work from morn to night
And live on hog and corn,
When one can pick up there at sight
Enough to buy a farm.

Chorus
O California! That's the land for me
I'm going to Californ-i-a the gold dust for to see.

There from the snowy mountain side,
Comes down the golden sand,
And spreads a carpet far and wide
O'er all the shining land:
The rivers run on golden beds,
O'er rocks of golden ore,
The valleys six feet deep are said
To hold a plenty more.

Chorus

I'll take my washbowl in my hand
And thither wind my way,
To wash the gold from out the sand
In Californ-i-a.
And when I get my pocket full,
In that bright land of gold
I'll have a rich and happy time;
Live merry till I'm old.

Chorus

CONTENTS

PART ONE

**OVER THE PLAINS,
ACROSS THE ISTHMUS,
ROUND THE HORN,
THEY CAME**

PART TWO

CALIFORNIA, THE GOLDEN LAND

AUTHOR'S NOTE

Six years ago when I first began my research into the California gold rush period, I realized that all too few of us really are aware of the life of that exciting time of our American past. A romantic story of these argonauts came out of it, a tale of those who were lured across a continent in answer to the call of adventure and the hope of a new life. *The Argonauts* recreates as authentically as possible the days of 1849 so that the modern reader may live with the people of that time as familiarly as with his family and friends in present day society. In so far as reference works, diaries, accounts and documents permitted, a historically accurate representation has been made of the details of the journeys along the three main routes taken to the gold fields and the particulars of pioneer life in California. The reference material furnished authentic background for the fictional characters. It also provided insights into the language, manners and customs of the Americans who migrated to the West in that time and made it possible for the United States to become a nation stretching from sea to sea.

Pines reach their full growth high on mountaintops;
Men tell the story, how the mountain pine
Could ever come to toss on fleeting waves.
Young men—the pick, and reckless young bloods all—
They swore they'd win the Golden Fleece away
From Colchis, even run their reckless race
Across a briny vastness after it
Aboard a ship, and sweep the sky-blue sea
With feathered fir: aboard the first ship ever
To dye the untried sea within her wake.
Her prow cut on, on through the wind-swept sea
To send white wave-sheen twisting past the oars
Until the very mermaids rode the swirl
Up from their depths to marvel, wild-eyed, white
With fear to see the Argo and her men.
Heroes they were, born in a hallowed age!
I hail a race of gods and not of men,
And cannot help but hail them, even now. . . .

Catullus LXIV, 1-23 (abridged)

tr. A. P. MacGregor
K. M. MacGregor
Indiana University

PART ONE

★★★★★★★★★★★★★★★★★★★★★★★★★★★★★★★★★★★

OVER THE PLAINS,
ACROSS THE ISTHMUS,
ROUND THE HORN,
THEY CAME

CHAPTER 1 INDIANA

Goldie Baxter sang happily as she pumped water into the sturdy tin-lined wooden sink. The kitchen, large and cheery, served well the needs of the few travelers and many permanent guests who stayed at the green-shuttered inn by the Wabash River. Long work tables set out with mixing bowls and huge cooking utensils ranged down its length. The fire burned low in the cast-iron cook stove along the wall; the smell of bacon still lingered in the air. Breakfast was over, and Goldie was washing the dishes.

This was the last morning she would be performing this chore, she thought with satisfaction. A new world was about to open up, and though it might hold many hardships, she did not imagine it would include washing hundreds of dishes over and over again. Tomorrow morning she and her brother, Gray, would join the other passengers on Big Timbers' canal boat to ride down the Wabash to Vincennes. Although she had spent all of her fifteen years in the State of Indiana, she had never been to the old Northwest territorial capital. Now she was so aglow with anticipation that she never imagined she might sometime look back with longing to the inn owned by her Uncle Bob and Aunt Opal.

Suddenly pensive, she thought back to her mother. She remembered her long wavy black hair and how the blue lights flashed out when the sun struck it. Goldie had always wanted hair like that instead of her own red gold color. She sighed as she reflected that the only thing her hair had in common with her mother's was the curl. A wave of longing for her mother swept over her. Along with it a cold shiver went down her spine, and excitement became tinged with fear. She looked about the kitchen. After today she wouldn't be here to see it. Quickly she turned back toward the sink, her eyes painfully misting. Yes, tomorrow she would leave forever Aunt Opal and Uncle Bob and the only home she had known since the death of her mother and father five years ago.

Glancing out the window into the cold March morning, she saw Gray in the woodyard energetically chopping logs into lengths

3

suitable for the hulking black kitchen stove and the many fireplaces. The morning sun glinting through the tall hickory trees revealed that her brother had shining copper-colored hair like hers. He was seventeen and also full of thoughts of the adventure lying ahead of them.

Seeking gold in California—he had been burning to go all winter. And now at last he *was* going and Goldie would accompany him. At first he had resented her injecting herself into what he considered essentially a man's adventure. But they had always shared their world, and somehow, even though Aunt Opal and Uncle Bob had been good to them for the last five years, he felt that Goldie and he belonged together. He paused in his work a moment to cast his eyes into the barn where sat the bright blue Conestoga wagon with its painted red wheels. Early tomorrow morning, they would load it on Big Timbers' boat to begin the first lap of their long journey. At Vincennes they would leave Big Timbers and for the first time in their lives would be on their own as they crossed Illinois to St. Louis where they would board one of the big floating palaces Big Timbers had told them about to ride up the Missouri. Everything was ready. Gray smiled as the ax bit deep into the wood and made the chips fly through the brisk morning air.

"Goldie Baxter, what do you mean just moonin' and idlin' with your hands in the water? Busy hands make no mischief. Remember, you're no fine lady in that California yet!" Aunt Opal's sharply nasal voice brought Goldie back to the reality of the big kitchen. She jumped and quickly began racking the breakfast plates on the long wooden drainboard. She had often marveled that her aunt and mother had been sisters. Opal was tight-lipped—"straight-laced" was the word for her, Goldie thought. She wore her dark hair parted in the middle and pulled straight back into a bun at the nape of her neck. Aunt Opal had long been frustrated by Goldie's curly hair, which refused to adapt itself to this severe treatment and now tumbled in a riot of waves and curls well below her shoulders. The startling color of their hair and the tall, lean bodies of these two children of her dead sister puzzled Opal. Nobody in her family had ever looked like them. "It must be the Baxter blood," she said dolefully to her husband on many occasions.

Like his two children, Jeremiah Baxter had been tall and lean. He and his wife had been termed a handsome couple in Fountain

4

County. They had loved life and each other. But stricken with fever five springs before this, they had died within a few days of each other, leaving Goldie and Gray, then ten and twelve, orphans. Ever since their parents' death, Uncle Bob had operated Jeremiah Baxter's farm for his niece and nephew, besides running his own Downey Inn. And when Goldie and Gray decided to make their life in the West, he had agreed to buy the farm from them. With the down payment they had bought their wagon and the necessities for the journey.

"I can't understand why you want to go way off there where you don't know anybody," sniffed Aunt Opal as Goldie finished the dishes. "You had a perfectly good farm here, and when you came of age you'd have had a nice start. I guess I don't understand you two." She gave the bread dough she was mixing a thump.

"We'll write often," said Goldie.

"Humph!" retorted her aunt. "You'd better start peeling the potatoes for dinner."

"I don't think I want to run an inn," said Goldie. "Too many potatoes."

"You could do worse," frowned Opal. "It's good honest work."

After preparing the vegetables for dinner and setting the bread to rise, Opal and Goldie, together with the hired girl, Hilda, scurried around the inn with brooms and dust pans cleaning the guests' rooms and making the beds.

Outdoors, Uncle Bob and Gray were putting the seed corn in the south field. By twelve-thirty they had finished plowing, and Gray glanced around at the rich land. It was just beginning to shake off winter. In the distance he saw the tall trees lining the Wabash, the river that would start him toward his destiny. He loved this country about him, he thought, and at once wondered why he felt so irresistible a pull to move on.

On the way to the inn for the noon dinner, Bob cautioned Gray about the people he would meet. "I would hate to see you become mean and stingy," he said. "But don't fall for every hard luck tale you hear. You've got a generous nature—kind of like your pa. Everybody liked your pa, but he wasn't a savin' man."

"I'll be careful, Uncle Bob," Gray grinned.

They put the team in the barn and had just finished washing up in the outside trough when Opal rang the dinner bell. Soon the dishes were being sent up and down the long trestle table, bright with a snowy cloth. In addition to hominy and potatoes, there were bowls of home-canned string beans and breaded tomatoes, large platters of fried chicken and crisp batter-fried perch from the river, and hot flaky biscuits, with plenty of butter and blackberry jam. This was accompanied by homemade dill and bread-and-butter pickles, huge pitchers of fresh milk, and steaming mugs of hot coffee and tea. When all of the dishes had been emptied by the hungry boarders, Opal, Goldie, and the hired girl appeared with huge wedges of apple and cherry pie.

About three o'clock that afternoon Goldie heard sleigh bells jingling down on the river. As if summoned by some magic call, she grabbed her brown cloak and started to run toward the sound, hoisting up her full skirts and displaying her long legs in white pantaloons.

The sound of the sleigh bells signaled that Big Timbers was bringing his barge to the dock. He was scarcely in when Gray leaped aboard and flung his arms around the bear-like man's neck. And before he righted himself another whirlwind assailed him in the form of Goldie.

The Baxters hadn't seen their old friend for some time, although messages sent up the river had told Big Timbers of their intentions. It was quite obvious by the affection that Gray and Goldie displayed for the big man that it was he who had supplanted their lost father and mother in their hearts. Big Timbers brought the lonely children candy and little gifts. But much more important, he listened to their dreams and encouraged them.

"So you're going to fly the nest?" he boomed. "Is it tired you are of waiting for me to marry you?" Goldie blushed. Big Timbers, sensitive to all about him, said, "Oh ho, so we are beginning to grow up!" He smiled, and a twinkle came into his blue eyes. "Maybe I didn't bring the right gift for a young lady." As he spoke, he reached deftly behind him and brought out a beautiful pair of deerskin moccasins.

"Oh, Big Timbers," Goldie cried in delight, "they're just lovely!"

"And I didn't forget my lad, either," said the giant as he produced a matching pair for Gray. "I think you'll find they'll come in handy when you get in the mountain country."

The next morning everyone traveling with Big Timbers was up

and moving about the inn before dawn. A fire was roaring in the cookstove, where Opal was busy slicing golden corn meal mush onto the sizzling black griddle. In the dining room where the traveling party was assembled the table was laid with large pitchers of blackberry syrup and plates of freshly churned butter. Scarcely aware in their excitement of the good-tasting food, Goldie and Gray attacked their huge portions of fried mush and country-cured ham with the hearty appetites of youth. In the wearing months ahead they would recall this sumptuous breakfast with longing, but now they simply accepted good and plentiful food as part of their inalienable rights.

After breakfast they and the three other passengers trooped down to Big Timbers' boat, *Annabelle*. Almost everyone who had known the Baxters was at the landing to see them off. Neighbors and boys and girls with whom they had grown up stood on the still winter-locked banks of the river to wish them well and press useless but treasured keepsakes on them. Looking at the weak sunlight filtering through an overcast sky on the dark undressed branches of the trees, Gray felt a lump rise in his throat. He was poignantly aware that he was giving up the security of the familiar and the acceptance of friends for the hazards of the unknown and the suspicions of strangers. He flung his arms around Aunt Opal and kissed her. At this, Opal hastily turned her back and surreptitiously lifted the corner of her neat apron to dab at her eyes. Then she briskly said, "Now mind, don't trust everybody you meet. There are all kinds out there. And you eat proper, you hear? You're too skinny. . .always have been!"

Goldie too felt a twinge of fear mixed with her excitement as she kissed her aunt and uncle goodbye.

"Do the washing regular," Opal admonished.

"I will," promised Goldie and hastily followed Gray onto the boat. As the current caught the *Annabelle* it rapidly drew away from the dock and pulled to the south. Soon Goldie and Gray could no longer see the dock clearly, but they strained, looking back, until the boat rounded a bend.

"Oh ho, there," boomed Big Timbers, alert to their feelings. "I need a couple of scouts for snags. You never know what the spring thaw might send down." Nor was Big Timbers supplying useless occupation. The river was high, full of logs and debris.

At noon they tied up at the bank for their midday meal. As

7

they were finishing, a small gray and white apparition emerged from the Conestoga wagon tied on the boat and with a wide yawn jumped gracefully to the deck and stalked elegantly down the plank to the shore. Gray stared at the intruder in dumbfounded surprise, then turned to Goldie. "What's Matilda doing here?" he spluttered. "She'll just have to go back."

"Now, don't be too hasty, lad," interjected Big Timbers as he picked up the small, dumpy feline in his big hands. "This may be providential. Not only that——" The big man looked at Matilda more closely. "Well, if this isn't luck," he chuckled. "She's pregnant. You can sell her kittens at one of the forts along the way. They're crying for cats out West. Rats and mice are eating up the feed and grain."

Goldie reached up and took the small bundle of loudly purring fur in her arms. "Besides, she's my cat, Gray, and I want her!"

"All right, but remember, *you* take care of her," grinned Gray as he stroked Matilda's white chin.

"Don't I always?" retorted Goldie.

Three more days of travel on the river brought the *Annabelle* and its passengers to Vincennes.

For her first visit to the old Northwest territorial capital, Goldie had put on her brown merino suit trimmed with rust-colored ruching, and had tied a little brown velvet bonnet over her copper curls.

"Is that the kind of outfit to wear when you're going to buy some mules?" asked Gray as he stood in his jeans and leather coat, hands on hips.

"Oh, let her have her fun," said Big Timbers. "She won't have much chance to dress up once you hit the trail."

"She's got to handle the team, too," grumbled Gray. "And I don't think we should buy anything until she sees if she can."

"Lookee here, son," cautioned Big Timbers. "You can't just barge into the livery stable and say you want six mules like that!" He clapped his hands for emphasis. "You gotta kind of feel your way around. Don't appear to be anxious or in a hurry."

"All right," said Gray. "But I don't want to take a lot of time. You wouldn't want us to get to California too late, would you?"

At the livery stable the noncommittal Big Timbers, followed closely and imitated by Gray, wandered among the mules, touching their flanks, occasionally lifting a hoof or peering into a startled mouth. Finally Big Timbers noted a sagging-looking pair and turned sharply to the proprietor. "How much for that span there?" he asked.

Gray visibly shuddered and began to doubt that Big Timbers knew much about anything except riverboats. The pair of mules stood with their heads down, their thin flanks heaving. Even the proprietor seemed embarrassed as he stammered an outrageous price of fifty dollars.

Big Timbers was no longer casual. He wheeled to face the man, his eyes glinting. Like lightning one big hand shot out and grabbed the huckster by his lapels. "Everywhere I went in this town and asked where I could find an honest livery stable I was told, 'Go to McCullough's, McCullough's will give you an honest price.' Well, here I am at McCullough's!" Putting his bewhiskered face close to the liveryman's, Big Timbers said more softly, "Now, you know and I know those mules ain't worth a dollar." Suddenly he wheeled and pointed to another span. "How much for them?"

McCullough's Adam's apple began to bounce up and down furiously until he ejected in a strangled whisper, "Ten. . .dollars. . . apiece."

"I'll give you fifteen dollars a pair for three pair," said Big Timbers. "My choice. Do you want to do business?"

"Yes. . .yes sir," stuttered McCullough. "Fifteen dollars a pair it is." Having recovered his composure somewhat, he walked over to another pair and said, "these is good workers. Wanta try them?"

"Gray!" bellowed Big Timbers, as though Gray were halfway across town instead of right behind him. "Better take this pair out and try them. Hard-mouthed, I betcha. . . .Gotta watch that!"

Gray, still standing dumbfounded, didn't respond fast enough to suit the big man. "Come on, boy," urged Big Timbers again. "Snap to it! Go try this team of mules!"

"Yes, sir," replied Gray. He hastened to bridle the pair in preparation for a trial handling on the flat land east of the livery stable. He soon had readied the animals and was off on a wild run across the prairie to the accompaniment of the hoots and hollers of several town buffs perched on the corral fence. At one point in his mad dash with the hard-mouthed mules, he fell down and was dragged. Gamely he refused to let loose of the reins.

Goldie was furious at the callous laughter of the men lining the fence. "Anybody can laugh!" she shouted at them. "Why

9

don't you try it and see how well you do?"

The men paid no attention to her, so she flounced back to the stable and began bridling a pair of mules for herself.

"Goldie Baxter, what are you doing?" demanded Big Timbers.

"I'll give them something to really laugh at," Goldie hissed through clenched teeth.

"You want to make a fool of yourself and ruin your new dress besides?"

"I'm going to drive this team of mules!"

"Well, let's at least hitch them to a wagon then."

"I hate for people to laugh at Gray," fumed Goldie, her eyes glistening with tears.

"He has to learn to handle those mules. He has to master them, and so do you. You can't afford to lose your animals where you're going. Now, we'll hitch these two to a wagon and go out and pick up Gray. And then we'll find another pair and see if we can make them all pull together." He handed Goldie a big red bandana. "Remember," he added, "people's laughing doesn't matter. What matters is what you do."

When Goldie and Big Timbers reached Gray and his recalcitrant team, the tyro had them responding to his rein as well as his "gee" and "haw." And by the time the afternoon sun was setting, the youngsters had a working six-mule team that both could handle despite blisters on their hands and a new soreness in their arms. As they returned to the stable in the waning light, Big Timbers pronounced them ready for the long trek to California.

That night, when Big Timbers heard Goldie's even breathing, he whispered to Gray to come out on deck. Gray was glad of the opportunity to talk, for tomorrow he and Goldie would be on their own. At seventeen he would have to assume the full responsibility of being a man, and he was more than a little afraid that he might not be equal to it. But Big Timbers had Goldie's welfare on his mind.

"Did your uncle ever have a talk with you about men and women?" he began gruffly.

"Well, yes, some," said Gray.

"Did he say anything about how men might feel about young girls like your sister?" Big Timbers continued.

"Well, not exactly," hedged Gray.

"Do you or do you not know what you have to do?" Big Timbers' tone was exasperated.

"I'm not sure," fumbled Gray.

"Well, I'll be——" Big Timbers was silent for a moment before continuing. "Some men are going to have only one thing on their minds when they see this ripe peach of a girl. She's been sheltered and won't suspect what it is. She'll think they're trying to be friendly. You're going to have to be able to sort the good apples from the bad ones, just like you did at home in the root cellar. Only these ain't going to be apples. . .they're going to be men."

"Gee whiz," said Gray. "We've been working in an inn for five years, haven't we? After all, we have seen a *few* types of people, you know."

"I know, boy," soothed Big Timbers. "But remember you and Goldie are going to be all alone. People may try to take advantage of you because you're young and green. You're going to have to protect your sister, and it may be hard sometimes. Now go on back and get your sleep. You'll need it for the morrow."

"Get my sleep indeed!" fumed Gray to himself as he climbed back in the wagon. He looked over at his sleeping sister almost with disgust. "Why did she have to come along anyway?" he began to wonder. He was sick and tired of everyone telling him he had to look out for her. He was ashamed of his feelings but could do nothing to overcome them. He fell into a troubled sleep.

CHAPTER 2 ACROSS ILLINOIS
AND UP THE MISSOURI★★★★★★★★★★★★★★★★★★★★★★★

After breakfast the next morning, Big Timbers untied the *Annabelle* and transported his young passengers and their cargo to the Illinois side of the stream, where a dirt track led off through the trees toward the Mississippi River and St. Louis. The early sunshine, which had promised a bright spring day, had disappeared

11

in heavy gray clouds by the time they had the wagon safely ashore. Goldie looked apprehensively at the dirt road which she knew could easily turn into writhing mud.

"Now remember," said Big Timbers, "just follow the main road through due west. It ain't as good as the National Road, but it's a heap shorter. You should be in St. Louis in five days. You can test how sturdy your mules are on this haul. If they're good workers and ain't too ugly in disposition, take 'em up the Missouri with you to Independence. If you find a bad one, though, sell him in St. Louis and get a replacement at Independence."

"We won't need any replacement for Ring, Tom, Diddy, or Do, Re, Me," said Goldie, patting the lead mule. "They're going to be just fine. They're going all the way with Gray and Matilda and me."

"Well, I'll be," laughed Big Timbers. "I never heard such names for mules afore. Come give your old friend a kiss, my lass. Then up on the wagon with you." Goldie clung to Big Timbers a moment, then whispered a strangled "Goodbye" as her old protector easily swung her up on the seat. Gray grabbed the reins and with a "Giddap" drove the big wagon into the curtain of trees.

As they plodded along the level road, an oppressive loneliness descended upon them. In this sparsely settled area they strained but did not hear the longed-for sounds of other human beings. They took turns handling the mules, and occasionally one or the other would get out and walk alongside to warm their numbed feet and escape the jolting of the wagon over the ruts. When they passed through wooded areas, the heavy gray of the sky seemed to press even closer against the naked branches of the bleak trees.

For their nooning they ate a cold meal of beef and bread and butter. As the heavy bread stuck in her throat, Goldie began to wonder about her romantic notions of this great adventure. The cold was penetrating, and the stillness only served to enhance her forebodings. She dreaded the rain that she felt sure must fall soon.

As the afternoon wore on and small talk became more difficult, they no longer made any attempt to cheer each other up. They were aching, tired, and miserable. A sharpness crept into their voices as each lurch of the wagon became more unbearable than the last.

"I don't see why we had to come this way," complained Goldie. "The road is just terrible. Why didn't we take the National Road?"

"Big Timbers said we'd get to St. Louis sooner on this road," reminded Gray.

"There isn't even any place to camp for the night," protested Goldie. "And it's getting darker by the minute."

"We don't want to stop yet," said Gray crossly as he hauled out his father's gold watch to check the time. "It's only four o'clock."

"Well, we ought to start looking. We do need water, you know."

"Oh, stop complaining!" said Gray. "Just stop complaining!" They both lapsed into a hostile silence.

About an hour later Goldie spied a clump of willows to the right of the road and knew that meant water nearby. To reinforce her opinion, she noticed that the land to the left had been tilled, and she also spotted a log cabin back some distance from the road. "Look, Gray," she said, "I'll bet that's a nice place to camp. I'll bet there's water there, too."

"It doesn't look like much to me," countered Gray, not at all willing to relinquish his dark mood. Nevertheless, he turned the wagon toward the trees. As they drew up in a small clearing in the center, they saw a clear bubbling spring.

"I guess it'll do," said Gray grudgingly as he climbed stiffly down from the wagon seat and began to unhitch the mules. There was no pasture here for the animals, so they would be forced to feed them from the precious supply of grain purchased in Vincennes. He fed them, then went to look for some firewood.

Matilda hopped down and sauntered over to the spring. After daintily lapping at the edge of the water, she strolled back to Goldie, and by mewing and rubbing against her, indicated that so far as she was concerned it was dinnertime. But Goldie had other things on her mind, for rain was now falling. She piled some stones together to form a fire pit on which to place her cooking surface of cast sheet iron. As the rain increased, she finally got one of the heavy tarpaulins from inside the wagon and wrapped it around her head and body Indian style. She set to work making the corn meal into cakes and dipping water from the spring for her iron kettle of salt beef and potatoes. By this time it was raining steadily. But she was able to start a fire with brush and small pieces of wood she found nearby. As she fed the fire, which was protected by the stones and the cast iron, her kettle began to boil, and soon the savory smell of meat and potatoes began to raise her spirits.

Just then a medium-size short-haired black dog with floppy ears and a wagging tail splashed out of the woods. Matilda took one look at the intruder and immediately climbed up the tarp to the top of Goldie's head, while the dog raced around her barking friendly greetings. A sodden but exuberant Gray followed, his arms full of logs and his short ax swinging from his belt.

"Look what I found!" he cried with obvious pleasure. "Isn't he great?" He dumped his logs by the fire. "He came up to me while I was chopping the wood. I think maybe he's a stray."

"Oh, no you don't!" yelled Goldie, picking Matilda off her head. "There's a farm over there." She waved her arm across the road. "I'll bet he belongs to them."

"I suppose you're right," said Gray dejectedly. "But he doesn't act like he belongs to anyone. He came right up to me."

"Oh, Gray," scolded Goldie. "You know all dogs do that with you."

"I'd sure like to keep him," said Gray.

"Watch out! Keep him away from my stew!" shouted Goldie. Despite the heat of the fire, the hungry animal was attempting to get at the pot. "You'd better give him some of the dried meat."

Their supper was consumed in heavy silence, and afterwards they both unhappily prepared for bed in the cold damp wagon.

After she had tucked herself in, Goldie called, "Gray."

"Yes," came the muffled answer.

"You can bring him in if you want to."

"What's the use? You're right, he probably belongs to the people at the farm."

"You could have him for tonight anyway."

"Oh, all right. Just to shut you up if nothing else! Come on, boy," he called to the dog standing forlornly outside looking up at the wagon. With a bound the dog was inside, leaping about and trying to lick Gray's face.

"His feet!" screeched Goldie. "Wipe his feet!"

"I'm trying to! Come on, boy. Lie down. There."

With the first light of dawn, both animals began to move about. Gray, who did not like greeting any new day, at first muttered sleepily for the dog to go away, then finally sat up and shouted, awakening Goldie.

14

Gray looked outside. "It's still raining. Nothing but puddles out there. Good thing we've both got boots."

It took almost two hours to prepare breakfast, fix the noonday lunch, feed the mules, and break camp, so it was eight o'clock before they were back on the main road. It now resembled a creek bed. They took a cut immediately to the left, which led to the cabin Goldie had seen the evening before. As they pulled up in front, an ill-kempt, unshaven man stepped out.

"What d'ye want?" he asked in a hostile voice.

"We were wondering if this was your dog," answered Gray. "We found him in the woods last night."

"Don't try to shove your loose animals off on me," said the man. "I've enough mouths to feed around here."

Goldie noticed three skinny, tousle-haired children standing barefoot and wide-eyed in the cabin door. The two girls were clad in frayed cotton frocks and the boy in patched Kentucky jeans and a tattered shirt.

"We weren't trying to shove anything off on you, mister," said Gray, beginning to flare. "We didn't want to take something that belonged to somebody else."

A thin, worn-out woman of unassessable age appeared in the doorway and shooed the children away. "Lem, you oughta be more sociable," she said in a high-pitched voice. "These are only younguns. Have you had your breakfast?"

"Now, now," protested the man.

"We ain't got much," continued the woman, "but you can have some nice hot cornbread and sorghum. It's good and fillin'. And I can make you some coffee soon as I run one of the children to the spring."

Goldie was horrified. She calculated that it was nearly three quarters of a mile from the cabin to the spring. "Don't you have a well?" she blurted out.

"I'm aimin' to dig one next year, mebbe," said the man, "iffen the crops grow good this year. That spring's the only water we got. Hope you didn't trample them mules around it and muddy it up."

Gray chose to ignore this remark. Turning to the pale, drawn woman he thanked her and said they'd had their breakfast and had to get on.

"Where you goin', son?" she asked.

15

"To California," replied Gray, unable to keep a note of pride from his voice.

"Bless you," the woman called as Gray turned the wagon away from the cabin.

"Well, I guess he's yours," said Goldie. "What're you going to call him?"

"I don't know. You got any ideas?"

"Yes, I thought of something last night. Why not Happy? Look at him." Happy obligingly beat his tail and looked up at the Baxters adoringly as he sat securely between them on the wagon seat.

"Do you like that, Happy?" Gray questioned his dog. Happy gave a bark of approval. And that settled the matter.

All that day the rain continued. But the following morning they were cheered to see it had stopped, although there still was no sign of the sun. As the day progressed the sky became lighter and lighter until finally, just before twilight, Gray excitedly pointed out a patch of blue sky in the west.

The next day was sunny but cold, and the road was much easier to travel as the ground hardened. The deep ruts still denied them riding comfort, but the improved weather had brought out the welcome company of other travelers, some on horseback, others riding in coaches or big farm wagons. Both Goldie and Gray would have liked to stop and visit with the people they met, but they knew they had not been making good time and must press on, so the encounters were all brief.

In camp that night both of them again were cross. They were so tired that they fumbled with the harnesses of the mules, taking twice as long as usual to get them unhitched. Gray dropped the feed bag and spilled the grain, and Goldie called him a clumsy oaf. Then she tripped over a tree root and fell sprawling. She began to cry in anger and frustration.

"Are you hurt?" asked Gray unsympathetically.

"No," she hissed back as she picked herself up and limped over to the lantern, which had flown ten feet through the air in front of her when she fell. The glass chimney around it was partly broken, but the flame was still going. She propped it right side up and in silence went about preparing the fireplace. Gray, equally malevolent and silent, scooped up as much of the feed as he could and put it back in the sack.

Soon the warmth and light from the fire gave a more cheerful atmosphere to the camp, and the smell of frying bacon and eggs summoned Gray, Happy, and Matilda. When everyone had had enough to eat and the wash-up was over, Gray went to the wagon and brought out Goldie's guitar.

"How about some music?" he asked.

"What shall we sing?" Her fingers strummed the strings.

" 'America,' " said Gray. Goldie struck a chord, and they blended their voices in the harmony they had learned as young children when their mother and father had taken them to singing school. For the next hour they entertained themselves with old and new hymns and songs, some of them gay and some of them sad. Finally they closed their song session with "Rock of Ages." The fire was low, but they felt a warmth and closeness they hadn't shared since they left Big Timbers back on the banks of the Wabash.

They were up well before dawn on the fifth day of their trek across Illinois, but didn't take time to build a fire. They breakfasted hastily on cold beans, bread, and water.

There was a change in the weather that day; the air was softer and warmer, and there was a smell of spring, of new fresh life all around them. As they relaxed in front of the fire after supper, they discussed something both of them were looking forward to—a shopping trip in St. Louis. Gray wanted a Sam Hawkins rifle. "I think we really need it," he reasoned. "That way, if we're attacked we'll each have one. Besides, I'll have a better gun to hunt with."

"You can have the rifle as long as you dress the meat."

Gray chuckled. He knew how Goldie hated skinning a deer or even a rabbit. It was a family joke how she even avoided killing and plucking a chicken whenever she could find an excuse.

"I've been meaning to ask you something too." Goldie said hesitantly.

"What is it?"

"Do you remember what Big Timbers said about riding on the big river steamers?"

"Yes, of course. He always made it sound like a wonderful life."

"What I want to know is, do you think we could spend some of the money to travel first class—just this once?" Goldie did not get the unfavorable reaction she had anticipated from Gray, for he also had a secret hankering to experience first-class treatment.

"I don't see why we couldn't," he said, "if it isn't too expensive.

17

It would be nice to sleep in a real bed once more."

"And take a bath in a real tub," sighed Goldie, reflecting on the luxury.

"Look, I'll tell you what. I'll bet we get to the Mississippi by noon tomorrow. Let't stop on this side, and you can do the wash, and we'll get all cleaned up. Then day after tomorrow we'll cross to St. Louis, buy our necessaries, and see about first-class tickets on a steamer!"

"That sounds wonderful!"

Gray's calculations proved correct, and before noon the next day they stood on the bluffs looking across the Mississippi River at the lovely white city on the other side. They could see tall church spires and the big dome of the state house. All along the river were steamboats and barges busily making their way up or down or pulling over to dock on the levee. They had never seen a river so broad, nor a city so large, nor so many boats in their lives. Tremendously thrilled, they also felt small and insignificant. Gray secretly wondered where he could shop with impunity in such a large city, and Goldie wondered if they could afford even deck passage on one of the big riverboats she saw spouting black smoke into the air.

The Mississippi ferry unloaded them at St. Louis the next morning. Goldie and Gray sat in their wagon not knowing exactly what to do. All around them was the bustle and confusion of the prosperous pursuit of business: there were barrels of sugar and bales of cotton piled high on the levee; there were big merchant wagons pulled by long teams of horses rumbling here and there; there were huge piles of furs, the first of the spring run, in front of long warehouses; and there were people scurrying in all directions, paying no attention to the bewildered Baxters.

"Hey, you!" Gray finally realized that the voice he heard was addressing him.

"Yes, sir," he said, as he looked around at a man who had drawn up his lumber wagon behind him.

"This is a loading dock. You can't sit here!"

"Oh, I'm sorry. I didn't know."

"You can pull over in one of those side streets," said the man more kindly, as he noticed Gray's forlorn look.

"Thanks, thanks a lot," said Gray, heading his team out into the stream of carts clogging the road.

18

"What'll we do? Do you think it's safe to leave the wagon?" worried Goldie. They had pulled off on one of the more quiet warehouse streets perpendicular to Front Street, which ran along the levee.

"I don't know," answered Gray, climbing down, "I sure don't think we can go driving this rig around."

"Maybe they'd know in there," said Goldie, pointing to an office.

As Gray started to enter, a Negro boy hopped up as if by magic and opened the door for him. Inside the office of the Bailey Fur Company, Gray approached a middle-aged man sitting behind a big desk. "Excuse me, sir," he began, "I've just arrived in St. Louis, and I was wondering if it was safe to leave my wagon in the street while I do some errands."

"We'll see that it's safe. Drive it up to the door, and I'll have Fred watch it for you." He pulled a rope by his desk, which was apparently connected to a bell outside, for the young black boy soon appeared again. "Fred, I'd like you to watch this young man's wagon for him while he's gone."

"Yas suh. What about the young lady, suh? You want I should watch her, too?"

"No, that's my sister," said Gray. "She's going with me. But we do have our dog and cat."

The man nodded Fred out. "Where are you bound for, son?"

"We're going to California."

"Gold fever, huh? I know what that is. If I were a younger man, I'd go myself. Pull your wagon up here and bring in your sister. Maybe I can tell you where you can find what you're looking for. I'm Price Bailey."

"Gray Baxter," said Gray, eagerly extending his hand. "I'm mighty glad to meet you, sir. . . .I won't be a moment."

Gray quickly fetched Goldie and introduced her.

"Delighted, my dear," said Mr. Bailey, offering her a chair. "And now, what errands do you two have to run before you head west? Up the Missouri, I presume?"

"Yes," said Goldie enthusiastically. "We'd like to know where the steamboat company offices are? And Gray wants to buy a Sam Hawkins rifle. . .only he doesn't know where to get it."

"Slowly, slowly," smiled Mr. Bailey. "I think you'd better work on your steamship passage first. I think Clayborne and Reed still

19

charge a fair price. Their offices are on Front Street, two blocks up. How soon did you want to leave?"

"Today, if possible," blurted Gray.

"You might, you just might do it. You'll have to check their sailings and also see if they have any space. . . .Now you two run along and take care of that while I see what I can do about finding you that rifle."

"Gee, thanks, Mr. Bailey," said Gray.

At the Clayborne and Reed offices the Baxters discovered that a steamer, the *Missouri Belle*, was sailing that afternoon, and they could secure deck passage for their wagon and mules and, for fourteen dollars extra, first-class stateroom passage for themselves. Delighted with the ease of the transaction, they returned to the fur company office. As they approached, they saw a carriage tied to the hitching post in front of their wagon. Mr. Bailey explained that he had found a good gunsmith shop and had decided to take them there since it was located some distance from the levee.

The bright-haired youngsters felt very important riding in the fine carriage. The treatment they received in the gunsmith shop made them aware that their benefactor was a person of some importance in the city. With this realization they both became shy and more formal.

"We've taken up an awful lot of your time, sir," Gray apologized as he carried his new rifle back to the carriage.

"Nonsense," said Mr. Bailey. "Makes me feel I'm sharing your adventure with you." He pulled out his gold watch. "But I'd better take you back now. We have just about enough time to get your things loaded before sailing time."

Shortly before three o'clock the Baxters' wagon and animals were put safely aboard. Minutes later the *Missouri Belle* cast off and backed out into the Mississippi to head fifteen miles upstream to the Missouri.

The youngsters waved and called out their grateful thanks to Mr. Bailey, then turned to examine the long white lacy boat. On the deck below them they knew their wagon and animals were crowded together with the many passengers who could only afford the much cheaper deck pass. On their own deck a lovely promenade enclosed by an intricately carved balustrade circled all around the outside of the ship. They could see two big paddle wheels, one on either side extending above the deck. Above them

20

was the hurricane deck crowned by the Texas, where the officers' quarters and the pilothouse were. Even higher, they could see the tall twin smokestacks belching their clouds aloft. And on the jackstaff forward, they thrilled to see the brilliant red, white, and blue of the American flag.

Goldie surveyed the gingerbread-decorated boat with delight. "It looks good enough to eat!" she exclaimed.

"I think I'll take a look at the Gentlemen's Cabin," said Gray. "Why don't you look at the Ladies'? I'll meet you there later."

"All right," agreed Goldie. "Besides, I want to straighten out some things in my stateroom."

Assuming an air of nonchalance, Gray entered the saloon in the Gentlemen's Cabin. Inside, the air was already thick with the blue smoke of many cigars. With the attitude that you are less conspicuous if you look like everyone else, he made his way to the highly polished bar at the other end of the cabin, where two Negro tenders were busily setting up drinks for the thirsty men. From one of them he bought a cigar. Observing a man close to him bite off the end and spit it into a convenient cuspidor, he clumsily imitated the action. The man lit the cigar and a smile spread across his face. Gray followed suit and deeply inhaled the acrid smoke. He quickly expelled it. His face became blood red, and despite all of his efforts to control himself, he began to choke. He turned to the wall in order to avoid being seen by the other men in the cabin. But a pair of sharp-eyed gamblers had already observed him.

His coughing fit finally subsided, and Gray moved through the cabin observing the other passengers. He noticed some Army officers talking excitedly to each other and paused a moment to watch an artist who was sitting to one side sketching the scene. One group of men dressed in fine suits was discussing the fur trade. He even detected a minister who, to Gray's surprise, was gambling with a group of other men. Almost before he could assess fully what was happening, he noticed more and more decks of cards appearing at the many tables.

This was the moment the two cardsharks picked to move in. One of them approached Gray. "Not much to do on this old boat," he said. "Sure does get boring after the first trip. Don't you agree, Mr. ——"

"Baxter," volunteered Gray, surprised and pleased at the friendly overture.

21

"My name's Haines," said the dark young man in the ruffled shirt. "You been up the Missouri many times, Mr. Baxter?"

"No, not many," bluffed Gray.

"Would you care to join me in a drink, Mr. Baxter?"

"No, thank you," said Gray quickly. At this point his Indiana Protestant background asserted itself. It was very difficult for him to conceive of drinking as anything except sinning.

"Don't you drink?" said Haines in mock astonishment.

"No, I didn't mean that. . .I just meant I didn't care for one right now."

"Oh, I see. Do you play cards?"

"Yes," said Gray, desperately trying to cover his blunder about the drink.

With alacrity, Haines found an empty table, sat down, took a deck of cards from his pocket and began to shuffle them. "Poker?" he questioned Gray.

"Why, yes, that's fine," said the innocent.

"What shall we make the stakes?"

"Stakes?" asked Gray in sudden alarm.

"Yes, you know, the wager, the bet. Or don't you gamble either, Mr. Baxter?" Haines' patronizing tone made Gray feel inadequate.

Having observed the progress of the baiting of the hook, Haines' partner stepped up to the table. "Is this a private game?" he asked politely, "or do you mind if I join you?"

"Delighted to have you, sir," said Haines. "My name's Haines and this here is Baxter. We were just discussing what our wager should be."

"I'm happy to meet you both. My name's Bryant." The newcomer extended his hand first to his partner and then to Gray. "May I suggest a minimum bet of a dollar, with say a twenty dollar limit. I'm not a wealthy man, I'll freely confess."

"Very reasonable, Mr. Bryant. I don't think Mr. Baxter or myself would count ourselves to be wealthy either. Do you agree, Mr. Baxter?"

Although Gray was horrified at the turn events were taking, nothing in his background had prepared him for extricating himself gracefully from a situation of this kind. He couldn't bear to get up and walk away from the two urbane young men and risk hearing their taunts of derisive laughter, although he knew that besides the steamship tickets, he had only twenty dollars in his pocket.

"Yes, that's fine," he finally blurted out as the two men sat staring at him expectantly.

True to the character of their trade, Haines and Bryant let Gray win a few modest pots. This served to make him more reckless, and he began to lose steadily. As three other men joined the game, Gray was holding a hand he thought to be very good, but when he reached in his pocket to cover his bet, he found he had no money. In desperation he asked the others to wait while he replenished his funds. Since he didn't dare approach Goldie, his only negotiable asset was the steamship tickets. He hurried to the purser, who gladly took them back. "I've got some folks anxious for staterooms," he said. "Couldn't give 'em anything but deck passage."

Tightly clutching the fourteen dollars from the purser, Gray rushed back to the game. He lost that hand and the next. With a sick feeling inside, he looked at the slick young men and knew he never had had a chance. Haines and Bryant, who no longer even made a pretense of being strangers to each other, nodded curtly as he left the game and stumbled over to the bar.

One of the bartenders said, "You don't look well, suh. You'd betta have a glass of brandy."

"Make it whisky," said Gray.

Goldie had been having the time of her life in the Ladies' Cabin. She tried several of the highbacked upholstered chairs, noted with pleasure the large ceiling painting of cherubs and ladies floating about in Grecian robes, and inspected the oil paintings depicting sights along the Missouri on every stateroom door. Then she retired to her own stateroom, where with equal delight she noted the details of its appointments, from the hand-painted washbowl and matching pitcher and the cake of lavender-scented soap on the washstand to the lovely lace bedspread, the charming little slipper chair, and the lovely rosewood writing desk. She was placing some of her dresses in the clothes cupboard when she heard a discreet knock on the door.

"Is that you, Gray?" she sang out and hastened to open it. "You should see the——" she broke off abruptly when she saw a middle-aged Negro man in a white steward's coat.

"Excuse me, Miss Baxter," he began apologetically, "but

I'm afraid there's some mistake about the cabin."

"Oh, am I in the wrong one? That's all right, it won't take me a minute to gather up my things."

"That's not it." The steward lowered his voice so the ladies in the saloon could not hear. "Your brother turned in your tickets a while ago. You don't have any cabin at all."

"Gray did *what*?" exclaimed Goldie in disbelief. She began to flush a deep red. "Do you know what happened?"

"Yes, Miss——" the grizzled head bowed a bit. "I'm afraid your brother fell in with some gamblers. And, well, they just took his money away from him."

Stunned, Goldie could only murmur, "I see."

"I'll be happy to help you gather your things together, Miss."

"No, that's all right. I can do it myself. But how do I get to where our wagon is?"

"The stairs are right outside the entrance to the Ladies' Saloon."

"Thank you, I won't be a moment." Goldie closed the door after the steward. Her cheeks were burning with humiliation, and she didn't know how she would get through the gauntlet of women in the saloon. She grabbed her belongings and threw them in her bags. She put on her hat and cloak and, grasping a bag in each hand, entered the saloon with her head held high. She looked neither to the right nor left as she walked the length of the room and out the door at the other end. But she imagined she heard titters and gossipy whispers as she passed along. Gray wasn't even there to help her, she reflected angrily as she made her way clumsily down the stairway to the main deck. Fighting the tears, she struggled toward the wagon. Just as she had almost reached her haven, a man in greasy black buckskins stepped in front of her.

"What's your hurry, Missy?" he asked.

She looked up into a dirty, unshaven face. Alarmed, she tried to pass, mumbling, "I want to get to my wagon."

"You can stop a minute and be sociable, can't you?"

Goldie looked at him in fright. At this moment she felt someone touching one of her curls. She whirled around to see another unshaven face grinning at her. "Now ain't that the purtiest stuff you ever did see?" he asked the first one. "You all alone, honey?"

She was speechless with fear. The first man who had accosted

24

her said, "Let's see some more of that purty hair," and ripped off her bonnet.

"Leave me alone!" she screamed. A woman appeared in the canvas opening of a wagon next to where Goldie was trapped. "What's the matter?" she inquired. Then her eyes narrowed in quick comprehension. "You roustabouts go on about your business and leave this girl alone!" she snapped.

"Mind your own business, you old bitch," said the second man.

"I'm making *this* my business," answered the woman, and raised her voice. "Tim, come here, Tim. I need your help, quick." But nobody appeared.

During the moment of distraction, Goldie tried to dart by, but one of the men grabbed her. "Not so fast, honey," he said. "How about a little kiss?"

"Let me go!" she screamed and swung her bag at him.

Although she made no contact, the man dropped his hold on her and cried out in pain. Dora Cunningham had grabbed the nearest thing to hand, a long bullwhip, and had applied a smart crack across the offender's back. The man darted toward the wagon, but another man in buckskins stepped in front of him. "Well, Chapman," said the new arrival, "it seems every time I run into you, you're stirring up some kind of trouble. And if it isn't Braddock," he continued in an unfriendly tone. "I might have known you'd be here too!"

"This ain't none of your affair, Peale," said Braddock.

"Let's just say I'm making it my affair, shall we?" said Peale, deftly removing Goldie's hat from Braddock's grasp. "Now, young lady, where were you going?"

"I'm trying to get to my wagon over there," she sobbed. Then she screamed as a knife flashed in Chapman's hand. But the weapon clattered harmlessly to the deck as Peale's knife pinned the sleeve of the troublemaker's arm to the wagon seat. Before the other man could do anything, Peale raised a rifle slung around his neck and pointed it at him. At the same time he withdrew his knife, releasing Chapman's arm. "Now, let's have you two get back over to the other side of this boat in a hell of a hurry!" he ordered. "And if I catch you over here again, I'll have the captain set you ashore. Is that clear?"

"You wait, Peale," threatened Chapman. "We'll get you one of these days!" But the two moved away with haste.

"You sure were a sight for sore eyes, Zack Peale," said Dora.

"I'm glad I happened to be coming by," said Zack.

When Goldie realized she had really been rescued, she began to shake all over and to sob uncontrollably. "There, Miss," said Zack. "It's all right now."

"There ain't been anybody in that wagon since we left St. Louis," observed Dora. "She may be by herself."

"Are you traveling alone?" asked Zack.

"N-n-no," said Goldie through her tears. "My brother——" She sobbed out the story of how she had lost her stateroom.

Zack said, "I'll bet I know what he's doing now." He turned Goldie over to Mrs. Cunningham and went off to find Gray.

When Zachariah Peale entered the Gentlemen's Saloon, all eyes were turned to him. Many tales of the exploits of the famous scout were babbled about the room. Zack, an extremely tall man with a light brown flowing beard and graceful mustache, was an imposing figure in his light-colored fringed buckskin jerkin and pants, complemented by high-topped Indian moccasins. He paid little attention to the stir he caused, but made his way directly to the bar and the copper-haired figure drooping at its end. "Are you Gray Baxter?" he asked.

"That's me, I'm just lil' ol' Gray Baxter. Waddya want?"

"Your sister needs you. Come on with me."

"Well, I don't need her. . .not one lil' ol' bit. So I'll just stay right here. But I like your looks. . .both of you. Why don't you have a lil' drink? That's funny," he mumbled, "there seems to be two of everything." He put his hand to his forehead. His knees started to fold just as Zack put his arms around his waist and hoisted him away from the bar.

By the time Zack managed to maneuver his burden down the companionway to the wagon, Gray was more like a sack of meal than a human being. But he managed to recognize his sister and began to cry. "So 'shamed," he said. "So 'shamed. . .didn't want to see you. . .couldn't tell you——"

Before she could reply, he trailed off to sleep. Zack laid him down on the feather tick.

"He'll be all right in the morning, except for his head," he said.

"I want to thank you, Mr. Peale, for everything," said Goldie gratefully.

"I'm glad I came along. And please call me Zack. . .All of my friends do."

"Could I ask you one more favor?" she hesitated, then rushed on. "Dora Cunningham said you were leading a wagon train to California. I wonder if Gray and I could join?"

"I don't see why not. I'm meeting with the company officers tomorrow morning, and I'll put it up to them."

Isaiah, the older Cunningham boy, who was twelve, appeared to invite Goldie to have supper. He stayed by the wagon to talk and confided that he had a younger brother named Adam and a sister named Ruth. "We had a farm in Kentucky," Isaiah went on, "but the land was too hard. I don't know. . .maybe Paw don't have a knack for farmin'. At any rate, when Paw heard about the gold, there was just no holdin' him, so here we are. We all kinda took to the idea. We sure couldn't be much worse off than we was."

From the lofty height of being three years his senior, Goldie marveled at the maturity and judgment of the boy. "I guess we kinda took to the idea too," she laughed.

She joined the Cunningham family for the simple supper of bread, bacon, and beans, then helped Dora do the dishes. Climbing back into her own wagon, she found Gray beginning to be sick, so she intermittently held a pan for him or applied cold cloths to his head for the next several hours. She could hear the sound of music and the gay laughter of the young people enjoying themselves in the upper deck saloon. As she listened and imagined the good time they were having, she couldn't restrain the tears that kept slipping silently down her cheeks.

The *Missouri Belle* had tied up at St. Charles for the evening, and many townspeople had come on board to enjoy the music and dancing and exchange bits of news and gossip with the cabin passengers, a pleasantness denied to those who merely had deck passage.

As the effects of the liquor wore off, Gray felt more and more miserable. He knew how much the trip up the Missouri had meant to Goldie, and he was furious because he had allowed himself to be duped.

"But you have no idea how it takes hold of you," he told her. "I can't explain why I sold our tickets. I guess it was because I knew you wouldn't give me any more money, and I simply had to

27

play. It was awful. . .seeing money go like that. . .awful!" After this confession he fell into a peaceful sleep.

In the morning when they were under way again, Gray found the noise of the pounding engines and the whistles from the pilot-house almost unbearable. But he managed an exploratory tour of their deck with Goldie. They stood in the bow for a while and watched how the pilot skillfully avoided the snags and sandbars in the treacherous turns and twists of Old Muddy, as they learned the Missouri was called.

At each fueling stop the roustabouts, a surly-looking lot, would leap off to hustle the cordwood on board for the huge yawning mouths of the furnaces, which consumed eighteen to twenty cords of wood a day.

When the *Missouri Belle* tied up at the German settlement of Hermann that night, Goldie and Gray were the first to leave the boat to make their way among the farmers and peddlers to purchase food. Goldie bought with care, however, because she knew their precious supply of gold was dwindling, and she felt as guilty as Gray over the loss of money the night before. For she reasoned if they hadn't been in first class, he would never have been lured into the card game.

Zack and Washington Lord, the elected leader of the company of pioneers headed for California, announced when they returned that the officers had agreed to let them join the train. Overjoyed, Goldie invited both men to supper, but only Zack accepted. The conversation turned to life on the trail. "We have to post a guard at night," he said, "so the Indians don't run off the stock."

"Do they attack?" asked Gray eagerly. "I've got a new rifle." He produced it for Zack's admiration.

"That's mighty fine," said Zack. "But it's unlikely the Indians will attack. They're more interested in stealing. We change the guard every two hours to discourage them."

"What do you do during the day?" asked Goldie. "I mean, how do you get the chores done?"

"It isn't easy, especially for the women. You do all of the cooking and cleaning up for the next day the night before. We have cold breakfasts and noonings. Occasionally we'll stop by a river for a day so you can catch up on the washing."

"I see," said Goldie.

"The main thing to remember," said Zack, "is that you're part

28

of a large group. We have thirty wagons here on the boat, and we're hoping to pick up fifteen or twenty more in Independence. We'll move slower than some of the smaller trains, but we'll have better protection. We already have about sixty armed men including you, Gray."

The tinkle of music interrupted their conversation, but this time it was not issuing from the upper deck. Apparently Goldie was not the only one who had felt left out on the previous evening. As they followed the throng of emigrants to the stern, they found a group of men and women engaged in a lively square dance. Somehow the passengers had managed to clear a space on the crowded deck for their merriment. After the first dance the musicians struck up a lively Virginia Reel, and Zack asked Goldie to be his partner. Gray looked quickly around but discovered the girls had all been snatched away. It was then that he noticed how few women there were. The men, he estimated, must outnumber the women four or five to one. Standing and listening to the gay music, he again felt a heaviness inside him as he thought of the long journey ahead and the responsibility, which he didn't want, of looking after his sister.

"Wow, I wanta dance with her," said one young blade to Gray's left.

"Which one?" asked another.

"That one with the shiny red hair."

"Yeah," said the second. "She's real purty, ain't she?"

Gray's scowl deepened, but soon he forgot all about Goldie as he vied with several other young men for the attention of a dark-haired girl with black-fringed eyes. Her name was Rachel Stevens, he discovered, and she too was traveling with her parents in the Lord and Peale train to California.

Goldie didn't go to the party the next night. During supper Matilda emitted several plaintive cries indicating that she was about to bear her kittens, and Goldie decided to stay with her. Gray went on alone. Scarcely had he gone when Zack came by. He seemed to want to talk, and Goldie asked him how he had become a scout. He told her he had run away to join the mountain men when he was sixteen, at first trapping, then gradually becoming more and more interested in exploring. He had been along the Oregon and Santa Fe trails and had even been lost in the great salt desert beyond the Mormon settlement.

"Yes, I've seen the gold in California," he answered in reply to her question.

"Why on earth didn't you stay and get rich?" Goldie demanded in surprise.

"What makes you think I didn't?" She looked down in embarrassment. "I've got a piece of land out there," he continued. "That's why I'm leading this wagon train. California's home to me now."

"Maybe it'll be home to me someday, too. I don't know. . .I feel all of this is leading toward something, but I don't know what that something is. I thought I knew what I wanted when we started this journey, but I'm not sure of anything now. Funny, isn't it?" She looked up at him through her thick gold lashes.

He had a sudden impulse to kiss her, but before he could give the idea further consideration, three young swains came over to the wagon, and he suddenly felt old among this scarce-shaven lot. Abruptly he said good night. As he walked away, he told himself he was a fool, that Goldie was only fifteen.

Goldie had completely forgotten Matilda, and was surprised to find when Gray returned that instead of one cat, she now had five. Without any assistance from anyone, Matilda had given birth to four little bits of wet fur. She announced her triumph with a noisy meow and purred with pride as Goldie made much of the tiny brood.

Gray seemed reluctant to leave the vicinity of the wagon the next morning. "What's the matter?" Goldie finally asked.

"Nothing. Can't I help you once in a while without something being wrong?"

"What's Rachel doing?"

"I dunno."

"Come on," said Goldie. "What happened last night?"

"She's a troublemaker!" came the hot reply.

"You can't expect her to give all of her time to you, Gray."

"That isn't what I mean. She's different. She promised every dance to at least five guys last night, and then when there was practically a fight, she got all flushed in the face, and her eyes got a queer glittery look. It gave me the creeps."

"She was probably scared," said Goldie.

"No, she wasn't. She wanted it to happen."

"Look for another girl, Gray. Dan Milford's sister, Mary, is nice."

"The trouble is, I still like Rachel," answered Gray.

That evening the steamer got only as far as Boonville. The boat had begun to encounter ice in the river to add to the other hazards. While the older people became more and more tense, the younger ones adapted to the constant danger and soon were pointing out the deteriorating shells of steamers wrecked earlier by the treacherous waters. Originally the emigrants had hoped they would get to Independence, Missouri, in five days. Now they knew it would be impossible to make it in less than a week.

Two nights later they had successfully navigated the twists and turns of Old Muddy as far as Lexington. Since everyone was especially happy on this evening, they dressed up in their finest. If their luck held, the pioneers knew they would be in Independence some time the following day.

Zack had stayed away from the Baxters for the rest of the trip. He hadn't even come to the regular evening festivities. But tonight he joined the party. Both men and women were dressed in Eastern clothes, possibly for the last time in many months. Gray looked especially tall and handsome in his blue coat, embroidered waistcoat, and fawn-colored pants over black boots. The starched ruffles on his best shirt gleamed in the lantern light, and crowning all was his shining red-gold hair. Goldie was less conspicuous only because of her height. In fact, it was difficult to find her in the midst of her special group of admirers. Finally Zack did see her and realized with a pang that she hadn't even missed him. She was dressed in a blue silk dress with a rose velvet sash. Her arms and throat had a white Dresden translucence with delicate shadings of pink, and her bright curls shot off firelight as she tossed her head laughing. Despite all of his resolutions, Zack made his way over, determined to have a dance with her.

He arrived just as the caller announced that the men should choose partners for the first dance. The younger boys fell away in confusion as Zack advanced into their midst and proffered his arm to Goldie. "The first dance will be a cotillion led by our own pathfinder, Mr. Zachariah Peale, and his charming partner, Miss Goldie Baxter," shouted the sharp-eyed caller to the loud cheers and hurrahs of the company.

31

After the opening dance, Zack left Goldie abruptly. But at the end of the evening, he asked her to be his partner in demonstrating a new dance called the waltz. As he put his arm around her waist and they stepped out to the lovely strains of the melody, she felt once more that he was trying to communicate something to her, but she had no time to think about what it could be as she concentrated on following him through the complex pattern of the new dance. Her huge skirt billowed out as they swayed back and forth and around, caught in the spell of the pulsating rhythm. There was loud and sustained applause for the graceful couple as they finished, facing each other in a deep bow and curtsy.

Zack insisted on keeping Goldie as his partner while the others were learning the new dance, much to the mutterings and sour looks of her other beaux. Goldie wondered why he was being so attentive and became uncomfortable. Zack sensed her tenseness in his arms and suddenly bid her good night at the end of this dance, leaving her to wonder if she had offended him. She determined to ask Gray what he thought of Zack. He seemed rather strange to her.

CHAPTER **3** INDEPENDENCE, THE JUMPING-OFF PLACE★★

At Independence the following afternoon, Zack directed the Lord train to a grove just outside of town to make camp. He knew that the company needed many lessons for starting, circling, and stopping on the trail and decided this was the night to begin. He ordered Wash, who was driving the lead wagon, to form a circle. Wash tried to turn his team to the right to do so. For more than twenty minutes the thirty wagons struggled to position themselves, only to end up sitting at different angles, with wide spaces between some and others so close together that they were practically standing with their teams intertwined.

Zack shook his head in despair as he stood in the stirrups on his horse and surveyed the mess. He rode to the center of the circle through one of the wide openings and addressed the company. "I want each of you to look at this," he exploded. "Just how much protection do you think this would afford out on the plains? Do you realize that it took you twenty minutes to make this—this——" Words failed him and he simply shook his head. "Now we're going to try it again. And you are all to bear sharply to the right. Keep a distance between you and the wagon ahead. . .and then close in by turning the teams toward the center after the circle is formed."

Eager to try again, the men started to jingle the reins. "Just a minute," shouted Zack over the din. "There's something to learn about starting too. When I give the signal to catch up in the morning, that means you hitch. After you're ready, you each in turn call out, 'All's set!' Then I'll give the order to 'Stretch out.' That's when you're to let the teams out. And when I call 'Fall in!' you turn your team into line and follow the wagon ahead. Has everyone got that?"

There was a general murmur from the pioneers.

"All right," said Zack. "Let's rehearse it from the beginning." He rode over to the Lord wagon and shouted, "Catch up! Catch up!"

There were enthusiastic jinglings of harnesses and chains and good-natured calls back of "All set! All set!"

The clamor grew as Zack called "Stretch out!" and they all let out their teams. At the signal to "Fall in!" the ragged string of wagons attempted to get into better order.

This circle was better than the first one, but Zack was still not pleased. He ordered them to go through the process again, and then again. By the fourth time through, he sensed the group had had enough, so he announced this would do for the night. Then he showed them how to picket and tether the animals and arrange the cook fires until at last the camp looked as it would every night for the many months they would be traveling across the plains. Men with rifles were stationed around the camp and on the picket line, children were playing within the circle by the firelight, and everyone was evidencing great interest in what was being made in the big iron pots and on the heavy griddles.

The next morning, after a wearying two-hour practice with the teams, Goldie and Gray went into Independence to buy supplies.

But there were far too many things to be priced and purchased in one day, so they made a list in order not to duplicate or, worse, leave out something vital, since they knew the wagon train would have to be a self-sufficient community during the three to four months they would be on the trail.

Independence was a booming town. Long one of the starting points for both the Oregon and Santa Fe trails, the merchants knew what to stock for the endless line of emigrant trains now gathering to leave for the West, no later than May if they could help it. There were stores and traders selling every item needed for the long journey. And even though there were thousands of emigrants in the town, competition had kept prices at a reasonable level. The long wooden walks were piled high with goods that couldn't be crammed into the stores. Everywhere people were hassling with each other over a can of axle grease, a length of rope, or a half dozen laying hens. There were mules, oxen, milk cows, and horses penned in huge corrals, as well as acres of bright-colored Conestoga and Pittsburgh wagons brought upriver from St. Louis. The traveler arriving with nothing could completely outfit himself in this trader's town on the west bank of the Missouri.

That night Gray had the watch from ten to twelve. He had been on duty about an hour when he thought he heard something in a small thicket. As he approached cautiously, he heard a woman giggle and the unmistakable sounds of two people making love. "Be gentle, be easy," he heard the woman entreat.

With a shock, he thought, Why, that's Rachel! He knew what was going on in the thicket, and he also knew that it was none of his business, but he was unable to move. His mind raced away, but his feet, as if weighted with lead, remained planted.

When they had finished he heard the man say, "God, but it's been long. When are you coming with me? I'm sick of this."

"Not yet, not yet, dearest," whispered Rachel. "You know about Daddy."

"I don't care," rasped the man. "I want you. We could be married."

"Soon, I'll be with you soon," sighed Rachel. And again Gray heard the sounds of passion.

Oh, God, he thought, and this time he did run. That wasn't the first time.

When he was relieved at midnight, he dragged himself back to the wagon with heavy feet and a sad heart. He hadn't recognized the man's voice, but he knew it was not one of his own friends.

Many of the footloose men were noisily returning from town, and among them was Zack, singing a bawdy mountain song slightly off-key.

"Howdy, Gray Baxter," he called out cheerfully. "How's the boy and that little hunk of gold he protects?"

This was Gray's second shock of the evening. His idol was drunk. "Howdy, Zack," he said uncertainly.

"That's a good boy. . . . You take good care of her," he mumbled as he trailed off toward his tent.

"Oh, I will," said Gray, not quite sure what Zack was talking about.

"What was that?" hissed Goldie from the wagon.

"It's just me, Sis," said Gray.

"I mean who was that?" asked Goldie as Gray entered.

"It was Zack," said Gray.

"He didn't sound right."

"Oh, Goldie, don't be such a prude. Look, Sis, men do drink. You'd better face it."

"All right, all right," she said and reached for the lamp.

"Don't do that!" he exclaimed.

"What's the matter?"

"Nothing!" he shouted. "Go to sleep!"

Within the next two weeks more and more wagons joined the train as the riverboats disgorged their passengers and cargos bound for the land of gold. On a bulletin board in the center of the camp supplies needed for the journey were posted. The pioneers were warned against having too much as well as having too little, for they were reminded of the mountains and streams that lay ahead, where an overloaded wagon could cause disaster. In addition, the bulletin board served as a handy place to leave messages or advertise services. The large train was fortunate in that they had a blacksmith, a carpenter, a harnessmaker, a lawyer, and a minister among their number. Many other men were moving West to open new businesses and were taking wagons piled high with goods for stores. Not everyone who joined in this great migration was interested in extracting the yellow metal from the earth. Many saw greater opportunity in extracting it instead from the hands of those who would do the digging.

Goldie awakened one morning to a balmy zephyr breeze which foretold a warm day. It was the last week of April. Suddenly aware of spring, she went to the woods to pick wild flowers for the wagon. She was gone so long that Gray became concerned and went to look for her. He found her, her arms full of flowers, standing on a knoll looking out over the river. Her skirt was billowing gently behind her in the breeze, and her bright hair glinted in the afternoon sun. She didn't see him at first, and he knew she was dreaming. Instead of scolding her as he had intended, he simply walked up and took some of the flowers from her arms. "Come on, Sis," he said, catching her now free hand. "It's time to go back."

"Oh, Gray," said Goldie enthusiastically, "don't you just love spring? Aren't you glad to be alive *now*?"

There was a general meeting that night at which Zack asked the men to make a rule outlawing drinking on the trail except at the forts. But despite his lengthy discussion of the hazards they would face and the need to be alert at all times, the proposal was defeated.

Zack stood silently a moment staring into the fire. The group became restive. Finally his head shot up and he looked keenly at them. "I've got an announcement to make," he said. "We now number forty-six wagons and one-hundred-thirty guns. In order to be among the first to catch the grass at its best along the way, we'll be pulling out next Monday."

Gray had not paid much attention to the liquor discussion, but now his flagging attention returned with a snap. As the company broke up, he rushed over to Zack to get his opinion about buying a horse.

"They do come in handy," said Zack. "Do you know anything about choosing an animal?"

"Well, I guess——" Gray started to bluster, then stopped. "Not much," he admitted.

"Why don't you ride into town with me tomorrow," said Zack. "We'll see what we can find."

The next few days were full of last-minute preparations. Supplies were checked and rechecked until finally there was nothing left to do except post last letters downstream on the riverboats to friends and relatives back East.

Gray bought the horse, and Goldie counted only thirty dollars left. But Zack told her the four kittens would be old enough to leave Matilda by the time the train reached Fort Kearney, and she should get at least ten dollars apiece for them. Selling the kittens had seemed a good idea when Big Timbers suggested it before they were born. But now she didn't want to part with them even though the money was needed. As she watched their sprightly pouncing on the feather tick, she consoled herself that Fort Kearney was a long way off and they might find another way of making money by then.

CHAPTER 4 WAGONS WEST★★★★★★★★★★★★★★★★★★★★★★★★★★★★★★★★

Finally Monday, the last day of April, dawned. After a cold breakfast that had been prepared the night before, Zack's voice could be heard, with the first rays of the sun, singing out the now familiar, "Catch up! Catch up!"

Washington Lord's wagon pulled out followed by each wagon in turn, until the train stretched for several blocks on the north side of the Kansas River. It would be many weeks before these people would see a sign of civilization, but few looked back. For most there was little behind, but ahead was the hope of a new and better life.

Goldie and Gray were sitting on the high seat of their wagon with Happy between them and Matilda and her brood in the back, while the newest member of the party, a pretty brown and white spotted pony, Sunny, was tied to the tail gate. Their wagon had place number eleven, and as far as Goldie could see behind, the other wagons followed in a long white ribbon rolling over the moist green turf.

Some wagons had cows tied to their tail gates. Many parties were bringing along extra animals for replacements or for meat, and some of the wagons were drawn by only a single pair of mules or a yoke of oxen. For those lightly loaded, it didn't matter, but others were too heavy for the straining animals. From the start these inevitably began falling behind.

Many wagons owned in common by four or five young argonauts were being used only to haul their supplies and gear. The owners were taking turns driving while their partners galloped their horses back and forth the length of the train, playing games or conversing with the girls.

Occasionally one of the riders would hoist a girl to the back of his horse. Caught up in the spirit of the frolic, Goldie untied Sunny to join a boy named Bob Cassidy in a romp. In their mad sprint, they passed Zack at the head of the column. Less than pleased with the hijinks of the younger men, some of whom were showing the effects of drinking, Zack was particularly annoyed with Goldie's performance. As she dashed by he called to her that they were in Indian country and she should stay with the train.

"Oh, pooh," she said, "You can see for miles. There's no one around."

"All right," said Zack. "Suit yourself."

Goldie realized how ignorant she had sounded. Chastened, she rode back and tied Sunny once more to the wagon. "I can handle the mules," she told Gray. "Why don't you ride awhile? But Zack says not to go away from the train because we're in Indian country."

As the day progressed the riders became more and more boisterous, now carrying their bottles openly on their saddles, and shooting at anything that moved on the prairie. The journey that had begun with such promise turned into a nightmare of drinking and shooting, and a silent and distrustful group formed their circle that night. Still the majority attributed the day's actions to youthful high spirits, and despite Zack's urging that they reconsider the no-drinking regulation before some real tragedy occurred, there was a reluctance to take any action. The carousing continued into the night, and no one got much rest till dawn when the merrymakers finally ceased their revelry.

It was a cheerless company that answered the call the next morning to another long day on the trail. A sense of foreboding had fallen on them, and many talked of turning back. Gray and Goldie stayed with their wagon all day, taking turns handling the mules and conversing only when necessary.

The morning passed peaceably because most of the carousers were still sleeping. But after the cold nooning, the young blades began rolling out of the wagons once more, and by midafternoon their actions were even more brazen than the day before. As the hostility of the rest of the company increased, they began drinking more and performing more daring feats to attract the attention and admiration of the young females in the train.

What everyone had feared finally occurred. Rodney Smith, one of the young rioters, enamored of a girl by the name of Betsy Fisher, raced up beside the wagon where she was sitting on the seat beside her father. "Look at me, Betsy!" he shouted as he leaped for the back of the lead mule. Even though the wagon was going at a slow pace, he missed, and the mules bolted. Rod was bounced down beneath their hooves, and as the wagon careened off, the rear wheel passed over his waist with a sickening thud.

Zack and some of the other outriders took off after the wagon, but before they could reach it, one wheel hit a depressed spot in the plain and it turned over, releasing the stampeding mules. Zack galloped on to catch the team while the others stopped to aid the Fisher family. Betsy had been thrown free, and although the wind had been knocked out of her and she was bruised, she seemed to be all right. But Mr. Fisher was pinned under the wagon with his left leg twisting off at an unnatural angle. Despite his obvious pain, he directed his rescuers to the inside of the wagon. "My wife, Lucy," he said. "And Priscilla."

Priscilla, the Fishers' six-month-old baby, had been protected by her mother and was fine. But a heavy trunk lay across Mrs. Fisher's back, and even after its removal, she was still unable to move. The men gently lifted her from the overturned wagon.

"Ollie," she gasped.

"I'm here, Lucy," called Mr. Fisher. "I'm fine."

Her eyes inquiring, Mrs. Fisher turned her head painfully toward her other daughter.

"Oh, Mother, I'm fine," sobbed Betsy as she knelt down beside her mother on the new grass.

Returning with the team, Zack directed the men to lift the wagon off of Mr. Fisher and right it. Two men carried him to his wife's side. Zack discovered that Mrs. Fisher had no feeling below her waist. "I think her back's broken," he said.

"Are you in pain, Lucy?" asked Mr. Fisher.

"No, I've no feeling at all. As long as you're all right, I'm satisfied." And she died holding her husband's hand. Sobbing uncontrollably, Betsy threw herself across her mother. Zack sent

39

one of the men back to the train to pass the word that they would have to camp there for the night.

Since he was the only one with even the rudiments of medical knowledge, Zack started to set Mr. Fisher's broken leg. He had not forgotten Rodney but had counted him as dead. When one of the men called out that the boy was still alive, Zack quickly showed another man how to make a splint, then rode over. Rodney's eyes were staring vacantly, and red flecks of blood trickled from the corners of his mouth. Zack knew there was nothing he could do, and ordered Rodney's wagon brought over so he could at least be made more comfortable. As his suddenly sober companions were lifting him in, Rodney gave a horrible shriek and lapsed into unconsciousness.

"Will he die, Mr. Peale?" asked one of the boys in fright.

"I'm afraid I can't do anything for him," said Zack. "He's hurt inside."

Doing the automatic chores of making the camp, feeding the stock, and starting the supper, it seemed to Goldie grotesque that everyone, including herself, should be continuing the regular routine. She thought there should be some mark, some change. A terrible tragedy had occurred, a family was bereaved, and yet the rest of the world was the same.

As the Fisher Pittsburgh took its place in the circle, the word was passed that services would be held for Mrs. Fisher. She must have flowers, thought Goldie desperately. No one should be buried without flowers. She flew out on the prairie, grasping the blooms tucked in the meadow grasses. The body of Mrs. Fisher was laid in a rude coffin, which had been constructed out of boards. Goldie dropped some of her flowers upon it. Mr. Carey, the minister who had joined the train in Independence, read the simple service, and then the wooden box was lowered into the Kansas sod. Ray Beame, the blacksmith, had made a rude cross of iron, which was hammered into the earth as a headstone. On it he had chiseled, "Lucy Fisher, born 1811–died 1849." Goldie placed the rest of her flowers on the newly turned grave, and a silent company returned to the chore of preparing a supper none wanted.

During the meal Washington Lord passed the word that there would be a general meeting immediately following. As the people assembled in the area framed by the wagons, Wash began to speak. "Friends," he said, "there is no need to go into the sad details of

40

what has happened, but there is a need to ask why. If you remember back in Independence," he gestured to the other officers, "we asked you to sign a pledge not to drink on the trail. I hardly need remind you how the vote turned out. Zack tried to explain in Independence that all of us must be ready for an emergency at any time. There was an emergency today, one that could have been avoided if young Smith had not been drinking. We are asking you to vote once more on whether or not there will be drinking on this train."

As he put the question for those opposed to drinking, the "ayes" were deafening. Wash declared, "The vote is against drinking, and henceforth there will be no drinking on the trail." He then said he was turning the meeting over to Zack because there were certain other laws that must be observed if the train was going to make it to California.

As Zack rose to speak, some grumbling young men in the back began to quiet down. "Folks," he said, "I want to talk about survival. First, there will be no more wild riding or tricks or showing off on the horses. The journey will be long, monotonous, and tiring for both animals and people. Wearing out animals now may mean not enough food at some later time. We'll need to scout ahead, and we'll have to hunt to replenish our meat, and this is why we need the horses. They are not playthings, and this journey is not a holiday outing. Every man must abide by these rules for the safety and well-being of this entire company. Any man not willing to do this will have to leave the train. I will guide only those who are willing to share this responsibility!"

There was vigorous discussion after Zack sat down. Most of the men, though young, had not participated in the undisciplined partying and were wholly in agreement with Zack. But there were some dissenters led by a man named Chuck Colby. He turned to his supporters. "No one's going to tell me what to do. Is anybody with me?" A group of sixteen inexperienced youths gathered around him, and Chuck announced they would form their own company.

"That's your choice," said Zack. "But there will be no further drinking here tonight." His clear eyes went hard. "Make no mistake on this. You'll not jeopardize another person on this train!"

"Then we'll leave now," boasted Chuck. "We'll be making our

claims in California when you're still trying to get across the first ridge of the Rockies!"

The small group broke away from the rest and began gathering their belongings. Rodney Smith's companions, who wished to accompany Chuck, had a problem to resolve first. They approached Zack in a group. "Since Rod's going to die anyway," said the spokesman, "we don't want to take him along with us. Would you see if someone else will carry him? We'll be willing to pay."

From his wagon Mr. Fisher overheard the callous proposal, and sent Betsy to ask Zack to come over. "I can't continue right now," he began. "So I'm taking my family back to Independence. When I get well, we'll join another train. Lucy would want it that way. We'll take young Rod back with us. Maybe somebody there can help him."

"That's mighty decent of you, Ollie," said Zack. "I'll tell the boys."

Obviously relieved to be rid of the barely breathing body, which only served as a reminder to them that life could end suddenly and unpleasantly, three of the young men quickly delivered their burden and hurried away to join the Colby group.

The following day was again long and dreary, and there was no rest in camp that night, for Zack informed them they would ford the Delaware River the next day and must stuff the cracks of their wagon beds with rags and papers in order to keep the goods inside as dry as possible. Goldie and Gray brought out the tub of marine caulking compound Big Timbers had insisted they take with them, remembering he had said, "If it's supposed to be a schooner, we'd better make sure it don't sink." And long into the night they worked diligently with a knife and a spoon applying the compound to the cracks between the boards in their wagon.

Just before noon the next day they arrived at the Delaware. While the pioneers waited on the bank, Zack turned his horse out into the river to measure its depth. After crossing back and forth, he told them to prop up the beds of their wagons ten inches with blocks of wood before attempting to ford.

When they were ready to go, Zack grabbed the reins of the lead mule of Wash's team and with a "Huzzah, huzzah, rah!" he led the mules into the water, riding with them. He called back for the second man on horseback to do the same. And so, one by one, each wagon was led across the ford by the mounted men. When it was Goldie's and Gray's turn, Gray grabbed the reins of the lead mule as he had seen Zack do. When they reached the other side, he asked Goldie to check the caulking.

"Bottom's dry," she reported cheerily.

After all of the wagons were safely across, Zack said they would push on as soon as they replenished their water supply. "Always travel with full water kegs," he warned. "Every time we come near water, I want you to fill those kegs."

The last two days had been so exciting and full of new experiences that Gray had had no time to ponder who Rachel's lover could be. But in camp that evening his thoughts returned to the mystery. The Milford wagon was next to the Stevens' in the train, so he decided to go see Mary. As he drew near, he heard loud voices. At first he thought the Milfords might be having a family squabble, but when he got closer, he saw them sitting quietly in front of their fire. The arguing was issuing from the Stevens wagon.

"What's the matter over there?" asked Gray as he joined the Milfords.

"Just listen," said Dan. "You'll hear."

"They're telling the whole train," grinned Mary.

"If you think I'm going to tie myself to him and work for him, you're very much mistaken," he heard Rachel say. "You may have to, you're married to him. But thank God, I'm not!"

"Oh, Rachel," wailed her mother. "We couldn't possibly keep up with the Colby group. It's all I can do to keep up with this one."

"And that's another thing," stormed Rachel. "Look at my hands! I'm through driving that filthy team! Let him do it for a change."

"But Rachel, you know he can't."

"Because he can't stay away from his damn bottle! Well, I'll tell you something, Mother. Either we break out and follow those men or I'll go alone. Take your choice." She hopped down from the back of the wagon and sauntered unconcernedly over to the Milford fire. "Oh, Gray," she said sweetly, "where've you been? That sister of yours must have you thoroughly domesticated."

Gray blushed to his copper hair line, stammering as he attempted to reply. But in a moment he regained his composure as he realized what Rachel was up to.

"Don't you think we're going awful slow?" she asked. "I mean, it looks like Chuck Colby had the right idea after all, doesn't it?"

"What makes you think that?" interjected Dan.

"Because they're ahead of us!" snapped Rachel. Then turning again to Gray she said, "Wouldn't you like to hurry along?"

"I guess we all would," said Gray. "But we're going as fast as we can."

"If we could get some horses," continued Rachel as if Gray hadn't said anything, "I'll bet we could catch Colby's group in no time. Would you do that for me, Gray?"

"I'd like to help you out, but I've got responsibilities here."

"Oh yes, I forgot," laughed Rachel. "Your sister." She made it sound like a dirty word. "There aren't any real men left in this whole wagon train. I guess I'll have to go alone."

"You don't have to do anything alone while I'm around, Rachel," said a youth who had joined the group just in time to hear Rachel's last remark.

"Why Henry Bowles," giggled Rachel. "You mean you'd desert this nice safe wagon train and ride away with me? My, aren't you dashing!"

"Ride away where?" asked the bewildered Henry.

"Why, to catch Chuck Colby," said Rachel. "And be in California in time to still get some gold."

"What about your folks?" asked Henry, looking apprehensively at the Stevens wagon.

"What folks?" sneered Rachel. "Will you take me, Henry? Or are you like the others?"

"If that's what you want, Rachel."

"Good! You get the horses while I gather my things."

Gray followed Henry as he started off. "Don't be a fool," he said. "She's only using you. She tried to get me to take her first."

"Shut up, Gray! You're my friend, but shut up!"

"It's not only that. . .I think she's got some fellow in the Colby gang."

"Look, Gray, just because you can't have her doesn't mean you can keep her from everybody else. Now leave me alone. I don't want to hear any more of your stories."

"It's not a story," shouted Gray. "It's true, you blind oaf! She doesn't care about you or me or anybody else. Can't you see that?"

Henry's fist suddenly met Gray's jaw. Staggering, Gray punched back. They squared-off and were fighting savagely when Wash Lord intervened.

"Here, you young blokes!" he shouted as he charged between them, shoving them aside with his burly shoulders. "What do you think you're doing?"

"Nothing," muttered Gray shamefacedly.

"You just mind your own business and leave me alone, Gray Baxter," puffed Henry. He turned to Wash. "Excuse me, I gotta get another horse. I'm leaving this lousy train tonight!"

As Henry walked away, Wash said, "What's he talking about?"

Gray told him. Wash snorted, "She needn't have gone to all that trouble. Zack thinks we'll catch 'em within the week. . . . Say, that's some eye you've got there, son. You'd better get that tended to while I tell Zack what's going on."

But Gray's concern wasn't with his eye. Henry had been partially right in his accusation. He would have liked to have taken Rachel, and he was jealous because Henry was doing it. He began to see part of Rachel's fascination. She knows exactly what she wants, and she'll stop at nothing to get it, he thought. He wished he could be like that and say, "To hell with Goldie. . .to hell with responsibility. . .I'm working for myself alone." But he couldn't. At this moment he was going back to Goldie to bind up his wounds, and he hated her for being there with the same unreasonable hatred he had experienced before, although he knew she wasn't responsible. "I'll never be anything. I'll never do anything!" he cried out in anguish.

When he climbed in the wagon, Goldie was immediately aware of the charged explosive within him, but the sight of his swollen eye and battered face sent her scurrying for their small store of medicines.

"What happened, Gray?" she asked as she bathed the wound.

"Oh, just a fight with Henry. It's not important."

"I'll bet Rachel was behind it."

"There you go. If anything goes wrong around here, it's always Rachel. You'd think she was the only woman on the whole train!"

"You're awfully loud if it wasn't Rachel."

"All right, so it was Rachel! Are you satisfied?" he winced as she applied a cold cloth to his eye.

"Well, aren't you going to tell me?" she asked.

"Rachel wants to leave the train and catch up to Colby's group, and Henry's taking her. . .that's all!"

"And you tried to stop him?"

"Yes."

"Why, Gray?"

"That's what I keep asking myself. Why should I care? She asked me first."

"I see. . . .I'm sorry."

"No, you don't see. I wouldn't have gone with her even if I hadn't had you to think of. It just wouldn't have made any difference."

"Why not? You give every sign of being in love with her."

"I guess I am. . .sort of. That's what's so hard to explain. She doesn't want me or Henry or anybody else. . .except maybe one person. She just wants to use us. She doesn't even see us. We're nothing. That's what I was trying to tell Henry."

"I think you're jealous," said Goldie. "Who do you think she cares for? And how do you know?"

"I saw something, or rather heard—a while back."

"Oh, come on, Gray, I know you better than that. What do you know about her?"

"She was with a man," said Gray, turning away. "Way back in Independence. It was late at night. . .when I was on watch. I think maybe she loves him, but I don't even know that."

"Who was it? Chuck Colby?"

Gray started to answer, then stopped as he thought back to that night in Independence. "I don't know," he said slowly. But at last he thought he did know. It *must* have been Chuck. "I didn't see anything," he continued. "I just heard."

Just then Dora Cunningham poked her head in the back of the wagon. "Goldie," she said. "Oh, I didn't know you was here, Gray. Have you heard the news? Rachel Stevens is running off with Henry Bowles. It's all over the camp. Let's go see."

Outside in the center of the circle they saw Rachel handsomely mounted on a horse with her black hair waving softly in the evening breeze. Henry was tying some provisions and Rachel's belongings on a pack mule.

Rachel's dark eyes were sparkling and she had a flush of pink on her cheeks. "Come on, Henry," she urged. "Don't be so slow. We've got to get going."

46

"Just a moment, Rachel," came Henry's uncertain reply.

Goldie detected that he was beginning to have second thoughts about this venture, so she walked over to speak to him. Just then Mrs. Stevens broke through the ring around her daughter.

"Rachel, please," she begged, "don't do this!"

"Oh, Mother," said Rachel coldly, "don't make a scene. I'm going and that's all there is to it."

By this time Goldie had reached Henry's side. "Henry," she said, "are you sure you want to do this?"

"Leave me alone, Goldie," said Henry. "I'm sorry about Gray, but leave me alone."

"I'm not speaking for Gray. She'll hurt you——" she broke off as she glanced up to see Rachel sitting above her with her arm upraised, holding a whip.

"Get away from him, you!" she said as her mouth twisted into an ugly grimace. "The Baxters seem to think Henry is their private property!" She brought her whip down, missing Goldie's head by less than an inch.

"There's no need for that, Rachel," protested Henry.

"Perhaps you'd like to stay. Maybe you're afraid, too," she sneered, a little gleam of fear flickering in her eyes.

"Oh, come on, let's go," said Henry as he mounted his horse.

Goldie detected a triumphant smile on Rachel's face as they passed out of the firelight and disappeared from view into the darkness beyond.

CHAPTER **5** THE PORT CITY OF NEW YORK,
MAY, 1849★★

It was nearly nine o'clock at night when the *Manhattan*, a smoky Hudson River steamboat, finally docked in New York in her berth just above the Battery.

Before Holt Compton quite knew what was happening to him, he was standing at the foot of the gangplank, a forlorn, bewildered figure surrounded by his possessions: a split cowhide trunk with brass corners and lock, a leather satchel containing three thousand dollars in gold coins, and a colorful carpetbag. It seemed to him that everyone had some place to go and something to do except himself. The tardy arrival of the steamer made it much too late to find his father's friend, Captain Hewitt, and the offices of his shipping firm on South Street would be long since closed. He didn't know the name of a single hotel or boarding house, and he was afraid to trust any of the hackney drivers to lead him to a safe place. He wanted to sit down on his cowhide trunk and hide his head and cry, but he knew that wouldn't do any good either. He was hungry, he was tired, and most of all he missed the solid security of his father. He had never known his mother, for she had died when he was born. But in his eighteen years of life he and his father had been nearly inseparable. He had wanted John Compton to come West prospecting with him, but he had said no, this was a young man's venture; he would stay home and keep the sawmill running. His father's lumberyard was in Albany, right on the Hudson. But though Holt had grown up within sight of the river, this was his first trip to New York, one-hundred-fifty miles downstream.

He tried to think what his father would do in a situation like this, but his mind was blank. As he stood there frozen in indecision, a tall man dressed in a nut brown frock coat and peg-legged trousers stepped up to him and shoved his beaver hat back on his head revealing crisp dark hair and fashionable long sideburns.

"I couldn't help noticing, kid," he said, "that you don't seem to know which way to go." His lips parted in a smile revealing a dazzling gold tooth that lent a certain malevolence to his appearance under the flickering lights of the whale oil flares and pine torches. Holt stared at him.

"You got a place to stay?" the man asked.

"No," blurted Holt, fighting desperately to keep his voice steady.

"Well, I know a nice boarding house out on Greenwich," said the man. Holt hesitated, and conscious of his suspicion, the stranger continued, "Honest kid, see I'm a detective." He pulled out a card and handed it to Holt. "Sam Henderson's the name."

Holt still couldn't bring himself to trust him.

"Look, kid," said Sam, "this is on the straight. All it'll cost is your cab fare. This is a legit place, and Mrs. Kerry might even give us a bite of cold supper if we sweet-talk her."

"Why do you want to help me?" asked Holt bluntly.

"I don't know," said Sam, taking off his hat and scratching his dark hair. "Maybe it's because I was once a green kid myself. But you better grab me while I'm hot. Sam Henderson don't do many free favors."

"I guess I've got to trust somebody," said Holt. "And I sure am hungry."

"That's the spirit," said Sam. He hoisted Holt's trunk lightly onto his broad shoulder and strode toward one of the cabs with its pale lights peering like two eyes into the night.

Sam Henderson's friendliness began to disarm Holt as they traveled to Mrs. Kerry's boarding house. Holt confided that he was sailing to California with Captain Hewitt.

"You'll be able to find the captain in the morning. I'll show you where the shipping offices are on South Street," said Sam.

Although it was nearly ten when the two knocked at the door of Mrs. Kerry's neat three-story brick house, they were quickly admitted by the owner, a small, round, middle-aged woman with light brown hair braided and pulled into a bun on top of her head. Her eyes were blue and her cheeks pink. She wore a crisp blue calico dress with a black sateen apron over it. Holt liked her immediately, and it was plain she had affection for the debonair Sam, for she treated him more like a son than a tenant. She scolded him for being so late then clucked in sympathy when he told her about Holt.

"And I suppose you're hungry?" she said.

Holt's eyes lighted up, and Sam said, "Haven't had a bite since midday. And this boy, you can see for yourself the state he's in. Lost and lonely. . ."

"Ah, the poor lad," sighed Mrs. Kerry. "You show him the room, Sam, and I'll make you both a bite while you freshen up." Then she turned back, her merry eyes twinkling. "But don't think I don't see through you, Sam, me boy. . . .Not a bite since midday, indeed!"

She scurried out to the kitchen while Sam, laughing uproariously, showed Holt up the stairs to a neat bedroom with a big double bed covered with snowy linen and a colorful quilt. The furniture was sturdy and serviceable and had been rubbed to a deep satiny brown by frequent polishing. There was a braided rug on the floor and fresh towels hung by the marble-topped washstand, which held a china pitcher and a bowl.

Holt looked around him in delight, and the burden of his homesickness started to lift. The dull thud of his empty stomach changed to a violent roar, and once again he felt the singing inside him that told him he was young, alive, and headed for great adventure.

"I told you you'd like it," said Sam.

"I apologize. I didn't trust you."

"Forget it. You had good reason. But I just couldn't see you getting rolled in one of those Cherry or Water Street holes."

"Do you think I could stay here till my ship sails?"

"Not only that," laughed Sam, "I've a feeling Mrs. Kerry will see to it personally that you're deposited safely on board. I can always tell when she takes a shine to somebody."

When the two returned downstairs, they were greeted by a banquet. Mrs. Kerry had a platter of sliced corned beef and homemade white bread with fresh churned butter. Besides these, there was a bowl of steaming scrambled eggs, a pitcher of cool milk, and a plate of puffy sugar cookies. She beamed with delight as her two boarders attacked and devoured the tasty supper.

In the morning Sam guided Holt down to the shipping offices of the Red Sun Line. Formerly the company had engaged exclusively in the China trade. But at present their ships were launched in a profitable three-way traffic carrying men and supplies to the gold fields in California, raw materials to China and India, and the rich fabrics, woods, spices, and teas of the East to London and the home port of New York. They had in operation two of the new fast ships called clippers, one of which, the *Sea Skimmer,* under the command of Captain Hewitt, would carry Holt to California.

As Holt entered the shipping firm's offices, a small, nervous clerk looked up from a ledger. "Yes, sir," he said. "What can I do for you?"

"I'm Holt Compton. Could you tell me where I could find Captain Hewitt?"

"Oh, Mr. Compton," the clerk sprang up. "Just a minute, I'll tell him you're here." He ran to a glass-topped door and tapped.

"Yes, what is it, Reeves?" asked a voice from within.

"It's Mr. Compton, sir. He's here."

50

"Well, by God!" A big, broad-shouldered and deep-chested man with close-cropped salt-and-pepper hair, long sideburns, and deeply carved sun and smile lines around his sparkling blue eyes brushed by the frail clerk and clapped Holt soundly on both shoulders. The captain was attired in fawn-colored trousers and a fashionable blue frockcoat, beneath which flashed a dashing red waistcoat draped with a massive gold watch chain. "Well, my boy, where *have* you been?" he boomed. Without waiting for an answer, he propelled Holt vigorously into the inner office. "Isn't he a fine lad?" he asked a gray-haired man with sparse chin whiskers. "McGill, I want you to meet the son of a lifelong friend. Holt, this is Hugh McGill, one of the directors of the Red Sun Line."

"How do you do, Mr. McGill," said Holt, respectfully holding out his hand.

Captain Hewitt wasted no more time on pleasantries. He snapped out his watch. "There's just enough time to show you the *Sea Skimmer* before lunch," he said.

Holt thrilled to the beautiful clipper-type ship with her tall slanting masts and long, slim lines. He gaped at the carved figure of a lady in flowing robes holding a torch high in her right hand, sprouting from the bow.

"Ah, she's our good luck piece," smiled Cyrus Hewitt in appreciation. "She'll see us safely through our voyage.

Below decks Holt marveled at the compact hold now being loaded with cargo and all the gear for a long sea voyage. Returning to the deck Captain Hewitt boomed in a way that was more a command than a query, "How about a bite of dinner? I'm hungry as an old tar can be."

"I'm sort of hungry too, sir. My father says I'm hungry most of the time."

"And why not? A fine strapping lad like you." He bounded to the street and forthwith captured a carriage for the drive up Broadway to the elegant Astor House opposite the park. At the famous eighty-foot black walnut bar in the rotunda, he ordered them each a rye whisky and proposed a toast to Holt's good fortune in California. The captain neatly downed his drink. Holt gamely imitated him, only to end up spluttering in red-faced embarrassment. But Captain Hewitt took no notice of this mark of inexperience. He immediately propelled Holt into the glittering crystal, gold, and white restaurant, where they dined sumptuously on Virginia ham boiled in cider and served with new spinach.

During their dinner Cyrus Hewitt told Holt that he had wanted to take him as part of the crew on the maiden voyage of the *Sea Skimmer*, but that John Compton had wanted Holt to travel as a passenger. "Your pa thinks the sea is brutalizing. He's a gentle man. I see that you are too," he sighed. "A pity—the sea can be a beautiful mistress. But your father is right too. You'll see some things on this voyage that you won't like. Sometimes a captain has to be rough. I want you to remember that, lad, and not try to interfere in things you may not understand."

"I won't, sir," promised Holt, not fully realizing what he was saying. Later he was to look back on his promise and reflect on how innocent he had been.

"And now, lad, do you think you can entertain yourself this evening? I had intended to take you to the Astor Place Opera House. . .the great English actor, William MacCready, is performing. But, unfortunately, the directors of the company are having an important meeting tonight which I must attend. We sail in three days' time."

"I'll be all right. There's so much to see here. This must be the most exciting city in the world."

"Then here are the tickets for the play. But be careful—they don't like the British here. It's a feud between MacCready and our own Edwin Forrest. And if there's trouble, you'd best stay away."

"Thank you, sir. I'll see if Sam Henderson can go. It should be safe enough with him along. . .he's a detective."

"Yes, but you'll be better off elsewhere if something serious develops from this foolishness. Now I must go."

That afternoon Kevin Adams, a blond, strapping, flint-boned farm boy from New England, was at his job in Mr. Jones' ship's chandlery on South Street and heard the talk about William MacCready. A rumor that the British were releasing crews from several men-of-war anchored in the harbor rippled up the street, and late in the afternoon a handbill appeared calling upon the citizens of New York to rally at Astor Place and Eighth that night "to prevent the dastardly MacCready from sullying the free soil of the United States." Kevin read the handbill but was not much interested. He was totally absorbed these days in his ambition to join the gold rush.

A poor supper of bread and cheese in his dank basement room half satisfied his hunger, but his restlessness and the unpleasantness of his surroundings drove him out onto the street. He knew that he didn't have to eat meagerly and alone. Nancy Lee would welcome him for supper at her Cherry Street establishment not only occasionally but every night. But he could not bring himself to become indebted to her in this way any more than he could take her money to buy his passage to California, for he felt this would surrender a measure of that personal freedom which he prized.

Out on the street he was surprised at the quiet. The only other person on the entire street was an old bum shuffling along. Curiosity drove him to speak to the derelict. "Where is everybody?" he asked.

"Why, down at Astor Place to see the excitement," laughed the old man. "Where you been, Mister?"

Then Kevin remembered the talk in the store that afternoon and the handbill he had read. He decided to walk up to Astor Place and see what was going on.

Holt had had an intoxicating afternoon. After inspecting Central Park he had gone back to the business district, where he watched the activity around the exotically named mercantile houses and the throbbing waterfront where some of the packets were casting off and dropping down the East River. He could see them anchored off the Battery waiting for the turn of the tide. The Battery was a lovely green strip, an oasis in the midst of all the sterile scurrying for money that surrounded it. Holt couldn't make himself leave this fascinating area until his hunger finally drove him to seek supper.

Sam Henderson was bolting some roast beef when Holt arrived back at Mrs. Kerry's place. "Gee, Sam," he said, "I hope you aren't busy this evening. Captain Hewitt gave me two tickets to see William MacCready, and I was hoping you'd go with me."

"I'm going to the opera house all right," said Sam. "I've been detailed to help beef up the police force. Some young galoots are threatening to start a riot over that MacCready. And you can bet we'll be ready for 'em if they do! We've got a detail of mounted men, and the Seventh Regiment of the National Guard Infantry will be standing by."

Holt's eyes began to shine with excitement. "Please, Sam," he begged, "take me with you. I've never seen a riot."

"And a lot better off you'll be if you never do. Besides, I can't be worrying about you in addition to everythin' else."

Not to be put off, after Sam left Holt asked Mrs. Kerry the best way to get to Astor Place.

"I'll not be havin' two of you out there to worry about," said Mr. Kerry tartly. "So, I'll not be tellin' you."

"I won't get involved, Mrs. Kerry," promised Holt. "I just want to see what happens."

"Curiosity killed a cat," retorted Mrs. Kerry. But when she saw he was determined, she told him the best route to take, cautioning him to keep his distance from any fighting.

Even with Mrs. Kerry's directions he was unable to follow the baffling turns of the streets and soon was hopelessly lost. He wandered about for some time, not knowing which way to go. Finally he heard a roar of clamoring voices and the noise of combat. He made his way toward the sound till he was standing near the opera house on Eighth Street. Not far away a mob of men, red-faced and screaming, were hurling paving stones and using clubs against a small band of police. The theatre looked as if it had been under siege. The big windows and fanlights were smashed, the paneled doors were beaten and battered, and the heavy walls were pockmarked. Part of the street was dug up, and Holt watched the piles of cobblestones diminish as the crowd angrily hurled them against the officials who were trying to fend them off.

Holt had never seen mob violence before, and he shivered. The street lights and torch flares picked out the contorted faces of the rioters. As he watched, men were felled by stones, their blood spurting from deep gouges and wounds. Though horrified, his own blood surged and pounded and he could not tear himself away from the scene. Just as it seemed the police could hold no longer, a small regiment of horse troops followed by a line of infantry charged into Astor Place. The angry rioters turned on them, hurling their stones and sticks. Many of the horses fell, others screamed and reared and bucked off their riders as they bolted.

The small band of infantry was wedged in tightly by the rioters. Some of the soldiers even had their guns wrested from their hands. Miraculously, despite its minute size, the company succeeded in driving the rioters down Eighth Street, clearing the back of the theatre. After they swept Eighth Street, a cordon of police was thrown across it, and the soldiers continued their march toward Broadway and back to Astor Place to clear the front of the opera house. When they reached the front, however, the crowd, which numbered in the thousands, turned on them again and forced them back toward the theatre.

Holt had gone around to Lafayette Place and had climbed on a lamppost to see what was happening. He heard someone shout an order to disperse or the soldiers would fire, but the mob only laughed derisively and flung more stones. Holt then heard a command to fire. At this moment he was grasped from behind and yanked to the pavement. As he fell he was aware of a bullet whizzing by him, and as he rolled over he saw his assailant was a shabby blond youth. It was Kevin Adams.

"What the hell——" he began, then stopped as he saw the blood gushing from a wound high on his rescuer's left arm.

"I heard them say to fire over their heads," Kevin said. "You were right in the line of fire standing on that lamp base."

"I don't know what to say," said Holt. "I guess I was a fool." He tore off a piece of his shirt to bind Kevin's arm. "My name's Holt Compton, and thanks for saving my life."

"Kevin Adams is my name."

The mob was advancing against the soldiers again. Kevin grabbed Holt with his good arm.

"Get back in the doorway!" he yelled. "They'll fire again!"

The next volley was directly into the ranks of the horde, and several young men slumped dead in the street. Some of the rioters turned and fled in panic. But the hard core wheeled again on the soldiers. Still a third volley was fired, and the crowd broke up and ran. Kevin and Holt huddled in the doorway away from the ricocheting bullets and the stampeding throng.

At last the area was quiet, and the two made their way out into the street. Kevin, his arm still bleeding profusely, said he'd go to Nancy Lee's if Holt got a cab. But the few drivers who paused only stared and then drove hastily on.

"Can we walk there?" asked Holt.

"Yes, I think I can make it," said Kevin. He directed Holt to the house on Cherry Street. But by the time they reached Nancy Lee's brightly painted pink door, Kevin was barely conscious. Holt rapped loudly.

The well-prepared smile of the Negro maid froze when she saw the bloodied Kevin awkwardly supported by a stranger. "Oh, Mistah Kevin," she shrieked, "what's happened?"

At the shriek Nancy Lee, a fragile looking golden-haired girl, came running from her office. Holt's eyes bulged at the low décolletage of her gown, a jet-trimmed brilliant pink taffeta that matched the vivid hue of her front door. Instantly she grasped the situation and dispatched the maid for the doctor. She helped Holt maneuver Kevin back to her fresh blue and white bedroom. While she wrested Kevin's coat and shirt off, Holt stammered out the tale of the riot and of how Kevin had saved his life. He had a strange feeling he knew what kind of place he was in but couldn't bring himself to ask.

Nancy Lee decided to answer the question that hovered in the air between them. "Yes," she said, "this is a house."

"I didn't mean to pry," said Holt, blushing a deep scarlet.

"You've never been in one before?"

"No, ma'am, I'm from Albany."

"I see," smiled Nancy as if that explained everything. "If you'd like a girl, it's on the house...I mean after your taking care of Kevin..." she trailed off.

"Oh, no thank you, ma'am," said Holt. "I guess if he's going to be all right, I'll be going."

Kevin roused. "Don't go," he pleaded.

Holt sat down gingerly on a rocker, awkwardly holding his hat on his knees.

The doctor came soon and cauterized Kevin's wound. "Lucky, that one," he observed. "The ball passed clean through the muscle...didn't touch a bone. He won't hardly know he was hit in a few days."

"That's a relief, Doctor," said Nancy.

"But see you don't try to use that arm for at least a week," he warned.

"I won't," said Kevin.

"Now you'd better take this. It'll make you sleep." He poured a strong dose of brandy.

56

"But I don't drink," said Kevin.

"All the better," commented the doctor and left.

In the aftermath of the riot Nancy Lee's business was suddenly booming, requiring her presence in the red velvet sitting room and enabling the two boys to become better acquainted. His tongue unusually loose because of the brandy, Kevin told Holt of his dreams of going to California and how he had tried but failed to gain passage by working as a deckhand. Holt offered to pay his passage, but Kevin vehemently refused. Finally he fell asleep, and Holt pushed his way out of the house. He returned to Mrs. Kerry's, brooding over how he could help his newfound friend get to California. But he could think of no way unless Captain Hewitt would be willing to sign him on the crew of the *Sea Skimmer*. I'll ask him, he thought and immediately fell asleep.

Captain Hewitt was in his cabin checking bills of lading on his cargo and puffing on a long Dutch clay pipe when Holt approached him the next morning. As soon as Holt told him how Kevin had risked his life for him the night before, the captain nodded in understanding.

"The fellow showed rare courage," he said. "I'll be happy to have him aboard, even if he is green."

"Thank you, sir," beamed Holt.

"But you'd best get the young buck down here in a hurry," continued the captain gravely. "Warrants have been sworn out for the arrest of anyone connected with the riot."

"But we weren't connected."

"I know, but the wound implicates Adams and would you, too, if this gets about. So bring him aboard. We sail day after tomorrow, and I'd like to have you both with us."

Holt sped off to the house on Cherry Street, where he discovered from a very groggy Nancy that Kevin, despite having the use of only one arm, had insisted upon reporting to his job. She gave Holt directions to the store on South Street.

At the good news, Kevin gripped his arm and said, "You'll never know what this means to me. I'll thank you the rest of my life."

"Have you heard about the warrants?" asked Holt.

"Yes, I found out even before I got to work. Nobody here knows about my arm."

"Good. Captain Hewitt says you'd better come to the ship and stay there till we sail."

57

It took little time for Kevin to sever his relationship with Mr. Jones, who wished him well and gave him a five-dollar gold piece for luck. Actually the gold piece constituted what Mr. Jones owed him in wages, but Kevin took it as a friendly gesture.

On board the *Sea Skimmer* Kevin met Captain Hewitt and entrusted him with his worldly wealth of twenty-seven dollars, to be deposited with Holt's three thousand in the ship's strongbox. The contrast between the two boys could not be greater: the tall, powerfully built, fair farm boy, and the not so tall, more slender, dark-haired merchant's son. Still, they were drawn to each other.

That evening Kevin insisted on going to see Nancy Lee once more and invited Holt to accompany him. On the way he asked if Holt would like to have a girl since it would probably be his last night ashore.

"You mean one of those girls?" asked Holt incredulously.

"Haven't you ever had a girl?"

"Not that way."

"Well, it's time you did. I'll ask Nance to pick you out a good one."

"I guess I'd really better get my things packed," gulped Holt. "You go on over. . .I'll see you on board tomorrow."

"Coward," said Kevin.

"It's not that at all!" protested Holt. Apprehensively he eyed the girls on the walk in front of the Cherry Street house they were passing.

"Then what?" asked Kevin.

"Oh, all right," he capitulated.

At the house Kevin whispered to Nancy Lee about Holt's virginal state. She nodded and sent the colored maid upstairs to fetch Miss Juliet, an exceptionally lovely girl with a cloud of dark hair and liquid brown eyes.

Each of Nancy Lee's girls had a spacious room or apartment in the house and commanded large sums for a night's work. Besides being beautiful, they were experts in their trade, trained in etiquette, language, and deportment as well as in the art of lovemaking. Her house was one of the top ones on the street. And a heavy payoff to the police and officials ensured that Nancy Lee could keep it that way without fear of being molested.

Juliet drew the bashful Holt slowly up the stairs to her room, while Nancy Lee sent the maid up with a bucket of iced champagne. Then laughing, she turned to Kevin. He drew her into her room and spilled out the news of his good fortune in signing on the *Sea Skimmer*. Hiding her disappointment, Nancy Lee asked in a steady voice, "When do you sail?"

"Day after tomorrow. But we'll be out in the harbor tomorrow night, so I guess this will be our last night together," sighed Kevin.

She couldn't help asking, "Will you miss me?"

"You know I will, Nance," said Kevin, running his fingers through her long golden hair. "I'll miss you more than anyone. It's been good between us."

"I've been wondering about going to California too," whispered Nancy.

"Yes," said Kevin, suddenly stiffening as he remembered what she was. "I guess it would be a pretty good place for a business like yours. . . . Plenty of customers."

Suddenly he was making love to her in a savage manner as if he were trying to revenge himself for some wrong she had done him. He didn't understand his feelings. He only knew that he was acting violently and gloried in it.

Up in Juliet's room which was lavishly furnished and decorated in pale pinks, Holt was feeling more uncomfortable by the moment. Clutching his hat tightly with both hands, he had seated himself on a small pink velvet slipper chair as far from the bed as possible. After a brief wrestling match, Juliet finally relieved him of his hat and hung it on the top bracket of a pink clothestree. Holt felt more insecure than ever. At Juliet's suggestion that he take off his coat and she slip into something more comfortable, he sprang to his feet in alarm. "Oh, no. . .I'm just fine, and so are you. That's a lovely dress. . .I like you just the way you are."

Juliet had stepped around behind him while he was making this speech and before he knew what she was up to had deftly slipped off his tailcoat. Small beads of perspiration began breaking out on his forehead, and he felt his hands grow clammy as Juliet unbuttoned his waistcoat and slipped that off too.

"There now, isn't that better? Let's have some champagne." She moved over to the champagne bucket, popped the cork, and poured two glasses of the bubbly nectar. Proferring one to Holt, she drew a pink chair close to the slipper chair where Holt had retreated after being relieved of his waistcoat.

"Thanks," said Holt, downing the glass so quickly that it tickled

59

his nose and made him sneeze. While he was apologizing and searching frantically for his handkerchief, Juliet had his glass refilled and again was offering it to him.

"Tastes good," said Holt lamely, tossing off the second glass as swiftly as the first. "I guess I was thirsty."

After the fourth glass Holt was becoming uncomfortably warm. "Wouldn't you like the window opened?" he asked.

"No thank you," said Juliet. "But this dress is heavy. Help me with the hooks, will you?" She turned her back to him.

Holt clumsily worked at unfastening the dress, breathing heavily at the scented nearness of the girl. As she stepped out of the dress and hung it in a clothes cupboard, he stole a secret look at her then looked quickly away. But he saw little more than he had already seen since she still wore numerous long petticoats and a chemise top. Feeling warmer by the moment, he reached for the bottle of champagne but found it empty. Juliet walked to the bed and pulled a silken cord. As if by magic, another bottle appeared. After pouring Holt a fresh glass, she sat on a chaise lounge and invitingly patted a place beside her. Holt was drawn toward her by his aroused desire, and under the expert tutelage of the girl, he soon found himself in the role of a delighted if clumsy aggressor.

His passion spent, however, he felt a pang of regret that his first sexual experience had been with a prostitute. Although this might be an insignificant detail to most men, for himself he wished that his physical satisfaction had been coupled with the joy of love.

The *Sea Skimmer*, manned by a skeleton crew the next day, sailed down the East River to anchor off the Battery. Before going ashore to get his final shipping orders, Captain Hewitt admonished the boys to remain on the ship even though they would not sail until the next morning on the first tide.

Kevin had already been befriended by an old sailor who was teaching him nautical terms. Holt decided to take lessons, too. There were the names and functions of more than twenty sails to be mastered on the three-masted clipper; and there were hundreds of lines leading up the masts to the yardarms that supported the sails. A sailor had to know them all. Besides sorting out the mainsail from the main topsail and the main topgallant sail, they learned which was the port and which the starboard side of the ship, and how the great wheel turned the rudder. It was a very busy day, and by dinnertime the boys were tired and more than

60

slightly confused by all of the information they were trying to cram into their heads. They retired soon after they finished the meal.

Below deck the majority of the space originally used to carry cargo had been carved into a cramped steerage cabin to carry fifty men in bunks three tiers high to the gold fields. For this dubious privilege of traveling steerage, the young men were paying three hundred and fifty dollars a head. Those more fortunate and better heeled could get cabins similar to Holt's on the main deck for six hundred to eight hundred dollars, depending on how many men shared the cabin. There were fifteen such berths available on the *Sea Skimmer.* In addition to some farming equipment bound for Valparaiso, the hold held a cargo of tobacco in five-pound tins, some short-handled shovels, and hundreds of kegs of various size nails, which the owners hoped would bring a high price in San Francisco.

As a result of the conversion of the ship to the gold rush trade, the crew's quarters were even more cramped than usual. Happily unaware of the distinction between himself and most of the men who shipped to California, Holt slept soundly and peacefully in his single cabin opposite Captain Hewitt's on the main deck, while below, Kevin was gently rocked to sleep in a tight berth in the crew's compartment.

CHAPTER **6** CROSSING THE BIG AND LITTLE
VERMILLION AND THE BIG
BLUE RIVERS ★★★★★★★★★★★★★★★★★★★★★★★★★★★★★★★

As Matilda's kittens became more lively and frolicsome, Goldie regretted more than ever that she must sell them at Fort Kearney. She couldn't bear the thought of parting with a gold and white tom whom she'd named Tag Along because he was always at her heels. "He's a people cat," she explained to Gray as they sat in front of their fire.

61

"He's just a plain moocher," assessed Gray. "He knows how to get anything he wants with that innocent stare."

Tag Along, sensing he was being discussed, climbed up Gray's pants leg to a cozy position in his lap. "See what I mean?" said Gray. "Who would have the heart to dump him? Now you're going to have to put more wood on the fire. I can't move."

"I know someone else who knows how to get out of doing something," said Goldie

They had to use heavy ropes and pulleys to lower the wagons one by one over the high, steep bank at the crossing of the Big Vermillion River, and faced the same kind of situation when they crossed the Little Vermillion. "That was just to get you in shape for the really bad one," said Zack after the crossing. "We should reach the Big Blue day after tomorrow, and there we'll have to build rafts."

At the Big Blue the company decided to build four large rafts which could carry several wagons at a time and some of the livestock that couldn't swim against the current. The men fell to their task with the ease of having worked together before, and soon they were ready to launch their first raft, rolled on logs down to the water's edge.

The animals were bawling and bellowing in terror. This din, coupled with the sound of the roaring river, began to set nerves on edge, and men and women began shouting and screaming at each other and the animals.

In order to make a safe crossing, Zack had several men ride into the river holding ropes attached to the raft, forcing their swimming mounts to help tow it across. Other men standing on the sides of the raft stuck long poles in the riverbed to stabilize the craft and propel it forward. Soon this first group was safely on the other side, where they rolled off the six wagons and went back for another load.

By this time the second raft was launched. The Baxter wagon was on this one. Gray was in the water on Sunny handling one of the ropes, while Goldie was taking her turn on one of the long poles. Except for one precarious moment when they seemed to stand still in midstream, their raft also made the crossing safely.

All was going well until the fourth raft was ready to make its first crossing. This one held the Stevens wagon. In midstream, under the unaccustomed motion, John Stevens, who had slept through all of the noise about him, wakened from his usual alcoholic somnolence. Since his wagon was on the end of the raft, when he peered out over the tail gate he saw only the roaring river beneath him. Screaming in fright, he toppled into the foaming water. Dan Milford, handling a pole toward the rear of the raft, saw Mr. Stevens fall and yelled, "Man in the water! Man in the water!"

Zack was leading some of the swimming mules across when Stevens fell. Quickly he turned his horse out into the current and grabbed the drowning man. He hauled the inert body up on the horse's back and swam the animal to the bank. He slid Mr. Stevens' body off onto the ground and began to extract the water from him.

The Stevens wagon was pushed onto the shore, and Rachel's mother ran up to where Zack was working over her husband. A wisp of her still fine light brown hair had blown across her white cheeks, and her delicate though work-hardened hands made slight fluttering motions like dying birds. Her enormous dark eyes gave off the stricken look of a wound too deep to bear. She never said a word, just stood there, small and fragile, as if waiting for the final blow that would strike her down forever.

Finally John Stevens sighed and opened his eyes. Zack looked up at her and said, "He'll be all right, Rose."

The frail woman sank to the ground in a faint.

"Here, some of you men," ordered Zack, "carry them both back to camp, and build a warm fire. We've got to get him out of those clothes. He could still catch a fever. And someone give that woman something decent to eat."

When the group of forty-one wagons started for the Little Blue the next morning, Dan Milford was driving the Stevens wagon, for Rose Stevens' fainting the afternoon before had heralded a complete collapse. Both she and her husband were bedded down in the back of the wagon with Dan's mother, Sara, ministering to them.

John Stevens, for the first time since the trip began, was sober. He was upbraiding himself for what he had done to his wife and kept asking about Rachel. Finally Sara told him that she had gone off with Henry Bowles to join Colby's group.

"Why wasn't I informed of this?" asked Stevens.

"You were informed, as you put it, Mr. Stevens," tartly replied Sara. "But it didn't seem to register."

"At least I'm fit to drive my own wagon now," said the stubborn man, attempting to rise.

"John, please," said Rose weakly. "Please let them help us. I'm so tired."

"For you, Rose," he said and gratefully settled back down.

Once more his wife had saved his pride, and once more he wanted a drink in order to reach that oblivion that kept him from facing his failure as a man. But this time he determined to withstand his craving in order to spare her more anguish.

For the first time since they started their trek, at their camping spot that night there were no trees and no wood for the fires. Zack pointed to the dried buffalo dung scattered about and directed them to build their fires from that, calling it "buffalo chips." To the greenhorns' surprise the chips made an excellent fire, relieving them of any further worry over finding wood. With the remainder of a great herd lying all around them, the pioneers began to long for a sight of the buffalo themselves, for many of the families had eaten no fresh meat since leaving Independence.

After supper Dan Milford came over and asked Goldie to take a walk with him.

"Go ahead, Sis," said Gray. "I'll finish getting the stuff packed for tomorrow's breakfast and nooning."

"We won't be gone too long," said Dan. "I have the watch at ten. Just thought it might be nice to look around. Would you like to walk to that little hill over there?"

"Yes, maybe we can see the Little Blue from the top."

Just before ten Zack came by the wagon. "Where's Goldie?" he asked.

"She and Dan Milford went walking. They must've got talking and forgot the time."

"Milford has the ten o'clock watch. Which way did they go?"

"Dan said something about going up on that hill out there. Maybe I'd better come too."

"No, you take Dan's place till I find him. Don't worry. . .I'll bring them back in a hurry." He walked swiftly off in the direction Gray had pointed.

It took Zack fifteen minutes of fast pacing to reach the spot where Goldie and Dan were sitting on the side of the hill. The entire way he kept telling himself that they were all right, but he knew that they very well could be in danger, and so he was angry with them for having left the safety of the circle. When he saw Dan sitting with his arm around Goldie, both gazing at the moon, he was furious. As he came softly up behind them, Dan bent over and kissed Goldie's upturned face. This was too much for Zack. He sprang forward and snarled at the culprits. "What do you mean by going off like this? I thought I had made it clear that no one was to leave the safety of the wagon circle at night. Do you think all I have to do is round up strays?"

"Gee, I'm sorry, Zack," said Dan, springing to his feet in embarrassment.

"And where should you be right now?" asked Zack, glowering at the lanky youth.

"Oh, my God," cried Dan. "Is it that late?" He turned to Goldie. "I clean forgot I have the ten o'clock guard. Could we sort of go back in a hurry?"

"You go on. I'll take Goldie back," said Zack.

"Thanks...I won't let it happen again," called Dan as he hurried off.

Goldie sat on the ground where Zack had found her with Dan. She had been experiencing the sweetness of a first kiss from a nice boy whom she liked very much. Having had no time to savor it, she felt disappointed and cheated. Since she showed no inclination to move, Zack finally said, "We'd better be getting back."

"Yes, I suppose so," she said listlessly.

Zack, sensing she was annoyed, tried to explain. "Why did you and Dan go off like that? You didn't even hear me come up. What if I had been an Indian?"

"It was such a beautiful night, and it was so good to get away. Anyway, it doesn't matter now. It's all spoiled. I won't do it again."

"What do you mean, *spoiled?*" asked Zack.

"You wouldn't understand...you're too old. But everything's new to us."

"Even a kiss?" said Zack quietly.

"Yes."

"I suppose that means you like Dan."

"Well, of course I like him! Do you suppose I'd let him kiss me if I didn't?"

"And how about me? Do you like me, Goldie?" asked Zack, pressing.

"Everybody likes and respects you, Zack. But that's different." She was confused as to where this questioning was leading.

"Is it?" Suddenly he stopped, took her in his arms, and began kissing her with the hungry mouth of a man. He was trembling, and Goldie began to tremble too as she caught the fire of his passion. She had never felt anything like this before. Dan's sweet tentative boy's kiss could not compare with what she was experiencing now. She threw her arms around Zack and gave herself completely to the ecstasy of the moment. She knew he could do anything he wanted to with her, and she wanted him to take her for his own. But at the height of her emotional surge, he broke and thrust her away from him. "That's what I'm trying to tell you," he said. "That could happen with anybody."

Goldie looked at him in shock, her eyes filling with tears. "Oh!" she cried. She turned and ran stumbling back to camp.

Zack remained motionless for a moment looking after her, trying to regain his composure. "Fool!" he said to himself. "You fool!"

How could a man do such a thing merely as an object lesson, Goldie sobbed to herself? She undressed quickly so as to be in her feather tick before Gray returned. If Zack had wanted to make her afraid of kissing, he certainly had succeeded. And how humiliating to think that he was capable of arousing such passion within her without feeling anything himself. And he knew what he had done. She didn't know how she could ever face him again.

Upon reaching the Little Blue River the next afternoon, the company turned northwest and followed the pretty meandering stream, lined with the now familiar cottonwoods, up toward its source. Since they had been traveling twelve days without even taking a break for the Sabbath, Zack said they could spend a day catching up on the washing and other chores.

For a change the appetizing odors of hot breakfasts wafted throughout the camp the next day, and by midmorning every bush and tree blossomed clean linens. Many of the women had set bread to rise, and the fires burned steadily as they cooked ahead for the long days when time would not permit planning or preparing tasty meals.

In the rush to catch up on all of the work, Goldie hardly had time to dwell on her passionate experience of the day before. Gray helped her with the washing. Then she took her soap and towel and went down to the river to bathe and wash her hair.

Shortly after, Zack went to the Lord wagon where he kept his belongings. He got some clean clothes, a towel, and some soap and headed for the river. A bend in the stream separating the men's bathing area from the women's was supposed to provide each sex with privacy. But as Zack approached the water, he heard the silvery voice of a girl singing. The sound drew him enchanted through the trees till finally he was looking at Goldie standing in the warm sun drying her long, shining hair with a towel. Although dressed once more in her serviceable butternut skirt held out by voluminous petticoats, above she wore only her laced chemise, revealing the lustre of her arms and throat. As he stood transfixed, she laid down her towel and began running a comb through her tangled curls. Zack had an impulse to go and help her, when with a jolt he realized that not only would this be improper, but also he shouldn't be there in the first place. In haste he withdrew to his own allotted portion of the river.

By three o'clock nearly all of the catch-up work had been completed. The clothes were clean, savory odors were drifting through the camp from the fires, and everyone was seeking some diversion. As if it were planned, one of the men watching the livestock sang out, "Wagon train coming."

There was an eager rush to see the new arrivals. They counted ten wagons in the approaching group, one of which was carrying supplies to the Army at Fort Kearney. Wash found out from their leader that they had been on the road a week from Independence. "We're all going to California," the man said. "Say, those Army boys are carrying some mail in their wagon. They might have some for you people."

"We'd be obliged if you'd see," said Wash to an Army sergeant.

"Sure," said the soldier. "By the way, is this the train headed by Zack Peale?"

"Yes, Zack's our guide."

"I'm Peale," said Zack, stepping forward.

"I got a message for you from an Oliver Fisher. We met him just outside of Independence. He said to tell you that they was doing fine, and that young Smith was still alive."

"How did they look?" asked Zack.

"The big man's leg looked pretty good," said the sergeant. "But that boy in the back of the wagon. . .well, I don't know about him. Must've been a real bad accident."

"It was. Real bad."

"Well, now just let me look through these letters," said the soldier.

Goldie and Gray pressed close hoping to have a letter from Uncle Bob and Aunt Opal or Big Timbers. At this moment they felt very far away from home. Finally their hoped for instant arrived as the sergeant called out, "Baxter. . .Goldie and Gray Baxter."

"Here!" yelled Gray and tripped over his own feet, falling flat as he grasped the letter. Willing hands helped him up. Embarrassed, he and Goldie retired with their prize to the woods.

"You read it to me," said Goldie. "I'm too excited!"

"It's from Aunt Opal," said Gray, glancing at the signature after he had broken the wax.

"Go on."

"Dear Children," Gray read. "It seems so long since you left and yet it was only last week. Big Timbers got back yesterday and reported he saw you on your way across Illinois. I do hope you are being careful." He paused and unabashedly dashed away a tear.

"Sounds just like her," choked Goldie.

Gray continued: "The spring planting's most all done and everything's leafing out real pretty now. We're all fine here. We got a new boarder. You'd like him, Gray. His name is Mr. Dandy. He's a theatrical man although right now he's selling some kind of cough medicine. You should hear him strum the banjo and sing a lively tune. The parlor's been right gay after supper since he came. Uncle Bob and I are fine except for missing you. Hope this finds you the same. God keep you. Aunt Opal. P.S. I do hope you're able to keep clean out in that wilderness. Keeping clean is almost as important as saying your prayers, you know."

"Well, she'd be mighty proud of us today," said Gray as he folded up the letter.

"Yes, she would," answered Goldie in a subdued voice.

As they walked back to the wagon, they hardly noticed the quiet that had descended on the whole camp. They were remembering the inn, the Wabash, and the farm. Even those who had not received letters were thinking back to the homes and families and friends they had left behind. It was difficult not to have doubts about what might lie ahead. The old life, the known life, from this distance looked safe and secure.

CHAPTER 7 THE STORMY ATLANTIC★★★★★★★★★★★★★★★★★★★★★★

Both Kevin and Holt were roused before dawn by the old seaman who had befriended them. In the first light they saw the Whitehall boats pull out from the lower end of the Battery with the crew and dunnage. Captain Hewitt arrived in the first boat and immediately disappeared below. The motley crew followed, some of them so drunk they had to be hauled over the side in bowlines. The young were frightened, the old were scarred, some looked mean and brutal, and none appeared capable of inspiring confidence or friendship.

The young men who had paid for passage came next. In a couple of hours all of the berths had been assigned, and all of the belongings—whether in handkerchief, canvas bag, or sea chest—had been stowed away. A crisp northeasterly breeze started to blow and the tide had begun to ebb when Captain Hewitt appeared again and ordered the first mate to man the windlass and heave short. Men sprang into action all over the boat.

The mate sang out, "Now boys, heave away on the windlass breaks, and strike a light. It's duller than a graveyard at midnight."

At this, Kevin and Holt learned their old sailor friend was the shantyman, who led the crew in the work songs. He began singing, "Shenandoah." A cold thrill crept up the back of Holt's neck prickling his hair as the sailors, hauling on the halyards to raise the sails and turning the capstan bars to weigh the anchor, took up the refrain.

As it rose, the canvas began to fill, and the slim *Sea Skimmer* turned on her heel toward Sandy Hook and the open sea. Faintly from the Battery came the cheers and shouts of the great crowd gathered to see the young men off for California. And on board the argonauts, protected by brand-new Bibles purchased from an enterprising hawker at the last minute by thoughtful relatives, waved and called back their last farewell.

At Sandy Hook the pilot and longshoremen debarked with a wish of "Godspeed," breaking the *Sea Skimmer's* last link with the shore. To the young men looking back, New York soon became a thin, wispy line, and they turned to each other to make new friends and to become acquainted with their ship. Holt was swept up by this exuberant group, while Kevin accompanied the shantyman to the forecastle, where he learned he had been assigned to the second mate's watch. The men called the second mate a rotter, and there was grumbling from those who were in his watch till a wiry Scot, who wore a tam-o'-shanter topped by a bright red pompon, jauntily bouncing like a flag of good cheer, intervened and told them if they bellyached so hard now, there wouldn't be any place for them to go by the time they got to the Horn. This served to break the ice in the forecastle, and the men started introducing themselves to each other.

The little Scotsman told Kevin and the shantyman his name was Jamie, and that he was on his way back to his bonny native land. In addition to him, the crew was made up of Irish, Swedish, British, and French sailors as well as native Americans, most of the foreigners having signed on for London because their one aim was to return to Europe. Though there were some old salts sprinkled among them, they were a youthful group for the most part, and the first night out tested their mettle. Heading southeast to pick up the favorable tradewinds, the ship encountered a storm of gale force. The rain fell in torrents and the mountainous water broke way above the bowsprit in a boiling foam. Besides ordering out the lifelines, Captain Hewitt had netting strung along the deck rails to sift out the lads who were swept away.

Kevin was not to work at the outset of the voyage. But White, the second mate, insisted he stand his watch along with the other men, so with the shantyman beside him he clung to a lifeline and watched as again and again the mate sent men aloft at the captain's orders to lay on more canvas. As the wind howled and tore the shouted words from his teacher's mouth, and the sea and sky seemed determined to find any space to extend their icy rivers beneath his oilskins, Kevin wondered if he would ever be able to do the work.

About two in the morning he felt a peculiar sensation in his stomach and managed to convey to the shantyman that he was ill.

"Get to the lee," said the old sailor as Kevin headed for the side. Kevin didn't hear him, and when he lost his supper, it all blew back in his face. The water was pouring over the deck at such a height, however, that it soon washed the scum away. But a worse problem confronted him. In his sickness he had let loose the lifeline, and before he could grab it again, he was washed off his feet and flung into the netting, where he lay sick and helpless, washed and strained again and again by the surging sea. Finally his mates ran out another lifeline and picked him out of the net. White, furious, handed him a rope and told him to tie it around his waist if he couldn't keep his feet any other way. "I'm tired of having you hold up the ship," he shouted.

Kevin meekly took the rope and obeyed, trying to forget his churning stomach and the longed-for haven of his bunk and some dry clothes.

During the storms and squalls of these first three days, like Kevin, most of the young men were miserably seasick. The lower deck was so foul smelling that to escape this hell hole the argonauts fled to the rolling and pitching deck, encumbering the hard-pressed sailors as they fought to keep the ship running before the wind. On the third day of the storm so many came on deck that Captain Hewitt had to order all passengers below for the safety of the ship.

Holt, one of the few men aboard who was hale, chafed at the confinement to his cabin and after a few hours of solitude approached Captain Hewitt for work. Looking up from the charts spread out before him, the captain didn't try to conceal his delight.

"We'll make a sailor out of you yet!" he exulted. "How'd you like to learn navigation?"

"I'd like that very much, sir."

"Then come over here." He pointed to the chart where he had been plotting the ship's course. "What do you think of that?" he asked, tracing a half circle far out into the Atlantic toward Africa.

"Why do you go so far east before heading south?"

"I'm following a route prescribed by Lieutenant Maury of the United States Navy. For years now he's been collecting data from the charts and logs of ships to find the best routes, and he's

71

discovered if we sail over here near the Azores before turning south, we go with the currents and winds instead of fighting against them."

"You mean it takes less time to go this way?" asked Holt.

"That's right. And it's easier on the ship, too. Lieutenant Maury's proving navigation's a science, not something done by chance. If this wind holds, we'll be in Rio de Janeiro inside of a month."

As if in defiance of the captain's words, there came an earsplitting crack followed by a crash that shook the already creaking ship. Close on Captain Hewitt's heels, Holt rushed out on deck. The foremast was two-thirds its normal size. McCarthy, the first mate, shouted that the fore topgallant mast and yards had clipped off and carried away, together with the main skystaysail and main topgallant crosstrees. All hands were called out to retrieve the loose canvas.

Captain Hewitt ordered the remaining sails trimmed as the *Sea Skimmer,* true to her name, still scudded lightly like a great bird before the roaring wind. But the storm was worsening. The sky became blacker, and angry bolts of lightning streaked in a jagged pattern through the heavy clouds. Terrible thunder followed. Rain pelted the crew so hard it hurt them. Below the decks, forbidden by the captain to come up, crouching in their filth, their belongings loosed to batter them, the thunder and the roar of the wind and sea deafening them, the hapless argonauts babbled in terror and beseeched God to save them.

By morning the squalls were less violent, and although the wind was still brisk and the skies overcast, the ship had steadied. Kevin, with Jamie and another sailor named Chip, was helping the sailmaker cut and sew new sails for the fore royal and skysails. To show where the sails went, Jamie pointed up to where spars were being fitted to the foremast and said they would hang from the second and third yards up.

On the second watch White ordered Kevin to join the crew attaching the yards to these new spars on the foremast. Though his injured arm was already overtaxed from handling the heavy canvas, he managed to reach the third yard up from the deck and plant his feet on the rope strung beneath it. He labored desperately to attach the gaskets for reefing the sail. But his strength gave out and he slumped forward unconscious, pinned to the rigging only by the wind.

"What's the matter, lad?" asked Big Blue, the old salt working beside him. Blood was staining Kevin's shirt. He cupped his hands and shouted below, "Send up a line. We've got a man hurt!"

Captain Hewitt had been explaining to Holt how he used dead reckoning and the compass when clouds obscured the sun or the stars. He heard Big Blue's call, and when the line came down, he ordered the limp figure carried to the forecastle.

"No," interjected Holt, "take him to my cabin."

The captain glared at Holt, then repeated, "Take him to the forecastle." Doctor as well as captain, he got out his medicine chest and treated the reopened wound.

Kevin opened his eyes and smiled wanly, "I'm sorry, captain, I'm not much good," he murmured.

"Nonsense, boy," the captain answered. "You'll be as good as new inside of a week. Now take this so you can sleep." He administered a dose of laudanum.

Out on deck once more he bellowed, "Send Mr. White to my cabin!" When the mate arrived, he looked at him icily, "By whose authority did you put Adams to work?"

"I thought him fit, sir," said White.

"I'll decide when a man's fit on this ship, Mr. White. And the next time you decide to act on your own authority, you'll find yourself under arrest for insubordination. Now get back to your duties."

"Aye, aye, sir," he said. But little beams of hatred darted from his eyes as he left the cabin.

The next morning the sun at last emerged through the clouds. Captain Hewitt took the opportunity to show Holt how to reckon longitude by use of the sextant and the chronometer.

"We're about fifty miles farther out in the Atlantic and farther south than I estimated by dead reckoning," he said, turning to the chart. "That's not too bad for four days of no sun or stars to steer by."

Sensing the captain's good mood, Holt thought this would be the right time to apologize for having interfered with the quartering of Kevin the previous day. He still thought the captain was wrong, but he recalled the promise he had made in New York not to interfere.

Since Holt had introduced the subject, Captain Hewitt sought to explain. "Supposing I had ten or fifteen men sick. Should I quarter them in the paying passengers' cabins?" he asked.

"Well, no," said Holt. "But— "

"Now, let me finish, lad. If I did quarter Adams in your cabin, what do you think the other members of the crew would think?"

"Well, I suppose that you were giving him special treatment."

"Exactly! You are beginning to learn. He is a deckhand and I can do no more or less for him than I can for any other man out there."

"I see. Then I guess that means he couldn't study with you like I'm doing."

"No, I'm afraid not. But I couldn't say anything if one of my passengers cared to teach him...when Kevin's off watch, of course."

"Of course," said Holt.

Thereafter Holt joined Kevin to learn about the ship from the shantyman. When Kevin was off duty, Holt taught him navigation.

CHAPTER **8** NEW ORLEANS AND THE LOWER DELTA, MID-MAY, 1849★★★★★★★★★★★★★★★★★★★★★★★★★★★★★★★★★

The candlelight threw ugly, meaningless shadows on the wall as Jacques Dupres clipped angrily back and forth across the polished cypress floor of the library, the crisp point of his black beard punctuating the voluble stream of abuse he was uttering. "He'd better not come back here. I'll have him whipped from the place!" His slender aristocratic hand decisively pulled on the bell rope.

Elizabeth Bailey Dupres sat quietly during her husband's tirade against their only son, Darcy, her anxious eyes belying the outward serenity indicated by her clasped hands. Now she spoke. Her voice was calm and low in pitch, with a compelling quality to it. The master of Shadow Lane stopped his pacing and listened to her.

"Jacques," Elizabeth said gently, "shouldn't Darcy be given a chance to explain?"

"Explain!" He seemed to be biting his words instead of

speaking them. "Explain that he thought it would be a great joke to make a wager involving the *wife* of a fellow planter!"

"But my dear, Andrew Bronson's the one who wagered his wife. It seems to me that Andrew's behavior was ungentlemanly, not Darcy's."

"Elizabeth, no gentleman would have accepted such stakes. There is no excuse for him."

Their faithful servant George entered the room. Through his many years of servitude, he had acquired a skill of making his presence known without intruding. He was dressed in navy blue livery, his gray kinky hair making a suitable silver frame for his antiqued bronze face.

Jacques turned to him, "George, I want you to send one of the boys to the overseer's house and tell him I want him and his drivers to come up here."

"Yes, suh, Mistuh Jacques, I'll send Lem down right away."

"And tell them to bring their whips!" Jacques snapped.

"Yes, suh," George replied deferentially as he left the room.

"Jacques, he's your heir. Why are you trying to destroy him?" asked Elizabeth.

"I live by the code, and so will my son! You weren't born here and don't understand these things. But in my family, the code and life itself are inseparable. The Dupres name has never been involved in scandal. And so help me God, it never will be. . .even if it costs me my own son!"

"Talk to Darcy before you condemn him. You would do as much for one of your field hands. Why not for your own son?"

"Elizabeth, he is no longer my son. I do not intend to lay eyes on him ever again."

She turned away, and he thought he heard, "Jacques, we are all nothing without love." But he was sure only of the whisper of her dress as she glided from the room.

The *Delta Dream* was slowly puffing her way up the Mississippi from New Orleans ablaze with light on all three decks. Darcy Dupres could easily read his large golden pocket watch. He had about one more hour before the riverboat arrived at the Shadow Lane landing. Standing by the railing outside the gentlemen's cabin of the grand saloon, he could see the dim shoreline, the levee, and the dark oaks trailing necklaces of moss. How beautiful and mysterious it was! Like a woman you didn't know, he thought The gay music of the Negro orchestra lured him inside to dance a quadrille with one of the pretty daughters of family friends, but he decided this was no time for frivolity since he must soon face his father and explain his behavior in New Orleans.

As Darcy looked out at the mist beginning to rise on the edge of the river, the nightmarish quality of that evening returned. He couldn't quite explain to himself how it had all happened.

Marie was so white that if he had not known she was the product of a liaison between a white man and a quadroon, he would have treated her as he would the sister of one of his friends. He had become her protector more than a year ago, and now they had a son. Of course, marriage was out of the question as they both knew. Darcy also knew that he didn't love Marie, although she was beautiful. She had soft brown hair, blue eyes, and an exciting body, sensuous and responsive. She dressed in the subdued pastel colors he associated with his mother and sister rather than in the more flamboyant scarlets, yellows, and greens that the quadroons usually favored. Darcy felt that Marie was different, and if he had troubled to analyze his feeling toward her, he would have discovered it was respect, despite their declassé relationship of lover and mistress. He maintained her small ménage on the Ramparts in New Orleans, and he planned to provide for the welfare of their son, Rafael, by giving him Bellflower, the plantation he had won.

On that fateful May evening Darcy and Marie had taken a carriage to the Quadroon Ball. Darcy felt like gambling. Marie didn't like his gambling, he knew, but he found her ideas irritating this evening. He joined a game of faro at a table where Andy Bronson was losing heavily. Soon Darcy won the deal, and as he began winning more and more, all of the other players with the exception of Andy withdrew. Normally he would have recognized how drunk Andy was and would have ceased playing with him, but Darcy had had a lot to drink himself, and something in Marie's disapproving looks drove him on and on. He wanted to show her and everyone else who the master of Shadow Lane would someday be. Bronson became a slobbering thing to be despised. His wife, Millicent, and her feelings didn't seem to matter either. Bronson bet his plantation. Darcy coldly looked across at the man only five years his senior who was blindly betting Bellflower on the turn of a card and accepted the bet. A stillness filled the small upstairs room at the establishment on Orleans Street. It was broken only by the movement of a young man who hastily got up and went down the staircase. A friend of the Bronsons and Treadwells, he knew that Millicent and her brother, Edward Treadwell, were just a few doors down the street enjoying an evening at the French opera. But by the time the messenger reached the Treadwells' box, Bellflower had passed forever from the incompetent hands of Andrew Bronson into the rash hands of Darcy Dupres.

Darcy rose and said, "I guess that's about all you had left to bet, Andy. Shall we quit for the evening?"

"Just a minute," said Andrew mushily, "I've got something else to bet." He rose shakily to his feet and faced the room of fascinated spectators.

Word of the loss of Bellflower had traveled swiftly not only throughout the ballroom but up and down Orleans Street. By this time Millicent Treadwell Bronson was alone in her box at the opera while her brother, Edward, was striding purposefully toward the Quadroon Ballroom. As he reached the glittering but deserted lower floor, he saw people hurrying up the graceful stairway at the end of the hall; he heard the slap of his polished opera slippers on the gleaming floor; and he heard the voice of his brother-in-law above. But he couldn't hear what Andy was saying.

Andy seemed pleased that he had the attention of many people crowded into the room and hallway beyond. He made an effort to clear his slurred speech and spoke more slowly. "Everybody knows I have a beautiful wife. Millicent is a beautiful woman, isn't she?" He looked at the crowd in pleased anticipation of his next statement. The faces of the men who looked back at him were the cream of New Orleans and Lower Coast society, but the women were all of mixed blood. There wasn't an all-white woman in the room. Andy had done the unforgivable. He had mentioned a lady's name at a quadroon ball. No one answered him. They simply stared. "Well, isn't she?" He looked at the crowd belligerently now.

One of the older men stepped forward. "No one is doubting that, Andy. Now why don't we go out for a walk?"

"No." Andy shoved his would-be benefactor aside. "Since everyone agrees that I have one of the most beautiful wives in the delta country, I aim to wager her against my Bellflower which Darcy now owns—may he rot in hell—and then we'll see who wins."

77

Darcy felt the charged atmosphere and the breathless hush in the jammed room. Everyone was gazing at him expectantly. A gentlemen should get up and walk away, he knew——But what if he didn't? Deliberately he sought and found Marie's scolding eyes. The urge to shock became irresistible, overriding prudence and manners, and he said, "All right, Andy Bronson, I'll give you a chance to win back your damn plantation. Cut your card."

Andy wet his lips with the tip of his tongue and reached toward the table. Carefully he drew out a card, but did not turn it face up. "You cut too," he said.

Darcy drew his card and turned it over. "It's a nine," the whisper carried around the room. Andy slowly turned up his card. "A tres! Andy's lost."

"Let me through," Edward shouted over the buzz. The men and women fell back forming a lane through which Edward approached the table. "What have you lost?" Andy seemed to wither and grow sober under his gaze.

Darcy answered, "I won Bellflower from him. . .twice in fact."

"And what did he wager the second time?" Edward's gaze was cold and hard.

"I simply gave him a chance to get back his plantation."

"Don't lie for yourself, Darcy Dupres. I heard my sister's name. You're no gentleman!" Edward's slap snapped Darcy's head back. "You may consider that a challenge. My second will call on you within the hour."

"I'll be happy to oblige you at dawn, unless Andy would like first honors?" He turned, mockingly deferential, to the drunken man. "I hope you understand, Andy, I had no intention of accepting your generous wager. I really wouldn't know what to do with another man's wife!"

"Darcy, stop it!" Marie was by his side. "You've said enough."

As the brothers by marriage stepped through the doorway, Darcy called, "By the way, my choice of weapons is pistols!"

Marie got him into a carriage and took him to the house on the Ramparts which they called home. It was she who sent for his cousin, Pierre Roguerre, to act as his second; and it was she who got Dr. Duvalier as surgeon. She also poured more than a dozen small cups of black, chicory-flavored coffee down him, repeating several times that it was quite apparent that Edward Treadwell had not been imbibing, and what a scandal the entire episode would make for the New Orleans and Lower Coast gossips to mull over. "Besides, you might be killed. That was a despicable bet to make."

"All right, Marie, I've said I was drunk and I didn't mean to take the bet. I'm sorry the whole thing happened, but I'm perfectly sober now. And I'd appreciate it if you would leave me alone so I can get ready for this duel."

She picked up the silver tray with the fragile china cups and coffee pot and started toward the door of their small sitting room. Although this night was the beginning of the end of their relationship, she had been too close for him to treat her this way, and he was ashamed. He took the tray from her and set it down. He looked into her face. "I want you to know I'm sorry. I was spiting you for some reason. I have been all evening. I don't know why. It's—well. . .I feel guilty somehow. Forgive me."

Marie turned around slowly. She knew what lay behind his words. Reaching up and touching his cheek, she said, "I know, my love, I know. Win your duel. Life still has much to offer you." She walked from the room, her head high. He would not see her cry. He would never know the despair in her soul.

Pierre and Dr. Duvalier arrived shortly before dawn. Marie drew aside the upstairs curtain to gaze at Darcy's tall lean figure, shrouded by his evening cape as he climbed into the carriage. Rafael slept soundly in his crib. He would grow up fatherless regardless of how the duel turned out. Marie bowed her head.

Marie's situation was that of untold other beautiful young quadroons. She wondered who could count the broken hearts along the Ramparts on this very night. Her friends had warned her that the arrangement she had with Darcy would be of the most temporary nature, but she had hoped their relationship would last. Now she knew that even if Darcy returned, it would only be from a sense of obligation or duty. And in the end a financial arrangement would be made. Darcy had had his quadroon fling, she thought bitterly. Now he would be considered ready for marriage.

Esplanade Avenue was deserted as Darcy and his party drove toward the park. When they arrived at the Dueling Oaks, Treadwell and his seconds were standing beneath the magnificent trees waiting quietly in the faint morning light.

The referee stepped between the two men and asked them to make up their quarrel. This was actually a formalized part of the ritual. No one expected them to stop now. But Darcy broke the customary silence following the referee's admonition and said, "Regardless of how this comes out, Edward, I want you to know I had no intention of dishonoring your sister. I'm sorry the whole thing happened."

The referee looked at Edward to see if he considered this an apology. Edward made no sign of having heard Darcy at all. He was gazing at one of the trees as if he particularly wanted to imprint each leaf on his brain.

"Very well, then," the referee continued. "Gentlemen, you will each take twelve paces and will turn upon the word 'fire.' May the right win."

As the referee shouted, "Fire," a bullet whizzed by Darcy's ear. Then he raised his pistol and took aim. The ball smashed into Edward's shoulder, spinning him around.

"Dr. Duvalier, go help him," Darcy called. "I aimed too high. I only intended to hit him in the arm."

All of the men rushed over to Edward. Dr. Duvalier first staunched the flow of blood; then he had him borne to his office on Royal Street. There Darcy learned that the ball had only nicked the edge of the collarbone. Edward and his arm would be all right. As Darcy left Dr. Duvalier's office and crossed the blue flagstone courtyard out onto the banquette, he decided to go to the St. Louis Hotel. He needed sleep badly, but he couldn't bear to face Marie again.

As he walked along, some of the old Negro peddlers were out selling their wares:

> Canta. . .lop. . .ah!
> Fresh and fine
> Just off de vine
> Only a dime. . . .

Suddenly he was starving. "Boy," he called, "I'll take one of those." Clutching his cantaloupe in one hand, he proceeded into the hotel. As he crossed the large alternating black and white marble squares of the lobby, he could see the small groups of chained Negro slaves lining the periphery of the room. Squatting on their heels, they were hunched over as they waited to be sold later in the morning at auction. This was a common sight to Darcy. He had bought many slaves who had been displayed on the block in the center of the room. This morning he scarecely looked at them; he was not interested in the raw material to run the plantation; he was simply interested in getting some sleep.

He had remained in New Orleans three more days, knowing his father would be angry, and not wanting to face him while the news of his escapade was fresh.

The cry of a sharp-eyed lookout interrupted his thoughts. "Spotter on the levee!" He looked across to the bank and in the light of several torches saw a Negro waving a white cloth from the Andres landing just below Shadow Lane. This was an unusual hour for anyone in the Andres family to be taking a trip, unless it was an emergency. It was also no time to be sending out produce on a steamer. The difficulty of loading at night restricted this kind of work to the daylight hours. In fact, the *Delta Dream* would not even be making this run if it were not for the full moon.

As the riverboat nosed into the landing, Darcy thought he saw George, his mother's old servant, standing on the dock. As the gangway was put to the levee, he heard George ask, "Is Mistuh Darcy Dupres on board?"

Darcy, who was standing directly above the old Negro, looked down and said, "Here I am, Uncle George. What is it?"

"Miss Elizabeth, she say you to please get off heh, Mistuh Darcy."

Darcy was puzzled but sensed an urgency in the faithful retainer's strange request. A colored boy in gleaming white soon appeared bearing Darcy's carpetbag and followed him at a respectful distance across the gangplank to the levee. After the boy had handed the bag to George, the old Negro, with a conspiratorial whisper, drew Darcy into the darkness.

As George talked on urgently, the blood rose into Darcy's face. He could not believe his father would actually post the overseer and slave drivers with their whips to keep him from landing at Shadow Lane. He had always felt that Jacques was overly harsh and demanding of him, and he was furious that his father chose to condemn his actions without giving him a chance to defend himself. He threatened to get back on the steamer to confront the overseer and the slave drivers. But George's soft voice was persuasive; he urged him to pursue the more subtle course of arriving secretly at the plantation. Besides, he knew his mother would not have sent the old Negro these several miles in the darkness if she had not believed that Darcy would be in jeopardy if he attempted to come ashore at Shadow Lane.

George had tied two horses in the protection of the towering pecan grove which was the pride of the Andres plantation. Jacques Dupres had openly coveted the trees for years. Riding the five miles along the levee to the Dupres land, Darcy's anger steadily mounted. He didn't care if he never saw his obdurate father again. If it weren't for his mother and his sister Suzanne, he thought, he would leave right now for the gold fields in California. He pictured himself returning to Shadow Lane wealthy by his own endeavors, his father, old and white-haired, asking his forgiveness for having so wronged him in his youth. But he brushed the scene away as fantasy. Such mind wandering would not help him in his present predicament.

George whispered, "We bettah tie our horses heh, Mistuh Darcy. Your papa, he have those drivuhs all along the levee above heh."

"I refuse to sneak back to my own home like this!" exploded Darcy, no longer able to control his pent-up indignation.

"Sh! Mistuh Darcy!" pleaded the old slave. "Your mama, she nevuh forgive me, and I let those drivuhs spot you."

Darcy respected the genuine anxiety of the old man. He had gone for comfort to him from the time he was a small boy. Uncle George had always had a soothing word and an undemanding love. "All right, Uncle George," he said, "you lead the way. I won't do anything to get you in trouble." He touched the thin straight old shoulders for an instant, and then the two men once more moved into the shadow of the trees.

As the conspirators stealthily approached the plantation house, Darcy was caught once again by its beauty. The mansion stood stately and impressive, its whiteness reflecting the moonlight. The four tall pillars across the front stood out as if from some ghostly ruin. But behind the pillars was the warm yellow light of candles and lamps bidding welcome.

They did not walk up the steps to the porch that stretched across the entire front of the house. Instead, George, raising his finger in caution, moved around to the back where a covered walkway led to the kitchen, which was in a separate building. Darcy followed George along the walkway, entering the main house through the butler's pantry.

In the dim room Uncle George found a stool for Darcy to sit on; then he went on silent feet down the rear hallway and climbed the back stairs to the bedrooms above. He found Elizabeth Bailey Dupres in her bedroom sitting on a small chair rolling cotton lint bandages for the medicine chest that stood on the floor beside her. As mistress of this great plantation, she was doctor and nurse as well as storekeeper and supplier to the slaves. At George's quiet tap, she rose quickly and asked him in, motioning him to close the door behind him

"He downstairs in the pantry," George said. "I got him off duh boat at duh Andres like you say."

"Is he all right?" Elizabeth queried anxiously.

"Oh he be fine," answered George.

"Things have grown worse since I sent you to flag the steamboat," Elizabeth said. "Mr. Dupres is downstairs drawing up documents to disinherit Darcy. I guess I've never really understood this code of his. Maybe you have to be born French. It was never like this at home. . .was it, George?"

"No, Miss Elizabeth. In Alabama we is different."

"We haven't much time now. I've been busy while you were gone. Go get Mister Darcy and bring him up here. Be sure no one sees you."

"Yes, ma'am," George said and silently disappeared.

As Darcy entered his mother's room, she eagerly clasped him to her breast. "I'm so glad you're safe," she whispered. "I don't know what's come over your father. He won't believe you couldn't do anything dishonorable. Now listen carefully and I'll tell you my plan. I must get you away from here before your father comes up to bed."

"But Mother, if I talk to him, surely he'll see that it was one misunderstanding leading to another until the whole thing became a snarled mess," Darcy pleaded.

"No, you mustn't see him, Darcy. He will act only with hatred in his heart. I need time to heal him. I've sent your things in a sugar hogshead over to the Andres plantation. I want you to take the steamer back to New Orleans tomorrow. Then I want you to take a coast packet to Mobile and stay with my family until I send word to you to come home."

"Why can't I just go to New Orleans until he gets over this?"

"Oh Darcy, my dear, it's different this time. I couldn't run the risk of his seeing you. You must go away."

"Away? All right, I'll go away. I'll go where he'll never see or hear of me again!"

"What do you mean?" Elizabeth looked at him anxiously. She was fearful whenever she sensed his wild spirit asserting itself. "Darcy, don't do anything rash!"

"It looks like I'm being pretty well cast out, doesn't it? If I have no future here, I'll make my future someplace else. New Orleans is filled with ships heading for the gold strike. Hundreds of men are going to California on them. They say you can pick the stuff up with your bare hands."

"But, my son," his mother looked at him sadly. "California. . . it's so far away."

"California! How exciting!" cried Suzanne, bursting exuberantly into the room, as usual without knocking. Her mass of dark curls was damp and atangle, and her cheeks were flushed. Over her blue sprigged muslin dress she was wearing a padded fencing jacket.

"So that's where you've been," said her mother as she eyed her attire. "You should have been in bed hours ago."

"Oh, Mother, I've been practicing. I'm rather good, Darcy. Take me with you to California. I'd really be quite an asset, you know."

"I'll tell you what," he said, lifting her by the elbows and swinging her around. "Some day you can visit me. Or better yet, I'll come home."

"It just isn't fair!" Suzanne flung out as Darcy set her back down. "Boys get to do everything!"

"Try to remember you are a young lady of marriageable age, and please lower your voice," Elizabeth admonished as she opened the top of her delicate rosewood desk and lifted out a box. She selected a key from the many that hung at her waist and unlocked it. Inside were several hundred dollars in gold and some paper money. She emptied the box and hastily counted out about three thousand dollars. "This is all I have to give you right now," she said. "But never fear, I shall see to it that you inherit Shadow Lane."

Once more George tapped urgently on the door of the bed chamber. Admitted by Suzanne, he closed the door carefully but swiftly behind him. "Mistuh Dupres sure moving around dat study." he said. "Look like he about to have some action."

"You must go," Elizabeth said. "He'll be up here shortly. He knows the *Delta Dream* has passed by this time. You can spend the night at the Andres...I sent a note over...they're expecting you."

"Thank you, Mother."

"Must it be California?"

His face became as hard and implacable as his father's. "Yes, Mother. I won't be dependent on him."

"Very well, but I can't let you go alone. I trust George more than any other living being. George will accompany you to California." She turned to the faithful old servant. "My father gave you to me, George, when I came alone as a bride to Louisiana. Now I give you to my son, who needs you as I did then."

"Yes, Miss Elizabeth," said George. "Don't you worry. I'll take care of him for you."

Neither Elizabeth, Darcy, nor George considered the hazards the journey to California would present to the old Negro. He had been born in servitude and he must go wherever his master or mistress chose to send him. Now, once again, he must say goodbye to his family and follow a white man to a strange and frightening place.

Elizabeth drew Darcy to her and kissed him. Her voice faltered slightly. "Goodbye, my son. God keep you. Now go quickly."

Darcy picked up his tiny sister, gave her a hug and a kiss, and followed George from the room.

When they reached the butler's pantry once more, George stopped and turned to Darcy, "Mistuh Darcy, would you wait heh a minute? I would like to say goodbye to my son, Lem."

Darcy suddenly realized that the old Negro was also leaving loved ones behind. It occurred to him that maybe it was unjust to force George to make this journey at his age. "Why don't you stay here, Uncle George?" he suggested. "I don't think I'll need valet services where I'm going."

"Oh no, Mistuh Darcy," George replied. "Miss Elizabeth say I to take care of you, and take care of you is what I intends to do."

"I could take Lem."

"Lem don't have good sense yit. I'd as soon send one of dem boys from de fields."

"All right, Uncle George, I guess I can't get rid of you," Darcy laughed.

"No, suh," George flashed his still beautiful white teeth in a smile. "I goin' to stick to you like de burr in de ole hound's ear."

He disappeared down the vine-covered walkway to the servants' quarters to say goodbye to Lem and his friends. His wife had died several years ago, so there would be no heartrending parting from her. He didn't mind serving Darcy, but he was tired and thought regretfully of leaving his cozy bed in his room over the warm kitchen.

Darcy mused that actually fate had dealt him an interesting hand. If he played it right, not only was there the prospect of excitement and adventure, but also a chance for untold wealth and power. Furthermore, this would simplify his breaking off with Marie, and he would be free from the round of activities of the plantation and New Orleans that had begun to pall on him.

The next morning as Darcy boarded the steamer at the Andres dock he heard the shout of the overseer in a nearby field. "Make a noise there!" The sharp crack of a whip cut through the sluggish air. Then for the last time he heard the plaintive song of Negro slaves working in the cane fields.

> I been workin' in de fields of cane
> Oh yea! Oh yea!
> De sun it hot and dere ain't no rain
> Oh yea! Oh yea!
> Yes, de sun so hot in de fields of cane
> Oh yea! Oh yea!
> But dere's water waitin' for me down dis lane!
> Oh yea, yea, yea!
> Oh yea, yea, yea!

The entire Andres family had come down to see Darcy off. It was a typical gesture for these warm and friendly neighbors, whom he had known all of his life, to muster themselves as stand-ins at a time when a family farewell was impossible. As the steamer left the landing, Darcy stood on the upper deck waving to Monsieur and Madame Andres, their five daughters, and their son, Roland.

It was late afternoon when the *White Lady* puffed up to her pier at New Orleans, joining a long white line of nearly identical sister ships, their tall black stacks at rest instead of belching fire, sparks, and sooty particles into the air. The jetty, full of interesting sights, sounds, and smells at all times and in all seasons, was not disappointing today. Nearby, black stevedores were unloading a banana boat in from the tropics. Another ship was being relieved of the coffee it had carried from Java. On the street, many peddlers and vendors mingled cries of their wares with those of runners from the small hotels and boarding houses. Darcy and George pushed their way through this volatile French-speaking throng, finally reaching a small tattered coach manned by an elderly Negro in a dirty cast-off hat. While George stowed their belongings in the hackney, Darcy directed the driver to take them to Marie's house.

Darcy knew that he would be received as the lord of his house, for Marie was always prepared for him. As he alighted from the coach and was admitted to the tastefully appointed sitting room, Marie entered, fresh and dainty in a rose silk dress, her light brown curls falling softly over the bare whiteness of one shoulder. She seemed scarcely to notice the trunk that had been deposited in the hall before George retired quietly to the kitchen with Marie's servant, Missy.

"Thank God, you're safe!" cried Marie, rushing into the hard and secure cradle of her lover's arms.

Darcy suddenly remembered that the card game and duel that had so precipitously changed his life had taken place only three days ago. To him it now seemed far away, a part of an old life he had already spiritually left behind. But to Marie that evening was still a recent and terrible ordeal. Seeking to regain their former familiarity, she said, "A hot bath will soothe you after your journey." She vanished into the kitchen to order hot water, which Missy already had on the stove.

Soon Uncle George and Missy, carrying steaming cauldrons of water, entered the upstairs sitting room that adjoined the large bedroom Marie and Darcy shared when he was in New Orleans. The servants poured the water into a tin bathtub, and Missy set out a stand with soap, towels, and cold water for Darcy to use to cool the tub to the temperature he desired.

Relaxing in the bath, Darcy's thoughts began to focus on just how he would tell Marie of his California trip. As had been her custom in their more intimate days, Marie interrupted his reflections by appearing to scrub his back. She had ordered Missy to prepare a welcome home dinner of his favorite foods, for she hoped that his arrival with manservant and trunk meant he had come to live with her permanently. Since he was now the owner of the fabulous Bellflower plantation, she reasoned, he need no longer depend upon the favor of his stern father, but could be his own master.

Aware of what she must be thinking, Darcy stated, "Marie, I've got something important to tell you."

"You have such strong shoulders, my love." Marie was applying the brush vigorously.

"I've been disinherited."

"It doesn't matter," was Marie's tranquil reply.

"But there's something else. I'm going away. . .to California."

Marie stopped scrubbing. "But why?" she asked in puzzlement. "You are now the master of Bellflower."

"We'll talk about Bellflower later. Right now I want you to understand why I'm going. I'll admit I probably would never have left here if my father hadn't given me the extra push. But now he has, and for the first time in my life I feel free to do as I want."

"Free?" asked Marie sardonically. She laid down her brush. "It seems a far ways to go to prove a point."

"Maybe," answered Darcy, his dark eyes flashing resentment. "But I'm going to prove to him and to everybody else that I can do something on my own."

"I understand," said Marie, quietly leaving the room.

Digesting the finality of Darcy's decision, Marie began to think in terms of herself and Rafael. Why not go to California with him? No one there would know of her background. This new land could be an escape from the bondage of that small part of her that was Negro. She and Darcy could be legally married, as there would be no law to prevent it, and she would be secure and protected for the rest of her life. At first she was restrained from broaching her scheme by the reasonable fear that Darcy would reject her. But as they were finishing their dinner, the hope of a new life and freedom rose up to overpower her caution. It was a moment of decision for her, as well as for Darcy. She must know if he loved her.

"Darcy?" She spoke almost timidly.

There had been a silence between them. He had been studying her furtively, wondering why the passion that had burned so hot in him only a few weeks ago had cooled to such disinterest. She was as attractive as ever, and yet he had no desire for her at all. She didn't stir him. He wondered, "Is this the way it always is? Is

88

there no such thing as love? Is sexual boredom just a step beyond the first pleasant intimacies?" He was puzzled and a little fearful of what a real marriage might mean, and was grateful not to be entrapped forever in this alliance.

"Oui, ma petite," he answered gently, because he could not shake off the feeling that there was something wrong with him.

"Could Rafael and I go with you to California? We could all start a new life together."

Darcy was dumbfounded. In all of his planning he had never considered the possibility of such a proposal. Hurried, violent protestations poured forth from his lips before he had a chance to sort and discard the unworthy ones. "I wouldn't think of it. Such a journey for a six-month-old baby? Marie, have you taken leave of your senses? Besides, we aren't married, and I'm going to have enough difficulty supporting myself at first without being bogged down by a woman and a baby!" Marie held up her hand as if to ward off blows. Darcy trailed off. "It just wouldn't be practical, Marie."

"It would solve so many problems for me and Rafael to start fresh in a new place."

"You mean pass for white?" Darcy's voice showed his shock.

"I *am* white!" was Marie's stinging rebuke.

And there it was. That was the crux of what was wrong between them. Her skin was whiter than his own. The Negro blood, that small portion, did not show in any feature. Yet she was an outcast, a misfit in both races. Darcy was beginning to sense that this was unjust and to feel guilty about helping perpetuate the system by siring Rafael. But though color may have contributed toward his unhappiness with Marie, there was more wrong between them than this. For if he loved her, her background would not matter. Since he didn't, it was an excuse for abandoning her and Rafael and paying off his conscience by deeding them Bellflower.

He hastened to inform her of his intent. "I haven't only been thinking of myself. I've made plans for you and Rafael, too. You can get away from all of this." He gestured to the little house, implying what it symbolized. "You can go upriver to Bellflower. Tomorrow my lawyer is drawing up papers making you my partner in the operation of Bellflower. And when Rafael's eighteen, he'll inherit the entire plantation. So you see, ma petite, I have been thinking of you and have provided a much more secure future for you than for myself. In just eighteen years Rafael will be the master of a fine plantation and the equal of any white man on the Lower Coast."

"Except that he'll never be accepted," cried Marie bitterly.

"I've given you everything I have to give. I can't do any more for you!"

Darcy threw his napkin on the table and stalked from the room. He was angry at Marie's correct interpretation of the motive behind his generosity. Every white man in Louisiana would say he had done far more than could be expected of him, but the ones he wished to thank him never would. He could hardly wait to get on a steamer and put this life far behind him. It posed questions too complicated for him to answer.

Long after Marie had retired he sat in the sitting room drinking brandy. The more he drank, the uglier he became. He had bought and paid for her, hadn't he? He was giving her everything he owned in Louisiana. He wouldn't see a woman for a long time—by God, he had certain rights! He lurched up the narrow stairs and kicked open the door to the bedroom. Missy heard him and lay cowering in her bed in Rafael's room. George awoke, but Darcy was the white man. And when the white man wanted something, no black man had better get in his way.

"So you're white, are you?" Darcy leered down at Marie.

Although Marie was afraid, she did not show it. "You're drunk and bestial," she said. "I can't discuss anything with you now!"

"Oh, my little innocent," Darcy gave an ugly laugh. "I didn't come here for a chat." He dropped heavily on the bed and began tugging clumsily at his boots. One which gave him particular trouble he sent crashing into the mirror across the room, shattering it into hundreds of pieces. Rafael began to scream across the hall.

Marie rose. "Now you've wakened the baby," she scolded. She started around the bed, hastily putting on her dressing gown. She had one arm in one sleeve and was trying to engage the other when Darcy caught it in a vise-like grip and spun her around.

"Missy can take care of him. . .your business is with *me.*" He flung her back on the bed. Marie struggled with him briefly. Then realizing the futility of resistance, she submitted to his brutal sexuality.

This was final proof to Marie, if she had needed any, that Darcy

90

held no love for her. This was rape. There was no solicitousness for her welfare, no gentleness toward her body. She was a thing to be used, not a person to be respected. Now she knew loathing for the man she had loved.

As soon as he was spent and asleep, Marie slipped out of bed and downstairs. Missy rose and followed to care for her mistress by applying soothing herb unguents to the bruises.

When Darcy awakened the next morning, the memory of his cruelty the night before shamed him. His action against Marie had deepened his sense of wrongdoing. He had acted against her in spite, in anger, even in hate. He could use his drunkenness as an excuse, but it would be an excuse and nothing more. Deep inside of him there was something that had enjoyed being cruel. Jacques Dupres had passed on to his son much more than strong shoulders and a lithe body.

Darcy skimmed through his morning ablutions and hastened downstairs to find Marie. Instead he found a note propped up against a small silver vase of aromatic orange blossoms at his place at the head of the table. He broke it open and read:

My dear Monsieur,

I have decided to accept the terms of your settlement for the sake of our son, Rafael. I shall see that Bellflower Plantation is run at a profit, so you need not trouble yourself any further over our welfare.

When your lawyers have drawn up the terms of the agreement, they may be brought to my mother's house where I shall be happy to sign them.

For reasons obvious to both of us, I believe it is best that we not meet again before your departure for California. I bear you no malice and have long ago forgiven you for any acts you may have committed. It is you who must forgive yourself and live with what you are in order to find contentment in your life. I wish you good fortune in this and in your future.

Faithfully,

Marie

In relief Darcy laid down the note and applauded Marie's

infallible sense of good taste. He didn't understand what she meant by the last part of the note, but the important thing was that she had spared him a painful scene of apology and contrition. As with the gambling and the duel, he did not have to face the consequences of his actions. He could now direct his full attention to preparing for his journey.

Darcy ate his breakfast in cheerful spirits and set out for the steamship office, nearly dancing along the brick banquette. At the waterfront he sought out the offices of the Panama Steamship Company, which he knew was now making regular runs to the American landing at Chagres. There were many other young men crowding the office of the company when Darcy entered, but the chief clerk at the counter made them stand aside and ushered Darcy into an inner office where the manager of the company reigned.

Since he was used to such treatment wherever he went, Darcy was oblivious to the mutterings and looks of resentment from the less wealthy men from Louisiana farms and trades. His tall beaver hat, white ruffled shirt, bright yellow vest, loose-fitting blue frock coat, tight gray trousers, and black pointed boots had identified him as a Creole gentleman. He needed no letter of introduction to any office or shop in New Orleans.

The manager pleasantly inquired the nature of Darcy's business, and when Darcy informed him that he wished to book passage from New Orleans to San Francisco via Panama, the manager was surprised.

"It is not a very pleasant journey," he remarked. "Although the company is doing its best, there is such a demand that we have not been able to get adequate facilities."

"I understand your problem," said Darcy, "but my needs are small. I shall simply require a private cabin for myself and my manservant on the ship. I am aware of the difficulties in crossing the isthmus, but I imagine we shall be able to manage without too much difficulty. I have heard native boats can be hired to take you up the Chagres. Is that correct?"

"Yes," the manager said hesitantly. "But their boats are crude, you know."

"It will only be a few days of inconvenience at the most. We'll manage." Darcy impatiently brushed aside these cautious objections. "Now, how soon can I book passage?"

92

The manager looked through his sailing schedule. "There's a ship leaving for Chagres the middle of next week," he said. "And allowing for emergencies, a ten-day crossing of the isthmus should connect you with a steamer that will sail from Panama City to San Francisco. Actually, the crossing of the isthmus should only take five days."

Darcy scowled. "Don't you have anything leaving sooner?"

"I didn't realize that you were in such haste," the manager apologized. "I presumed you might like time to get your affairs in order before taking such a—er—hazardous journey."

"My affairs are in order," Darcy snapped.

"Well, in that case," the manager smiled ingratiatingly, "I do have a ship, the *Bluebird*, leaving day after tomorrow."

"That's the one I want to be on." Darcy beamed his radiant smile in the direction of the manager, who likewise began to smile. But as he looked down his passenger list, he began to frown.

"I have a space in a double cabin," he faltered.

"That just won't do," Darcy insisted. "What about my man?"

"We could make up a pallet for him," ventured the manager.

"It is rather short notice," Darcy agreed. "You can assure me a private cabin from Panama City to San Francisco though, can't you?"

"We shall endeavor to do our best for you, Monsieur. Your ticket will read 'one first-class cabin' on the first steamer leaving port after you reach Panama City. The voyage to the mouth of the Chagres River takes about a week." The manager suggested Darcy accompany him to a nearby coffee house while the clerk wrote up the ticket. Having been trained to conduct business in this leisurely manner, Darcy accepted the manager's invitation.

Within the next two days Darcy wound up his affairs. He converted all the money his mother had given him to gold, adding another thousand dollars to the supply; he made the legal arrangements for Marie's operation of Bellflower and for Rafael's eventual inheritance; he looked at mining paraphernalia but decided against getting any since there was so much conflicting information about what was needed; and he paid a visit to the Basilica of St. Louis to ask a blessing for his journey. This last act was the only indication of any doubt on his part about the outcome of his venture. For although a Catholic, he had depended mostly upon his mother to keep the communication line open between him and the Almighty. But from now on there would be no family or friends for him to turn to in case of need or trouble. For this reason his faith assumed, but only temporarily, an importance which it had hitherto not known.

CHAPTER **9** INDIAN COUNTRY AND FORT KEARNEY★★★

Although several members of the wagon train came down with fever on the morning after the wash day by the Little Blue, Zack said they must move on to Fort Kearney with as much speed as they could muster. From the diarrhea, vomiting, and cramps of the victims, he deduced that the group had been struck by a form of cholera brought on by a change of diet and water, a common malady along the trail.

"It's important that they don't get all dried out," he told the well ones. "You must feed them water laced with vinegar. If it is the cholera, we should be done with it in a few days."

While Goldie and Gray were breakfasting the next morning, Isaiah Cunningham stuck a scared face out the front of his wagon. "Ma, Pa, and Ruth are sick," he said. "I don't know what to do."

"You and Adam hop down and help me hitch your mules," said Gray. "Can you drive?"

"Yes, I've done some."

"Good boy. I'll see if I can get somebody to help you out though."

But when he approached Bob Cassidy's group to help, none of them demonstrated any eagerness, and Gray realized they were afraid of catching the fever.

"You're a fine bunch," he said in contempt. "I hope you need help someday and nobody turns aside for you." He turned to leave.

"I'll come, Gray," said Bob quietly.

"I'll spell them, too," said one of the other boys.

"That's better," said Gray.

94

Goldie put in some hard days nursing the Cunninghams, but within a week they and most of the others who had been ill were up and around. Only the Stevenses failed to respond to treatment. They remained bedfast in the back of their wagon, and Zack grew increasingly apprehensive as the days went by.

Approaching the Platte, the emigrants heard a sound like distant cannon fire and almost immediately saw a massive herd of buffalo cross their trail a mile ahead. The eager ones wanted to take off after the great animals, but Zack restrained them.

"They've too good a start," he said. "They may turn. If they do, we'll have some meat. If not, we'll just have to wait."

But sighting the herd made the young men restless, and they spent the nooning cleaning and priming their guns. About an hour later the pioneers again heard the thunderous noise, and this time it was much closer. Zack's head went up like an animal smelling water, and he called to the would-be hunters who were leaping onto their saddled ponies, "Follow me!"

Scarcely taking time to hand the reins of the mules to Goldie, Gray grabbed his rifle, leaped over the tail gate onto the startled Sunny's back, and went tearing off across the plains after Zack.

The roar grew louder. Goldie spotted the herd ahead, and her heart began to pound as she saw why the animals were stampeding. A large band of Indian warriors was riding after the buffalo, drawing their bows and firing their arrows in quick succession into the thick hides.

As Gray, his rifle clutched tightly in his hand, raced after Zack and the herd, he had only one thought: he must kill a buffalo; he must prove his manhood. Sunny's instinct for running was sure and true as she began to gain on the buffalo. Gray saw Zack, with his horse in full gallop, raise his rifle and fire into the herd. A big brute dropped. As Zack continued to load and fire, others fell. By this time Gray had come full on the herd and had turned Sunny to run with the animals. He raised his rifle as he had seen Zack do and fired into the head of one of the huge creatures. To his delight and amazement, the big brown beast dropped. He pulled up Sunny to let the herd pass so he could better see his prize. Excited as he was, he didn't think to kill more. He was proud that he had killed one. It was only then that he noticed the band of Indians riding on the opposite side. The horde passed, leaving Gray's bull and a number of other dead carcasses in its wake.

Gray leaped off Sunny to get a closer look at his trophy just as Zack came riding up.

"Good boy," Zack said. "How many did you get?"

"Only this one," confessed Gray.

"One's better than none. If you'd care to come over here, I'll show you how to skin it and cut it up fast."

As Wash and a number of the other men joined Gray for the lesson, Zack saw Harley Fisher arguing with a Pawnee over a buffalo that lay between them.

"Excuse me a minute," he said, wiping his knife on the matted brown fur of the animal at his feet.

Casually but rapidly he strode over to Fisher and the brave and spoke a few words in Pawnee. The warrior pointed to an arrow sticking out of the dead buffalo.

Zack turned to Harley. "Why are you claiming meat you haven't killed?"

"I thought I shot him. He dropped just about the time I fired."

"You must have missed."

"How do you know I missed? He could have come along and shot him after he was already dead." The Pawnee stayed back. Zack went over the huge body carefully.

"There's no other wound in the hide," he said sternly.

"Well, ain't that somethin'? A white man takin' the word of a thievin' Indian over that of another white man."

The Indian looked inquiringly from one angry face to the other. Zack explained in Pawnee that Harley had made a mistake and the buffalo was no longer being claimed. The brave nodded in satisfaction as Zack drew Harley back toward his own group.

"Cool off!" said Zack. "We're on their land. We have plenty of meat without that buffalo."

"Dirty thievin' savages," said Harley. "We shoulda shot them instead of the meat."

"Harley could be right," said one of the other men. "You can't trust 'em. They'd probably like to murder us."

"That's enough of this," said Zack. "How many of you have ever known an Indian?" He looked around at their noncommittal faces. "All right, come on, how many?"

"That ain't the point," said one of the men. "You don't have to sleep with a woman so to speak to tell what she is."

"Well, there's something you don't know," said Zack, "and

96

that's if an Indian claimed a kill that wasn't his, he'd be thrown out by his tribe. Now come on over here, we've got work to do."

Following Zack's instructions, Gray cut up his trophy. But loading it on the wagon, he felt a pang of disappointment. It looked just like all of the other hunks of meat. There was nothing to mark his moment of triumph, and no one had seen it to remember. Some of the savor went out of his first hunt.

That night the camp became a meat packing plant. The marrow was dug out of the bones with sticks and packed in kegs, long slices of the meat were salted down in barrels, and inch-thick strips were hung on racks before the fires to dry.

By tradition each successful hunter was given one of the prized tongues, while the remainder were distributed by lot to holders of lucky numbers. Goldie felt fortunate when both Gray and Zack presented her with a tongue to fry in the savory marrow, and she began cooking them beside the stew and the large ham she had roasting over the fire. What had seemed like a lot soon vanished under the voracious attack of Gray, Zack, and the Cunninghams. Even frail Dora cleaned her plate and asked for more of the delicate flavored tongue.

As the company was about to depart after the nooning the next day, Goldie discovered Matilda and Tag Along were missing. She put her hands to her mouth and called, "Kitty, kitty, kitty." Receiving no response, she struck out to find them, pausing every now and then to call, for it was impossible to see anything move in the tall grass.

She had wandered some distance from the wagon train when an Indian suddenly rose from behind some bushes holding two cowed cats by the scruff of their necks. Goldie observed that he was extremely tall and young. He was dressed in fringed buckskin trousers and moccasins, and two feathers stuck out from his long shining black braids. His cheeks were pink under his faintly bronze complexion, and his eyes were a deep sea blue.

"Your dinner?" he asked, thrusting the two stiff cats, with their hind toes curled back, toward her.

"No!" she shouted in horror, "my pets!"

"Oh," said the Indian, "not much good."

"They are so," she protested. "They eat rats and mice. They're very valuable." Just then she noticed the Indian's horse tied to a small tree. "Your dinner?" she asked, pointing to the beautiful animal.

"No!" replied the astonished Indian, "my horse."

"Oh," said Goldie, "not much good."

"Why, I ride him," replied the Indian. Suddenly he got the joke. His face formed into a broad smile, showing white even teeth. "One should never presume," he said. "I am Running Wind. How are you called?"

"Goldie," she said, "Goldie Baxter. I'm mighty glad to meet you. I'm sorry I can't stay and chat, but we're about to start up again. Thanks for finding my cats. I hope I see you again some time."

"You will, golden one," said the Indian as he watched her running through the grass, parting it with her skirts as she went.

Gray had harnessed the mules and was sitting in the driver's seat waiting for the signal to stretch out.

"Where have you been?" he asked crossly.

"I was looking for Matilda and Tag Along. And guess what? I made friends with an Indian. Look, see. . .over there." She pointed to a white horse galloping away in the distance, bearing its brown owner on its back.

"You mean you were over there all by yourself? You know good and well the Indians capture people who stray away from the trains. How many times has Zack warned us about that?"

"He was nice. He found Matilda and Tag, and he spoke English. . .just as good as we do. I wonder where he learned it."

"Boy, just wait till Zack hears this one."

"He needn't hear. . .unless you tell him. Please, Gray, I couldn't bear to go off and leave Matilda and Tag."

"All right, but don't do it again. Promise?"

"I promise."

Next afternoon at Fort Kearney Zack found an open space to camp among the other wagon trains clustered around. Then he rode into the fort seeking a doctor and facilities for the sick Stevenses.

Although Gray wanted to go in and see the fort, he stayed to help Goldie with the chores. Finally tired of the way he was mooning around, she told him to ride in and see if Zack had found a doctor. Inside the gates he saw Zack's horse tied up in front of the only two-story structure in the whole fort. Zack was on his way out in the company of an Army officer.

"Oh, Gray," said Zack, "this is Doctor Seitz. He's going to show

98

me an empty building over here where the Stevenses can stay till they get well. Why don't you come along?"

They crossed the parade ground and entered a long, low hut with an earthen floor and a sod roof resting on brush-covered poles.

"We can move a few beds and fixings in here," the doctor said, "and make this quite habitable. . .yes, quite habitable indeed."

"Fine, Doctor Seitz," said Zack. "I'll bring in your patients in a couple of hours."

On the way to the gate they were arrested by a familiar voice calling out, "What's your hurry?" Rachel Stevens was standing in front of the combination post office, store, and saloon.

"We're worried about your mother and father," snapped Zack.

"What do you mean by that?" bristled Rachel.

"I mean they're sick," said Zack. "Have been for weeks. At least now maybe you can take care of them."

"What have they got?"

"I don't know. If you come on out to camp with us, you might find out. We're going to move them into the fort so Doctor Seitz can look after them."

"I'm with Chuck," said Rachel. "I'll have to tell him."

They found the wagon train abuzz with the news that Rachel and Chuck Colby were being married that evening. Gray wondered if she'd go through with the marriage in the light of her parents' illness.

"I suppose you'll be taking your parents back home now instead of going on?" he suggested later as they were moving the sick to the fort.

"Home," snorted Rachel. "What home? Oh, I feel sorry for Mother, but what can I do about it? Chuck and I are heading West anyway."

"You mean you're going to leave your mother and father here all alone?" he gasped in astonishment.

"We all have to leave the family fold sometime, sonny boy," retorted Rachel defensively. Seeking sympathy, she turned to Zack. "Honestly, what can I do? I can't take them with me, and Chuck certainly isn't going to wait here till they get well. They'll have good care here. The truth of the matter is, the sooner I get to California the sooner I can send back some money. Isn't that right?" She looked at their disapproving faces and then flared, "I

99

suppose you think we should all starve genteelly together. It's awfully easy to judge someone else, isn't it?" Sparks shot from her eyes. "I don't care what you think. . .Chuck and I are still being married tonight and you can come or not as you like!" She turned away and flounced into the saloon.

In her blood-red taffeta dress falling well off the shoulders and half-baring her full white breasts, Rachel was the unchallenged belle of her wedding party. Her black hair fell in soft waves over her creamy shoulders, and the red in her gown accented twin spots of excitement in her cheeks. Chuck had wanted everyone to come and see the prize he was getting. With some justification, he felt himself the envy of every man present.

Rachel was not to be tamed. After the ceremony she showed no inclination to behave any differently than she had before. She danced and flirted with every man present.

Gray had told himself he shouldn't go to Rachel's wedding, but he easily lost the battle, and now he stood on the sidelines, a fascinated spectator to the results of her flirting. Humiliated by her refusal to pay him any attention, Chuck had been a constant attendant at the punchbowl. Now thoroughly drunk and jealous, he decided to fight for his wife's attention by attacking her latest partner. With a bull-like bellow, he charged. But the man stepped aside and the sodden bridegroom ran into a post, knocking himself out. Rachel's face registered the first sign of concern Gray could ever recall seeing on it. She ran over and knelt down beside Chuck. His eyelids fluttered and he began to move. Rachel's old mask reappeared instantly. Gaily she asked, "Will some of you carry my husband to our tent?" Singling out Gray, she lowered her long fringed lashes and said, "You will. . .won't you, Gray?" He found himself unable to refuse.

Inside the tent Rachel detained Gray. "It looks like my bridegroom is going to sleep through our wedding night," she said.

"It sorta looks that way," he replied.

"A bride shouldn't be left alone like that," she said, pressing close to him.

"Well, you did it, you know," said Gray uncomfortably.

"I don't like to be alone," she pouted, putting her arms around him. "I'm cold." She looked up at him expectantly.

It was more than he could take. Suddenly he found himself crushing her to him and kissing her passionately. Almost before he

100

knew what was happening, Rachel was drawing him down beside her sleeping husband. "Oh, my God," he cried, "I've got to go!" To the accompaniment of Rachel's laughter he dashed out of the tent and ran headlong into Henry Bowles.

They stood looking at each other awkwardly, then Gray blurted, "How've things been going?"

"Just fine," said Henry, looking curiously at the tent.

"I didn't see you at the wedding," Gray quickly continued. "I wanted to apologize about what happened the night you left."

"Oh, that's all right. I've wished a hundred times I could tell you how sorry I was about it."

"Why don't you come on back with us on the train? I know everybody would be glad to have you."

"I've made my choice now. I guess I'd better stick with it. I'm afraid I don't have a very high opinion of anybody anymore." He looked toward the tent once more, then down at the ground.

Gray followed his gaze. "Yes," he said, "I know what you mean." He clasped Henry's hand. "I'm glad I got a chance to see you anyway."

"Yes, so am I. Good luck to you, Gray."

All was quiet when he got back to camp, and in the morning Colby's group was gone.

With more than three weeks of rough trail behind them, the gold seekers with overloaded wagons now realized their folly, for many of their animals were worn out. But fortunately supplies were low at Fort Kearney, making it possible to sell much of the surplus goods instead of having to dump them and bear the loss, as would many of those in trains following. In addition, the women at the fort, starved for the things they were accustomed to in the East, had relieved the argonauts of some of their heavy furniture, paying them well. But there were few replacements for the tired mules and oxen, and though lightened, the problem of heavy loads would continue to plague them as they reached rougher terrain.

Midst the bartering on this warm May morning, Zack and the company officers went from wagon to wagon collecting what the people could spare to pay for the care of the Stevenses. Those who could not give money donated supplies. By noon the men had collected forty dollars and enough rations to last a sizable party for several months.

101

After donating a dollar to the fund, Goldie and Gray had only twenty-nine dollars left in their stake, and Goldie knew she could delay no longer the unhappy task of selling the four kittens. Sorrowfully she put them in a basket and went to the fort, where she was immediately mobbed by people vying to buy them. A soldier who happened to be in the trading post when she arrived rushed over to tell the commandant about the kittens, and he sent back word that the Army would top any offer.

To Goldie it seemed barbaric to offer her pets to the highest bidder. But when the Army offered a price of fifty dollars for all four of them, she accepted and accompanied the young officer to the two-story building. In exchange for her basket of kittens, the Army quartermaster gave her fifty dollars in gold. With tears in her eyes, especially over leaving Tag Along, she clutched the coins and hurriedly left the fort.

Back at the wagon she showed Gray the money. But he displayed no more enthusiasm for it than she had.

"I think I know how Judas felt," he said finally.

"I almost couldn't go through with it," she said and picked up Matilda, who peered into her face with huge yellow eyes.

"I'm sorry, Matilda," she said, "I had to."

That evening they walked into the fort to post their letters home. When they returned, Goldie gave a cry of delight, for curled up on her feather tick between his mother's protective paws was Tag Along. How he had found his way back to the wagon she could not guess, but she was determined not to give him up again. "I simply won't do it!" she exclaimed.

"I guess if we gave them back the twelve-fifty, they'd let us keep him," said Gray.

"I'll return the money first thing in the morning," she said, patting the sleeping kitten's head.

Before dawn, while Gray was hitching up, Goldie hurried to the fort to explain to the commandant what had happened. He told her to keep the money, for he was glad to have three potential mousers now and was looking forward to having a whole platoon by fall. She smiled her thanks and returned to the long line of wagons already stretching out toward the Platte River.

During the previous day two more large trains had pulled into the fort, and Zack firmly told the Lord group they must keep a steady pace from now on if they were to remain in the vanguard

of the great migration. He warned that both water and grass would
be scarce ahead, and those who were there first would be the ones
to benefit from the meager supply. From now on there would be
few rest days, he said, and those who could not keep up would
have to be left behind.

CHAPTER **10** IN NEPTUNE'S WATERS★★★★★★★★★★★★★★★★★★★

As she charged toward the tropical latitudes, running before brisk
winds, the *Sea Skimmer* was averaging fourteen knots. On the
morning of May twenty-fifth, Captain Hewitt sent for Kevin to
report to the wheelbox station and had him remove his shirt. The
captain flexed Kevin's arm and felt the wound.

"It's coming along fine," he announced and turned to White. "I
want this man put on light duty."

"Aye, aye, sir," said the second mate.

"Did you understand my meaning, Mr. White?"

"Aye, aye, sir. Light duty it is, sir."

White was very careful to follow the captain's orders explicitly,
but there was no mistaking his animosity toward Kevin and
toward Holt, who was always at Kevin's side.

At the end of the week of light duty, the captain called
both Kevin and White to him and informed them that he
thought Kevin was now ready for regular seaman's duty. Kevin
sensed there would be hard days ahead as White chirruped, "Aye,
aye, sir."

The ship was now wafted along by gentle breezes, and the air
was soft and hazy instead of brisk and clear. During this balmy
spell most of the passengers lolled on deck, considering it too
much effort to do anything, and most of them had nothing to do
anyway. As their boredom increased, they sought to create
diversions, usually by some form of practical joke. A favorite trick
was slapping a sunburned companion smartly between the
shoulder blades or propping a bucket of seawater over a hatchway

and waiting for an unwary victim. But these pranks only momentarily lifted their boredom.

The first of June dawned hot and muggy, and by noon the vessel had become becalmed in a flat oil-like sea that shimmered infernally under the relentless sun. Stopped in her great circle movement toward Cape St. Roque off South America, the ship was wallowing in her beams near the equator out in the Atlantic. Since the first great storm there had not been a single drop from the sky. Drinking water was scarce and had a foul smell and taste.

At dinner time one of the men in steerage sniffed his tea and said, "This ain't fit for a dog." He hurled the fetid cup at the steward, who fled up the ladder to the next deck. Two men leaped after him and yanked him down, hurling profanities at him.

One man started beating the table with his spoon and chanting, "We want pie—we want cake—we want brandy!" The others took up the refrain and also began pounding the table. "We want brandy! We want brandy!"

Suddenly an enraged man picked up one of the kettles of the sailor's stew called *lobscouse* and emptied it over the steward's head.

"I want something fresh!" he screamed. "You can keep your hardtack, salt beef, potatoes, and onions. I've had enough!"

The madness mounted. Men hurled stew all over the cabin and at each other, turning the mutiny into a war among themselves. At the height of the fray Captain Hewitt fired a shot above the hatchway. A stillness descended on the group as intense as the previous racket. The men looked up to see the captain, his mates, and several of the crew ringing the hatch, pointing guns down into the hold.

"Come on up here, Mr. Smalling," said Captain Hewitt to the steward, who, still dripping *lobscouse*, slowly climbed the ladder.

Cold and hard the captain continued, "I'm closing this hatch. You men can either live down there in that filth locked in like animals, or you can clean it up and come and go freely like human beings. The choice is up to you." He stepped back and the hatch was covered, sealing in the men.

Captain Hewitt had no sympathy for the steerage passengers' complaint; for ship food, their fare was far above average in both quality and quantity. In first class, steerage and the crew dining quarters everyone was served two substantial meals a day, plus afternoon tea with hardtack.

Captain Hewitt believed in serving his men—passengers and crew—an ample quantity of as good food as was available. He had shopped carefully for his stewards. What they were able to achieve, considering the scarce six-foot square galleys and tiny stoves on which they had to work, he thought miraculous. Furious over the treatment Mr. Smalling had received, he determined not to let the men out of the stifling hold until they were thoroughly penitent.

In silence, the argonauts sheepishly began to look around at what they had done. Some of those who had not participated in the fracas now assumed leadership, forming work gangs to clean up the bunks, the bulkheads, the tables, and the deck. By four bells that night they had even cleaned up the steward's tiny galley Their barrel of water was empty, and they were all famished.

Satisfied that their quarters could stand inspection, the leaders announced they would like to send a commission to see the captain. When the committee told him the riot had been brought on by the bad-tasting water coupled with the monotony of the food, Captain Hewitt said, "You're getting the best shipboard food available. If it lacks variety, I'm sorry, but it can't be helped. There is no means for preserving fresh food or keeping water sweet at sea."

"There'll be no further trouble from the lower deck, sir," said the leader. "And we would like to apologize for our treatment of Mr. Smalling."

"You can do that in the morning when I open the hatch," said the captain.

By eight bells the stars went out and a breeze started up, foretelling a tropical storm. So Captain Hewitt opened the hatch once more to give the steerage passengers the advantage of the expected downpour. The men streamed on deck bearing pots, pans, and any kind of vessel that might serve to collect rainwater; they even helped the crew roll out the water barrels. Shortly the sky spilled over, and for a solid hour it poured. As the rain slacked off, a strong wind filled the sails, and the *Sea Skimmer* once again began eating up the nautical miles on her southwesterly race toward the equator and Cape St. Roque.

Ashamed that they had compromised their Yankee sense of law and order by participating in the riot, some of the steerage passengers sought to improve their situation. One group started a newspaper, another formed an orchestra to entertain in the evenings, and many of them began to take an interest in sailing The mates soon found they had too many hands hoisting or reefing the sails, and they implored Captain Hewitt to assign the volunteer seamen to watches. Holt was already serving a watch with Kevin, and twenty eager neophytes soon joined him. What they lacked in knowledge, the fledgling sailors made up in zeal. Although this procedure was unorthodox, it was better than having the youths sitting idly about, and Captain Hewitt preferred to run his ship this way.

As they neared the equator, the crew made elaborate preparations to initiate all of the novices at the crossing. One hot bright morning the captain announced Neptune and his court would be honored by the ship and ordered everyone to assemble on the upper deck.

A sailor blew on his pipe, and Neptune, wearing a long canvas gown cut from sailcloth and fastened in the middle by a piece of rope, a string mop dyed green for his hair, and a crown fashioned from a brass ring and a mutilated copper pot, lumbered over the side and with assumed dignity walked toward a throne that had been constructed amidships.

When he reached his throne, he proclaimed, "I am the master of all I survey, I command the elements. When I tell the wind to blow. . .it blows." A sudden shift of the sails by mariners posted above caused a breeze to waft across the assembled passengers and crew. They laughed in appreciation and pressed closer to Neptune.

"And when I tell it to rain. . .it rains," he thundered. Two sailors doused the unsuspecting novices with a hogshead of seawater, and their laughter became more strained.

"You are all my subjects," continued Neptune, brandishing his scepter made out of a ship's instrument "and must now bring me tribute or pay the forfeit."

Beginning with the crew, his clerk began to call the names of those who had never crossed the equator before. After lathering the face of the first sailor with a paint brush dipped in grease, then shaving him with a barrel hoop, Neptune asked him for tribute and was promptly handed a bottle of brandy, whereupon he

106

announced, "You are now a member of the order of Free Sons of the Sea and may travel anywhere within my domain "

Then the clerk called, "Kevin Adams."

When Neptune asked, "And what tribute have you to offer, my son?"

Kevin replied, "Nothing, your majesty.'

"Nothing," roared Neptune. "Blindfold this whippersnapper!"

Two seamen sprang forward, tied a cloth over Kevin's eyes, and seated him on a plank above a large wooden tub of water in front of Neptune's throne.

"Now," said Neptune, "do you wish the freedom of my domain?"

"Yes," replied Kevin.

"Very well, then give it to him, lads!"

The two seamen upended the plank, ducking Kevin in the tub. As he was fished out, Neptune announced again, "You are now free to travel in any part of my dominion."

"Thank you, your majesty," spluttered Kevin.

A party followed the initiation ceremony. Captain Hewitt added a barrel of rum to Neptune's collection of fifty bottles of liquor, and the stewards brought out pastries and pies and several huge wheels of cheese.

The next morning Holt heard from Captain Hewitt that they had successfully avoided the Roccas Shoals and a good wind had carried them safely around Cape St. Roque on the hump of Brazil.

"We'll be in Rio de Janeiro within a week," he prophesied. "Even with this mild breeze, the Brazilian current is strong enough to carry us."

From the day of the rounding of the Cape, Mr. White began assigning Kevin extra duty. Whenever anyone was called to climb the masts to loose the gaskets to free the topsails or to reef and tie them down again, Kevin was sure to be among them. He was lucky that during this period the ship did not require too much tending, for sadistic mates or captains could lose a man from sheer exhaustion by riding him as White was now riding Kevin. The entire forecastle was aware of what was going on, but the men were afraid to speak up lest they be subjected to the same treatment.

On the morning of June twelfth the *Sea Skimmer* was lying off Rio waiting for the pilot to take her in. The vast crescent-shaped harbor dotted with islands spread before them. Jamie, the Scot, noted Kevin and Holt's admiration and commented, "Ah, yes, she's a beauty the first time you see her."

As he spoke the ship began to move again, and soon they saw the city of Rio de Janeiro and some small towns on the other side. As they came to anchor in the harbor they counted at least fifty other ships. Captain Hewitt was at the rail to receive the customs men from a boat that had pulled alongside. They all went below.

Holt asked Jamie, "How soon can we go ashore?"

"Probably not till tomorrow," said Jamie. "They have some funny regulations." Holt was disappointed, but when the customs men left, a sailor informed him Captain Hewitt wanted to see him.

"How would you like to go ashore with me, lad?" asked the captain as he entered the cabin.

"There's nothing I'd like better, sir, only,——" Holt hesitated.

"Only what, son?" asked the captain.

"Could Kevin come along too?" Captain Hewitt simply looked at him. "I'm sorry, sir, I keep forgetting. If you'd still like to have me, I'd like to come."

"Very well, then. Get your best clothes out of your chest. We're going to dine with a friend of mine."

An hour later, under the envious gaze of Kevin, Holt and the captain left the ship and rowed toward the pale lights that outlined the shore. As they disembarked on the busy harbor street, a slim figure rustled toward them in a green silk dress. When she came nearer, it was evident to the captain that the dress was spotted and the Brussels point lace collar, though genuine, was wilted. She was obviously a lady in distress.

"Captain Hewitt," she ventured as she looked up at the older man. (She had taken the trouble to find out the name of the skipper of the newly arrived vessel in the harbor.) "I'm Mirina Black," she said, "Mrs. Mirina Black." There was a wide gold band on her left hand third finger. "I've been stranded here, and I throw myself on your mercy." Her speech seemed well-rehearsed, as if she had uttered it many times.

"I'm sorry, ma'am," said Captain Hewitt, "but my ship is overloaded as it is. I haven't even got an extra berth, much less a cabin for a lady."

"But, sir," the girl faltered, and her hazel eyes began to fill with tears. "I've been here three months now. You see, my husband got sick on the voyage and the captain put us off here. John was too ill to protest. And. . .he died. We spent all of our money for our passage. We were abandoned."

"I'm sorry, ma'am," said the captain more kindly, "but I really don't have the room. Come along, Holt." He pulled Holt toward a waiting carriage.

The girl hurried after them, "The American consul will guarantee my passage," she called as the carriage drove off.

"Can't we do something for her?" asked Holt earnestly.

"I admit she's in a terrible situation if her story is true," said the captain.

"We could check with the consulate, couldn't we?" asked Holt.

"Yes, it would be easy enough to get the truth. But even so, I've no place to put her. She won't be the only sad case we'll encounter while we're in Rio. Since the gold rush, taking on new passengers and leaving the old ones on the beach has been common here. I'm sure our firm has a waiting list of abandoned men who'll be begging me tomorrow to get on our ship."

As they continued through the hot streets toward the suburbs, Captain Hewitt pointed out some of the splendid buildings and gardens. But Holt scarcely paid attention. He couldn't forget the girl with the tears in her eyes.

On the outskirts of the great city they drove up to the estate of José Valataigo, a wealthy importer and friend of Captain Hewitt. As the carriage swept down the long avenue of giant palm trees past the well-kept tropical gardens, Holt couldn't help but be impressed. They drew up in front of the *casa grande*, a large two-story building with a soft pink stucco exterior topped by a red tile roof. Attached to the house on one side was a chapel with a cross at the apex of the roof; and on the other side some distance behind was a low, rambling building which Captain Hewitt said was the slave quarters.

A black woman servant ushered them to a large inner courtyard where elaborately dressed men and women were clustered in small groups sipping wine. Most of them were speaking in Portuguese, but José Valataigo greeted his new guests in English and conducted them to a small group of Americans surrounding the American consul.

Finally forty people had assembled, and Senhor Valataigo led his guests to a room adjoining the court, where all were seated at a huge mahogany dining table draped in snowy linen and adorned with shining silver and glittering crystal. Holt saw there was ice in the water glasses, and sweating pitchers on the sideboard heralded that more was available. He took his first bite of food and discovered the reason for this generous supply of water. His mouth was on fire and his face turned lobster red. Unbidden tears sprang to his eyes, and the two well-developed girls he had been placed between at the dinner table began to laugh. They chattered animatedly at him and over him, but he couldn't understand a word they said. Mercifully they taught him to alternate the bland rice and beans with portions of the highly seasoned fish and meat. Following their pantomime, he fared much better, although he observed the Brazilians used copious amounts of pepper in nearly everything. But he enjoyed this unusual meal after the dull food on the ship. And when the desserts were served, he was delighted. There were ice cold pineapple and melon sherbets and endless pastries and sweet cakes. Following these, delectable chocolate candies, marzipan, and bonbons were served. Except for the sensitivity of his Yankee nose to the odor of his companions and wishing he might remove his coat before he ruined it with sweat, he was thrilled to be dining in this strange house in this strange country.

The banquet finished, the guests streamed outside to hear the Negro slaves sing, a common form of entertainment Holt learned as Senhor Valataigo told him these were the work songs of the field hands on the big sugar plantations or of the stevedores who unloaded the vessels in the harbor.

Following the serenade the guests retired inside to play cards or talk. Holt had been hoping to speak with the American consul concerning Mrs. Black but was unable to get near him. Late in the evening the consul at last appeared to be free, and Holt quickly approached.

"Ah, yes," said the consul. "She's a very sad case. . .a young widow. Quite comely, too. . .a fact I suppose you noticed."

"Yes," said Holt eagerly.

"What she told you is true. The captain of her vessel sent her and her husband ashore, ostensibly to get medical attention, and then upped anchor and sailed away. Her husband died three days later, leaving her practically destitute. Poor girl. . .you can't help feeling sorry for her, though I don't believe she comes from the best background."

"How does she live?" asked Holt

"I've taken a small room for her near the waterfront, and she's being supported by the charity of a few Brazilians. They're basically a good-hearted people."

Holt, suspecting the sorry lot of the Negroes he had seen under Senhor Valataigo's roof, doubted the veracity of this statement.

The consul turned to Captain Hewitt, who had just approached. "You wouldn't happen to have room for a poor little widow on your ship, would you, Cyrus?"

"I'm sorry to say I do not," said the captain. "And I told her so down at the dock."

"A pity," said the consul. "I've really got to do something about her."

For once Holt was formulating a plan in his mind without voicing it for everyone to hear. Since he had a single cabin, he didn't see why he couldn't give it to the widow and bunk someplace else himself. But before proposing his plan to Captain Hewitt, he decided to discuss it with Kevin.

After a slight hassle with Mr. White the next day, Holt got Kevin released from duty and told him about Mirina Black as they rowed ashore. Kevin could see Holt was already infatuated with the young widow and decided he had better meet her before giving advice. Though she wasn't at the landing, Holt had got her address from the consul, and they went around to her room. She wasn't there either. Holt proposed to sit on the stoop and wait for her, but Kevin wanted to see the city.

The bells from the many cathedrals chimed a pleasant accompaniment as they walked through the streets, and they satisfied their craving for sweets by stopping on the corners to buy candy and cakes from the trays of the big African women vendors. At the central grocery market they bought wines, brandies, and chocolate. By midafternoon, their arms laden, they decided to go back and deposit their treasures in Holt's cabin before returning to the city.

On their way they turned a corner and suddenly found themselves at the huge Rio central slave market. They stood in amazement at the sight of the long lines of chained slaves being

111

auctioned off as hands for the big sugar plantations. The half-naked, rib-protruding bodies of the slaves and the sight of the brutal purveyors assaulting them with whips and clubs made them ill. But though they hurried away from the miserable place as fast as they could, they could not escape other gangs of slaves bought for the seaboard plantations shuffling through the streets, heavy chains dragging from their wrists and ankles, and their bodies striped by the snaking whips.

Recalling the singing of the Africans at the Valataigo estate the night before, Holt asked Kevin, "How could they possibly have sounded so happy?"

"Maybe it's the only thing they've got. Maybe if they didn't sing, they'd die."

"I'll bet they do that anyway."

"I don't ever want to see anything like this again," said Kevin, shuddering. "I'll never forget the way those slaves looked as long as I live."

Though their zest for exploring the city had died, they returned late that afternoon in search of Mirina Black. Holt spotted her on the pier, and together they approached her. She was dressed the same as she had been the day before.

"Mrs. Black?" Holt said.

"Yes," the girl turned toward them. Her face lit up. "You're the gentleman who was with Captain Hewitt yesterday, aren't you?"

"Yes," said Holt. "This is my friend Kevin Adams. We were wondering if you'd have supper with us? We think we can help you."

Kevin cut in. "The fact is, Mrs.——"

"Call me Mirina."

"We don't know if we can help you or not. Holt here has a plan, but we don't know if Captain Hewitt will agree."

Disappointment clouded her eyes, but she quickly rallied. "At any rate I'd enjoy the supper," she said. "It's a long time since I had a good meal."

Mirina led them to a small restaurant, clean and inexpensive. The food was good, but they still sputtered over the hot condiments. Mirina volunteered bits of information about herself and her late husband. "We were going to go to California to get rich. We were always going to get rich. . .at the next place."

"And yet you want to go on?" asked Holt.

112

"Why not?" she said with a shrug. "There's nothing back there. You see, Johnny was a gambler. We didn't have any real home so to speak. But we were married rightly enough," she added as though she detected some doubt in Kevin's mind. Kevin noticed that he seemed to be the one that she was trying to convince. Holt was already totally sympathetic. The more he saw of her the more lovely she seemed; a perfect lady to be rescued.

Kevin was concerned about something else. It had been a long time since he had been with Nancy Lee, and he found Mirina very desirable. In hope of having her to himself for awhile, he suggested Holt go back to the ship and work out the plan with Captain Hewitt.

"We'll wait for you in Mirina's room," he said.

"When I get back your troubles will be over, Mrs. Black," said Holt as he hurried off.

Within the privacy of the room, Kevin immediately commenced his conquest. However, he did not figure on Mirina. At first she dodged him, asking for news from the States and questioning him about his background. But finally, when she saw this was not working, she bluntly laid out her hand.

"As I understand it, Mr. Adams," she began coolly and formally.

"Kevin," murmured Kevin, trying to embrace her.

Firmly she put down his arms and stepped back. "As I was saying, Mr. Adams, you don't have any money, do you? I mean, if I understood correctly, you're working your passage to California."

"What's that got to do with you and me?"

"I'm sorry, but I'm afraid. . .everything." She smiled at him. "You see, I'm not interested in just an affair with you or any other man. . .no matter how entertaining it might be. Holt is interested in me, and I think he'll take me out of this miserable hole." She looked around with obvious distaste. "I mean, Mr. Adams, I intend to get to California on your ship. Holt's the one who can help me. . .not you. It's as simple as that."

"And you think he'll marry you?"

"Yes."

"Not if I have anything to do with it."

"Oh, but you won't."

"You'd use a man. . .just like that. . .to get what you want?"

113

"Why not? You were going to use me to get what you wanted a moment ago, weren't you?" She stared at him with penetrating eyes. "Oh, I see," she laughed. "I'm a woman, so I'm supposed to be soft and pliable. Well, Kevin," she purred, "you'll see that I can be very soft and pliable *after* I get what I want. And now, good night." She walked to the door and opened it. "I suddenly find I'm very tired. Holt can bring me the good news in the morning."

"I hope you stay here and rot!" shouted Kevin in a hoarse, angry voice. He slammed his cap on the back of his head and stalked out, to the accompaniment of her low, throbbing laughter, which penetrated his anger and stirred him all the more.

Burning with aroused and unsatisfied passions, he didn't want to see anyone when he got back to the ship. But Holt was out on deck, peering dejectedly into the black water.

"He won't agree," he said dully. "Said it wouldn't do to have an unmarried woman on a ship full of men. It's not so!" He looked up at Kevin, his eyes blazing. "He just doesn't like her or want to help her. He's a snob like all the rest!"

"Forget her," said Kevin. "She's a pro."

"What do you mean by that?" cried Holt, grabbing him by his shirt. "What do you mean?"

"Let go of me!" shouted Kevin. "I'm warning you." He threw up his arms, breaking Holt's hold, and the two started to punch. They fought bitterly up and down the deck until finally Captain Hewitt appeared and thrust his brawny form between them. "What in the name of God has got into you two?" he asked.

"He insulted Mrs. Black," cried Holt as he took another swing at Kevin.

"Now cool off, both of you!" exclaimed Captain Hewitt, picking up a handy bucket of seawater and dousing them.

"He called Mirina a pro," said Holt more quietly. Turning to Kevin he added, "I'll never forgive you for that."

"Kevin may know a mite more about women than you do, son," said the captain. "Maybe now you can see why I don't want a woman on my ship. They're nothing but trouble."

"Everybody judges her," said Holt. "Nobody wants to help. She may not be perfect, but neither are we."

With a flash of insight Kevin saw two things: the depth of Holt's interest in Mirina, and that his own attack on the girl was only driving Holt toward her. As a result, he did a rare thing for him.

He walked over and extended his hand. "I apologize, Holt," he said. "I was judging her. I won't say anything more against her."

Holt grabbed Kevin's hand in boyish zeal, and his face contorted in a crooked grin, for his upper lip was beginning to swell.

"That's better," sighed Captain Hewitt. "But you look like a couple of shipwrecked derelicts. Get below and clean up."

The fight had washed away much of the bad feeling that had been building up. But Holt's infatuation with Mirina left Kevin out, and on the last day in Rio, some four days later, Kevin went ashore with Jamie and Big Blue. By evening he had become thoroughly drunk on *aguardiente*, the potent native brew made from sugarcane. He wanted a woman badly, despite the warning of his shipmates about the diseased Brazilians.

"It's time we all went back to the ship," said Jamie, trying to disentangle Kevin from the arms of an obliging copper-skinned whore.

"Leave me alone," hiccoughed Kevin. "You're prettier'n Mirina," he confided to the girl.

"Come on, Kevin, me boy," wheedled Jamie, "tell her goodbye. . .Now that's a good lad, and we'll all go home."

"Go to hell!" barked Kevin, taking a drunken swipe at Jamie.

"Ah, well, if that's the way you want it," sighed the Scot, nodding to Big Blue, who picked up a bottle and swung it down heavily on Kevin's head.

"Ooh, not so hard," winced Jamie. "You might've broken his pate."

They picked up Kevin and half-dragging and half-walking him between them made their way back to the waterfront.

If Kevin had been aware of Holt's plans for the last day in Rio he would have tried to stop him. But by the time Holt, dressed in his best clothes, appeared on deck and got in one of the skiffs, Kevin had already gone ashore with Jamie and Big Blue. How appropriate that it was Sunday, he thought as he rowed ashore. The air was soft and balmy, and even the sunlight seemed to be diffused in deference to this day of days.

He and Mirina were married that afternoon, and at nightfall made their way to the ship, for Holt did not want to encounter Captain Hewitt until they were well out to sea the next day.

Safe in his cabin he started to make awkward love to her, but

Mirina pleaded a headache from nervousness over their fate and asked him to wait. Reluctantly, he left the cabin to make an uncomfortable bed on some ropes coiled on the deck. But he was not unhappy, for he believed everything would be all right the next night.

Around two o'clock in the morning Kevin awakened with a throbbing head and a raging thirst. After quenching it at the forecastle water barrel, he wasn't sleepy anymore and wondered if Holt, feeling badly over leaving Mirina, also might be awake. He made his way to Holt's cabin and reached down to the bunk. A very feminine shriek caused him to leap backwards.

"What the blazes!" he yelled.

"Oh, shut up before you wake the captain," whispered Mirina, lighting a lamp.

"What are you doing here?"

"This," she said and held out her hand, displaying a new gold wedding band. He knew it was different because it was heavily worked with entwined flowers and leaves, whereas the old ring had been quite plain.

"You married him!"

"Yes, aren't you pleased? Now you can see me whenever you want."

"Holt's my friend."

"That's all the better. You were the one I wanted. But you couldn't have got me out of Rio, could you?"

She drew him down on the bunk. Her lips parted beneath his. His head was pounding and he wanted her badly, but he tore himself away.

"I knew you were a pro," he said. "I told Holt so. He should have listened."

"You swine!" she spit out, clawing at him. "Get out of here, or I'll scream!"

"No you won't," he smiled, "because you don't want Captain Hewitt to know you're here. And now let's see how good you really are." He reached out and tore her nightdress from her body. "Not bad," he said as she stood naked and trembling before him. "Not bad at all."

"Get away from me," she hissed. "Leave me alone. . .I'm warning you."

"Oh, no, my dear, I'm warning you," he said, slapping her face. "Get into bed."

He grabbed her roughly and deposited her like a sack of meal on the bunk. By turns he vented his love and his hate upon her until they both lay exhausted. Toward dawn he pulled her by the hair toward him and kissed her once more passionately and feverishly. Then he said, "And if you ever tell Holt about this or try to come between us in any way, so help me, I'll kill you."

"I hate you," she whimpered, crying softly.

"No you don't. . .you love me."

Kevin left the cabin abruptly, and Mirina spent a frantic hour trying to cover her bruises with powder and repairing her torn nightdress so Holt wouldn't discover what had transpired. She needn't have worried. In his eyes she was perfect, and he had no suspicions of her at all.

CHAPTER 11 THE BLUEBIRD'S FLIGHT TO CHAGRES★★★★★★★★★★★★★★★★★★★★★★★★★

Shortly after nine in the morning the *Bluebird* pulled away from the *batture* and out into the swift current of the Mississippi. She would travel one-hundred-twenty miles from New Orleans before reaching the Gulf of Mexico. Darcy was standing at the railing gazing back at the Crescent City for the last time when he heard a commotion from the direction of the cabins. He turned to see George flying through the doors of the saloon, rolling his eyes wildly. In pursuit of him was a feisty elflike man dressed in an orange plaid suit cut with loose trousers and a sack jacket. His tall cream-colored hat was set at a jaunty angle on his head, and he boasted the most bristling set of rusty side-whiskers Darcy had ever seen.

"I ain't sharin' my cabin with no nigger," the man screeched in a high piping voice. "I paid for first class and I aim to have it!"

As George darted behind him, Darcy brought the man up short.

"Sir," he said calmly, "my name is Darcy Dupres."

"Pleased to meetcha." The little man thrust out a hand as soft and white and well-manicured as a woman's. "The name is Rip Packet. Ain't got time for socializin' though. . . .Gotta see about my cabin!"

"I believe you're sharing a cabin with me, sir," said Darcy. He turned to George. "This is my man, George. He was straightening my things."

"All I want to know is, where does he sleep?"

"He'll sleep on a pallet between our berths, if it's all right with you, of course."

The gnome looked warily at George and then at Darcy. "Do you mean to tell me you let him sleep in the same room with you?"

"Why, of course," Darcy laughed. "I've known Uncle George all of my life."

Rip's narrow eyes opened wide, and he started backing away from Darcy. His eyes darted back and forth like those of a cornered animal desperately seeking a way of escape.

Darcy was laughing uncontrollably, his dark eyes flashing and his white teeth giving him a fiendish look in Rip's view. He started to edge past, but Darcy stopped him once again. "Don't be afraid, Mr. Packet, we won't harm you. George isn't my real uncle. He belonged to my grandfather, and now he belongs to me."

"Oh," said Rip cautiously. He still didn't know whether or not to trust this Southerner, for he was from the North and had always been suspicious of Negroes.

"Couldn't he sleep outside the cabin in the saloon?" he asked, jerking his thumb toward George.

"I think that could be arranged, Mr. Packet. But I assure you he's harmless."

"You say. . . .But I'd still be obliged if you'd have him sleep outside."

"Your servant, sir," said Darcy. "Say no more about it."

"There's one other thing," Rip said. He was wily enough to seek an advantage.

"Anything within reason, Mr. Packet," said Darcy.

"I was wondering if you'd mind if I set up my game in the cabin, Mr. Uh—"

"Dupres," filled in Darcy. "Darcy Dupres."

"Oh, yes, Dupres....Dupres? Say, are you the one who won that big plantation? And the duel? I hope you ain't sensitive. Everyone in New Orleans was talking about it. Say, what in the world are you doing here?"

"The same thing you are, I imagine."

"I'm going to the diggings," Rip announced proudly. "Lot of money to be made there."

"So I've heard."

"I'm not thinking of it in the usual sense. You see, I'm a gambler—I mean by profession. That's why I want to use the cabin. I need a quiet place to engage in my business."

"I don't know. That wouldn't give me much privacy. Why can't you use the saloon?"

"Too noisy—can't concentrate." He pushed his fancy hat back on his head and thought again. "I'll tell you what," he said. "If you let me use the cabin, I'll give you ten percent of the take."

"No," Darcy countered. "But I'll agree for fifty percent of what you make, plus letting me watch you."

"You drive a hard bargain, Mr. Dupres. But I accept." He grasped Darcy's hand, then moved off among the other passengers thriftily sorting and culling the young men like so many apples to find the ones sweet enough for his bite.

Throughout the day Darcy remained on deck watching the green shore slip by. At dusk the steamer reached the tidelands leading out into the Gulf, and he returned to the cabin. He found it packed with seven men. A table had been shoved between the two bunks, and the men were sitting on either side. Rip, who was dealing, fastidiously lifted a long thin cigar from his mouth, smiled at Darcy, and beckoned him to a favored spot at his side on Darcy's bunk.

"My associate," he announced.

The men barely nodded to Darcy as they waited for their cards. During the next few hands Rip won very little, and Darcy began to wonder about his partner's expertise as a gambler. Suddenly Rip announced the game was at an end. The other players protested, but Rip picked up his cards and his money, turned his back, and said tightly between his teeth, "My associate will show you out." Darcy stood up and nodded curtly toward the door. Still grumbling, the men filed out.

Darcy turned to find that Rip had slid beneath the table. His

119

face was a peculiar green color, and he was moaning faintly. Darcy gently shook him.

"Sick. . . terribly sick," Rip groaned.

"Here, let me help you to your bunk," Darcy said. "Damn this table! I'll move it out into the corridor first."

"No," protested Rip. "I had a block jack of a time getting it, and I'll not find another. Leave it be."

"You may be in no condition to play any more games, Mr. Packet. You're seasick."

"Pshaw!" said the bantam predator. "I've been traveling the Mississippi for years. You don't get seasick on a river. It's that blasted hog bilge we had for lunch. . .that's what it is!"

"We've been in the Gulf at least half an hour," Darcy informed his cabinmate. "You're seasick." He extricated Rip and laid him on his bunk, loosening his cravat and removing the prized hat. Darcy decided it was best to leave him alone, but before going out he made sure the wash basin and slop pail were handy.

At dinner the captain divulged that although this route was new to him, from studying his charts he believed it was best to sail west of Cuba and then due south through the Caribbean Sea straight into the mouth of the Chagres River.

"If the good weather holds, we should be there in five days," he said.

"That's good," said one of the Northerners, " 'cause I don't think I could take more than five days of this hot food."

"I hope you got plenty of wine, Captain Mason," said another. "It's the only thing that's keeping me from burning up."

Darcy was surprised at the Northerners' reaction to the spicy Creole cuisine. But he enjoyed the wine as much as they for it helped the flow of conversation, and he was soon on a first-name basis with the entire table.

Completely forgetting Rip's predicament, he invited his new friends to the cabin for a game of cards after dinner. He found George sitting by the bunk wringing out cool cloths and applying them to Rip's forehead.

"What's the matter with him?" a ruddy-cheeked fellow asked.

"Sh! Sh!" Darcy held his finger to his lips. "He's seasick."

"You sure that's all?" queried another suspiciously. "You sure he ain't got the fever?"

"George and I've seen lots of fever, haven't we, George?"

"That right, Mistuh Darcy," George corroborated. "We sure has."

"Just the same," the first man insisted, "I ain't playin' cards in here."

"Of course you won't," said Darcy. "I wouldn't dream of disturbing Mr. Packet in his inconvenience. We'll move out there."

Now that a plan of action had been introduced, the high spirits of the wine-bibbing men returned. With much tussling, pulling, and shoving they got the table outside the door. Some of the men appropriated benches from the main saloon and shoved them around the table, completely blocking the passageway. During the remainder of the voyage, the feelings of the players frequently ran high when a passenger not inclined to cards, but definitely wishing to gain access to his cabin, would step up on the table, walk the length of it, and step down at the other end.

For the next three days Darcy's luck with cards held, and he won two thousand dollars. Rip was still seasick.

The *Bluebird* had passed the western tip of Cuba and was well out in the Caribbean when the weather worsened. Like a block of wood with no directional force of its own, the ship was tossed end to end. The ranks of the card players became decimated as one after another of the young men succumbed to the peculiar malady of the sea. Only Darcy, Captain Mason, and a few hands thrived on the vicissitudes of the storm. The ship was inevitably driven off course.

Eight days out from New Orleans the weather finally cleared, and the sea and sky became a bright blue once more. But there was no sign of land. Fearing he had sailed too far south and would soon strike the coast of South America, the captain ordered the ship's course altered to a northeasterly direction.

"We shall soon strike land," he said confidently to the worried passengers. "We should be only a few miles from your debarkation point."

Actually the ship had not made much headway during the storm. Instead of being south, she was still north of her destination, caught in the backward curve of land lying above the mouth of the Chagres River. By midmorning the tropical shoreline was clearly visible, but there was no river and no indication of human habitation. Upon checking the land curve on his charts, Captain Mason reset his course to travel south once more. He announced they should sight Chagres by nightfall. His calculations proved correct. Being unfamiliar with the anchorage, he decided to wait until morning and engage a pilot to take the *Bluebird* into the American landing on the river. Then, to pacify the eager argonauts who wished to debark at once, he ordered several cases of French champagne opened.

In a plethora of indecision after dinner, Darcy didn't know whether to get rip-roaring drunk, pack his belongings in order to be ready for an early debarkation, or have one last glorious game of cards. He glanced across the table at Rip who, although up and well, seemed strangely troubled and preoccupied among all of the smiling and joking colts.

Grabbing a bottle from a steward, Darcy went over to him. "Come on, partner," he said, "it's all over. You won't have to see a ship again for at least a week."

"Oh, that——" Rip smiled bleakly. "That ain't what's taken the pleasure out of me. . .not entirely, that is. It's the game. Look at all of 'em." He gazed pathetically at the happy faces surrounding him. "I never got one chance. . .not one." His voice broke with sorrow.

"Well, I'll fix that," said Darcy in sympathy.

Grabbing a gong from the sideboard and beating it loudly, he stepped up on a chair. "Gentlemen," he said, "I have a very serious announcement to make. This is your last. . .absolutely your very last chance to be parted from that which you hold most dear. Gentlemen, I am referring to that which has lured you half-way round a continent. Does anyone know what I'm talking about?" His flashing smile encompassed the room as the men began to laugh.

"Yea, Darcy," one boy cried.

"Let's show him," said another.

Darcy struck his gong again. "Whoever wishes to test his luck may join me and Mr. Packet in the companionway."

Men came to the table and departed, some in anger, some in sadness, until four o'clock in the morning. Darcy's luck was phenomenal, but Rip lost heavily. Finally only the two of them were left.

Rip stared bellicosely down the length of the table. "Well, partner," he said, "since I've nothing left to bet except our partnership, I'll bet my half against yours."

"Oh, come on, Rip, let's quit. We've got a lot of money to divide."

"No! I didn't win it!" Rip, possessed by an uncontrollable rage, spat out the words. Then he choked, "One cut—that's all I ask."

Darcy's eyes glittered. "All right," he said. He carefully shuffled the cards, then shoved them down the table. "Cut," he said.

Rip took his cut, then threw the card down, sobbing. He had drawn the deuce of clubs. But Darcy held him. "Wait," he said. Rip stood shaking in front of him. "I haven't had my cut yet. Gentlemen always extend the courtesy of seeing the other man's hand." Although he knew he was being cruel, he felt compelled to show this greedy little toad. He reached out carefully and took a card. It was the ace of hearts. "I now declare this partnership officially dissolved, Mr. Packet," he said coldly. Then he turned and entered the stateroom.

Feeling as though he were being smothered, and at the same time aware that he was being shaken, Darcy struggled to come awake. He was soaking wet, the air was thick and still, and he felt no motion. These thoughts tumbling through his mind, he peered blearily at the perspiring face of George, who was saying, "Mistuh Darcy. . .Mistuh Darcy. . .it aftuh noon, Mistuh Darcy. I got some nice hot coffee heah."

"Past noon! Where are we? Why didn't you wake me sooner?" Darcy sprang up. Sweat was running down his broad chest, and his hair was wet. "My God, how hot it is! Where is everybody?"

"Too tired to move, I 'spect. We anchored off duh mouth of dat rivuh, but dere's no pilot."

"Well, how does the captain expect us to get ashore? Swim?"

"No, suh," George grinned. "A man, he come out in a boat and say he send out more boats to take us in. It just a mattuh of money."

"We pay his price or stay out here and rot, I suppose."

"Dat about it. He and duh captain been goin' at it good and propuh. Heah, Mistuh Darcy, I got some nice fresh watuh for you to wash up. We had some buckets of rain a while ago."

"Thank you, George. Go see what progress they're making with our transport ashore while I shave."

As George went out, Darcy began singing softly to himself. "Oh, Susannah, don't you cry for me. For I'm goin' to

123

Californ-i-ay with my washbowl on my knee." He carefully gathered and smoothed the bills and put them in his purse. There were over two thousand dollars. Then he opened his trunk and began counting the gold coins. He had collected a total of nearly fiteen thousand dollars. A nice little start toward a fortune in California, he thought. Hearing footsteps in the companionway, he quickly closed and locked the trunk, slipping the key on the chain of the saint's medal he wore around his neck. He had just turned to the washbasin when Rip rushed into the cabin.

"Tarnation! Can't get ashore. About to die of the heat," he said, removing his cocky hat and fanning himself vigorously. "Malodorous place. You ought to go on deck. . .stinks clear out here."

Darcy's good humor having returned, he was amused by the petulance of his cabinmate. "Don't you enjoy anything?" he asked. "You know, I don't think I've ever seen you smile."

"To answer your first question," Rip put his hat back on his head, "I enjoy only one thing. Trust me with your wife or sweetheart or mother, but never ask me to hold your money. As to your second remark, I ain't seen nothin' so far to smile about. I'm practically penniless in the most Godforsaken spot on earth. *I* didn't win everybody's money last night."

"I'll tell you what, Rip," Darcy said as he finished washing. "I'll stake you to Panama City. You can pay me back later."

"You may regret it. It looks like it's going to be a mighty expensive journey."

At this moment the steward came striding down the passage beating his gong. "Captain would like to see everybody in the saloon, please."

Rip looked at Darcy. "Sounds like they've struck a bargain at last."

Most of the other passengers were lounging or sitting in the tightly closed, airless room when Darcy and Rip entered. The captain was standing at the head of the long center table talking vehemently in Spanish to a fat, oily-looking man, who was mopping his face frequently with a once white silk handkerchief liberally sprinkled with large purple dots. The man's suit, likewise once white, was spotted and grayed, and two dark wet stains showed beneath his armpits. His pudgy hands fingered the handkerchief nervously, but his avaricious eyes glittered as he counted the heads of the men in the saloon.

"Gentlemen," the captain addressed the assemblage, "I have finally made an agreement for your transport to the American landing at Chagres at fifty cents apiece. I regret that I cannot take the ship in any further because I have been given to understand that the pilot of this so-called port cannot be released from jail. It seems he got drunk last night and destroyed some property, though I can't imagine what there could be here that could be that valuable. In fact, I think the whole thing is a cock-and-bull story. . . .But there you are. I could do no better than fifty cents a head. Are you agreeable to that?"

"We know you did your best, Captain," said one of the men.

"All right, all in favor say 'aye'," said Captain Mason.

A chorus of "ayes" filled the cabin.

The captain said a few words in Spanish to the fat man, who stuffed his handkerchief in his pocket and left the saloon smiling broadly.

"The boats will be here at three o'clock, gentlemen," the captain said. "Meanwhile we'll have dinner."

During the meal Darcy gleaned from Captain Mason that the native bungo boatmen who would take them up the Chagres to either Gorgona or Cruces were charging ten dollars per passenger at the present time, although there was some indication that the rates were flexible and could be reduced. The captain warned all of the men to drive as hard a bargain as they could. "I'm loosing you into a den of thieves," he said, "so you'd best guard your belongings."

Captain Mason's warning beat insistently in Darcy's brain as he retired to the cabin after dinner, and he decided to transfer his gold to his small leather handbag. By the time he had finished, the first boats were drawing to the side of the ship.

The brown and black men swarmed aboard and George, though he didn't speak a word of Spanish, soon had two of them hauling Darcy's trunk out of the cabin and lowering it by ropes into a waiting boat. Darcy, clasping his leather satchel, and Rip, clutching his carpetbag, followed the trunk down. As soon as George was aboard, the boat shoved off.

As they approached the isthmus the smell of rotting vegetation became more offensive. The odor was soon forgotten, however, in the drenching they received from a sudden tropical shower. The

125

rain ceased as quickly as it had begun, and by the time they reached the shore, clouds of steam were rising out of the lush green jungle to meet the hot rays of the sun.

The boatmen deposited Rip, Darcy, and George on the beach and returned to the ship for another load. The three looked around, not knowing exactly what to do. Finally they picked up the trunk and struggled over to a group of thatched buildings standing on stilts in the midst of a stinking swamp.

Hanging dismally from a pole in front of one of the evil-looking huts was a sign, HOTEL AMERICAN. The two white men gaped at the sign, then shrugged their shoulders and climbed up the rickety ladderlike steps to the dark interior. Coming from brilliant sunshine, their eyes were unable to make a quick adjustment to the gloom. Rip struck a match.

A deep voice boomed, "Put that damned thing out! Do you want every flying and crawling thing in this swamp to descend on me?"

Startled, Rip dropped the match and started to back out of the hut, in the process stepping on Darcy's toes. Darcy cursed and gave him a shove, catapulting him to the foot of a cot upon which he could distinguish a figure lying prone.

"Are. . .are. . .are you the proprietor?" he stammered.

"That's as good a name for me as any," the figure replied.

Darcy came forward. His eyes having become more accustomed to the dimness, he noticed that the man had several days' growth of beard, and that his cheeks and jowls were puffy. On a stool beside the cot stood an empty bottle, and since the man made no attempt to rise, Darcy assumed he was drunk. He started to turn away.

Rip, however, was not to be thwarted. Getting on his feet, he addressed the man once more. "We'd like some information."

"What?" said the man, sitting up. "It's this fearsome heat and this beastly place. It gets to you after a while."

"Why don't you leave?" asked Darcy.

"Can't. . .represent the Chagres River Company. They're going to run steamers up to Gorgona. I'm waiting for them to bring them down from Baltimore. I surveyed the river, you know. It's feasible—very feasible. A lot better than those native bungo boats."

"Where do we engage the boatmen?" Rip asked.

"Oh, they're upriver a little ways, but they won't want to start tonight. . .too late. You'd better stay here." Despite his lethargy the man assumed a managerial air.

"I don't see any rooms," said Darcy.

The man began to laugh. It was a big laugh but not mirthful. "I have cots," he said, "and you're lucky to get 'em. Plenty of buckos spend their nights on the beach." He pointed to ten cots crowded side by side on either side of the doorway.

"How much?" Darcy demanded.

"One dollar. One Yankee dollar a cot, and it's dirt cheap."

"What about my man?"

"He can sleep on the floor. It's not much worse than the cots. Spent plenty of nights there myself. If it ain't the fleas, it's the mosquitoes. Plenty of liquor. . .get plenty of liquor. That's the only thing keeps the fever away." Suddenly he stood up. He was a large-boned man with good features that had sagged into a blurred softness.

"We'll take three cots," said Darcy with distaste, looking around the long, low bamboo building with its palmetto thatched roof.

"That'll be three dollars in advance," said their host.

Darcy paid the sum and started out. At the door he met George trying to shove the trunk up the steps. Darcy grabbed the upper end, and between them they got it inside. The old Negro staggered as he entered the hut, and Darcy told him to rest while he and Rip went to engage a boat.

Rip deposited his carpetbag on one of the dirty cots. "You said we'd find the boatmen up the river?"

"That's right—up there." The man ambled to the door and flapped his bottle in the direction of the jungle.

Darcy's white suit, already hanging in wet, rumpled folds, soon became spattered with mud as he and Rip set out squishing through the swamp in the direction of the river. The mud sucked at his feet; he would have lost his boots had they not been a tight fit. Only his wide-brimmed planter's hat seemed to have borne up under the assault of the rain, sun, and steam. On the other hand, Rip's outrageous plaid scarcely showed the wrinkles and stains, but his beloved beaver hat had wilted, no longer advertising the dapper spirit of its owner.

Arriving back on the beach where the walking was easier, they

127

turned upriver, soon coming to a small clearing. Steam was rising from lakes of water; bedraggled houses with matted tops huddled over sticklike legs; naked children in varying shades of brown and black mingled with pigs, chickens, and dogs splashing in the puddles and mud; the smell of rot and decay hung heavy in the air. Darcy was both repelled and fascinated.

Glancing toward the river, Rip observed, "The boats are down there."

On the bank they saw a lone man sticking a long pole into the bed of the stream and bending it back and forth. They approached and began addressing him in English.

Smiling broadly at them, he said, "Yankee doodle."

"Yes," Rip replied. "Now what we want to know is how much you want to take us upstream in one of those things?" He pointed to the hollowed log canoes tied along the bank. The bungo boats were flat-bottomed with a broad edge running the length of either side. In the middle many of them had little thatched shelters in imitation of the village huts.

The brown man smiled and nodded. "Susannah, don't you cry for me," he piped.

"Here," Darcy said, pulling a gold piece out of his pocket.

The native's eyes glittered and narrowed. He ran to one of the boats and pointed to Darcy and Rip then upstream.

Darcy and Rip both nodded their heads up and down.

"Forty dollar," said the brown man.

Darcy shook his head negatively. He held up his two hands, the fingers outstretched. "Ten dollars. . .three of us and all of our gear," he said.

The native frowned. He pointed to Darcy and Rip, then looked back in the direction from which they had come.

Darcy held up three fingers and then made motions he hoped the native would interpret as indicating luggage.

After watching Darcy attentively, the man made a circle with his arms and said questioningly, "Thirty dollar?"

"That's too much," Darcy said to Rip. "We'd better look for somebody else." He started to walk away.

Recognizing that he was about to lose his customers, the native shrugged his shoulders and smiling broadly said, "Twenty dollar."

Darcy nodded his head affirmatively. The native pointed upstream and made motions as if to start.

"That old drunk back there!" Darcy exploded. "Extracting money from us for a night's lodging. I guess we'd better start or we might lose the boat."

"I think we can wait till morning," Rip said. "After all, you've paid for those cots."

Darcy pantomimed to the boatman that they would start in the morning. Several other brown men began approaching from the huts. One came up to the man they had engaged; obviously they were partners.

Then other men from the ship began emerging from the jungle by twos and threes, and Darcy again became concerned they might lose their transportation if they delayed leaving until morning.

"I'd like to get a good night's sleep before starting up there," said Rip. "How do we know what's ahead?"

Darcy peered up the jungle-encased river. "All right. It is getting late," he agreed. They returned to the Hotel American where they found George sitting on the trunk clutching the brown leather bag between his knees. Realizing that the old servant had been on guard since they left, Darcy ordered him to lie down on one of the cots and get some sleep.

The proprietor, whose name was Thorne, brought out some native brandy. "You'd better stock up," he said. "This is the only thing that'll keep away Panama fever."

Though he doubted the efficacy of the remedy, Darcy bought a few bottles. He had a couple of drinks and put the remaining bottles in his trunk. Then he lay on his cot intending merely to rest. But after a while the droning of the insects lulled him to sleep.

For an impatient man, Rip waited a long time before making his move that night. Long after the hut was quiet, his way lighted by the moon, he silently arose and slipped the brown leather bag from beside Darcy. With it in one hand and his carpetbag in the other, he stealthily backed out the door and down the ladder to the swamp. Just as he was about to flee for the river, he felt a powerful grip on his arm. He would have screamed in terror, except that another huge hand closed over his mouth and he was lifted bodily and borne dangling like a puppet to the edge of the jungle before being set down. Speechless, he stared into the face of the proprietor of the American.

"I figured you was up to something," said Thorne. "Now let's

129

see what you've got in the little brown bag."

"It's mine," spluttered Rip.

"Why of course it is. That's why you were takin' your leave solo, and so nice and early." He opened the bag and whistled softly. "Now that's what I call right friendly of you. Imagine wanting to share half your fortune with me so's I can get out of this stinking hell hole and back to Baltimore." He unrolled a canvas bag he had stuck beneath his belt. Then he removed approximately half of the gold and put it in it.

"You shan't have it!" Rip hissed, pulling out his toy gun.

Thorne laughed. "Now you wouldn't want to use that," he said. "I don't think your friend up there would take kindly to your running off with his money. There's enough for both of us. And for my half, I promise you I won't tell him where you've gone." He gave his ugly laugh again, then turned and walked away.

Rip, shaking with frustration, not daring to use his derringer, put it away. With a sigh and a shrug he closed the bag containing the diminished fortune he had risked everything to steal and hurried down to the river and into the jungle.

CHAPTER **12** UP THE PLATTE TO FORT LARAMIE✶✶✶✶

Winding up the sand hills away from Fort Kearney, Goldie and Gray realized more clearly why Zack had hastened their departure. Across the river on the Mormon Trail a long line of wagons and riders was strung out as far as the eye could see, while on their side a similar long line was following in the wake of their own train on the Oregon Trail.

On the first of June the argonauts forded the south fork of the Platte and continued on the next day, following the trail between the North and South Platte rivers.

Just before the noon rest period Zack, who had been scouting the route ahead, came riding back at a gallop shouting, "Buffalo!" He ordered the train to form the wagons in a wedge pointing west and for the men with horses to come to the head of the train with loaded guns.

By the time the pioneers had carried out Zack's instructions, they heard the ominous roar rolling toward them.

Zack directed the men to form a flank on either side of the point wagon facing the oncoming herd. "There are thousands!" he shouted. "Fire your guns to divert them as they approach. If you get some meat, so much the better."

The wagon train was directly in the path of the bison and in a matter of moments was engulfed in a flood of huge animals running in crazed flight. The frightened mules and oxen reared and plunged, and the men on horses filled the air with continuous whooping as they shot lead into the great herd that parted and flowed on either side. Gray thought he saw a horse without a rider go by him, but he wasn't sure. It took all of his strength to keep Sunny pointed toward the herd, since every instinct in the horse was telling her to turn and run too. Unable to reload his gun, he slapped his hand to his side and screamed until the dust choked off his voice. He thought he saw one great animal falter and fall and wondered if there would be anything left of it by the time the deluge passed. He also found himself wondering if it ever would pass. All he could see was buffalo pouring toward him.

The men fought to turn the animals aside, but the bison kept closing in, pressing against the sides of the wagons. The great prairie schooners were rocked and buffeted as if by hurricane winds. The screams of the men, women, and children added to the braying of the mules, the bawling of the oxen, and the trumpeting of the buffalo. Happy was the only quiet being in all this mass of terrified people and animals. Silently trembling, he sat on the wagon seat beside Goldie, looking over the side with wide brown eyes.

Although all of Goldie's strength was engaged in fighting for control of her team and clinging to the violently swaying wagon, she was aware of a crash on the other side of the line. Turning, she thought she saw a wagon disappear in the sea of bison. Instinctively she started to look back at her own side of the wedge, but was checked as a crazed buffalo suddenly careened into the side of the wagon. As the stout Conestoga teetered perilously back and forth, she clutched the reins until her knuckles whitened. Just as she thought she could hold no more and that her arms would surely break, the buffalo were gone. The ordeal had lasted a half hour, the longest in her life.

While the reality that she was still alive and well was trying to establish itself in her mind, she looked over to the other side of the wedge. A gaping hole in the column testified that one of the wagons was gone. Turning to her own side, she ran her eyes up and down the line until she was satisfied none other was missing. As soon as Ring, Tom, Diddy and Do, Re, Me had quieted, she climbed down to see what had happened to the missing wagon.

Gray's feeling of relief that the herd had passed turned to sickness when he saw the lifeless body of a man lying about fifty yards from him on the plain. Quickly he rode over. As he dismounted he was joined by several other men, who identified the dead man as Bill Malcom, knocked from his horse and trampled to death in the stampede. Bearing Bill's body back, Gray noticed another group gathered around the Baird wagon, third in line on the right side of the point. Beneath it, Zack was rendering first aid to Abe Lewis, who accidentally had been shot. He would be dead too if he hadn't fallen under the Baird wagon.

Thoroughly alarmed by this time, Gray rushed over to his own wagon to see how Goldie had fared. Not finding her there and noticing the crowd of people gathered around the open space on the other side of the wedge, he ran over, frantically shouting Goldie's name. The wagon he approached was a pile of kindling. Goldie was standing on the edge of the circle that surrounded it. She turned at his call and rushed into his arms. For a brief moment they clung to each other.

Goldie shivered and said, "I didn't know such a thing could happen. Jimmy Mathews and Mel Brady are dead. Nobody knows how Lawrence Mathews and Marshall Whitman survived. Their team just suddenly turned right out into the stampede. It's horrible."

The word was passed along to form a circle and for the men to come and prepare the dead for burial and to cut up the meat of the felled buffalo. The needs of the living and the dead stood out in stark contrast as the argonauts silently turned to these tasks.

The beauty of the wild region through which the company traveled for the next few days helped restore their fallen spirits. More than once they were awestruck by the vision of the mountains that lay ahead. But before their confidence had completely returned, another fever struck. As before, the well attempted to care for the sick, but it was more difficult in this rugged terrain where most of the time the pioneers were outside the wagons, walking or helping to push them over particularly rough places.

Undermanned as the fever took more victims, they had to negotiate the descent into Ash Hollow. The mountains were so steep around this depression along the south side of the North Platte that the company had to employ ropes and windlasses once more to lower the wagons into the valley. Although they had used this method successfully at the stream crossings, they were awed by the steepness and length of the trail down, and some were ready to give up in despair. It seemed that before they could surmount one difficulty, they were confronted with another more terrible one. With the blacksmith, Ray Beame, and Wash supervising, the men set to work constructing a crude machine of gears and an extra wagon wheel around which they could loop ropes and pay them out slowly much like a capstan on a ship, as each wagon was lowered into the hollow. Finally all were down.

The next day during the nooning Wash picked up a cow's skull with some writing on it. Recently the argonauts had been seeing more and more of this form of communication peculiar to the trail. Bone-writing was done either to inform friends how the pioneers ahead were faring or to impart news of the terrain. Sometimes scraps of newspapers also were left under mounds of rocks. And even though the papers scarcely held anything that was any longer news, they were read avidly because they were a touch with the country from which the travelers now felt so remote.

This skull Wash found was dated two days earlier. On it the writer stated that they feared they were carrying smallpox on their train of fifteen wagons and advised those behind to give them a wide berth if they came upon the group encamped.

With this news the healthy members of the company began to look at the fever victims in their own group to see if they bore any of the tell-tale signs of the dread disease. Although they found none, Wash called a meeting to find out how many of the company had either been vaccinated or had survived the disease. When he asked for a show of hands, he found that only one-fourth of the group had been immunized. Among these were Goldie and Gray. Aunt Opal had stated before having them vaccinated that there were enough things going around to kill a body without ignoring what medicine had found to keep a body well and alive.

Fear riding with them once more, the emigrants no longer stopped at the tents they passed to inquire whether they could be of service. But their spirits rose three days later when most of the fever victims were up once more. And on this same day they passed two famous trail landmarks, which further elated them. In the morning they saw the wind- and rain-carved sandstone monolith called Court House Rock towering above the plains. Then late in the afternoon, having passed by other weird rock formations that looked like the ruins of a great city, they saw the slender spire of Chimney Rock rising from the peak of a sandstone hill. As they gazed at it in wonder, the rays of the setting sun turned the shaft a deep red. On the following day they were treated to a view of the magnificent Scotts Bluff rising eight hundred feet above the Platte. But they did not pause to climb the escarpment, for now the smell of Fort Laramie was in their nostrils.

Robidoux Pass, which they climbed the next day, appeared mild to them after their ordeal at Ash Hollow. Beyond the pass they met a small party of traders and trappers just out of Fort Laramie.

"There's a sizable herd of buffalo about a day's ride ahead of you," a grizzled old trapper informed them. "It's on the right of the trail. You might get some fresh meat if you're hankerin' for any."

"Thanks," said Zack, "we could use some all right. How's the trail ahead?"

"Crowded," said one of the traders. "There were four trains at the fort when we left, and we've passed another four or five before gettin' to you."

"Any sickness?" asked Wash.

"Yes," said the trapper. "There's a group just ahead of you in a bad way. Hear they've got smallpox."

"We heard about them," said Zack. "How about the other trains?"

"They all seemed to be fine so far," said another man.

"Sure hope you folks get through all right," said the trader.

"Thanks," said Zack. "Good luck to you, too."

As the party turned to leave, Goldie came running up. "Wait a minute, please," she said. "Would you mind carrying some letters east for us? You're the first people we've seen going the other way in a long time."

"Glad to," said the trader. Goldie pressed two fat letters she and Gray had written to Aunt Opal and Big Timbers into the trader's hand.

"Anybody else?" asked the trapper. "We're going all the way to St. Louis."

Nearly everyone on the train rushed to seal their scribblings into letters, and as the men rode off, their saddlebags were bulging with the mail.

Robidoux Pass marked the beginning of the high plains. The emigrants would be traveling across this vast area at an altitude between four and five thousand feet until they reached the Rocky Mountains. The soil was dry and sandy, and sagebrush became so familiar that they soon took no notice of it. Summer was approaching, and the trail grass was drying out. The mules and oxen kicked up clouds of dust as they plodded along, and Goldie and Gray choked on it day after day with no respite. Sometimes, to add to their misery, the wind blew in gusts about the wagon, driving the alkali powder into every nook and cranny. They tried closing the canvas in front and opening up the back to keep the dust out, but their efforts were in vain. Their mouths were dry and parched, and when they bit down, their teeth ground on the grit. Casting about for anything that would help them breathe, Gray wet his handkerchief and tied it over his nose and mouth.

"It does help some," he told Goldie. "Why don't you try it?"

"Why not?" said Goldie, tying a bandana over her face.

One by one the other emigrants followed suit, until the whole train looked like a band of masked bandits.

Three days later, Gray felt a lump in his throat when he saw the stars and stripes billowing out red, white, and blue high above the stockade of heavy timbers that was Fort Laramie. Constructed of heavy logs reinforced with adobe, and with blockhouses mounted above the main gate and at diagonal corners, the fort towered above the plain at the confluence of the Laramie and Platte rivers.

It looked far more imposing than Fort Kearney, Gray thought. Clustered around it he counted five other wagon trains and a scattering of Indian tepees.

Impatient though he was to explore the fort's interior, he knew he must first prepare the wagon for crossing the Rockies. The wheels, loosened, rattling, and squeaking in the dry air, needed their rims tightened; the mules needed shoeing; and the brittle leather of the harnesses and reins needed mending. Ray Beame already had his small forge glowing when Gray arrived to ask him about tightening the wheels and shoeing the mules.

"Bring over your wagon and team in about an hour," he said.

Dora Cunningham had never regained her strength after her bout with the fever. Tim learned there was a doctor in the fort and wanted her to see him. But Dora already knew what was the matter with her and was trying to keep her overburdened and impoverished husband from finding out. She protested that they couldn't afford it, and that she'd be all right after a few days' rest. But Tim was adamant, and after asking Goldie to care for Adam and Ruth, he took his wife to the fort.

The doctor confirmed what Dora already knew. "You're pregnant," he said, "and if you continue this hard journey you might lose the child. You don't have the strength. The only way for you to regain your health is to take a long rest."

Dora almost laughed at the sobering words. "Rest!" she said. "Doctor, do you know how much money we have? Twenty-five dollars. That and our wagon is everything we own. Do you think we can stop?"

"I'm not able to relieve your financial burden, Mrs. Cunningham," replied the doctor. "I can only tell you what will very likely happen if you keep on at this time. I don't like to say this. . .but it could mean your very life."

"I'm afraid that doesn't frighten me much anymore," she answered. "Just one thing. Please don't tell Tim. If everything turns out all right, he'll know. And if it doesn't. . .well, that won't matter much."

"I will tell him you need rest. Have you any other children?"

"Yes, three."

"They'll have to assume a greater share of the camp burden from now on."

After informing Tim that Dora must not do any heavy work,

136

the doctor brusquely brushed aside any payment, saying, "I didn't do anything."

The train remained at the fort two days. On the second evening Zack, Wash, and the company officers called a meeting to discuss the terrain ahead and how they would proceed.

Zack addressed the group: "We'll continue along the North Platte till it bends down toward the Sweetwater. Then we'll follow the Sweetwater to South Pass at the foot of the Wind River Mountains, and finally we'll wind our way down to Fort Bridger, which will be our next stop."

"How long will it take to get to South Pass?" asked one man.

"If we move right along, it should take less than three weeks," replied Zack.

"Any Indians between here and there?" asked another.

"Yes," answered Zack, "and don't expect them to be friendly. They're branches of the great Sioux Nation that were pushed off their ancestral lands by white settlers. They bear us no love, so won't miss an opportunity to harass or even kill any stragglers. We'll have to be more alert from now on. . .especially at night. Nothing would make these tribes happier than to steal our livestock."

"What about meat?" asked Wash. "Can we expect to find any more buffalo?"

"Yes," said another man. "Since we missed that herd the trappers at Robidoux Pass told us about, we've all been wondering about that."

"If we don't run into any herds on this side of South Pass, we won't have much fresh meat. There won't be any buffalo once we cross the mountains," replied Zack. "And as you already know other game is scarce."

During the day four more wagon trains had rolled into Fort Laramie. "You can all see how the trail's getting," he continued. "We'll have to move out tomorrow at dawn."

As Goldie and Gray were returning to their wagon, they encountered Isaiah.

"Why, whatever are you doing up so late, Isaiah?" exclaimed Goldie.

"I've been helping Mr. Beame," responded the boy. "And look what I've got." He brought out two dollars, which caught the light of the dying fires.

"That's wonderful, Isaiah," said Gray. "But have you been working all of this time?"

"Yes, lots of folks from the other trains wanted work done, so Mr. Beame closed up just a little while ago. He shoed all of our mules, too. That was part of my wages."

"I'm sure your mother and father will be very proud of you," said Goldie.

"You'd better run on home now," said Gray. "We're leaving at dawn tomorrow."

As Isaiah ran off, Goldie felt guilty. Compared to the Cunninghams, her time at Fort Laramie had been easy. Slight Tim Cunningham had been hoisting heavy feed and grain sacks at the trading post for two days in order to earn money to replenish the family's meager supplies. She'd asked Tim why he didn't just help himself from the growing stockpile of food discarded from overloaded wagons outside the fort, but he had replied forthrightly that he couldn't take what wasn't his or what he hadn't earned. With such strict standards she feared he wouldn't be any more of a success in California than he had been in Kentucky.

That night as she went to bed, cuddling the purring Matilda, she determined to be more watchful over the Cunninghams and to try to help Dora, who, after swearing Goldie to secrecy, had told her she was carrying a baby. Although this was hardly a subject on which Goldie was an expert, she had a feeling that riding on a jolting wagon was not the best treatment for an ailing, pregnant woman.

The Laramie River was forded the next morning, and the emigrants continued along the south bank of the North Platte, looking with awe at the rough rocks and the distant peaks they soon must cross.

On the day the *Sea Skimmer* left Rio de Janeiro, Holt and Mirina waited until afternoon before confronting Captain Hewitt. The captain stared at them with undisguised frigidity.

"I'd like to present my wife," said Holt. "We were married yesterday."

"I see," said Captain Hewitt. "And now you have got your passage to California, haven't you, Mrs. Black?"

"Mrs. Compton," corrected Mirina.

"Ah, yes, Mrs. Compton. . ." He brought out a decanter of whisky and poured two glasses. Lifting his, he said, "To your happiness, Holt." Downing the glass neatly, he dismissed them, saying, "Go tell the steward to make a cake or something. I've got work to do."

The news of the marriage speedily traveled from one end of the ship to the other. Though some of the men were delighted at the prospect of having a female to look at on the long voyage ahead, others shook their heads prophesying trouble. And Kevin, thoroughly ashamed of what he had done, fervently wished her back in Rio de Janeiro.

For several days the *Sea Skimmer* made her way deep into the southern latitudes with both wind and current in her favor. At times she was making sixteen knots, and the men were predicting an easy passage around Old Cape Stiff. By keeping the ship well off the South American coast, Captain Hewitt was avoiding the unfavorable land winds and tides and retaining the favorable Brazilian current. Aware that they would soon be in a bad gale and squall area fighting the northern sweep of the Falkland current, he was not as optimistic as his passengers and crew about their quick passage around Cape Horn.

During this time Holt spent his days with Kevin and Captain Hewitt. For though Mirina shared a berth with him, she showed no inclination to share his interests. Hers, he quickly discovered, lay in a different direction. An accomplished faro dealer, she could be counted among the players whenever there was a hot game going on the deck or in the saloon. At first he thought it an innocent enough pastime, although the thought that nice girls didn't do this sort of thing kept nagging him.

Early in the morning of the fifth day out from Rio the weather changed. Off the mouth of the La Plata River in Patagonia a squall hit. The fierce land pamperos were blowing far out to sea, and the hands were pelted with icy rain as they altered the sails for working dead to windward.

As the *Sea Skimmer* drew further into the southern latitudes, the air grew steadily colder, until on the morning of the Fourth of July the men found ice on their washbasins.

Mr. White took no notice of the holiday, and during the early watch he sent Kevin aloft alone to loosen the topgallant sail on the mizzenmast. The gaskets were frozen to the sail, and after nearly an hour of work Kevin's hands were raw and bleeding from breaking away the ice. He had loosened all of the gaskets, but the sail still would not come free. Working carefully with his feet along the walk rope strung beneath the reefed sail, he felt with his hands around the yard to find the trouble. Suddenly far below him, White gave the order to the crew to give another heave on the halyards. With a mighty crack the great sail broke the ice that was imprisoning it, pinching Kevin's hand under a gasket and bruising it as he frantically jerked it free. The hurt hand dangling useless, he fought his way back to the masthead and slowly began his descent.

Knowing there should have been more than one man working on the yard, his shipmates watched him apprehensively as he painfully worked his way down. The watch was changing by the time he reached the stern deck, and Mr. McCarthy's men had joined White's. The first mate asked what had happened. When Kevin explained, he nodded his head and told him to report to Captain Hewitt to have his hand bandaged. White, livid at McCarthy's usurping his authority, stalked below.

The door to Captain Hewitt's cabin was ajar, and Kevin could hear Holt's flat, metallic voice accusing Second Mate White of trying to kill him. Knocking sharply in order to interrupt the barrage, he entered, angrily glaring at Holt.

"You're a lucky one. I don't think anything's broken," Captain Hewitt said after gently feeling the hand. "But I'll have to remove you from the duty roster for at least three days. Can't have you in the rigging with that."

"Aye, aye, sir," said Kevin.

"Do you wish to enter a complaint against Mr. White?" continued the captain as he bandaged the hand.

"No, sir," replied Kevin.

"Very well," said Captain Hewitt, "that ends it."

"But why not?" demanded Holt. "Mr. White deliberately ordered the men to pull when he knew you were in a dangerous position."

"What proof do I have of that?"

"All the men know. They're your proof."

"I stand on what I answered to you, Captain Hewitt," said Kevin and scowled at Holt as he left the cabin.

"I know White tried to kill him. . .and he'll try again," said Holt.

"I'll keep an eye on him," said the captain. "But that's all I can promise. White's carried out his duties aboard this ship with dispatch. I can't expect more from a second mate."

Late in the afternoon of the ship's celebration of America's seventy-third Independence Day, the temperature dropped sharply again and black clouds scudded overhead, darkening the sky. Noting the steadily rising wind, Captain Hewitt issued a call to Mr. McCarthy to close-reef the topsails, and McCarthy sent White below to get a crew.

In the forecastle White barked out the names of several men. Then he spotted Kevin in his bunk. "Adams," he called.

"But I've been relieved from duty," protested Kevin.

"I've issued you an order," said White.

"Here now," said Jamie, "you'll not be quarreling on your country's birthday. I'll furl the sail."

"But you're not on this watch. And you've been celebrating too," said Kevin.

"Not so much I can't walk like a cat," said Jamie with a wink.

"All right then, let's go," said White, and he went out followed by the crew he had selected. On an impulse Kevin followed and from the shelter of the companionway watched them climb the mastheads. He could hear the wind whistling through the rigging, and peering up into the darkness he saw the crew was struggling to reef the topsails.

The wind mounted to a high-pitched scream, and the ship heeled over with a shudder. Kevin heard a rip and crack signaling a sail had split. As he sought to find Jamie and Big Blue on the mainmast, he felt the sting of hail on his face. The stones were sharp, and he could imagine what they were doing to the sails; the decks would be covered if the seas weren't washing them off with each dip of the ship into the wave troughs. Through the wintry curtain he could occasionally see Captain Hewitt near the wheel giving orders to the helmsman to keep the ship in the wind

The hail turned to snow, and still the men did not come down. Kevin couldn't see them in the storm, and he became more and more alarmed. Then he heard an ominous crack followed by a crashing of splintered wood and tangled ropes to the deck. The mainmast had lost its top and now gave off a creaking sound indicating the mast had been sprung. McCarthy and White ran to the spot, directing the deck crew to cut the ropes and clear away the canvas. At the same moment Captain Hewitt issued a call for all hands, and Kevin quickly stepped out into the storm to avoid being trampled by the men who began pouring out of the companionway.

Jamie and Big Blue had been among the men working on the mainmast, but since no one had fallen to the deck in the debris, Kevin assumed they were all right. But his relief was short-lived, for he now spotted Big Blue climbing down the mast bearing a body. Forgetting his hurt hand and the danger of the slippery deck, Kevin rushed over. It was Jamie the big sailor was carrying. "Take him to my cabin," briskly ordered Captain Hewitt.

But Jamie, who was still conscious, said, "No, Captain, I'm afraid there's something pretty smashed up inside of me. Just lay me easy on a bit of deck, Blue, me lad." Big Blue laid him down on one of the torn sails in the shelter of a hatch. "I guess I was na' intended to have me lass or me land," said Jamie with effort.

Kevin felt tears stinging his eyes. Big Blue was openly and unashamedly weeping.

"Here now," said Jamie, "never a tear for me. I'll be all right, you know."

Amid the howling winds the men were aware of the presence of death. Big Blue picked up the body of his friend and carried it below where the sailmaker would prepare it for burial.

Later Captain Hewitt asked him for a report.

Blue explained, "I was working on the topgallant and Jamie was above me on the royal. When the top of the mast went, it toppled

Jamie and his yard down on my yard, squeezing him in between. Then his yard fell away, and I grabbed him to keep him from falling with it." He shook his head in amazement. "For a moment I thought we was both goners. I don't know why the yard we was on didn't break too."

"Thank you for the report, Mr. Blue," said the captain.

The rest of the men had returned to the deck and were crowding around to hear Big Blue's story. Since the ship was now close-reefed and riding the storm well, Captain Hewitt ordered, "Everyone get below and dry off. There's nothing more we can do here."

Back in the forecastle the superstitious sailors talked of nothing but what had happened to Jamie.

"She's an unlucky ship," said an old salt, nodding his head. "They always comes in threes, you know."

"What?" asked Kevin. "What always comes in threes?"

"Why deaths—accidents," said the old tar. "Jamie's only the first, and we ain't even reached the Horn. You wait and see. There's trouble ahead."

Kevin looked around at his shipmates. There was fear in their eyes, and he knew they believed this was only the first death the ship would have.

Captain Hewitt read the brief burial service in the morning, and Jamie's body, sewn up in canvas, was committed to the deep.

The entire ship missed the cheery little Scot. In the forecastle or on the decks, his optimism and merry wit had endeared him to everyone and had lightened many a bad situation or show of ill-feeling among the crew. Now there was no one to take his place, and with each passing day the men became more despondent.

Three days after Jamie's death Captain Hewitt spotted the Falkland Islands in his glass. Aware that everyone needed a diversion, he had McCarthy call out the hands and the argonauts so they could see the islands as they passed in the channel between them and Tierra del Fuego on the southernmost tip of South America.

For a moment a glimmer of sunlight struck through the clouds, and those aloft called down that they could see the mastheads of three ships in her harbor.

"They must have put in to make repairs from the storm or to pick up water," said Captain Hewitt. "We'll not stop, though. We're making good progress with the new sails, and I expect we'll be flying full canvas again by the time we round the Horn."

"How soon will we be there?" asked Holt.

"This westerly wind is still against us. But if it changes tomorrow, we should be able to negotiate the strait without being driven back."

There was no easterly wind behind them on the next day, so the ship, her wings poised for flight, simply marked time. On July ninth they finally found themselves in the Le Maire Strait, where they could see the land of both the island of Tierra del Fuego and Staten Island, though the seas were violent and high. Just as it seemed they might double the Cape on this one day, they were hurled back by the fierce opposing winds. Though he had worked the ship hard all day, in midafternoon Captain Hewitt decided he would make one more try before dark.

In addition to the wind they were now hampered by fog, and lookouts were posted aloft while other hands were making soundings to keep the *Sea Skimmer* off the rocks of the Wallaston Group, one of which was Cape Horn itself.

Both of the mates had been on deck with the crew all day carrying out the captain's commands. The men were exhausted from scrambling up and down the ropes of the masts, and Kevin had been continually singled out by White to go aloft. Once more angry over the second mate's treatment of his friend, Holt went to Captain Hewitt to complain.

"My God, boy, I've been out here for more than twelve hours myself!" the captain exploded. "I'm trying to double the Cape. Don't bother me with your petty complaints about my officers!" He abruptly turned back to the helm.

Feeling foolish, Holt returned amidships. Several hands were ordered up the masts to lay on more sail, and White again picked Kevin for duty. Holt scrambled up the masthead directly behind him.

As they were loosening the mizzen royal, White, standing way back by the mainmast, cupped his hands and shouted up at them. First Mate McCarthy, with a crew ready to hoist up the main royal as soon as it was free, also was standing by the mainmast, his eyes aloft, waiting for the signal from above. As soon as he got it he ordered his crew to give a mighty heave. For some unknown reason White was standing on the main royal's rope, and as McCarthy's men pulled, it uncoiled, sending White up in the air and depositing him in a heap on the deck. At the same time the ship heeled far over on her side, and a great wave washed high over the lee rail, taking him out to sea.

A sailor shouted, "Man overboard!"

McCarthy and several of the men rushed to the side to throw over lifelines, but they couldn't even see White.

Captain Hewitt ordered a boat lowered with McCarthy in command. Without thinking, both Holt and Kevin, who had scrambled down from the mizzenmast, volunteered to go. Because of the thickening fog, Captain Hewitt ordered the boat not to go beyond the sound of the ship's bell in their search.

As the longboat pulled away, the volunteers soon saw what the captain meant. Less than fifty yards out they could no longer see the *Sea Skimmer*, and could only identify where she was by the sound of her bell. The distance between the peaks and troughs of the waves seemed interminable. Repeatedly McCarthy cupped his hands to his mouth and shouted White's name, and all of the men tried to pierce the fog. But they could not find the second mate. An hour passed as they rowed in ever-widening circles.

Suddenly Mr. McCarthy said, "Ship your oars." His head went up, listening intently.

Then Holt realized he hadn't heard the bell from the *Sea Skimmer* for some time. The men looked at each other apprehensively. After a moment McCarthy rang their own small bell. But except for the wind and the wash of the waves against the boat there was no response. The fog closed thickly around, and now it was dark.

McCarthy reckoned their direction on a small compass he carried, then ordered the men to row once more. They dipped their oars in the cold, gray water as lightly as possible. Not a word was spoken. Every few minutes McCarthy sounded the bell, but the hoped-for answer never came.

Another forty-five minutes passed, and though the men listened as intently as ever, a deep foreboding began to grip them. Kevin sensed that the atmosphere in the boat had changed. He looked at Holt to see if he had noticed. Holt gave him a fleeting smile but didn't say anything. He was wondering what foolhardy gallantry had led the two of them to volunteer for such a hazardous mission, especially since White had been an enemy.

As the minutes passed the men's despair became as bleak as the

145

fog and darkness that surrounded them. Then Kevin thought he heard something. Yes, there it was again, faint but unmistakable above the sound of the waves. "Sir," he said to McCarthy. "I think I hear a bell ahead on the starboard side." The men turned to him, hope flickering in their eyes.

McCarthy sounded the bell and, with the rest of the men, lifted his head to listen. But nobody heard anything. Still McCarthy ordered the men to pull in the direction Kevin indicated. Then the wind died down completely and they all heard it. They were almost upon the ship before they saw her. But instead of the welcome sight of the *Sea Skimmer*, they were looking up at a derelict drifting helplessly in the water, prey to the wind and waves. Wrecked but not sunk somewhere off the Cape, she rocked back and forth, empty and silent except for the funereal tolling of her bell.

"A death ship," whispered one of the sailors.

"It's a sign," said another. "We'll never make it back."

A young deckhand began to cry hysterically. All of the men started shouting and talking at once. One of them had to be physically restrained from leaping over the side. With difficulty Holt choked back his own panic. Was it all to end here? His feet were numb, and he could feel the cold creeping up his legs. If they didn't find the *Sea Skimmer* soon they'd all freeze to death. He thought about Mirina, and for the first time honestly saw their marriage. I was only the way out of Rio to her, he said to himself bitterly—nothing more. And now she would see California, while he. . .by God, he couldn't give up. He couldn't die now. He sat up and squared his shoulders as McCarthy clanged his bell for order.

"I'm so cold," whimpered a young sailor.

"All right," said McCarthy, "you're all going to have to exercise or you'll get frostbite. Rub your hands and feet and get up and down by spells. But be quiet. We've found one ship—that means we can find our own."

The crew calmed down. McCarthy resumed sounding his bell, and the men once more bent to their oars.

Half an hour later the sound of a bell again cut through the fog. Since McCarthy's compass assured them they were not going in a circle, they knew it could not be the derelict luring them once more. McCarthy signaled with their bell, and an answering ring brought the men shouting to their feet, nearly capsizing the small

146

boat. As the *Sea Skimmer* hove in sight, the entire ship was lining her starboard rail, shouting and waving. And soon the little crew was scrambling up the ropes to the welcoming arms of their shipmates above.

Mirina hurled herself into Kevin's arms as he climbed aboard ahead of Holt. "I thought you were lost," she cried.

At her touch he forgot where they were and that she was married to Holt. All that mattered was that he was alive and they were together. He bent down to kiss her. Then he saw Captain Hewitt watching them closely. Abruptly he thrust her from him and said, "Your husband's back too."

She stood hesitant a moment, blinking at him. Then her eyes hardened and she returned to the side to welcome Holt aboard. Silently cursing his longing for her, Kevin went below.

Captain Hewitt followed Mirina over to Holt. "Egad, boy," he said. "I thought I'd lost you. Didn't know how I could make an accounting to your father, either. Mighty glad I don't have to." Then he turned to his first mate. "Mr. McCarthy, I'll have your report in my cabin."

"Aye, aye, sir," said McCarthy as he followed the captain below.

In their joy at the return of the search party, the ship had almost forgotten the man who was lost. But as the evening wore on, they remembered.

"There's two gone," said the same sailor who had whispered superstitiously after Jamie's death. "I told you they always comes in threes. And we ain't around Old Cape Stiff yet!" The smiles left the faces of the men, and fear once more took hold in the forecastle.

Again the ship fought fierce winds and sky-high waves the next day. Finally Captain Hewitt told Holt, "I'm going to move the ship south. We're getting nowhere beating against the wind here in the shadow of the Cape. Sometimes there's an easterly to the south."

But further south the wind died completely, and the following day the *Sea Skimmer* lay becalmed in the subzero temperature of the Drake Passage. Here the ship encountered its first iceberg, an awesome sight with its top over two hundred feet high, all white with snow shading to a deep indigo blue where its base entered the ocean. It was hundreds of feet in diameter, and every now and then a huge chunk would break off with a loud crack and form a new iceberg to float away in the current. Like the icebergs, all day the ship rocked helplessly in the sea, the intense cold penetrating above and below decks. With no work to keep them active the crew became sluggish, and Captain Hewitt ordered Mr. McCarthy to have them play games as a preventive for frostbite.

"All hands skylark!" came McCarthy's crisp command.

Instantly the ship sprang to life as the men began devising games. One sport became particularly popular. Two men were tied by their waists on ropes hung from the mainsail yards about ten feet above the deck. The object was for one to cut the other down without being cut down himself. The other men stood around below making wagers on which man would successfully dump the other on the deck. As they laughed, stomped their feet, and talked, they forgot how cold they were and how precarious their lot was.

That night in the forecastle there was more cheer and talking than there had been in many a day, and around four o'clock in the morning the prayed-for easterly began to blow.

"All hands on deck!" sang out Mr. McCarthy.

The men jumped to unfurl the sails. As the *Sea Skimmer* sped westward and north, the wind held fair, and in the late afternoon she rounded Cape Horn. Captain Hewitt sighted the bleak rock island through his spyglass and then handing the glass to Holt said, "There she is—not much to look at, but a siren just the same."

As the ship passed into the Pacific the men could feel the strong pull of the current toward the north, and they gave a mighty cheer. They had conquered the greatest hazard of the voyage and within a few days would make their second shore stop, at Valparaiso, Chile.

In the steaming hut in the swamp near the Chagres River, Darcy came awake with a start. George was shaking him.

"What is it?" he asked loudly.

"Sh! Mistuh Darcy," George admonished him. "Duh others is still asleep. Duh day not come yet."

"Then what the——?"

"It Mistuh Rip. He gone. Where you bag? I can't find it."

Darcy hastily felt over the cot, but the bag was not there. George lit a candle, and they quietly but desperately searched the entire hut.

"It's no use," Darcy finally whispered. "The little weasel's stolen the money and deserted us. We'd be stranded if it wasn't for this." He took out the purse containing the two thousand dollars in bills and patted the gold coins he had stuffed in his pockets. "But by God, we'll catch him. And when we do, he'll regret the day he met me. Come on, help me with this trunk. We're leaving."

Objects were barely visible in the early morning light as they approached the native landing by the river, and Darcy excitedly pointed to one of the boats.

"Look," he cried, "that's the boat I engaged yesterday afternoon. I wonder why he didn't take it—unless he's still here. Just wait till I catch him!" He looked around sharply.

"What you goin' to do, Mistuh Darcy?" asked George anxiously, for he had grown fond of the little gambler.

"Kill him!"

"No, Mistuh Darcy, you mustn't do dat. He can't help hisself."

"Uncle George, I don't have time to argue. I've got to find my boatman."

An old native was coming down to the river, and Darcy went to meet him. He pointed to the boat where George was standing. "Upriver. . .I want to go upriver," he said, making paddling motions with his arms.

"Sí," said the man, beckoning him to follow.

"You stay here with the trunk, Uncle George," Darcy called "I'll be back in a minute."

As they walked along to the village, he questioned the native. "White man," he said. Then with his hands he indicated smallness. The native smiled broadly and began dancing up and down and shouting. The words came out in Spanish, but it was a perfect imitation of the little gambler. At the end of his performance he pointed upstream, indicating Rip had gone.

They had arrived at the cluster of huts, and the native motioned for Darcy to wait while he climbed inside one. In a moment he reappeared with the man Darcy had engaged the previous afternoon. Darcy gave the old man a coin and turned to the boatman.

He pointed to himself. "Dupres," he said. "My name is Dupres."

"Reny," said the boatman, imitating Darcy's gesture.

"All right, Reny," said Darcy. "We start now." He pointed to the river. Then he raised two fingers to indicate there would only be two passengers. Reny nodded and climbed back in the hut, soon emerging with his partner.

"Brother," said Reny. "Palu."

"Sí," said Darcy. "Now we must hurry."

Darcy and George climbed into the bungo boat; Reny and Palu pushed it out into the water. Standing on each side of the boat, they shoved long poles into the riverbed, braced them against their shoulders, and walked the length of the boat on the long broad rims, propelling the canoe forward. Since they were fighting against the current, it was a slow method of navigation, requiring strong application of muscle.

As they were about to make their second trip along the side of the canoe, they were stopped by the screaming of a girl running toward the river. In one hand she was carrying a big iron pot, and in the other, a bundle and a rolled mat. Laughing uproariously, Reny and Palu skillfully poled the canoe back toward shore, and the girl splashed out to it and climbed aboard.

Reny said, "Tamura. . .sister."

"All right," said Darcy, "but let's go. We're wasting time."

When Tamura unrolled her mat and bundle by the small charcoal stove beneath the canopy, George was glad to see that she had brought food for the three days' trip to Gorgona. Darcy, in his anger, hadn't even thought about preparations for eating.

Tamura held up a package to show George. "Café. . .nice," she said. "Soon." She pointed to the small stove.

George nodded, but when Tamura handed him a banana for breakfast, he found he wasn't hungry and laid it aside without touching it. I'm just tired, he thought. If I have a little nap I'll feel better. He closed his eyes, and Tamura did not disturb him when the boiled coffee was ready.

Displeased with the slow progress they were making, Darcy kept urging Reny and Palu on to greater speed. He couldn't understand why they periodically tied the boat along the bank and jumped into the river. Dark, unhappy looks came over the faces of the natives as the hot day progressed, for every time they took a plunge in the stream to cool and restore their tired bodies, the black-eyed white man shouted at them from the boat. And though he insisted they travel into the evening dusk, he complained when they had difficulty finding a place to tie up for the night.

Scarcely conscious of those around him, George, who had not been restored by sleep, was unable to eat any supper. The others also had little appetite, for with evening, swarms of biting insects had descended upon them. Miserable, Darcy crawled beneath his blanket to escape, but his mind continued to brood over catching and punishing Rip.

Awake before dawn the next morning, he routed out his sleepy boatmen and Tamura and demanded that they immediately eat breakfast and be off. Impatiently he paced around the camp while Tamura fixed the meal. As soon as he had drunk his coffee, he ordered them to pack up and leave. Sullenly, and in silence, the natives did as he bid. George had forced himself to drink some coffee with sugar, but he was barely able to pull himself back on the boat.

They were tied up for the noon rest period when Darcy noticed for the first time that Tamura was sweetening the coffee by chewing the ends of some cut sticks of sugarcane and spitting the juice out into the cups. His stomach gave a wrench as he realized he had been drinking coffee made this way for over a day. When the coffee was sweetened to her satisfaction, she approached him and extended the cup.

"No," said Darcy. But Tamura stuck the offensive beverage right under his nose. "I said no!" he shouted and knocked the cup out of her hand into the water.

Tamura's eyes widened briefly and her nostrils flared. She lunged at him like a tigress, pushing him backwards off the boat

151

into the water. Her anger dispelled, she stood above him on the edge of the canoe laughing in high glee. Her brothers came running to see what had happened. The sight of Darcy treading water, his white ruffled shirt ballooning in front of him and his coattails billowing behind, set them also into wild spasms of laughter. They turned to George and in rapid-fire Spanish told him to come and look. But all George could manage in response was a faint smile and a slight lifting of his hand. Fine beads of perspiration had broken out over his face.

Annoyed with Tamura, Darcy reached up and grabbed the girl by the ankle, pulling her off into the river. She went in headfirst and came up spluttering but still laughing. Darcy began to laugh too, and his ugly mood dissolved. As he climbed back on the boat he extended his hand to Tamura, who had dived down and retrieved the cup from the river bottom. Holding it triumphantly, she grasped Darcy's hand and came aboard. Reny and Palu nodded their heads in satisfaction.

When the boat tied up for the midafternoon rest period Darcy joined the natives in the water. He had borrowed a brief wraparound garment from Reny, which he wore the rest of the trip. Suddenly realizing that George must be sweltering back on the boat, Darcy swam over to the side and said, "Come on in, Uncle George. It'll revive your spirits."

"I can't swim, Mistuh Darcy," George whispered.

"Then dip up some water and pour it over you. It'll make you feel better."

"Yassuh," agreed George as Darcy swam back to the middle of the stream. But the old Negro didn't have the strength to obey.

After a while Tamura swam over to the bank and beckoned Darcy to follow. Reny and Palu, diving and splashing in the middle of the river, took no notice. Tamura climbed the bank, parted some vines and leaves, and flung herself down in a hidden bower. As he crowded in beside her, Darcy noticed the soft diffused light, the deep green of the plants, and the brilliant hues of the flowers. He plucked a scarlet bloom and tucked it behind her ear.

Holding out her arms to him, she kissed him slowly and passionately. Enticed by the feel of her firm brown breasts, he pressed his body close and began making love to her. She responded in a way he had not felt from a woman before. At last, sated, he fell asleep but soon was awakened; Tamura was brushing his ear with a

152

flower. He pulled her down once more and kissed her. Laughing, she pushed him away and darted out from their hiding place. When he reached the boat she was sitting demurely under the thatch combing her long black hair. Reny and Palu sat up and stretched. They picked up their long poles, and the party proceeded upstream at the usual slow pace.

That evening they tied up to the bank early. After supper Reny brought out a small stringed instrument and together with Palu began to harmonize on some old Spanish ballads interspersed with the American tunes of "Yankee Doodle" and "Oh, Susannah." Darcy caught Tamura's hand and drew her away from the fire into the incredible green of the jungle.

During the remainder of the trip he did not think finding Rip was nearly as important as he had three days earlier. Although he had intended to go by water only the forty miles to Gorgona, he now decided to push on by boat the extra five miles to Cruces, extending this pleasant part of his journey.

George nodded gratefully at his change of plan, for he hoped the extra time on the river would give him a chance to recover. He knew he had to face mounting and riding a mule the remaining twenty miles to Panama City. After the first day, Darcy had been so engrossed in the pursuit of Tamura he had been oblivious to the drenching rains, the thick heat, and even the biting flies and mosquitoes; but George had had no such pleasant distraction. Old and homesick, he was seized with alternating chills and fever, and his body was a mass of welts from the insect bites.

With all of the desires of his hot young blood, Darcy made the most of his final evening on the river. He had enjoyed his affair with Tamura. She gave herself freely, and he believed there were none of the unpleasant complications that had spoiled his liaison with Marie.

At Cruces the next morning Darcy paid Reny and his brother the agreed-upon twenty dollars, patted Tamura on the head, and stepped ashore. On the other side of the clearing near the start of the trail leading off into the mountains some mules stood in a corral. Outside the rope enclosure a man was emptying water from a bucket into a trough. As Darcy approached and began dickering about the animals, Tamura came up beside them. Suddenly aware that he had vastly oversimplified his relationship with the girl, he grabbed her by the arm and hustled her back to the river. To his relief he found the brothers had not left, and he wildly gestured that he could not take Tamura with him. Reny frowned; he and Palu had a long consultation.

Finally they pointed to Tamura and the boat and motioned downstream. "Forty dollar," they said in unison.

"All right, you pirates," said Darcy. "I'll give you twenty."

"Bueno," said Reny, taking the money. He motioned to Tamura.

"Adiós," she chuckled, stepping into the boat.

Having now paid forty dollars for passage and extra benefits and suspecting he had been tactically outmaneuvered by Tamura and her wily brothers, he returned to the muleteer, his ego deflated. After a half hour's haggling, the owner agreed to a price of twenty-five dollars for three mules plus his services as a guide to Panama City. With his last bit of strength, George helped the man put up Darcy's trunk and mounted his mule.

Although the first part of the ride across a tableland was rough, they soon entered a dim forest where the ground was soft and pulled at the mules' every step. Coming out of the forest they entered a narrow canyon with sheer rock walls on either side. Darcy had learned from Thorne that they would be following the old Spanish gold route. They began climbing cliffs so steep that the mules sometimes scrambled up on centuries-worn little stone steps carved in the solid rock. Much of the time George simply closed his eyes and hung on. There was no relief from either the blistering sun or the torrential downpours that had constantly assailed them since starting across the isthmus.

In some of the narrow rain-washed ravines they could touch both of the cliff walls rising on either side of them. When the passage became too narrow, Darcy would lift his legs from the stirrups and sit cross-legged on his mule's back like a Turk riding his magic carpet, but George paid no attention to his knees scraping on the canyon walls. The only thing that would startle him out of his half-conscious state was the periodic hallooing of the guide when they reached the narrow cracks, to warn anyone coming through the other way that they were about to enter. Darcy wondered what it would be like to try and back a mule through one of these slits, since there was no place wide enough to turn around. Fortunately, they never had to find out. At last they broke out of the confining cliffs and canyons and saw lying below them the city of Panama, gleaming in the afternoon sun.

"Look, George," Darcy called. "There it is. Soon we can be rid of these pesky mules."

But George did not hear. As Darcy turned around, he saw the old slave melt from his mule down toward the wet, sticky earth like a candle guttering out. Leaping from his saddle, Darcy caught the sick old Negro as he settled. George's eyes were glazed, and the perspiration was streaming from him. But worse than this, for Darcy was sweating also, was the gray cast of the old man's face. Darcy could tell that the poor worn-out body was racked with fever.

"Uncle George. . .Uncle George," he crooned, cradling the old man's head in his lap. "I didn't know. You were so quiet. Don't give up now. We're almost there."

"Panama fever. He got Panama fever," said the guide briefly.

"We've got to get him to a doctor," said Darcy. "Is there a doctor down there?"

"Give quinine." He gave Darcy some of the pills, and Darcy tried to administer them with some water from the canteen. George was unable to swallow.

"We go to town. You put to bed," said the guide.

"You're not afraid?" asked Darcy.

"Why afraid?" The lined face of the guide showed puzzlement. "Cannot catch from him. Catch from swamp. . .not from man."

He shook his head at the stupidity of the white man. Then he got down and held Darcy's mule while Darcy, carrying George, mounted. The frail body in his arms was scarcely any weight at all. He tried to remember if George had always been this thin or if this was the result of the journey.

As they entered the town, Darcy realized that its large and spacious appearance from the hills was an illusion. The old Spanish city was crumbling into gray decay. Narrow and dirty streets lined with cheerless native bark huts sprouting signs for lodging, eating, and gambling crowded in upon the once fine buildings.

Though his guide shook his head, Darcy entered several of these dank dens in search of lodging. Inside he was even more repelled. The hotels were nothing more than long, low-ceilinged huts lined with bunks two tiers high. Fifty or more would be crowded in a room, and there were no sanitary facilities. The grinning owners usually announced they were full. But even when they weren't, they refused to take in a sick man. In despair, Darcy returned to the guide, who had remained with George.

"Come," the guide said, motioning for Darcy to mount again. They rode to high ground outside the city, where there were trees and they could see the harbor. It was getting dark, but the guide did not seem to need the light. He stopped in front of a hut. Although Darcy had seen other shacks and shanties as they passed, this one appeared more permanent, more lasting. The guide dismounted from his mule and walked to the door.

With a gracious, dignified gesture he turned and said, "Enter my house."

Darcy carried George in and placed him on a plain but clean cot at one end of the single room. While the guide covered George with quilts and blankets, Darcy glanced around and saw the house had a wooden floor, a stone hearth, and a cast-iron cook stove.

"I get some water," the guide said.

He took the bucket from the planed wood table and went out. When he returned he tried to force some of the quinine down George's throat, but the sick man choked.

"A doctor—he's got to have a doctor," Darcy insisted.

"You stay," said the man. "I know of one who is true. I will go and see."

Darcy nodded and turned back to the bed. He began applying cloths wrung out in the cool spring water to George's head as he remembered seeing his mother do for fever victims. If only he hadn't been so engrossed in his own pleasure on the river, he upbraided himself. He would have seen George was sick. George who had always cared for him and loved him. . . unquestioningly. He sighed and glanced down at the ghostly face. When had George last eaten, he wondered? He couldn't remember having seen him eat at all on the trip up the Chagres. He got up and looked in the small cupboard for some food, but there was nothing there except a little flour, some sugar, and some coffee. Maybe some hot coffee with sugar in it might revive them both.

For the first time in his life he realized how helpless he was. He didn't have the least idea how to make coffee. He cast back in his memory to the big plantation kitchen where, as a child, he had liked to watch great big Aunt Sukie prepare the food. First he knew he had to grind the beans. He found the coffee mill, and as he ground the beans, he tried to remember what Aunt Sukie had said as she spooned the coffee into the big pot. She always finished with a little rhyme: "One for you, and one for me, and one to make the pot happy." Darcy started to spoon the coffee into the pot, but stopped himself. No, he thought, this isn't right. Then he remembered. Steam was rising from the pot when Aunt Sukie added the coffee. He must boil the water first.

Soon he had readied a cup of hot coffee sweetened with sugar. With an arm under the old man's shoulders, he lifted him up. George opened his eyes—and this time they weren't staring vacantly. "Here, Uncle George, drink this," he urged. "It'll make you feel better."

George swallowed. Darcy fast followed with a dose of the quinine. But George was disconsolate.

"I's failed mah trust," he said dejectedly. "Miss Elizabeth nevuh forgive me." He drifted off into a troubled sleep.

Self-reproach raged through Darcy. He should never have brought George to this pestilential land so far from home. He kept on applying the cold cloths to George's head, as if this alone would cure him. At last he turned to see the guide and a doctor entering the small hut.

The doctor examined George, then shook his head. "He's too old and frail to withstand the force of the fever," he said. "I don't know how he's managed to live this long." He opened his bag and took out some quinine and another drug. "I'll leave you these, but I'm afraid they won't do much good."

"You can't let him die!" cried Darcy.

"I'm sorry, my boy," said the doctor. "We know so very little. Some day—maybe yes—but now?" He shook his head and shrugged. "I am as helpless as you." He turned to go. "There are hundreds of sick men in the city, and I can do almost nothing." At the door he patted the guide on the shoulder. "Good night, Miguel. I am sorry."

"Good night, señor," Miguel replied.

Until early morning Miguel and Darcy worked with the quinine and cold cloths to break the fever, but to no avail. About three, rallying some, George turned his deep, tragic eyes on Darcy.

"I sorry, Mistuh Darcy, I can't go on with you," he said. He sighed deeply and quietly died.

Darcy turned away from the bed, tears streaming down his face. Finally he straightened his shoulders and said, "The world seems so much smaller."

"And so it grows with each passing of those we love," said Miguel.

At first light, Darcy and his stranger friend, a brown man of only two days' acquaintance, dug a grave in a nearby grove of trees and laid George's body to rest. It was the first hard manual labor Darcy had ever performed, and he had performed it for his slave. He took out his knife and carved on the crude wooden cross: George—faithful friend—June 19, 1849. As they were settling the marker in the loose earth, a horseman came flying up the trail. Darcy could not mistake the small figure in the sadly soiled beaver hat. Five days ago he had wanted to kill Rip. Now the sight of the little gambler didn't even stir him.

Rip fell off his horse and rushed toward Darcy, clutching a bouquet of flowers in one hand and a small wrapped box in the other. "I come to see George," he screamed in his high-pitched voice. "I brung him some medicine." He held out the box. "And these." He proffered the flowers.

"You're too late, Rip," said Darcy. "We just buried him."

"What?" screeched the little man. "I come as soon as I heard. Doctor was attendin' somebody in my hotel—told about George—said he was out here last night. Where is he?"

Darcy pointed to the grave. Rip stared at the cross and began to cry. "He was the only one who cared about me. I coulda died on that boat and nobody to know. He used to say, 'Mistuh Rip, you gonna be fine, you'll see.' He fed me, kept me fresh, and never complained about the mess I made. He was the only friend I had. . .the only one who didn't laugh. You laughed—I knew." Laying his flowers by the cross, he stood up, wiped his spotted sleeve across his nose and eyes, and faced Darcy. "All right, here I am, Darcy Dupres. I've stolen your money and I lost it all. You can kill me now. That's what you aim to do, ain't it?"

Darcy wearily shook his head. "I don't want to kill you, Rip. All I want is to get out of here and on to California."

"You are welcome to stay in my house until your ship comes," said Miguel. "You have a fine view of the harbor from up here."

No longer fearing his immediate demise, Rip began to recover some of his usual ebullience. "They're expectin' the steamer any day now," he volunteered. "Sure you ain't mad at me, Darcy?" he asked, still unbelieving.

"No, I'm not mad."

"Do you think you might consider takin' me on as a partner again? You see, I not only lost the money, but I wagered my passage. . .and I lost that, too. You never seen anything like the stakes they play for here. They just swallowed me up."

Darcy was so astounded at Rip's audacity that he scarcely knew how to reply. "Mr. Packet," he finally managed to say, "if I bear you no malice, I bear you no friendship, either. And it would make me very happy if you would just bow out of my life permanently. I want no relationship or association with you whatsoever."

"Can't say as I blame you," said Rip, turning to go. "Still, I can be useful in my way. I just might be able to get us a place on that next steamer. There's over a thousand men in Panama City tryin' to get passage."

"You haven't even got a ticket. What do you want to do now? Gamble away mine?"

"No, I don't—I got other ways. But if you ain't interested, I'll just go my way and you can go yours." He began grappling with his nag.

Looking beseechingly at the sky, Darcy inquired, "Why, oh why? All right, Rip. I'll stake you one more time. But you'd better be sure that we have berths on that steamer."

Rip danced up and down chanting, "We will! You'll see. We will!"

That afternoon they went to Panama City to find out when the next steamer was expected. But once they reached the narrow warren of streets, Rip said he had some unfinished business to attend to and would meet Darcy at the steamship office later. Alone, Darcy continued to the waterfront, where he entered a flimsy building bearing the sign PANAMA STEAMSHIP COMPANY. Inside he found a sweating clerk trying to calm the horde of men clamoring for attention and waving tickets marked first class. Among them Darcy recognized many of the passengers on the *Bluebird*. One of them broke the news that the company had oversold the passage, and that many of them might be stranded on the isthmus for weeks.

"The *American*'s overdue and expected any day," the young man said. "The clerk's been trying to get some of the men to transfer to sailing ships."

"But that would take weeks longer," protested Darcy.

"I know," said the youth.

When Darcy reached the desk he waved his guaranteed passage under the harried clerk's nose. "What are you going to do when the steamer arrives?" he asked.

"I don't know! I don't know! I don't know!" the clerk kept shouting.

Darcy was forced to give up his place at the counter to the man behind him, who was likewise clutching a first-class ticket with guaranteed passage.

Rip had not returned, and Darcy wandered through the alley-ways in search of him. Then he started checking the gambling dens and finally found a man who knew where Rip had been staying. In the dark, windowless hovel he saw Rip sitting on a bunk opposite a bunk where another man was lying.

"He's dead," Rip said.

"I'm sorry," said Darcy conventionally. "Was he a friend of yours?"

"Didn't know him at all," was Rip's startling reply. "But he's got a ticket to San Francisco."

"What?"

"Ain't no use to him now."

"Then why didn't you take it?"

"Scared. Wouldn't want to get cursed." He surveyed the dead man once more. "Do you think he'd mind?"

"I don't think he would if you buried him."

"That's a fine idea. I'll bury him out there in that grove next to George."

The next morning Darcy awakened early and rushed out to look down at the harbor. The *American* was sailing in. The steamer looked terribly small and slow, but he thought it must be the distance that made it appear this way and called Rip to come and see.

"It's beautiful!" screeched Rip as he danced up and down and threw his beloved hat high in the air.

Without breakfast they hastened into town and down to the docks. Still some distance from the shipping firm's offices, they were halted by the press of the crowd. Ahead they could see a man standing on a rickety platform made of boxes screaming the company's proposals at the stranded men; it was impossible to hear what he was saying over the din. Pressing, wriggling, and shoving, Rip with Darcy in tow oozed toward the platform, where they heard the man say, "All of you with first-class tickets are to write your names on these slips of paper and drop them in this hat. The company will accommodate all first-class passengers. The type of accommodation each of you will receive will be determined by drawing your names out of the hat. Some of you will have to ride on the decks, and some of you will have to ride in the hold. If there is any space left after we have taken care of those holding first-class tickets, we will portion it out by lot to the second-class and finally to the steerage ticket holders." The man held up his hand for silence but didn't get it. "In the meantime," he shouted, "for those of you who do not wish to wait for future steamers, we have been able to secure passage on two packets now in the harbor."

Most of the men with the cheaper tickets turned away in disappointment.

Darcy and Rip dropped their names in the hat. They learned that the *American* would not be sailing until the next day because of a maintenance problem. Wondering what that meant, they started toward the water to get a better look at the ship. On the way Darcy collided with a man rapidly walking toward town.

"Would you mind directing me to the nearest place where I can get transport across the isthmus?" he asked. He was carrying a leather satchel and was dressed in worn miner's boots, dungarees, a plaid flannel shirt, and a flat black hat.

"Did you just come in on the *American*?" Darcy inquired.

"That I did," the man replied, jettisoning a brown stream of tobacco juice neatly through his teeth and halfway across the street.

"We're supposed to leave on her tomorrow," volunteered Rip.

"Well, the best of luck to ye both—damned stinking tub," responded the man cheerfully.

"We're on our way to the diggings," Darcy said, "If we walk along with you to get your transport, would you tell us about it?"

"It figures," said the man looking at their eager faces. "Green as grass now. You'll learn out there in a hell of a hurry."

"Can you pick it up right off the ground like they say?" asked Rip.

"Not exactly," chuckled the ex-miner. "You gotta dig it and you gotta wash it and if you're lucky, you may get sixteen to twenty dollars a day, which will be just about enough to pay for the grub to keep you alive. But don't believe me." He started to laugh as he looked at the two shocked faces. "Go see the elephant for yourselves. That's what I did." By this time they had reached one of the larger stables, and with a cheerful, "Thankee," the man entered the dark interior.

"He must have been exaggerating," Darcy said.

"Sure," said Rip. "After all, he got his, didn't he?'

Darcy and Rip were at the Panama Steamship Company offices at dawn the next morning to watch the hat lottery. After Rip's name was drawn for the last berth in the second-class accommodations, Darcy's spirits drooped. But within half an hour, as the drawing continued, he deemed himself the luckiest of men. His name had been drawn for a hammock slung in the aft rigging. He was to be spared the foul steerage quarters.

Elated, he hoisted his trunk to his shoulder and, with Rip still carrying his worn carpetbag, made his way down to the small boats that would row them out to the *American*. Although in his soiled clothes he little resembled the Creole dandy who had set out from New Orleans only three weeks ago, he still believed he was a superior being entitled to special treatment. The death of George had only partially chipped away the veneer of his belief in his infallibility.

CHAPTER 15 REGROUPING AT FORT BRIDGER★★★★★★★★

In midafternoon of the third day out from Fort Laramie, the wagon train came to Bridger's Crossing. Zack explained that they must ford the North Platte here because from this point on the north bank would be easier going. Propping up the wagon beds twelve inches, they began crossing one by one, with the Cunninghams as usual following Goldie and Gray.

In midstream, midst the shouting and bellowing that always accompanied a crossing, Gray thought he heard a scream. Quickly he looked behind and saw the back end on the right side of the Cunningham wagon tilting into the water.

"Must be a broken wheel," he told Goldie. "I'm going back to help." The other wagons were already going around as he rode up. Zack was lifting Dora Cunningham out onto his horse. Gray could see that her dress was soaked with blood.

At sight of his mother's blood, Adam sighed and fainted. He would have tumbled into the water if Gray hadn't caught him. The Milford wagon pulled alongside. "Can we help?" asked Dan.

"Get the rest of them out of that wagon! We'll fix it later," shouted Zack as he wheeled his horse and plunged for shore. Gray followed with Adam, who had revived.

"Here, bring her here," cried Rebecca Lord when Zack reached the bank.

Goldie finished the crossing and wheeled the wagon into its place in the circle. She jumped down and ran over to the Lord wagon. "She was carrying a baby," she gasped.

"Oh, dear," said Rebecca. "She must be having a miscarriage. But I've never done any midwifing."

Just then the Milford wagon bearing Tim and the other two children rolled up. White and shaking, Tim said, "She should've told me. I never knew."

Mrs. Milford climbed down. "Here, let me see if I can help. I saw it happen once." She got into the Lord wagon and began ministering to Dora.

A few minutes later she emerged. "Bleeding's not so bad now," she said. "But she really needs a doctor."

"We're no more than sixty miles from the fort," said Wash. "Maybe somebody should ride for the doctor there."

"I'll go," volunteered Gray. Zack nodded and Gray took some pemmican and rode off.

Since the company was composed primarily of young men without wives or family responsibilities, they had little to do after they had dragged the Cunningham wagon from the stream and repaired its broken wheel. As the hours ticked by, they began gathering in restless little groups, chafing at the delay.

Goldie heard there would be a general meeting after supper but paid little heed until Isaiah said, "Let 'em go. We don't need 'em. Ma used to say you might as well not have friends as fair-weather ones."

"You mustn't say that, Isaiah. They wouldn't dream of deserting you," said Goldie, giving him a hug. But privately she began to wonder.

A few miles from camp Gray ran into a band of Indians headed upstream. Engrossed in his mission, he would have passed by without stopping if he had not come face to face with Running Wind.

"Ah, you must be the brother of Miss Baxter," said Running Wind, pulling his horse up short.

"Yes," said Gray. "How did you know?"

"Her cats," smiled Running Wind, "way back there."

"Oh, so you're the one," said Gray.

"Yes. But you are going the way you came. Is there trouble?"

"One of our ladies has lost a baby. I'm going for the doctor at the fort."

"Perhaps help is nearer than that," said Running Wind as he called a middle-aged woman over and spoke to her in Cheyenne. She nodded her head and called to two other squaws. She gathered a few articles, and all three mounted horses.

When they arrived at the camp Gray identified himself to the guard and led the three squaws over to the Lord wagon. One of the women put a pottery vessel with some water and a sprinkling of herbs on the fire while the other two climbed into the wagon to minister to Dora. As soon as the herb mixture was steaming, the squaw who was tending it passed it in to the others who, by this time, had packed Dora and elevated her feet.

After Dora was resting quietly, the old squaw reported in halting English, "She have lost much blood, but will be better now. She need rest and this." She pointed to the herbal tea. "Also give buffalo for strength."

"Can she travel?" asked a man from the group who had gathered around.

"She lie flat." The Indian demonstrated. "And soft." She plumped her hands up and down. "It all right."

"Would you come with us a ways?" pleaded Tim.

"You husband?" asked the squaw, whose name was Mother of Eagles. Tim nodded. "I go with two, three days." Then she noticed Goldie standing with the three children. "These hers?" she asked, pointing toward the wagon.

"Yes," said Goldie.

"Mother be all right," she said to the frightened children.

As everyone began drifting away, Goldie realized the group had not been tested as to whether they would abandon a stricken member.

During the next few days Mother of Eagles demonstrated great skill not only in ministering to Dora but also in caring for Tim and the children. She spoke little English, but Goldie was so fascinated by her many capabilities that she tried hard to communicate with her. Mainly by means of sign language, she found out that the squaw's tribe lived southwest of the mountains—but Goldie couldn't tell what mountains. And she could find out nothing about Running Wind.

Equally impressed with the skills of Mother of Eagles, Zack said, "The tribe must have been influenced by a white man. . .a very unusual white man."

"They looked prosperous," said Gray. "They were driving good wagons."

"That proves they've been influenced by a white man," said Zack. "Indians hereabouts drag their goods on litters."

Questioning Mother of Eagles in Cheyenne, he found out someone by the name of Marshall had lived with the tribe. He could get no further information though, and concluded, "It must have been a long time ago. I've never heard of him."

Six days after she had joined the train, the old squaw said to Dora, "You be all right now. I go."

"Couldn't you stay a little longer?" pleaded Tim as the children noisily clamored about her.

"Must go to my people," she said gently. Nodding off Tim's thanks, she mounted her horse and rode away.

On the Mormon Ferry the train crossed the Platte for the last time. Now headed up the Sweetwater toward the mountains, the pioneers began talking eagerly about climbing Independence Rock to add their names to the growing roster on its top. Zack was more concerned about finding meat. He had scouting parties out from early in the morning until sunset. They ranged far from the train, but the men could find no buffalo. Then on the afternoon of July first the company reached the historic trail marker. Zack recalled how he had climbed the huge whale-shaped monolith nearly ten years ago to add his name to those of the trappers and mountain men already there. Now it was the autograph book of the Oregon Trail. Suddenly it became very important to Zack to have Goldie sign her name by his, and as soon as camp was made he hurried over to ask her to climb the rock after supper.

"Can Gray come too?" she asked.

Though Zack had hoped to have her to himself, he said, "Of course Gray can come. The more the merrier."

They scrambled up the huge granite boulder, and Zack showed Goldie and Gray the spot near the center where he had carved his name.

"Would you mind if we cut our names by yours?" asked Gray.

"I'd be pleased," said Zack.

Goldie and Gray began scraping at the granite. Nearby, other members of the train also were scratching their names to preserve for posterity, and Zack wryly reflected that it would not have been an auspicious place for a romantic rendezvous after all.

When Goldie finished she walked over to where Zack was looking down at the wagons far below. "They look so tiny," she gasped. "Like toys."

"Yes," said Zack. "We've climbed high. Look over there." A vast mountain range rose in the distance.

"Do we have to cross those?" asked Gray.

"Those are the Wind River Mountains," said Zack. "South Pass lies at the foot of them."

The sun was sinking. They watched as the hot reds shaded into deep purples, and the shadows of the distant peaks became indistinct. They sat still on the rock to await the rising of the moon.

"Are you going to guide more trains to California after this one?" asked Gray.

"No," said Zack. "My wandering days are over. I'm going to settle down on my ranch." His voice deepened with feeling as he described his land. "It lies in the foothills of the Sierra Nevadas. I'll show it to you when we get there. You've never seen anything like it—rolling hills, timber, plenty of water and grass. . .it's beautiful!"

"Won't it be kind of lonely way off from everyone?" asked Goldie.

"Why, he won't be lonely," said Gray. "He'll have men working for him, and there'll be other ranchers around—just like back home. And someday he'll probably have a wife and kids. I think ranching would be great."

"I've always thought I'd like to live in a city where you can have lots of friends," said Goldie. "Oh look," she sprang up.

"Look at the silver on the river, and see how the moon is lighting up the canvas on the wagons." She stood transfixed a moment, drinking in the strange beauty of the vast land broken only by the small human imprint of the twenty-nine wagons circled below them. "It doesn't look real, does it?"

Disappointed in her lack of enthusiasm for his ranch, Zack abruptly said, "We'd better go. It's getting late."

It was still dark when Gray went on watch the next morning, and when the sun rose he could hardly believe his eyes. Within a mile of the camp a herd of buffalo was grazing.

"Buffalo! Buffalo! Buffalo yonder!" he shrieked, dashing around the wagons brandishing his gun aloft. Half-clothed, the sleepy-eyed men came tumbling out of the wagons with guns in hand. Zack quickly gathered them together.

"All right, all right, calm down," he said. "Let's try to do this so's we don't cause a stampede. Now everybody mount up. We'll get upwind of them so they don't get our scent and then move in quietly."

By noon the first wagonloads of meat were brought in to be prepared, and by four o'clock most of the edible parts of the twenty-four buffalo killed had been stowed away for future consumption. But some of the fresh meat was set aside for the Fourth of July, a day the pioneers considered equally as important as Christmas, and now only two days off.

They forded the Sweetwater River at the Three Stations Crossing on the afternoon of Independence Day, then began preparing their communal feast. On a long table, made from boxes and barrels covered with tarpaulins and ranging down the middle of the circled wagons, miraculous things began to appear. There were precious jars of jellies and preserves and homemade pickles; there were loaves of thick-sliced bread, made on the day of the buffalo hunt; and by the time the meat was ready, there were also mammoth stacks of biscuits and hot plates of cornbread. At the last moment the women placed the dried fruit and molasses pies down the center of the table to cool. Then with the fires leaping toward the stars and the lanterns reflecting the stars in their eyes, the argonauts sat down, nearly a hundred strong, to honor their country.

One of the Lord children complained of not feeling well the next morning, but Rebecca attributed the upset to too much

167

feasting the night before and dosed the lad with molasses and vinegar. As the day drew to its close, however, the boy was coughing and became hot and feverish, and his mother feared some new malady was striking the train. That night the fever mounted, but there still was no indication of what ailed him. Zack admitted he was as puzzled as Rebecca and Wash were. By the next morning the boy had broken out in bright red spots all over his body.

"Measles," sighed Rebecca in relief. "Oh, dear, I suppose that means all the rest of the children will get them, too."

Besides the four Lord children and the three Cunninghams, there were five other children under the age of twelve traveling with the company. "Would you like to stop?" Zack asked Wash.

"No, we could be here for weeks while it works its way through the children. It's only a simple childhood ailment."

"Sometimes measles can be dangerous," said Zack. Although he thought it would do little good now, he ordered all the parents to keep their children isolated. Four days later when they were climbing through the long, green valley of South Pass, three more children became ill.

But that afternoon when they reached the Continental Divide at the summit of South Pass, where they could clearly see the rivers falling away to the west, the argonauts forgot their latest trial. Several of them fired their guns, and they all shouted their joy over having surmounted the Rocky Mountains.

For several days they wound down the western side of the Rockies, first following Pacific Creek to the Little Sandy Crossing, then following the Big Sandy to Green River. There the pioneers found a commodious ferry, capable of carrying six wagons and their teams across at one time, operated by an enterprising mountain man and his crew.

"These folks are kinda poor, Ben," said Zack.

"My goin' price is a dollar a wagon," said the mountaineer. "But seein' as how you're a friend, Zack, me and my boys'll take your group across at half price." The two shook hands, and soon all of the wagons had been ferried across.

"I feel kinda queasy," said Gray the next morning. "Would you mind driving a while?"

Goldie felt his forehead and said, "You've got a fever. You'd better lie down in back."

"Oh, I'll be all right," said Gray.

"There's no sense in your sitting here when you feel miserable. Now go on and get in the back." Gray made no further protest but did as he was told.

Zack tied his horse to the tail gate later and climbed in to see if he could do anything.

He felt Gray's head and said, "I think you're getting the measles."

"I'm too old for that," protested Gray.

"Nobody's too old," said Zack. "Now you've got to stay quiet."

During the night the fever mounted and Gray became delirious. Instead of breaking out in spots as the children had done, he kept the disease internally, and by morning Zack, who had seen scores of Indians die because the fever would not break, had become highly alarmed. Dora Cunningham was unable to help Goldie because all three of her children now had the measles. But Dan Milford came over and began helping Goldie hitch up the mules. Gray lay in the back wildly tossing, his cheeks flushed and his eyes burning. Intermittently he raved about imaginary sights or lapsed into a coma.

"Stay with him," said Dan. "I'll drive the wagon."

The party had to make the two crossings at Ham's Fork and Big Muddy Creek that day. After the wagons were over Big Muddy, Zack dropped back to check on Gray.

"How soon will we get to Fort Bridger?" asked Goldie.

"We should be there in two or three days at the most," replied Zack.

"I sure hope there's a doctor there."

"So do I. Gray can't stand much more of this. Pile some more blankets on him. Maybe we can sweat it out of him."

Though she did as she was bid, it was to no avail, and all the next day the fever remained high. That evening everyone passed the wagon quietly, and it suddenly occurred to the distraught girl that they all thought Gray was going to die.

She flung herself on her knees beside her spent brother and sobbed, "Oh God, please don't let him die. . .oh, please!" Just then she felt a comforting arm around her shoulders, and through her tears she saw Dan sitting beside her.

"Come on, Goldie," said Dan, awkwardly patting her. "He isn't gonna die. He's too tough. He hasn't come all this way just to die now. And I'll tell you something else. My mother used to say, 'It takes three days to break a fever.' It's going to break tonight. I just know it is. You get some sleep. I'll sit by him and call you if anything happens."

Awakening before dawn, Goldie dimly made out a figure sitting with bowed head beside Gray.

"He's dead," she said fearfully, making her way toward Gray's pallet.

"No," said Zack. "The spots have come out, but there's still something wrong. His breathing's hard. He may have lung fever."

"What do we do about that?"

"I don't know. Just keep him warm and pray for a doctor at Fort Bridger. We should get there this evening."

"Where's Dan?"

"I sent him to bed. He was dog-tired."

"What about you?"

"Never was much of a sleeper."

"Zack, whatever happens, I'm so grateful to you."

"Don't you worry," said the weary scout, "We'll get him well again." He glanced out the back of the wagon. "It's dawn—time to hitch up. I'll stop by later." He squeezed her hand and climbed down to the ground.

Steadily winding its way along Black's Creek toward Fort Bridger, the wagon train arrived just before sunset. Since it was a private fort operated by the famous trapper Jim Bridger, there were no soldiers around the stockade. Much smaller than either Fort Kearney or Fort Laramie, it was constructed in a square shape entirely of split logs. Though primitive, to Goldie it was a beautiful sight jutting above the barren treeless ground.

The fever had taken its toll of Gray. He was so thin that Goldie noted his wrist and forearm were smaller than hers. Protesting these signs of deterioration, she whispered fiercely, "I'll not let him die!" Then wondering if she was blaspheming and if God might punish her, she pleaded, "Please. . .oh, please." Happy, who had scarcely left his post at Gray's feet since his master had been stricken, sought reassurance by putting his nose in her hand.

As soon as the wagons had formed their circle, Zack rode swiftly into Bridger's Trading Post. At the store he asked about a doctor.

"No, there ain't no doctor here," said one of the men. "What's the trouble?"

"I think I got a man on my train with lung fever," said Zack.

"Well, now, just a minute," said a grizzly-haired old veteran with a peg leg. "I believe one of Marshall's Indians is camped outside."

"Would he know what to do?" asked Zack.

"Dunno," said the trapper. "But Marshall sure would. I'll take ye to him if ye like."

"Thanks," said Zack, following the old fellow out.

"The name's Beaver-Tail Jones," volunteered his guide, stumping out of the fort. "Marshall's a doctor, though he don't like to be called that. But if it weren't for him, I wouldn't be here aside you right now. You see, several years ago I was caught in a blizzard in the mountains north o' here. I was tryin' to make it back to my camp when I fell off a ledge. I hurt my leg bad but had to keep on or freeze. Well, I made it to my camp, but then I got a fever, and I don't know how long it was afore Marshall and his Indians found me. He said I had gangrene and he'd have to take off my leg. I told him to chop away. Well, he did. . .and here I am."

"But who is he?" asked Zack. "I've never heard of him before this trip, and now I seem to run into everyone who knows him."

"Ain't surprisin', he and his band of Cheyennes kept mostly to themselves until the last coupla years. Like I said, he's a genuine doctor, but he went with the Indians a long time ago. Nobody calls him anything but Marshall. Well, anyway, I owe him my life and mebbe he can help that young fella you have. Here we are." Beaver-Tail stepped up to an Indian campfire and raised his hand in greeting.

After introducing Zack to Falling Water, the old trapper returned to the fort. Zack explained to the Indian as much as he could about Gray's illness and asked him if he thought Marshall might come and help him.

"Marshall is always ready to help people in trouble," said Falling Water. "But he is a day's ride away in the mountains. Two days before we come back."

"Could we take our man up to him?" asked Zack.

"Too rough for a wagon," said Falling Water. "It would take longer."

171

"Will you go for Marshall, then? I will pay you well."

"I will go, but I do not do it for money. That is not the way we believe. I will leave now."

"One of your people has already helped a woman in our group. Tell your chief and Marshall we are most grateful."

"We know Zachariah Peale to be a man of honor."

"Thank you. . .Godspeed."

By the time Zack returned to camp everyone had eaten supper, but Goldie had kept some stew and cornbread hot for him. Zack told her what he had learned about Marshall.

While he was eating, Wash came by and asked him to come to his wagon as soon as he was finished. When Zack arrived he was not surprised to find a large and vocal group of men gathered there.

"How long are we gonna be stuck here?" asked one.

"The doctor probably won't arrive until the day after tomorrow," said Zack.

"It's past the middle of July," said another man. "There's already too many ahead of us on the trail."

"Yeah, if we don't get a move on the waterin' holes is liable to be dried up," argued a third.

"All right, you've made your point!" said Zack angrily.

"Would you step over here a minute, Zack?" asked Wash. As the two withdrew, he continued, "We all know how you feel about Gray, but you've done all you can. Now it's up to the doctor and Providence."

"Hang Providence!" shouted Zack. "If Gray dies, Goldie will be all alone!"

"There'll be other trains along," said Wash. "Your responsibility is to us."

"You could at least wait till the doctor gets here."

"I'm sorry, Zack, but the men have asked me to put it to a vote. I'm calling a general meeting."

The word was quickly passed along the train. The test Goldie had wondered about when Dora became ill was being made. During the meeting Isaiah, still broken out in spots, came by.

"I'm sorry we made Gray sick," he said.

"It's not your fault, Isaiah."

"Oh, yes it is," said the boy gravely. "If we hadn't got the measles, Gray would be well now. I wanted to go and tell them that, but Ma said it wouldn't do any good. She told Pa though, that for once she wished he'd speak his mind."

Goldie was brought back to the reality of the situation with a jolt. Of course, you ninny, she thought to herself. Why else would they have a meeting but to discuss moving on. Suddenly she knew very clearly that the others would abandon them. At first she was both angry and afraid, but then she only felt despair, and finally all feeling left her.

When the meeting broke up, Dan and Mary Milford came by. "We just wanted to tell you how we feel," said Mary. "We voted against it and aim to stay, too. Pa says he's got no use for the others."

"Oh, no," said Goldie, "you must go on. There's no reason for you to stop because of us."

"We'd rather take our chances with decent folks," said Dan. "They'll all break up anyway when they get close to California and think they won't need help anymore."

"Zack won't let that happen," said Goldie.

"I don't know. . .Zack got pretty mad at the meeting," said Mary. "Called them deserters."

The Milfords had gone when Zack came by and sat down near the fire. For a long time he stared pensively into it. Then he spoke quietly. "I never thought I'd be trapped by my own rules."

"I know you did all you could," said Goldie. She got up to tend Gray. As she passed Zack, impulsively she reached down and touched his shoulder. His hand reached up and covered hers for an instant, then she passed on into the wagon.

While she was sitting beside Gray wiping the perspiration from his face with a cool cloth, he had one of his rare lucid moments.

"Goldie," he said heavily, "where are we?"

"We're at Fort Bridger, and we've sent for a doctor who's going to make you well."

"It's hard to breathe."

"Zack says you have lung fever."

"You all right?" he asked, touching his sister's hand weakly.

"I'm fine. . .everybody's fine. Now you just rest."

"Yes, I am tired. Gotta get well to do my share," he sighed, and drifted off again.

Zack climbed in the wagon. "You get some sleep," he said. "I'll watch him."

A few hours later she awakened abruptly and called, "Zack."

Zack glanced out the back of the wagon. "It's almost daylight," he said. "As long as you're up, I'll go check the camp."

"It'll soon be time to hitch up. Zack. . ." Would he stay if she asked him? She wavered a moment, then fought down her panic. "There's one more thing," she gulped. "Make the Milfords go. I don't want anybody else to suffer because of us."

"All right, I'll take them."

He climbed out of the wagon, and Goldie waited until he was safely out of earshot before breaking down into sobs. After a moment she heard someone rustling at the tail gate.

"It's me, honey," came the sprightly voice of Dora Cunningham. "There now, don't you cry." She put her arms around the girl. Goldie put her head down on Dora's shoulder and wept uncontrollably. "You ain't goin' to be alone. Me and Tim and the children are stayin'."

"Oh no, Dora, you can't. You must go. You haven't got any money."

"After what we've been through, I think we'll make out all right," said Dora. "Now don't you fret none. We all need the rest. Why, our animals are just plain tuckered, and the children ain't got over the measles yet."

"Oh, Dora," said Goldie, throwing her arms around the gaunt woman. "I hope Tim is the one who finds the pot of gold if there is one."

"Don't much matter," said Dora. "Just feels good to be alive."

Before dawn Zack returned once more. "I've drawn a map of the route for you to follow when Gray gets well," he said. "Keep it safe, and don't lose it. And here's fifty dollars in gold. You may need it for more supplies."

"Oh, I couldn't take your money."

"Well, call it a loan. You can pay me back later."

"But how will I find you?" asked Goldie, a lump rising in her throat as she began to feel the impact of the parting.

"I'll find you," said Zack. "I promise you that."

Then he lifted her out of the wagon and walked her a short distance away. He kissed her as he had done that other evening on the Kansas plains when she felt so young. Was it only two months ago, she wondered? She had thought he was just teaching her a lesson then. But this kiss, and the question in his eyes stirred a

174

response deep inside her she had never felt before. She trembled. Zack held her for a moment, with renewed hope that perhaps something lasting was emerging between them.

"Goodbye, Goldie," he said and was quickly enveloped in the dark.

Goldie stood looking after him with an overwhelming feeling that she had been abandoned. How could she take care of Gray, she asked herself? How could they possibly get through alone? "Wait!" she wanted to cry out. "Wait, don't leave us!" But the words died on her lips. Suddenly she remembered, tomorrow—no, now it was today—was her birthday. She was sixteen. A wave of homesickness for Aunt Opal and Uncle Bob and the cake and presents that always marked a birthday at the inn swept over her. She tried resolutely to shake it off. "You're here!" she said fiercely to herself. "You've got to face things here!"

As the wagons broke camp and pulled out, she peeped out of the canvas one more time. Seeing the tall figure in white buckskins riding at the head of the column almost broke her resolve, for she wondered desperately if she would ever see him again.

Gray stirred fitfully. "Got to hitch up," he said. "Didn't you hear the call? Why aren't we moving?"

"We have to wait," said Goldie. "We have to follow later."

"Oh," said Gray, satisfied, as he drifted off again.

As the Milford wagon passed in the long line, Dan leaped off and came over. "I want you to know we would've stayed," he said. "But Zack said it'd only complicate things for you."

"Goodbye, Dan," said Goldie. "I hope we meet again."

"Me too," said the tall, rangy lad. He reached up and kissed her. Then in embarrassment he turned and ran after the retreating wagons.

On the day after rounding Cape Horn the *Sea Skimmer* crossed fifty degrees south latitude and almost immediately the temperature rose twenty degrees. With the favorable winds and currents the ship was making her northing in record time. She was flying all her sails except for those of the missing top of the mainmast, and Holt found it awesome as well as beautiful to look aloft and see the acres of white canvas filled with wind. He went below to fetch Mirina to see it too.

When he got to the cabin he could hear Mirina inside laughing with a man. Flinging open the door, he saw her standing with her back to Albert Duane, one of the other cabin passengers. Her right hand was raised to her hair in a coquettish gesture.

"Get out!" he shouted furiously at Duane, clenching his fists.

"I just came to fetch my shawl," protested Mirina.

Duane smiled in a chummy manner, "Honestly, old man, there's nothing wrong," he said.

"Get out!" shouted Holt again.

Duane quickly eased himself into the corridor.

Holt slammed the door before Mirina could follow. "Just a minute, Mrs. Compton," he said, fighting for control. He had no memory of ever being as angry as this.

"You were unforgivably rude," said Mirina. "I don't wish to discuss anything with you until your manners have returned."

"Oh, no, my lady," said Holt. "There are a few things we're going to get straight. You're never going to have a man—any man—in this cabin again!"

"You're my husband, not my master," screeched Mirina. "Nobody, not you or anybody else, is going to tell me what to do."

Holt could contain his fury no longer. He grabbed her hard by the arms and shook her. "Yes, I am your husband," he said. "And I'm beginning to think that I'm just the ticket you needed to get out of Rio, like everybody's been saying!"

"You're hurting me," whined Mirina.

"You'll obey me in this, or I promise you you'll regret it," he said, throwing her roughly aside.

"Now may I go?" she asked coldly. With what dignity she could muster, she swept out. She had not apologized, and she had not denied his accusation.

As the *Sea Skimmer* raced for Valparaiso, Kevin observed the breach widening between them. Holt still worked the ship, but without enthusiasm. When he wasn't working he was either down in the cabin or tucked away in some wind-free corner alone and brooding. And Kevin looked on helplessly, unable to speak lest he betray his own involvement with Mirina. So he watched and waited in silence, hating his longing for her.

Gradually Mirina came to the unpleasant conclusion that she was pregnant. Because she wanted to, she believed the child was Kevin's. Still, she was married to Holt and now for some months would need the care and protection of a husband. With this in mind she decided to make up the quarrel with him.

In their cabin that evening she played the injured wife, pouting and sighing. Then she told him she had forgiven him. But Holt was not as easy to woo back as she had thought he would be, and once more she found herself acknowledging that she had married a stranger with depths she could not fathom. As a last resort she deliberately set out to seduce him. Finally Holt became so aroused he clawed at her clothes and tore them from her body; and as his passion blotted out the inhibitions of his mind, she found how strong and lusty a man she had married. His desire made him rough and greedy, and Mirina found herself responding to him with a great passion of her own.

The next morning Holt appeared on deck for his watch whistling cheerfully. Spotting Kevin, he clapped him heartily on the back and asked, "Where've you been keeping yourself?" Kevin heaved a sigh of relief that the crisis was over, at least for the present.

Captain Hewitt announced they would reach Valparaiso the next day, and he would need four days in port to repair the ship and trade some of the cargo. At this news the men cheered, for they longed for the feel of land under their feet once more.

Holt asked Kevin, "What are you going to do in Valparaiso?"

"Big Blue's going to show me a cockfight," said Kevin.

"Could I go with you?"

"What about Mirina?"

"I'm taking her in the first day, but I'd like to spend the next with you."

177

"Sure, come along," said Kevin.

Valparaiso was dramatically situated on the base of a spur of the Andes, jutting out into the ocean. On the cliffs high above the business section of the town, composed of white-walled buildings with red tile roofs, were the beautiful and spacious residences of the well-to-do citizenry; and to the south were the three infamous conical hills nicknamed The Foremast, The Mainmast, and The Mizzenmast, where the sailors' boarding houses, the brothels, the bars, and the gambling dens were located

The *Sea Skimmer* anchored among ten other American vessels, and Kevin's watch was given immediate shore leave. Donning a clean shirt, he joined the mad scramble to be among the first to set foot on land.

Holt had gone to Captain Hewitt's quarters. "I'd like you to dine with Mirina and me tonight, sir, if you're free," he said.

"Sorry, my boy, but I can't," said the captain. "I'm meeting a business acquaintance. But the Cruz del Sur has very good food, and I think you and Mirina would enjoy it."

"What are you trading here?" asked Holt.

"That farm equipment I have in the hold. . .going to fill the space with grain. Flour's at a premium in California—should bring a handsome profit."

Holt located the Cruz del Sur shortly after they arrived in the city. But Mirina protested, "I don't want to eat in that stuffy old place. Let's go where they have music and dance the fandango."

They peered into many eating places, but none of them measured up to Mirina's expectations. Finally they met some Yankees from one of the other ships in the harbor who told them where to find the kind of café Mirina wanted. Mirina was the only woman besides the Spanish entertainers in the rough barlike cabaret, but this didn't bother her in the least. Her eyes lit up as she eagerly watched the dancers executing the lively steps of the fandango.

"What would you like to eat?" asked Holt.

"I'm not hungry anymore," said Mirina. "This is too exciting."

"Well, I am," said Holt.

"Then go ahead and eat, dear."

Holt ordered some meat and vegetables from a man who looked like a waiter. Mirina darted her eyes around the dimly lighted, smoke-filled room until she spied a table in a corner with five men

178

huddled around it. Turning to Holt, she said, "I'm going over there for a minute."

Before he could answer, a black-eyed girl had drawn him out on the floor, where he awkwardly tried to follow her in the Spanish dance. When he returned to the table, Mirina was not back but the food had arrived. The greasy mess soon took his appetite and he pushed the plate away. The place was getting noisier and more crowded by the moment, and he couldn't see Mirina anywhere. Getting up and circling the room, he located her back in the corner gambling with three Americans and two Chileans. Furious, he approached and said, "Come on, we're getting out of here."

"But I'm not ready to go yet," she said.

"I don't care, you're going anyway."

"Now, that's no way to talk to the little lady," said one of the Americans.

"Keep out of this, mister," said Holt. "I'm talking to my wife."

"Sorry, brother," said the man. "No offense meant. I've got one of 'em myself. Didn't know she was married—the way she come over here."

Holt reached down and grabbed the man by his collar, lifting him up out of his chair. "What did you mean by that?" he asked.

"Nothing," stammered the man. "Nothing, honest. Go on, lady, please—get him out of here."

"Come on," said Mirina. Holt dropped the man back in his chair. He grabbed Mirina's arm and walked swiftly from the gambling den.

"I didn't think you'd mind," said Mirina. "You didn't seem to on the ship."

"Well I *do* mind," said Holt, still panting with anger. "And I don't want you to do it anywhere anymore. Do you understand? People get the wrong ideas."

"All right, if it upsets you so. I was only doing it to pass the time. Let's go back to that place Captain Hewitt suggested."

"I'm not hungry now. We're going back to the ship." Knowing it was useless to argue, and hating her dependence on him, she followed along meekly.

When they got back to their cabin Holt began undressing her. She made no protest because by now she had learned he considered her body his to use whenever he desired and would brook no nonsense about headaches or resistance of any kind. In fact, if she did try to resist him, he seemed to enjoy using force. Never-

179

theless, when he touched her body she couldn't help but respond. Actually their best times with each other had become the times when they were in bed. When Holt was satisfied he always became gentle and tender, and she felt relaxed and safe within his arms.

Holt had discovered that sex was an enjoyable part of life. No longer the embarrassed, fumbling boy of the call house in New York, he was accomplished and sure of himself. That night he wondered if he would enjoy making love to someone else as much as he did to Mirina. Once the idea had popped into his head, he found it irresistible and decided to have himself a Spanish señorita before he left Valparaiso.

At daylight the next morning shipwrights and workers were swarming all over the *Sea Skimmer* repairing the masts and tightening up the sleek clipper for the voyage out into the Pacific. Holt took Mirina ashore to see the sights and do some shopping. She was gratified to find that he did not have a penurious nature. She used all of her charms to give him complete satisfaction that evening. She was both angry and hurt the next day, however, when he informed her he was going ashore with Kevin to see the cockfights and wouldn't be back until late.

At the cockpit the betting was loud and furious on the two handsome birds being held up for inspection by their owners before being released to fight each other to the death. Kevin had attended the fights the day before; now he explained to Holt how the long spurs on the cock's feet were used for cutting and slashing. The fight began, and both of them laid down bets. At first when the birds attacked, feinting, dodging, and slashing, Holt felt it was much like a prizefight. But as their deadly weapons began taking their toll, and the fresh blood of the combatants began splattering the pit and the spectators, he found it not much to his liking. Looking around at the other men, he was horrified and fascinated. One little man was wetting his lips continually with his tongue and rubbing his hands together. Others were breathing hard, their mouths formed in fixed half-smiles. One man darted his eyes around to be sure to see all of the blood freely flowing. Another was slack-jawed, with saliva dripping from the corners of his mouth. The remainder were yelling and screaming and jumping up and down. No one except Holt took his eyes away from the attraction, and he found himself wondering what lay deep within men, including himself, that could respond to this kind of slaughter with such obvious enjoyment.

After the fights Holt said, "Let's go find some women."

Surprised, Kevin blurted out, "Don't you and Mirina——" Then he stopped himself.

"Of course," said Holt in a debonair manner. "But a man needs variety."

Kevin took Holt to a bar on Mizzenmast Hill where he had spent the two previous evenings. As soon as he came in, a small girl with a heart-shaped face named Maria attached herself to him, and after a few drinks they started for the stairs that led to the upper rooms of the brothel.

"I'll see you back at the ship," Kevin called over his shoulder.

Holt selected a well-developed girl, equally as pretty as Maria, and followed Kevin upstairs. His girl, named Felicia, was an accomplished prostitute, and Holt learned a few new tricks. But when he got back to the *Sea Skimmer* some time later he kissed the sleeping Mirina lightly on the cheek as he slipped in beside her and whispered, "But you're much better, honey." Somehow his conscience didn't bother him for having cheated on her.

While escorting Mirina around town the next day, however, he pondered his relationship to her. Had he only pitied her right from the beginning, he wondered, and never really loved her at all? Whatever had happened, he knew he did not feel the same way about her as he had the day he married her. Now he longed to be off and away with the unfettered Kevin.

By evening Mirina was tired and suggested, "Let's go back to the ship."

Happy to have his freedom, Holt said, "You can go back if you like, but I'm staying." He took her to the waterfront where one of the boats was waiting and departed.

Mirina was seething with rage. Instead of having a lovesick swain dancing to her bidding, her husband couldn't be quick enough to be rid of her and off to his own pleasures. While she sat in the skiff waiting for more passengers, one of the other boats rowed in, and riding in it was Albert Duane. As soon as he had alighted, he stepped over to Mirina.

"What an unexpected pleasure," he said. "Don't tell me you're going back already. The evening's in its infancy."

"We decided we'd had enough sightseeing for one day," replied Mirina.

"But where's your husband?"

"I'm expecting him any minute."

"I'll just keep you company till he comes."

"Oh, no thank you. I believe I'll not wait any longer. He can get the next boat."

"I'll see you later then," said Albert, giving her a wink.

She was disturbed by the wink all the way back to the ship, but she was too tired to think and so put it out of her mind as she quickly undressed and slipped into the bunk. She viewed the cramped cabin with loathing. What she would really like would be to sleep in a bed on dry land and never set foot on a ship again. With this comforting thought, she had almost drifted off to sleep when she heard someone moving stealthily in the companionway. The silence of the nearly empty ship had not bothered her when she had come aboard, but now she was terrified. Soon she heard the latch give, and the door slowly opened.

"Mirina, my dear, are you there?" came the voice of Albert Duane.

Suddenly vociferous, Mirina shrieked, "Get out of my cabin."

"Not just yet. You've been issuing me an invitation ever since you came aboard, and I'm here to collect."

"I don't know what you're talking about. Now get out or I'll call Captain Hewitt."

"He's ashore," whispered Albert. "I checked."

"I don't care. Go away and leave me alone!"

"You weren't so distant the other day before your husband came in."

"If Holt finds you here he'll kill you."

"But he isn't here, and he won't be for a long time, will he? So why don't you relax and enjoy yourself?" Breathing hard, he lunged for the bunk. Mirina leaped out on the floor, but he caught the shoulder of her nightdress and tore it. She screamed.

"So you're one of those," said Albert savagely. "Arouse a man but don't want to deliver. Well, you're not going to get away with it this time!"

He grabbed her again and was attempting to wrestle her down when once more the door to the cabin swung open. Kevin stood in the frame holding a ship's lantern above his head. Deliberately setting the lantern down, he picked up Duane by the collar and threw him against the side of the cabin. Duane raised his arms to

182

defend himself, but Kevin gave him a punch that sent him flying out of the open door to land in a heap against the wall of the passageway. As Kevin was about to attack the senseless man again, Captain Hewitt came down the companionway.

"What's going on here?" he boomed.

"He was trying to rape Mirina," gasped Kevin. "I heard her scream."

Sobbing and half naked, Mirina flung herself into the captain's arms. "Get something to cover this woman with!" the burly man roared. Kevin grabbed Mirina's cloak from the cabin and threw it over her shoulders as she stood there shivering. Duane finally opened his eyes and sat up. The captain glowered at him. "Get your things and leave this ship, Duane," he commanded. "And I'll be making a full report of this escapade at the consulate, so you'd best not be running there to make any charges of abandonment."

When Holt came aboard a little later, Captain Hewitt called him into his cabin and told him the story.

"Where is he? I'll kill him!" yelled Holt.

"He's gone," said the captain, "And that wouldn't do any good anyway." He leaned back in his big chair behind his desk full of charts and maps and peered out at Holt from beneath his bushy brows. "You're responsible for what happened tonight."

Holt looked startled and guilty at the same time. "Me?" he said lamely.

"Yes, you. You are no longer a gay young bachelor, though to observe your behavior, nobody would ever know it. You have taken on the responsibility of a wife. . .and it is a responsibility. Whether you were ready for marriage or not has nothing to do with it now. The fact is you are married, young man." He put his palms flat on the desk and leaned forward. "And it is your duty to see that your wife is protected at all times."

Holt felt his face grow hot. He had no answer for the captain.

Captain Hewitt rose from his desk and walked around toward him. In a more kindly tone he said, "You've chosen your course, son. You can't turn back now." He placed his hand on Holt's shoulder. "Now go to her. She's had a terrible shock and needs you."

Chastened by Captain Hewitt's lecture, Holt apologized to Mirina for having left her that evening and promised he would not leave her unprotected again. Sensing the change in him, Mirina nearly broke down and told him about the baby, but fear held her back.

By the next evening Captain Hewitt's Chilean wheat was stowed away and battened down, and all of the ship's repairs had been finished. Even though he had been unable to get a replacement for White, he determined to sail with the early tide.

In the morning under a clear sky the shantyman began singing,

> In Val-prai-so there lived a maid,
> Mark well what I do say
> In Val-prai-so there lived a maid
> And she was mistress of her trade
> And I'll go no more a-rov-ing
> With you, fair maid!

And the men took up the chorus as they fell on the ropes and turned the capstan bars, weighing the anchor and hoisting the huge white wings of the *Sea Skimmer* once more.

> A-rov-ing, a-rov-ing,
> Since rov-ing's been my ru-i-in,
> I'll go no more a-rov-ing
> With you, fair maid!

"Turn her into the wind," sang out Captain Hewitt to the helmsman, and the great bird skimmed out to sea on the final leg of her flight to San Francisco.

CHAPTER 17 TRAVELING FIRST CLASS ON THE AMERICAN★★★★★★★★★★★★★★★★★★★★★★

The granting of gambling concessions on its steamers was against the policy of the Panama Steamship Company. But on the overcrowded *American,* where men were sleeping two to a berth in the cabins and steerage, on the tables and benches in the saloon, and on the decks and in the rigging, a gambler from Panama named Forbes had a whole table for his faro game, and his partner

Blaine's roulette wheel turned incessantly in a private cabin. This favoritism Darcy suspected meant the captain had made his own arrangement with the two gamblers. And Rip insisted these same two were the cheats who had fleeced him in Panama.

"Then let's give them some competition with an honest game," said Darcy.

Through Darcy's skill they gradually began to recoup Rip's Panama losses. But Forbes and Blaine, anxious to add Darcy's winnings to their hoard, made several attempts to lure him into their high-stakes games.

Nine days out from Panama they stopped at Acapulco, a pretty town nestling by the sea beneath towering cliffs that seemed to overhang the shore. Eager to leave the cramped ship, Darcy and Rip joined the wood-gathering party. But on shore they discovered that very little of the wood needed for the next fifteen hundred miles of steaming to San Diego had been cut. Although like Darcy many of the argonauts had never done a hard day's labor in their lives, they fell to with zest to cut and saw the timber into suitable lengths for the greedy steamer boilers.

In the heat Darcy stripped to his waist to work, and soon his back and chest were liberally oiled with sweat and dotted with black flies. "How do you like traveling to California first-class style?" he asked Rip.

"Not much," groaned the small redhead. His now limp hat was a poor sunshade, and dark stains showed where his shirt was plastered to his back and his sleeves clung to his arms.

"Why don't you take off your shirt?" asked Darcy. "It'll rub you raw."

"Better that than gettin' sick," said Rip, breathing heavily. "Can't take the sun. . .never could."

For three more days the work proceeded, the pace becoming faster as the bodies of the men became stronger. Then at the midday break on the fourth day, the captain declared they had enough wood to steam to San Diego, and the work party quickly stowed themselves in the small boats to row back out to the ship. Within an hour the little sidewheeler had a full head of steam. The argonauts left the snug harbor with scarcely a backward glance, and the *American* steamed on up the coast.

The Fourth of July dawned, a day to be commemorated by drinking, eating, dancing, and noise. By evening of the glorious

185

day of celebration, the decks, the companionways, and the saloon were littered with the bodies of the celebrants. Some were snoring as loudly as they had earlier laughed, some were sick and lying asleep in their own mess, some wore that particular pale green color which signified they were about to be sick, while others were draped weakly over the rails as they heaved. It was a miserable and smelly end to such a gay beginning, and yet oblivious to all that lay around them, a few men still were gathered near the bow quaffing and laughing and singing. Around nine o'clock to the soft strains of "Auld Lang Syne" they, too, staggered off to bed, and the ship settled down into the quiet of the night.

Darcy no longer slept in innocent oblivion as he had when he left home, and around midnight he came awake suddenly. He knew he had heard an unusual sound. Quietly he slipped from his hammock and piled some clothes beneath his blankets to make it appear he was sleeping there. Then he drew his derringer and positioned himself behind a rum keg a few feet away. A figure crept toward the hammock. Just as the intruder buried a knife deep in the bedclothes, Darcy stepped up behind him.

"Raise your hands, sir," he commanded.

The man whirled around and slashed at him with the knife. In reflex Darcy fired his gun, hitting his assailant in the shoulder and sending his weapon clattering to the deck. Instantly the ship sprang to life. The would-be assassin started to run, but the deck-riders grabbed him and forced him into the center of a close-packed ring.

"You ain't leavin' just yet," said one.

Someone brought over a lantern and Darcy saw Blaine holding his hand over a spot on his right shoulder where blood was beginning to darken his shirt.

"Can't you see? He tried to kill me," blustered the gambler.

"Then why was you in such a hurry to leave?" said the man who had collared him.

"I'll tell you what I think," said another man. "He wasn't satisfied with taking all our money. He wanted Darcy's, too. That right, Darcy?"

"He wanted more than my money," said Darcy. "He tried to kill me." He kicked the knife with his boot.

"A thief and a murderer!" shouted another man. "Somebody get a rope!"

At this moment the captain appeared brandishing a gun. "Back away!" he ordered the belligerent men. "There'll be no lynching on this ship!" He grabbed Blaine and pulled him to his side. "Now what's this all about?" he demanded.

Darcy told the story and showed him the knife

"I can't handle a murder charge," the captain said. "I'll have to turn him over to the military authorities at San Diego."

"When will we get there?" asked Darcy.

"In a week or so."

"What about all the money he's taken?" asked one of the heavy losers.

"I'll take that and lock it in the strongbox till this thing gets straightened away," said the captain. "Now everybody go on about your business."

As the men started moving away, Forbes brushed by Darcy. "This ain't going to be the end of it, Dupres," he said.

Before Darcy could reply, Rip came stumbling up on deck. "What's going on?" he asked.

Darcy began to laugh. "You've just missed the most exciting event of the whole voyage," he said. "I don't understand it. You try harder than anybody else to be in on everything, and yet you always miss out."

But on the morning the ship was due in San Diego, Rip was passing the captain's quarters when he heard Forbes and the captain shouting at each other.

"Be damned!" yelled Forbes. "That money belongs to Blaine and me. All you're entitled to is your ten percent." Fascinated, Rip pressed his ear close to the door.

"My ten percent went up the other night," said the captain. "When I gave you the gambling concession on this boat I knew I was dealing with a couple of crooks, but I didn't know I was dealing with murderers." Rip heard a well-aimed stream of tobacco juice hit the spittoon by the captain's desk.

"I won't leave this ship without my money," said Forbes.

"Oh, but you will, sir," retorted the captain. "You'll leave on the same boat that picks up Blaine. Frankly, I'm surprised at your ingratitude. I saved Blaine's life. And if you don't snatch this opportunity of getting away, I shall be forced to turn you over to the men as a cheat. Now get out of my cabin!"

Bursting with his news, the eavesdropper ran out on deck.

187

"Darcy, Darcy," he cried. "We was right about the captain bein' in cahoots with them gamblers."

Darcy listened carefully. "What makes you think the captain intends to keep the money?" he asked.

"The way he did it. He said they was cheats and threatened 'em. Oh, he aims to keep it all right. What should we do?"

"For now, nothing. Let's see what happens between here and San Francisco."

The *American* was already steaming into the fine natural harbor at San Diego, and the two joined the other passengers at the rail. Ringed by green, low-lying hills, the bay was a beautiful sight to behold. Within minutes after the steamer had dropped anchor, the government officials rowed out and came aboard. After the customary amenities, the captain handed over the handcuffed Blaine to the authorities, along with the formal written charges. But Darcy noticed he did not hand over any money.

"We'll be meeting again, Dupres," threatened Blaine as he was led over the side.

"Yeah, damn your hide!" spat Forbes as he followed his partner down into the officials' boat.

The captain turned to the argonauts. "You'll be happy to know that the wood for the next stage of our voyage is cut and ready for loading. We'll sail on the first tide tomorrow," he said.

A week later the ship passed Monterey in the early morning just as the sun was rising over the town. Although the former center of the Mexican government in California was an established stop, the captain said he had enough fuel to reach the harbor in San Francisco. Urged on by his eager passengers, he directed the steamer past the large bay dotted with many ships.

Darcy decided it was now time to alert the other argonauts that the money they had lost to Forbes and Blaine was still reposing in the ship's strongbox. Rip heartily agreed and spent the next hour buzzing like a happy bee from group to group spreading the word.

Gathering aft, the men milled around for some time protesting ineffectually. At last a leader emerged. Sam Wackem, a generally mild-mannered carpenter from Philadelphia, was a huge man standing six-and-a-half feet tall.

Holding up his big hands for silence, he finally got their attention. "I've got a plan," he said. "Each of you must write down on this slip of paper what you've lost to Forbes and Blaine. Then we'll take it to the captain and make him give us ninety percent of the money. That'll still leave him with his original ten percent profit." There was a chorus of angry protests. But Sam continued, "I know it wasn't legal, but he has been taking care of it for us and this'll make the parting less painful. And don't forget he still has to take us to Frisco."

They cornered the captain in his cabin. A wily man, he sought to put them off. But the men became threatening, so he tried to bargain with them. "Suppose I give you seventy-five percent. Now that would be reasonable, wouldn't it?" he asked.

"We want the whole sum. . .every damn penny of it," said Sam.

The captain glanced at the angry faces around him and capitulated. Bringing out the box, he handed Sam the money, which Sam carefully doled out to each loser according to his claim.

Now eagerly anticipating their arrival in San Francisco that evening, the argonauts began packing their meager belongings. By late afternoon they were off Yerba Buena point, and Rip shouted, "There she is. We're coming in!"

A huge cry reverberated throughout the ship. Their long journey was nearing its end, and the gold that had lured them so far was beckoning.

Since the fog was way out to sea, the captain took on a pilot to guide them safely through the Golden Gate into the great harbor. The hour was late and no other ships were entering the bay, but when they rounded Clark's Point, the men could see many small boats putting out from the town, and before the *American* was halfway to her pier at the foot of Sacramento Street, many tradesmen and merchants' agents had swarmed aboard, as well as earlier emigrants, hungry for news of home.

Before the new arrivals were quite aware of what was happening, these men were bidding on their old, well-thumbed newspapers. Papers that had been bought in the Eastern seaboard ports for one cent were auctioned off for as much as a dollar and a half. Cries of, "Anyone here from New York? Philadelphia? Boston?" and names of other cities a continent away rang across the decks. Response brought forth a warm clasp of the hand. The questions and answers flew back and forth. Some few actually met old acquaintances and the greetings were long and loud.

The captain was besieged to open his mail bags and deliver

189

long-awaited letters from home. This he flatly refused to do. Finally, out of fear for the safety of his already badly overloaded vessel, he ordered the sailors to pull up the ropes and ladders and not let any more aboard. But they were unable to carry out the command, for as soon as the tradesmen found out the ship carried only human cargo, they wanted off. Thus for the next forty-five minutes the little steamer labored toward its berth, its progress hindered by a constant stream of men climbing up and down its sides.

Before they reached the dock Darcy had been approached by half a dozen employers offering him jobs that ran the gamut from carpenter to waiter. Though the wages he was offered were fantastically high, this meant nothing to him because he had never worked for pay. But Rip's eyes popped and his mouth dropped in astonishment when he was offered ten dollars just to clerk in a store for one day.

"Do you know that's a week's wages back home?" he asked.

"Why don't you take it then?" teased Darcy.

"Not me, I'm a gambler," Rip scornfully retorted. "You know, there's somethin' strange about all this though. Everybody who's come on this ship has tried to buy somethin'."

"You're right," said Darcy, looking at the groups of bargainers with more interest.

"There ain't one person who's come up and said, 'How's about stayin' at my hotel?' "

"And nobody's said anything about a restaurant either. Yet they all know that the men who get off this boat have got to find a place to eat and sleep at least for one night."

Having worked their way aft where it was quieter to wait until they could debark, they were interrupted in their speculations by Sam Wackem.

"Hide me quick," the giant pleaded as he ran up. "I shouldn't have told them I was a carpenter. I find it very hard to say 'no.' "

"Get in this hatchway," said Rip. He and and Darcy stood innocently in front of the hatch blocking any view of Sam. A harried-looking man panted up.

"Did you see a big man come this way?" he asked anxiously. "I believe I almost had got him to work for me."

"Sorry, we ain't seen anybody," said Rip pleasantly.

"I don't suppose either of you is a carpenter," the man said wistfully.

"I'm afraid not," said Darcy.

"That's too bad," murmured the man, wandering forward. "I'm trying to build a store. It's the very devil to get anybody to work nowadays."

As he disappeared, Darcy and Rip pulled Sam out of the hatch. "If it's this bad on board, I wonder what it's like on the streets?" remarked Darcy.

"I don't know," said Sam "You suppose there's safety in numbers?"

"That's a good idea," said Rip. "Let's all go together."

Just then they felt their ship wedge itself tightly against the pier. And as soon as the gangplank was down, the three argonauts ventured out on the dirt streets of the raw city of San Francisco. It was late July, 1849.

CHAPTER 18   TO THE LAND OF MORMONS★★★★★★★★★★★★★

An hour after the wagon train left Fort Bridger Goldie started to build a fire for breakfast.

"No use in cookin' just for yourself," called over Dora. "You may as well eat with us from now on."

"Only if you'll let me share my stores," said Goldie.

"If you like. Now come on over and have some coffee. You look plumb wore out. I'll set with Gray a spell."

After breakfast Tim said, "I think Gray might be more comfortable in a tent. And we oughta be able to rig some kind of bed so he could be sittin' up more."

"I've got him propped up with pillows," said Goldie, "but they keep packing down."

"He'll breathe easier in a tent," said Tim.

He put Isaiah to work, and within an hour they had constucted the tent from their tarpaulins. Tim fashioned a bed with a sloping back, and carried Gray out.

"Is it time to start?" asked Gray weakly.

"No, not yet." Tim was evasive.

All day Goldie and Dora took turns sitting by Gray, listening to his rasping cough but unable to do anything to relieve the congestion in his lungs. Goldie fed him some broth, and her heart sank when he tried to take the spoon and could not hold it.

"Oh, God," she prayed. "Send the doctor soon. Gray hasn't got any strength left."

Late that afternoon a white man accompanied by a number of Indians came riding down from the mountains toward the fort. He sat tall and straight in the saddle, and for a moment Goldie's heart skipped a beat. She almost thought Zack had returned. But when the group drew nearer, one of the Indians pointed toward the two wagons, and she knew the man must be Dr. Marshall. He rode up, tipped his light wide-brimmed hat courteously, and dismounted. The Cunninghams gathered round, but the man spoke directly to the girl.

"You must be Goldie Baxter," he said, looking at her bright curly hair. "I don't mind telling you my son is quite smitten with you."

"Your son?" asked Goldie, puzzled.

"Why, yes," said the doctor, gesturing toward the band of Cheyennes. And then Goldie recognized Running Wind.

"You mean Running Wind is your son?"

"Yes, he's my son. Well now, where's the sick lad?"

"It's my brother," said Goldie. "He's over here in this tent. At first we thought he had the measles, and I guess he did. Then Zack Peale—he was our guide—thought he had lung fever. He's awfully weak, Doctor. He. . .he can't hardly breathe." Tears welled up in her eyes.

The doctor examined Gray. Then he told one of the women to brew an herbal tea. Sometimes speaking in the Cheyenne tongue and sometimes in English, he indicated how he wanted the tent prepared. Both he and the Indians slipped effortlessly from one language to the other, absolutely amazing Goldie. At last he stepped outside the tent and drew Goldie out with him.

"Your brother is very weak and his lungs are badly affected," he said. "But I think his youth will help. I'm going to fill the tent with herbal vapors, which I hope will relieve the congestion in his lungs. Then we'll build back his strength with teas and broths."

"Then he. . .I mean. . .everybody thought——" She stopped and bit her lip.

192

"Nobody can be sure. But he's fought well by himself, and with our help. . .I think he'll recover."

"Oh, thank you, Dr. Marshall. You've given me the first hope."

"And David," said Marshall. "You didn't introduce yourself properly to Goldie before." Then turning back to the pioneers he said, "This is my son, David Running Wind Marshall, a bridge, I hope, to the future."

Suddenly it registered on Goldie that Running Wind's eyes were blue like his father's. "I should have known," she thought. "Indians don't have blue eyes." She felt those eyes intensely upon her and blushed. But Running Wind made no other approach.

Nonetheless after dinner, when Dr. Marshall and Rustling Leaf, Running Wind's aunt, returned to Gray's tent, Running Wind claimed Goldie. "Where is the rest of your wagon train?" he inquired.

"They had to go on," answered Goldie. "And Gray was too sick."

"I understand, Miss Baxter," said Running Wind.

"Goldie, please. Everybody calls me Goldie. Miss Baxter sounds unfriendly."

"My father says you should always call unmarried ladies 'Miss,' and that it is presumptuous to call a young lady by her first name unless she asks you to. I shall be delighted to call you Goldie. It is a most beautiful name."

"Thank you. What shall I call you?"

"My mother and father always called me David. You call me that too."

"Very well," said Goldie. "But I think Running Wind is a lovely name."

"But it makes me alien, doesn't it?"

Goldie colored. "Yes, I guess in a way it does."

"Oh, I know it isn't just that. It's my clothes and my hair as well."

"You may look different, but that doesn't mean you are."

"My father said to me once, 'Someday you will see a woman and she will be the only woman in the world for you.' I thought that day I saw you out on the prairie you were that woman, and now that I have talked with you, I know you are. I want——"

"Don't," Goldie broke in, "please don't. All I want right now is for Gray to get well so we can go on together like we planned.

Please forgive me." She turned away and ran over to the tent where Dr. Marshall was working over Gray.

Inside she heard Gray coughing, but the cough already sounded less harsh to her. She went back to the wagon and an hour later Dr. Marshall came by

"You can see Gray now," he said. "He's much relieved and has even been able to eat a little. But you can only stay for a moment. He must rest." Goldie rushed over to the tent.

Opening his eyes, Gray said, "I guess I've been a real trial. How's everything going?"

"Fine," said Goldie, squeezing his hand. "You're going to get well now that Dr. Marshall's here."

"First time I've been able to breathe without hurting," said Gray, closing his eyes again

"He soon be strong again," said Rustling Leaf.

"Thank you," choked Goldie. "I'm so grateful."

When Dr. Marshall returned to his tent, he found Running Wind morosely sitting on his heels and staring off into space.

"Don't blame her too much, son," said Dr. Marshall. "She's very young."

"That's not the problem. I thought if I loved her, she would return my love. . . .But it doesn't work that way."

"I doubt if she knows what love is. And until she does, she won't make anyone a good wife. I think you had best forget her."

"I don't know if I can."

"I guess I always thought you'd marry one of our girls. I don't want to hurt you, son, but your life is here. I'm counting on you to make some kind of agreement to ensure this land for our people in the future, for white men will come and try to take our land away as they have before."

"Then why can't I be a white man?" cried Running Wind.

"I'm sorry, David—I didn't give you much choice, did I?" He bowed his head.

"It is I who should apologize, Father," said Running Wind, quickly contrite. "You gave me life and an education. That is enough." And yet both knew that David Running Wind Marshall would always be part of two worlds but belong to neither.

In a few days Gray's cough disappeared. But his strength returned slowly, and Goldie still was permitted only brief visits with him. Then one morning she awakened to a pouring rain, reminding

194

her that summer was on the wane and they must start on soon if they were to cross the Sierra Nevadas ahead of the snows. Throwing on her cloak during a lull in the storm, she sloshed over to Dr. Marshall's tent to find out how soon Gray could travel.

At Dr. Marshall's invitation she entered. "Ah, my dear," he said, "I was beginning to tire of this book. I guess I've read it too many times. I'm delighted to have an excuse to put it down. What can I do for you?"

"I came to see you about Gray. This storm. . .we must get on. But he still seems so weak."

"He's doing better than you think. I'd say you'll be able to leave in four or five days."

"Really?" she said in delight. "I hate to admit it but I was scared of getting caught in the mountains in a snow."

"You should get through them well before the snows come."

"I've heard from some of the men at the fort that there's a shorter route than this one." Goldie brought out the map Zack had made showing the northern route which wound up to Soda Springs and Fort Hall and then turned down the Snake River to the Humboldt to join the California Trail.

"You must be thinking of Hastings Cut-off south of the Great Salt Lake across the desert," said the doctor.

"Yes, that's the one."

He shook his head. "It's very hard. It's about ninety miles from Salt Lake City to the first springs at the foot of Pilot Peak. Still, if you could carry enough water and feed for your animals, it is a shorter way. Some of our men could show you the Mormon Trail through the mountains to Salt Lake City, and from there on I think you'd find the trail pretty well marked."

Although Dr. Marshall objected, Running Wind insisted on being one of the three guides to lead the Baxters and Cunninghams through the Wasatch Range.

"The longer you are with her, the more deep will be your hurt when you finally must part," said the doctor.

"It is my hurt," said Running Wind.

And so on the morning of the twenty-sixth of July the Baxter wagon driven by Running Wind, followed by the Cunningham wagon driven by Tim, pulled out of Fort Bridger. Thanks to the advice of Dr. Marshall they were well equipped for the ordeal that lay ahead after they left Salt Lake City. They had purchased oats and grain for the animals and were carrying empty casks and barrels to fill with water at Salt Lake City and again at Muskrat Springs before the long trek around the lake.

At first the road they were traveling from the fort was well marked, many of the grades having been smoothed by the hardy Mormons in order to make the trip through the Wasatch Range easier for their brethren. But as the journey continued into the second and third days, the terrain became more rugged and the way less distinct. Goldie was grateful for their Indian guides, for she now saw how easy it would have been to miss a trail marker and lose precious days wandering in the maze of canyons and ravines.

Following Dr. Marshall's instructions, Gray had spent the first day in the back of the wagon except for a brief ride on Sunny before the noon stop. But aware that they would soon be on their own, he resolved to do more the next day and increase his amount of work every day until he was once again strong. His naturally optimistic nature began to reassert itself as day by day he felt the energy slowly flowing back into his body. And on their last night in the mountains while they were camped in Emigration Canyon, he told Goldie that from now on he would be able to do his share of the work. Bright tears shone in her eyes as she looked at his filled-out body and realized what he said was true.

"Come on, Sis," he said gruffly. "What are you doing that for?"

"I'm so happy," she said. For a moment their hands touched in quick understanding.

The next afternoon the two wagons crested the last rise in the trail and they saw below them shining in the sun the Great Salt Lake and the valley before it, made green by the Mormons. But beyond they could also see the desolation of the salt flats.

Knowing how he felt about her, Goldie had found it difficult to talk to Running Wind on the rugged trip. But now she found it even more difficult to say goodbye. Mutely she held out to him and the two braves three fringed buckskin vests decorated with silver and mother-of-pearl buttons which she had made during Gray's confinement at Fort Bridger. She handed Running Wind a second vest. "This is for your father. He wouldn't take any payment, but I hope he will take this as a gift from our hearts."

"He will be honored," said Running Wind.

"Goodbye, David. We shall never forget your many kindnesses."

"Godspeed, golden one. I hope you find what you are looking for."

The three young Indians vaulted onto the backs of their horses and were soon out of sight around a bend in the trail, while Goldie and Gray and the Cunninghams went forward alone to grapple with the desert.

Before sunset the two wagons had come to the first cultivated land, and soon the travelers saw a house. Warned by Dr. Marshall that the Mormons were not friendly to people not of their faith, they approached with caution.

Standing in the barnyard of the farm was a man dressed in dark pants held up by galluses stretched over a gray work shirt, black boots, and a flat brimmed hat. He had a gentle fringe of beard that encircled his chin like a ruffle from ear to ear, and his eyes twinkled above his apple-pink cheeks as the two wagons drove up.

"He doesn't look so fierce," thought Isaiah, so he ventured a question. "You a Mormon?"

"That I am, sonny," said the man.

"We was wonderin'," said Tim, "if you'd mind if we camped by your stream?"

"Help yourself," said the farmer.

"We're obliged," said Dora.

"Be you in a trading mood?" asked the Mormon.

"Depends on what you got to trade," said Tim.

"I've got some nice lettuce and green beans in my garden, and I could sell you a chicken for your supper and some eggs."

"That certainly would taste good," said Goldie. "We haven't had anything like that for ever so long."

"How much are you chargin'?" asked Dora.

Within a few minutes a bargain was struck. For a dollar he gave her two chickens, a couple of dozen eggs, a mess of green beans, some roasting ears, and a bucket of lettuce.

"Got any fodder for your mules?" asked the Mormon.

"Yes," said Tim, "we've got some oats, but we could use some more. You sellin'?"

"I'll fill your wagons with hay for fifty cents."

"Agreed," said Tim.

"How's the trail?" asked Gray.

"Well marked with the truck and castoffs of those who've gone before you," said the Mormon. "You won't have any trouble

197

makin' your way along. Water's the real problem."

"We aim to fill all our barrels and kegs at Muskrat Springs," said Tim.

"Best fill them all here," said the farmer. "That way you'll only have to fill what's empty at the Springs. The water ain't sweet tastin' there." Then nodding his head in approval as he turned to leave, he said, "You're better prepared than most."

The next morning at the shore of the Great Salt Lake, they couldn't resist running out to taste the salty water. They found it as unpalatable as they had been warned and quickly spat it out. Camping on the shore that night, they discovered that in addition to offering no water, the salt flats also offered no fuel for their fire, and were grateful to Running Wind for warning them to bring wood along from the mountains.

They were up and away before dawn the next morning, but it had been so much cooler during the night that Gray wondered if it wouldn't make better sense to travel during darkness. The more his skin burned under the blazing sun, and the more his lips cracked in the alkali dust, the better his idea seemed.

All day and well past sunset the sweating animals and humans toiled toward Muskrat Springs. But when they finally reached the oasis they found it a ruin. The dry grassy area surrounding the waterhole was littered with trash and abandoned household goods, and the spring itself, lined with the carcasses and bleached bones of animals, was polluted also with wagon chains, harnesses, and other debris that had been thrown into the water. Fortunately they had used less than a quarter of their water supply and needed to take on only a few barrels of the rank-smelling stuff.

With the setting of the sun there was an instant cooling of the dry air, and Gray, remembering his idea of traveling at night, proposed it to the others.

"Sounds right sensible," said Dora.

"Sure does," said Tim. "It'd be a lot easier on the animals not to have to pull the wagons in this heat."

"Only thing wrong is I'd hate to start out again now," said Dora.

"We could sleep a while and start out again later tonight," said Goldie.

"We've got to have shade for the mules if they're supposed to rest during the day," said Tim. "They can't just stand out in the sun."

"How about our tarps?" said Dora. "We ought to be able to rig somethin' outa those."

"Yes, let's do it," said Goldie.

"All right," said Gray. "We can sleep four hours now, then start."

As a small party they knew they were a good target for marauding Indians, so the rest period was divided into four one-hour watches. Dora took the first, and the others stretched out to sleep.

Four hours later they cleared their eyes with water from the spring and started out again. The moon lighting the phosphorus in the bones that lined the trail turned the desert salts to silver. It was an eerie, chill world, but far better than the scorching one they knew awaited them when the sun rose.

By ten o'clock, when they pulled to the side of the trail to make camp, the mules were panting. Gray and Tim quickly rigged the tarpaulins into awning shelters. Then, except for Goldie who took the first watch, they all lay down to rest. Around four o'clock they rose, had long drinks and something to eat, and started off again

In this manner they continued across the Great Salt Lake desert. But on the fourth day, with their water supply dangerously low, they dared not rest. By midmorning they began passing wagons with men, women, and children in them; some vehicles were still attached to dead or dying animals, others were standing alone like marooned ships. All, they discovered, were waiting for someone to return with water. Although besieged with pleas to share their scanty supply, Goldie and the Cunninghams shook their heads in refusal—over Gray's protests.

"We can't do it, Gray," called Tim grimly. "We'll be in the same fix ourselves if we don't get to that spring mighty quick."

Turning to Goldie, Gray observed the firm set of her mouth. Staring straight ahead she said, "Tim's right. We've only got part of a barrel left. We've got to keep moving till we get to the spring."

Although logically he knew Tim and Goldie were right, instinctively Gray drew up on the reins as they approached another wagon. Pulling them away from him and shaking them over the mules' backs, Goldie said firmly, "We've got to go on, Gray. We haven't enough to share. This time we have to think of ourselves."

They continued to pass stranded wagons, and by noon as Goldie felt her resolve to persevere draining away, the mules' heads suddenly went up, signifying they had smelled the spring beneath Pilot Peak. They bolted, running pell-mell for the water. Gray strained on the reins but could not slow them down. On the seat beside him Goldie clutched the wagon in terror. They came up short at the water's edge, careening and nearly overturning. Goldie and Gray leaped down and quickly unhitched the animals. Happy, Matilda, and Tag Along were already down at the edge of the spring lapping away. By the time they led their mules to the water, Tim and Dora rolled up at a much more leisurely pace with Isaiah, Ruth, and Adam chuckling gleefully over the way the Baxter wagon had shot off.

Their thirst satisfied, Tim and Gray began talking to some of the other men filling water kegs at the spring, and discovered that they had actually overtaken and passed at least one wagon train.

One of the men said, "We've got to hurry back if we're goin' to save the animals. The folks'll be all right as soon as they get a good drink, but the animals is dyin'."

Assuming that two more men who were loading a wagon with barrels of water must belong to the same group, Gray went over to talk with them. "That's a real good idea," he ventured as he came up. "That way you can haul a lot of water to help your people."

"They ain't our people," said one man, pausing to wipe the sweat from his face. "And we ain't offerin' charity."

"Then what's the water for?" asked Gray.

"To sell," barked the second man. "These fools need water and we supply it. . .a dollar a drink. Now get out of the way, we're busy!"

His mouth gaping, Gray retreated. He couldn't believe that men would actually capitalize on the sufferings of others this way. Back at the wagon, he exploded to Goldie, "Sell it, will they? I'll show them!"

"Why, Gray, what's the matter?" she asked. When he blurted it out, she was as horrified as he had been.

"Help me unload the wagon," said Gray. "I'm going to fill our barrels and take the water back to give to the people who couldn't make it to the spring."

As they began dropping goods out the back, Dora called out, "What're you doing?" Goldie told her, and she replied, "We'll help too. Come on, Tim. And you children can start fillin' those water barrels."

Two hours later when they had the wagon loaded and Gray was ready to start, Isaiah said, "Can't I go, Pa? I could help Gray."

"All right, Dora?" asked Tim.

"All right," said Dora, "Hop up, son."

"Don't go too far, Gray," cautioned Goldie. "Remember you have to get back here yourself."

"I'll take care of him, Goldie," said Isaiah.

"We should be back by late tonight or by morning at the latest," said Gray. "Don't worry, Sis, I'll be sensible."

As the day wore along, more and more emigrants straggled to the spring. Some were on foot by this time, while others were leading their animals to the water. A few wagons rolled in, and when their drivers learned that Gray and Isaiah belonged to Goldie, Dora, and Tim, they blessed them for their charity.

By evening a sizable group had gathered, and with the horror of their recent travail behind them, they began exchanging information and rumors about the trail ahead. Goldie and Dora chatted with the other women while they did a long overdue washing; the children found playmates among the wide-eyed group that came in on the wagon train. Tim, after checking their equipment and mending a harness, enjoyed a visit with some of the men. At supper it was pleasant to see the neighboring fires around the spring; already they were nostalgic about the days when they had been members of a wagon train themselves.

As the night wore on, Goldie's eagerness for the return of Gray and Isaiah turned into anxiety. Unable to sleep anymore, she rose at four, filled several canteens with water, quietly saddled Sunny, and after leading her out of the camp, mounted and rode off down the trail to the east.

Gray and Isaiah had had a gratifying afternoon stopping their wagon intermittently along the trail and ministering to those in need. But wisdom was slowly replacing the imprudence of boyhood in Gray, and now realizing it would be folly to extend their distance from the spring too far, he drew the wagon to a halt and scanned the horizon to the east beneath the darkening sky. Isaiah,

201

following his example, looked all around them at the desert.

Finally Gray said, "I don't see any more wagons out there. What do you say we have our supper while the mules rest and then head on back to camp?"

"Yes, I guess we've done just about all we can do for now," said Isaiah, trying to sound grown-up and looking about once more. Though the light was dimming, something caught his attention to the right of the trail. "Hey, Gray," he said, "I think I see somebody over there. It looks like a man!"

"We'd sure better see," said Gray, turning the team from the trail in the direction Isaiah was pointing. It was indeed a man, stretched out on the desert floor. Gray drew up the wagon, then hopped down, cautioning Isaiah to remain until he found out what was the matter.

Turning the man over, Gray was appalled to find that it was Henry Bowles.

"Water," rasped Henry in a thick voice.

"Isaiah, quick. . .water!" shouted Gray. Grabbing a canteen, Isaiah leaped from the wagon and ran over.

Turning back to Henry, Gray noticed that the skin on his face was peeling off like layers of paper, his clothes were ragged and torn, and though he still had his boots, they were worn completely through. Gray put the canteen to his parched lips and he gulped greedily. He sat up and stared.

"Gray," he whispered hoarsely. "My God, what are you doing here?"

"The same for you," said Gray. "I thought you'd be in California long ago."

"I guess the others are," gasped Henry, reaching for the water again.

"Can you walk?" asked Gray. "We want to get back on the trail while there's still enough light to see it. Then we'll make camp for a while."

"I guess so," said Henry weakly. With a boost from Gray and Isaiah, he managed to get into the wagon. They rode along in silence for a time, while Henry lay exhausted in the back. Soon he noticed all of the barrels and spoke hoarsely. "What are you, some kind of missionaries?" he asked.

"We've been givin' people water all afternoon," said Isaiah

"Thank God you were," said Henry.

202

"What were you doing out on the desert all alone?" Gray asked.

Haltingly Henry told of his adventures. "We heard about Hasting's Cut-off at Fort Laramie, and naturally everybody wanted to take it. So after we crossed South Pass, we headed down to Fort Bridger. . .like you must have done. Everything went fine until we were winding through the Wasatch Mountains. Then several of the fellows, including Chuck, got sick. We called it Mountain Fever. Rachel didn't get it, and she sure got upset with the rest of us. We must have been delayed for nearly a week. Finally most of the boys except three of us were well enough to push on, so they did."

"You mean they left you?" asked Isaiah.

"That's what I mean," said Henry. "Both of the others died, but somehow I hung on, and three days later a wagon train came by and took me down to Salt Lake City. I guess I would have died too if they hadn't come along. Anyway, a Mormon family cared for me until I was well enough to travel again. Then four days ago I started across the desert with a horse and a pack mule. I was doing fine, had plenty of water and was making good time. Then last night some Indians came up out of nowhere and stole my animals. The only thing I had left was my bedroll and a canteen of water. I don't know where I dropped the bedroll, and after the canteen was empty, I guess I just wandered. I'd 've died if you two hadn't come along."

Isaiah and Henry dropped off to sleep, and Gray also found himself dozing as they plodded along the trail in the white moonlight. The sky was paling when he was jarred awake by the sound of Sunny's hoofbeats.

"I was worried about you," Goldie cried as she pulled up.

"Doggone it, Goldie," he scolded, "what do you mean by riding off from camp all by yourself? When are you going to get some sense? But guess who's aboard? We found Henry Bowles almost dead back there on the desert."

Isaiah and Henry stirred as Goldie tied Sunny to the tail gate and climbed up on the high seat. But both dropped off to sleep again, and Gray too climbed back with the water barrels to catch a nap.

They arrived back at the spring just as the wagon train they had helped the day before was pulling out. Despite their hardships, these people were not delaying any longer. Awake once more,

Gray agreed with Tim that it was important their group also press on. And although it was afternoon by the time they had repacked their wagons and filled their water barrels, they decided they should be able to cross the pass over Pilot Range while it was still daylight, and so set off for the Humboldt River and the California Trail.

CHAPTER **19**   FRISCO BAY AT LAST★★★★★★★★★★★★★★★★★★★★★★

Captain Hewitt headed northwest from Valparaiso in order to take advantage of the upward sweep of the Peruvian current and the southeast tradewinds. The passage was fair, and he was beginning to dream that the *Sea Skimmer*'s name might be entered in the books for a record run to San Francisco. At times he could scarcely keep from patting her wheel as she skimmed lightly over the sparkling ocean to complete the first lap of her world conquest.

Except for a violent morning nausea and loss of appetite, Mirina had been enjoying the smooth passage north toward the equator more than any other part of the trip. But Holt, who at first thought she was seasick, became alarmed as the days went by and she grew no better. And finally one morning after she had had a particularly bad spell, he went to Captain Hewitt.

"Come in," boomed the hearty voice at his knock.

"I'm sorry to bother you, sir," said Holt and wondered why every time he stood before the captain he felt like a disobedient schoolboy with his cap in his hand brought before the master. He tried to be more manly, but as usual only succeeded in blurting out his problem.

"It's Mirina, sir, she's awfully sick. . .every morning. And she's losing weight, and her skin looks funny. . .and, well, I'm afraid she's sick. I mean really sick."

"Avast!" said Captain Hewitt. "You say she's sick every morning?"

"Yes, sir."

"Maybe I'd better talk to her. Is she in the cabin now?"

"Yes, sir."

"All right. Now you go out on deck, and I'll see what's the matter."

"Shouldn't I come too, sir? In case you need any help."

"Help!" shouted the captain. "You can help by going out on deck like I told you."

Captain Hewitt couldn't restrain a chuckle as he thought how surprised Holt would be when he found out what was really the matter with Mirina. He tapped on the door and entered the cabin across from his own.

"Well, my dear," he said in the most kindly tone he had ever used to her. "Why haven't you told your husband?"

"Told him what?"

"Come now. . .a green boy might not know what's the matter with you, but a man of my years has had considerably more experience. How long have you been pregnant?"

"I think almost since we left Rio," said Mirina in relief. She began to cry softly, for she hadn't realized how much she needed to have someone else know and understand.

"I think you'll be all right soon," said the captain. "But you've got to eat. We can't have you wasting away."

"I'll try."

"That's a good girl. Now I don't think you should keep the father in the dark any longer. He thinks you've got some serious illness."

"Oh, I can't tell him—not just yet. You see, Holt doesn't love me. He only married me out of pity. He'll think I'm burdening him."

"Nonsense! You're manufacturing nonsense in your mind. He'll be delighted. Any man is proud to become a father."

"I'm afraid," said Mirina. She grabbed the captain's hand. "Please give me a little more time! Don't tell him."

"All right," said the captain. "But you'll have to break the news soon."

"I will. Just give me a little more time."

Two weeks from Valparaiso the ship crossed the equator once more, and the argonauts began to speculate about how soon they would get to San Francisco.

But as Captain Hewitt pointed out to Holt in his navigation lesson that morning, "From now on we'll be fighting against the downward sweep of the California current and also the desert winds off the coast of Mexico. We may have to go out toward the Sandwich Islands and north of San Francisco in order to come in on the westerlies."

"Is it possible to sail due north without westing?" asked Holt.

"At rare times," said the captain. "The next few days will tell us if this is to be one of those times."

Then suddenly the wind died and the *Sea Skimmer* was becalmed just north of the equator in the Pacific as she had been in the Atlantic. All day the ship wallowed in the swells beneath the burning sun, with no escape for her passengers except the stifling cabins from the blinding blue sky or the equally blinding blue water. Heat and boredom shortened tempers until Captain Hewitt feared a repetition of the *lobscouse* rebellion.

But early the next morning the wind began snapping through the rigging and a torrential tropical rain flooded the decks and poured through the open hatchways and ventilators. Sailors scurried to hoist sails and close hatches at McCarthy's commands, and the argonauts hustled out with pots, pans, and other vessels to catch the rainwater

Welcome as the storm was, it shoved the ship further west; Captain Hewitt had no choice but to follow the fickle wind and hope to gain some degrees north also. By daylight the clipper had been blown to 121 degrees west longitude, but also well above the equator, and fresh new winds were carrying her north at a good rate.

With California now so near, the argonauts began overhauling their belongings, long stowed away in trunks and boxes. Some of them brought out the strange-looking gold-washing machines they had bought in New York, and it was not uncommon to see three or four men with their heads together pondering an instruction sheet and trying to figure out how a machine was supposed to work. Others were industriously sewing leather pouches out of old vests or even boot tops to put their gold in.

One acquaintance let Holt and Kevin copy a map of the gold region. Although they didn't know whether it was accurate, they thought it was better than nothing. They had decided to become partners, and despite Kevin's lack of capital, Holt insisted it be on a fifty-fifty basis. As they made their plans, Mirina, feeling left out, pouted, "And what am I supposed to do while you two are running up and down rivers looking for gold?"

"Why, you'll stay in San Francisco and live off the fat of the land," laughed Kevin.

"It's not fair," said Mirina. "You'll have all the fun and be together while I'll be all alone." Although she wanted desperately to tell Holt of her condition, her fear of being deserted held her back.

Another squall blew up, pushing the ship farther out in the Pacific and knocking the passengers and crew about. Once more the rails were awash with foam. But Captain Hewitt refused to take off any sail. "We have to take advantage of this," he said. "We're still not getting the westerlies." And so the *Sea Skimmer* got a little more westing with her northing, but she was doing better than twelve knots now.

Another week passed. Captain Hewitt calculated they were now off the southern California coast at 126 degrees west longitude. He recognized that this should put them in a good position to drive for the Golden Gate, providing they got the westerlies. "We'll be in sight of the Farallone Islands and Yerba Buena Bay within a week to ten days if this keeps on," he announced.

Again he approached Mirina about informing Holt of his forth-coming fatherhood.

"I don't want to be left alone," said Mirina, beginning to sob. "He'll go off and leave me if I tell him."

"He's not that kind of a lad," said the captain. "He'll figure it out pretty soon, you know. It's a fact you can't hide."

"I know. But I just can't tell him now. Promise you won't say anything."

"I'll not interfere," said the captain and left the cabin to return to the helm. She is a good ship, he thought to himself as he stood looking up through the sails at the sky. Better than a woman. She charts her course true.

"How goes it?" he said aloud to the helmsman.

"It goes well, sir," came the grave reply.

With the voyage so near completion, the weariness of the long months at sea and the little creeping fears of how they would fare when their mettle was finally tested combined to make the argonauts edgy and irritable. Their equipment and belongings had been checked and rechecked and then checked again. They had traded goods with each other so many times that some things had found their way back to their original owners. There was nothing left to do. And so they took out their frustrations and impatience to end the journey by finding fault with one another. New friendships were formed and broken over the slightest thing. Those who had come from the same areas and had planned to work together could no longer stand the sight of each other. Captain Hewitt prayed for a quick landing so that he might be rid of the whole quarrelsome, cantankerous lot.

Through all this, the serenity and steadfastness of the friendship between Kevin and Holt was remarkable. It was as if their doubts and mistrust of each other had been resolved during the voyage. Although they were as eager as any of the others to sight land, they quietly pored over their map, trying to decide where they should go to seek their fortune.

Mirina in the meantime had decided to accompany Holt to the mines. She didn't bother to work out any details as to how she was going to accomplish this, but simply resolved she would take advantage of whatever opportunity presented itself to thrust her presence into the search for gold.

At last the long-sought westerlies began to blow, and the *Sea Skimmer* sped toward San Francisco. Late one afternoon the captain announced they were approaching their landing and posted men aloft to keep a sharp lookout for the treacherous Farallones.

"I haven't brought her this far to wreck her now," he told Holt.

He had scarcely uttered these words when Kevin, who was atop the mainmast, sang out, "Rocks—rocks to the south!"

"That'll be the islands," said the captain.

Then Kevin sang out again, "Land—land to the north!"

"It looks like we're in the right position," breathed Holt excitedly.

"Yes," sighed the captain. "But we can't make it before the fog sets in. The gate is narrow, you know."

By this time the layout of the land surrounding the Golden Gate was clearly visible some thirty miles away. But Captain Hewitt gave orders to pull north to the shelter above the Farallones known as Drake's Bay.

"We'll anchor there and take her in in the morning," he said.

Excitement was fever-high on board that night. The cook-stewards prepared the most bountiful repast they could with the stores they had left, and the men brought out the last of their liquors, jellies, and sweets to share. Passengers who hadn't spoken to each other for days now greeted one another with smiles.

"We made it! We made it!" The murmur swept back and forth with wonder and pride.

In the forecastle the seamen were equally excited. Like Kevin, many of them had signed on just for this leg of the voyage, and others were planning to desert, even though it meant they would get no pay. Kevin was singing inside and could scarcely keep from shouting aloud. His dream, nurtured in his grubby surroundings in New York, was about to come true. Impatiently he waited for morning so he could be about the business of shaping Kevin Adams, Esquire.

In their cabin, despite sharing the narrow, intimate bunk, Mirina felt the remoteness of Holt, who, like Kevin, was so full of dreams of a grand future that he hardly knew his wife lay beside him. He didn't convey any of his hopes to her, but simply lay there, happy, excited, and eager for the morrow to begin. Mirina feared the end of the voyage but clung to the thought that she would go along with Holt and Kevin in their adventures, no matter what.

Drake's Bay was shrouded in fog the next morning. At ten o'clock it lifted, and under a strong breeze with forty men aloft unfurling the great white sails, the *Sea Skimmer* swung around. As they weighed in the anchor for the last time, the old shantyman began "Oh, Susannah." And with the song of the argonauts swelling from over one hundred throats, the ship drove southeast for a perfect sighting of the Golden Gate. As they rounded Point Bonita, the pilot came out and was boisterously welcomed aboard. He pointed out to Captain Hewitt that the semaphore telegraph station on Point Lobos had already relayed to the Telegraph Hill station that the ship was coming in.

Since he was working, Kevin had little time to devote to seeing the bay and the land he would call home. But Holt and Mirina stood at the rail eagerly scanning the shore for hospitable signs.

Suddenly Holt shouted joyously and pointed off the starboard bow, "Look!" On the bluff above them, Mirina saw the American flag waving proudly in the stiff wind.

They passed beneath Telegraph Hill, where they could see the semaphore signals flying from the mast of the telegraph station, and across the bay, Alcatraz Island. Finally they rounded Telegraph Hill and saw Yerba Buena Cove, its harbor crowded with the hulls of dead and dying ships. Holt gasped at the forest of masts;

even in New York he had not realized the enormity of the gold rush.

As they slipped into their anchorage, scores of little boats carrying merchants scrambled alongside; the men ascended like so many spiders climbing their webs up to the ship's deck. They were bidding on the cargo before the anchor was dropped and before some of them even knew what it was. But the rush was on to get ashore, and these merchants were a hindrance to the crowd lining the railing and calling down to the boatmen to see how much they would charge to row them into town.

Midst this milling throng, Kevin finally found Holt and Mirina, and they collected their belongings together in one neat pile on deck. Holt, who had approached Captain Hewitt for his money while the captain was being pursued by several merchants, was told he would have to wait. So despite their impatience the trio sat down on their luggage while acquaintances bid them hasty good-byes and clambered off the ship to the waiting lighters that stood by to row them in at three dollars a head.

An hour later the ship was relatively quiet, and Captain Hewitt called Holt and Kevin to his cabin. He gave Holt his money and Kevin his savings plus thirty-five dollars in wages. "Godspeed," he added and shook their hands warmly.

"Thank you, sir, for everything," said Holt.

Captain Hewitt accompanied them back on deck and called for one of the ship's boats to be lowered to row them in. As they pulled away, he shouted, "If I were twenty years younger, I might join you. Good luck, lads!"

CHAPTER **20** THE BROWN HILLS OF CALIFORNIA★★★★

Several days out of Pilot Springs and only a few miles along the Humboldt on the California Trail, Isaiah, who was investigating the rocks and pieces of bone by the side of the trail, found the jawbone of a cow with a message for them written on it. He took it to Gray who read: "Hey, Gray, we been going along here ight smart. Zack says keep following the river till he tells you where to turn—Dan."

"August fourth," said Tim in delight. "Why, they're only a little over a week ahead of us."

They continued along the river and a week later found a message from Zack saying: "The river turns south here, and you might say we're on the final leg of the journey. Hope your wagons and mules are holding out. We've lost some I'm sorry to say—Zack—August 11, 1849."

From then on the trail was lined with the carcasses of cattle, and the number of abandoned wagons increased, their owners having transferred what goods they could onto the backs of their remaining animals in order to hurry along.

"Sure hope our mules don't play out," said Tim. "I'd like to take the wagon all the way in."

"We're going to make it all right," said Dora. "These animals still got plenty of sass in 'em. Too bad about the folks that's having' to leave their things though. Just look at that dresser over there. It'll soon be ruined settin' out in the weather. Mahogany, too."

At the crossing of the Humboldt they found another message from Zack indicating they should now veer away from the river to avoid the Humboldt and Carson sinks. "There's sixty miles of desert ahead before you reach the Carson River," the note continued. "Fill everything you've got with water here, and don't take water from any of the springs along the way. They're poisonous."

After four days of searing heat, their mouths powder-dry and their eyes aching from the glare of the sun, they finally arrived at the Carson River. Hardly pausing at the edge, both animals and humans plunged into its refreshing coolness. Never did water feel so good, thought Goldie as she sank down to her neck in the stream.

On the second of September they negotiated Carson Pass in the Sierra Nevadas and turned south to follow the steep trail down the western side of the range. Gradually the slopes became more gentle, and at a fork in the trail they found another message from Zack telling them to turn northwest toward Hangtown.

The next day a man on horseback approached from the west.

"I'm a trader," said the man. "How're you fixed for supplies?"

"We have plenty to get us there," said Dora, suddenly wary that the man might be trying to sell them something.

"Got any bacon?" asked the trader.

"Some," she said.

"I'll give you sixty cents a pound for what you've got left."

"Why, that would be robbin' you," said Tim. "I only paid eight cents a pound for it in Independence."

"Well, now, let me tell you a thing or two," said the trader, tapping a button on Tim's shirt. "I can get a dollar fifty a pound retail for that bacon in Sacramento."

"Well, then, Mister," said the wily Tim, "it appears to me you'd be doin' the robbin'." Both men began to laugh, and the trader slapped his knee.

"Buyin' bacon isn't all I've got in my kit," he said. "How'd you like to sell your mules and wagon for. . ." He paused dramatically. "Say fifteen hundred dollars?"

"What'd you say, Mister?" exclaimed Dora.

"I said fifteen hundred dollars. . .cash!" said the man. "I may as well tell you 'cause you're goin' to find out as soon as you get to Sacramento to pick up your supplies for the mines anyway. Everything's scarce here. Prices are like nothin' you ever heard of before. That's the reason I ride out here to meet the incomin' trains."

"Well, I'd sure like to sell this rig for that kind of money," said Tim, "but I've got to get my family to Sacramento, and that's a piece yet."

"I'll tell you what," said the trader. "You make a deal with me now and just deliver the wagon to my warehouse. The same goes for you, young feller," he said, turning to Gray. "The money'll give you a good start in the mines."

"I don't know." Gray was suspicious. "I'll have to think it over."

"You folks don't want to be hampered with a wagon at the mines. You'll see what I mean when you get to Sacramento. Here's my address. The deal will still hold when you get there."

"Jumping Jehoshaphats, Goldie!" burst out Gray when the trader was out of earshot. "Did you ever hear of so much money for a wagon and six mules?"

"No," she answered soberly. "I'm beginning to wonder if we can afford to dig for gold."

They continued on toward Hangtown. But now with their goal

so near, their minds were filled with misgivings about this strange, inhospitable-looking land. The grasses on the hills and in the valleys were brittle, brown, and dry; the few unfamiliar scrub trees, mostly manzanita and California oak, were gray from lack of water; and there was never any rain to lay the ankle-deep dust of the road.

Hangtown did nothing to dispel their trail weariness and misgivings. The main street was dirt and was lined with ramshackle buildings made mostly of canvas displaying signs such as: RED DOG SALOON, DRY DIGGIN'S CASINO, and MINERS' SUPPLIES LTD. As they drove through the town, Goldie realized the trader had told them the truth about the prices. A barrel of flour sitting in front of a store prominently displayed a sign of five hundred dollars, and a tag attached to a side of bacon marked it at twenty-five. She gulped and looked at Gray.

"Don't forget the trader offered us fifteen hundred dollars for the wagon and mules," he said. Now, though, he privately wondered how long even that amount would last.

From Hangtown the trail led ever downward through the brown rolling hills until finally they were in the broad, fertile, but still dry valley approaching the Embarcadero of Sacramento. Each day they met more people, but all were intent upon their own business and none paused to greet or offer aid to the newcomers. It was a land of strangers, and they felt unwelcome. . .except for Dora. She looked around in delight. "Such land," she said over and over. "I never saw such land." But she failed to generate any enthusiasm in the others, and the last night on the trail she upbraided them. "I never saw such a hangdog-lookin' crew in all my life. This is no time to be back-lookin' and moanin' about what we left behind." She looked at her husband. "As far as we're concerned, Tim Cunningham, what we left wasn't much." Tim stared dolefully at the fire.

"It ain't what we left that's botherin' me," he finally volunteered. "It's that I feel foolish. . .like some kid chasin' rainbows."

"Well, what'd you expect?" said the exasperated Dora. "Sure the stories were crazy. But we're here, ain't we? All of us, alive and well with a chance to be somethin' different than we was before. This is new country even though it ain't like what we knew. We should be thankful instead of regrettin'. I'm ashamed of all of you—especially you, Gray, and you, Henry." She stared at

213

them, her steely eyes snapping. "You almost died to get here, and now you're tuckin' your tails between your legs. I suppose you believed the roads were going to be paved with gold all the way to Sacramento City?"

"It isn't that," blurted out Gray. "The land doesn't make you feel welcome. Well, doggone it—it isn't pretty. Paradise is supposed to be pretty, isn't it?"

"Whatever gave you the idea that you were going to be livin' in Paradise? It's up to you to make somethin' of the land. It ain't gonna give you any gifts. You all act like you thought gettin' to California was goin' to end your labors, and you'd just lay down and rest. Well, let me tell you somethin'. . .God didn't intend for it to be that way. If you want the *gold,* you're all goin' to have to go after it." She looked from one self-pitying face to another and sniffed in disgust.

In the morose silence that followed, Isaiah got Goldie's guitar and timidly asked her to play and sing for them. To please him, Goldie began the tune, "The Maid of the Greenwood," and Gray joined the chorus. They followed this with "The Rag Man," and soon everyone was singing the popular songs they all had sung so many times along the two thousand weary miles of the trail. Finally the one song above all others that had sustained them when their hearts were heaviest bubbled cheerfully out of Goldie's throat to the strong accompaniment of her guitar: "Oh, Susannah, oh don't you cry for me, cause I'm goin' to Californ-i-ay with my washbowl on my knee."

Under the spell of the music, the spirit that had impelled them to leave the safety of their known world and plunge across more than half a continent revived. Once more they felt they were Fortune's children and looked forward to seeing the city on the delta on the morrow.

With suppressed excitement Goldie awakened the next morning. It was September eleventh, Gray's birthday, and she wanted to surprise him by having all of their friends to a real dinner in a hotel in Sacramento tonight. During the hitchup she told Dora, who promised to keep the secret and have everyone ready that evening.

During the day Gray found it hard to hide his disappointment. Today he was eighteen, and Goldie hadn't even wished him a happy birthday. He had never thought she would forget like this.

214

As they drew nearer the city he became more despondent, and several times Goldie almost broke down and told him of her plans. But she managed to keep the picture of his surprise in her mind and held her tongue.

Had they not already seen Hangtown they would have been sorely disappointed in Sacramento, which was also almost entirely a city of canvas. But the place was bustling; the dirt streets were glutted with people and wagons, the stores and walks were piled high with goods, and the banks of the river were lined with merchant ships and smaller craft.

Goldie anxiously scanned the signs on the canvas buildings and was gratified to see that there were several eating establishments. Though afraid of what she might find inside these places as to bill of fare and price, she clung to the belief that somehow she would be able to make Gray's eighteenth birthday an event. Most of all she wanted a cake, though she realized this might be too much to hope for.

After they had found a pleasant camping site in some sycamores near the river, Goldie said, "I'm going back into town and get a real bath and wash my hair."

"Where?" asked Gray.

"I saw a sign on one of those tents that said 'Hot water baths —twenty-five cents,' that's where.'

"Mind if I come along?"

"I hope they have enough hot water for three," said Henry. "I'd like to come too."

When the three of them got to the makeshift bathhouse, Goldie deposited her things with the proprietor, dodged the boys, and went out to arrange her dinner party. She stopped at a large canvas building with the name, ROYAL RESTAURANT painted across its front, but inside she found the place was royal in title only. The tables consisted of rude wooden planks resting on barrels with more long boards serving as benches on either side. These all stood on a dirt floor, and there wasn't a tablecloth in sight. Dismayed but still determined, she made her way to the back of the structure, where some noises coming from behind a canvas sheet indicated there might be a kitchen.

"Can you make a cake?" she asked one of the men working in the back.

For a moment the man stared at her as if she had lost her

215

senses. Then he recovered and looked at her more closely. "You just get here?" he asked. She nodded. "I thought so," he said. "Try the La Portal, miss. It's one street over."

The La Portal was also made of canvas, but unlike the Royal it had a wooden floor and real tables and chairs. A round little man with scant tophair but long side whiskers, dressed in a dark suit and wearing glasses, was sitting on a stool behind a counter by the door.

Goldie approached him. "It's my brother's eighteenth birthday," she said in a rush. "Gray, that's for Grayson, Baxter."

"Yes," said the little man in an encouraging tone of voice.

"You see we just arrived from Indiana. . .I mean just now. . . and I'd like it to be something special with a cake and everything for eight. I mean, there's eight in our party." She looked at him expectantly. "Three of them are children."

"Yes," said the man, "I think it could be arranged. I think I know what you mean. You're from Indiana, you say?" She nodded assent. "Yes, I'm sure we can do it. You leave everything to me."

She gulped. "How—how much will it cost?"

"Let me see," pondered the little man as he sized up his young and apparently destitute customer. "You say three of your guests are children?"

"Yes."

"Do you think ten dollars would be a fair price?"

"Oh, yes," she sighed in relief.

"Then shall we say seven o'clock?"

"Yes, yes, seven would be lovely. And you won't forget the cake?"

"No, I won't forget the cake."

"You do mean ten dollars for everything, don't you?" she questioned.

"That's right," said the restaurant owner.

"Oh, thank you, Mr.——" She broke off.

"Ogilvy," supplied her benefactor. "Horace Ogilvy, and I'm more than pleased to serve you, Miss Baxter."

"Thank you, Mr. Ogilvy," she smiled.

Henry was already outside waiting when she arrived back at the bathhouse.

"I did it," she said "Everything—even the cake! We're all to go at seven."

"That's great," said Henry.

"Can you keep Gray busy for another hour or so? It's going to take me a long time to do something about this." She gestured to her shabby dress and tousled hair.

"Take your time," said Henry. "We can walk around and see the town."

For ladies, the manager of the bathhouse generously supplied a dressing table and a mirror, but Goldie almost wished that he hadn't when she first looked at herself in it. Her hair was bleached to a dry, brittle straw color on the ends; her face was red and peeling, which made the liberal sprinkling of freckles across it even more ugly to her. She looked down at the raggedness of her clothing. Her calico dress was frayed beyond recognition, her boots were worn clear through, and her socks had holes in them beyond repair. With a sigh she realized how badly she had let herself deteriorate these last few weeks on the trail. She resolved that never again, no matter what, would she allow herself to become so dirty and unkempt.

She kicked her beggar's tatters into a corner of the canvas room and carefully unwrapped a bar of lemon-scented soap she had been saving for this day. Then she stepped into a real tin bathtub for the first time since March. She washed her hair and soaked and lathered her bony frame all over several times. Finally she took the scissors and snipped the strawlike ends off her copper hair and arranged it in the long curls she thought becoming. As she put on her clean underwear, her white stockings and black slippers, and her yellow sprigged muslin dress with small puffed sleeves and a big yellow sash, she viewed herself once more in the mirror, this time with much more satisfaction.

When she emerged to pay the proprietor, the man said, "I was gonna charge you extra, but young lady, it was worth haulin' all that hot water to see a sight like you now."

Outside both Gray and Henry stood staring at her as if transfixed.

"Gosh!" said Gray finally. "You look wonderful! It doesn't seem right to take you back to the wagon looking like that."

"You're not," said Goldie. "I've decided you're going to take me to one of those restaurants to eat tonight. We're here! Do you actually realize, we're here! And we're going to celebrate."

Henry, suddenly grown shy, asked, "Could I carry your

things back to the wagon for you, Goldie?"

"Thank you, Henry," said Goldie. "I'd almost forgotten."

"Forgotten?" asked Henry in surprise. "Forgotten what?"

"What it's like to be treated like a girl." She paused dreamily—but then came back to the present moment.

"Bring the Cunninghams, Henry. We're all going out to dinner!" she cried.

At the La Portal Mr. Ogilvy had a startled expression when he saw Goldie in her new attire. He grandly ushered the Baxters, Henry, and the Cunningham family to a table in the back. Goldie almost cried when she saw the table set with a snowy linen cloth, the crystal and silver shimmering and sparkling in the candlelight, and the fragile translucence of the white china. She knew Mr. Ogilvy had gone far beyond the promised dinner and cake. At each place was a hand-printed menu stating, "A dinner commemorating the eighteenth birthday of Mr. Grayson Baxter." As Gray looked up after reading it, Goldie threw her arms around him and said, "Happy birthday, Gray. I hope it's the best year ever."

Gray was dumbfounded. He felt ashamed and owned, "I thought you'd forgotten. I've never been so surprised in my whole life."

Most of the other diners had departed by this time, and Mr. Ogilvy deployed two of his waiters to serve them. It was truly a feast for any time. There were oysters and salmon for a first course, and following that, platters of fried chicken and roast pork, and bowls of creamed potatoes, garden-fresh green beans, and vine-ripened tomatoes. Just when they all declared they couldn't eat another bite, Mr. Ogilvy brought in an extravagant cake frosted and festooned with a snow-white icing and supporting eighteen candles on its top.

Gray felt a lump rise in his throat. "Even a cake," he said quietly.

"It's plumb beautiful," said Dora. "Be a shame to cut it."

"No, it won't, Ma," said Isaiah. "It'll spoil if we don't eat it."

Everybody laughed. Then Goldie said, "Make a wish, Gray, and blow out your candles."

"Make it a good one," said Henry.

"I have," said Gray. Then he blew, and all of the candles went out.

"Gray gets his wish. . .Gray gets his wish!" chanted Ruth.

"It's the best birthday I've ever had," said Gray to Mr. Ogilvy as they finished. "Last night and all day today I was wondering why we'd come out here. Now I know. You've made me feel at home."

"It was my pleasure," said Mr. Ogilvy.

"I gotta confess I had my doubts about this California too," said Tim. "I think it was all of the folks hurryin' that was gettin' to me. But when somebody takes the time to do what you done for Gray and us tonight, Mr. Ogilvy. . .well, it's got to be a pretty good place."

"I enjoyed it," said the little restaurant owner. "This is the first real party I've given since I opened. Glad I had some good waiters tonight. It's hard to keep help. They keep leaving for the mines. But I'll have a fine restaurant someday."

"You already have," said Goldie

Contented and happy for the first time in many months, Goldie and Gray slept peacefully that night on their feather ticks in their prairie schooner moored beneath the rustling sycamores. Their long trek was over, and tomorrow they would begin a new life.

PART TWO

★★

CALIFORNIA, THE GOLDEN LAND

In July of 1849 when Darcy, Rip, and Sam Wackem stepped
ashore in San Francisco, the city was thronging with thousands of
men all in need of lodging, food, supplies, and entertainment.
Constructed of insubstantial materials, the embryonic city appeared to be a boom town doomed to disappear when the yellow
stuff that had made it was no longer there to sustain it. But those
with vision saw the beginnings of a great city rising on the hills
behind the wide bay.

"Don't seem to have any rain," observed Rip as he waded
through the dusty street.

"Don't seem to have much of anything else either," said Sam,
eying the tent buildings with distaste.

"It's getting late," said Darcy. "We've got to find a place to
sleep."

He stepped into a flimsy structure labeled HOTEL, and approached a man sitting behind a board counter. "Have you any
rooms?" he asked.

Rip noted the accommodations were similar to Panama's and
tugged at Darcy's coat. "Ain't no rooms," he said. "Just them
shelves." He pointed to the rows of planks lining the canvas walls
of the establishment.

"How much for one of those?" amended Darcy, gesturing at the
boards.

"My goin' price is five dollars a night, but I ain't got any space,"
said the man.

"Five dollars!" roared Sam. "For one of those?"

"Yes," the man answered placidly, "and I'm cheaper 'n most. I
don't fancy gouging folks. You might try up the street. But a lot
of ships have come in the last couple of days, and I don't reckon
you'll find anything."

For more than an hour the three searched for sleeping space,
only to be refused wherever they inquired. At the edge of the
town they stopped in a saloon to ponder their next move, when
they were distracted by the entrance of a slim brown-haired girl in

a faded calico dress. She was carrying a battered milk pail. Darcy noticed that every man in the place was staring unabashedly at her.

"Cracky!" exclaimed Rip. "A woman! Do you realize she's the first one we've seen since we got to this place?"

"And from the looks on the faces of these men we aren't likely to see many more," said Darcy.

The girl smiled and nodded to the bartender. "Evening, Mike," she said.

"Milk's all ready, November," said the man behind the bar. "But Daisy didn't give as much tonight."

"Sure hope she isn't going dry." The girl stepped behind a corner of the bar and set her pail on the floor. While she was ladling the milk from the saloon's container, a paunchy tippler suddenly circled around behind her and pinched her behind. She straightened up quickly and her cheeks flushed. Both Darcy and Sam, instantly on their feet, started toward the drunk, who was laughing uproariously as he grabbed for the girl. Darcy yanked him away and with a single blow knocked him to the floor. Right away Sam picked him up by the scruff of the neck, carried him to the door, and tossed him out into the street.

"November, you all right?" asked the bartender.

"I guess so, Mike," the girl managed to reply. But she was still furious.

Darcy stared at her for a moment, speechless. She couldn't be termed beautiful except for her large and luminous eyes. But there was something else about her—a spirit—the way she held her head. It reminded him of someone, and he was deeply resentful that she had been pawed like a barmaid. Slowly he took off his hat. "My apologies, Miss November," he said. "Some animals don't seem to recognize a lady when they see one."

"You're so right," said the bartender. "And I sure do appreciate what you and your friend did. I'm Mike Flaggerty. I own and operate this place. And this is Miss November York."

Darcy bowed to November and extended his hand to Mike. "Darcy Dupres," he said. Then turning to Sam, he added, "This is Mr. Sam Wackem of Philadelphia."

"If you don't mind my askin', miss," said Sam, "Whatever are you doin' in a place like this?"

"I come over every evening to get the milk for our rooming

house. Mike Flaggerty is one of the luckiest men in San Francisco. He keeps a cow and is kind enough to sell us his extra milk."

"Did you say you operated a rooming house?" asked the ever-alert Rip, approaching with his carpetbag in hand.

"Rip Packet," said Darcy to November.

"Pleased t' meetcha," said Rip, and doffed his battered hat as he had seen Darcy do. "We three come in on the *American* this evening and we can't find no place to stay."

"The place where I work belongs to Ma and Pa Brown. We're full too, but. . ." She smiled. "I think Ma would like the cut of your jibs."

Ma Brown's rooming house, like the rest of the hotels, was nothing more than a large tent stretched over a wooden frame. There was some privacy provided, however, by sheets of muslin hung between the beds, and the tent had a plank flooring, distinguishing it from most of the other buildings.

Ma Brown was a striking woman, tall and thin, about forty-five years of age, with light brown hair streaked with gray which she wore drawn back in a bun. Her deeply tanned face showed the signs of a hard life, but her hazel eyes were twinkling and were set off by deep smile creases at the corners. A woman of tremendous foresight and energy, in her six-week residency in San Francisco she already had acquired the wooden floor of her building and intended to have a hotel made entirely of wood before the year was out. By moving some of the muslin partitions, she managed to squeeze the newcomers in.

"It'll be cramped," she said. "But at least you're in off the street."

Almost immediately Darcy caught San Francisco's fever. If he had ever doubted the tales about California, they were dispelled, for in the untamed town gold was king and flowed like a never-ending river. Daily he saw enterprising men engage each other in the streets and conclude fantastic deals involving thousands of dollars with a handshake, a man's word being his bond as it had been in Louisiana. But even more incredible were the number of gambling establishments, all crowded with men eager to risk their earnings on the spin of a wheel or turn of a card. Why, he thought, should he rush to the gold fields when the miners laden with their dust from the diggings seemed so anxious to get rid of it here?

Rip was not of the same mind. Impatient as ever, he grumbled during one of Darcy's daily pilgrimages to the post office, "When are we gonna leave for the mines? You been puttin' me off all week."

"I'm not going yet, Rip. I've decided to start my own gambling place right here in San Francisco. This is where the money is. Look around you."

"But if we're goin' to look for gold, we should do it in the summer."

"There's always next year."

"But it may all be gone by then!" screeched Rip.

"Well, then you go on," said Darcy. "You don't have to stay here just because I do."

"Maybe I'll do that," said Rip and left in a huff.

Darcy looked after him and laughed, then joined the long queue extending out into the square from the post office. An hour later his wait was rewarded with a letter from his sister, Suzanne.

Bubbling with plantation gossip, her sprightly account had the effect of making him homesick. Then unaccountably he thought of November. Of course, that was it! She was like Suzanne. Suddenly home no longer seemed so far away. He smiled and pocketed the letter. It was time to set his plan in motion. He hastened to Mike Flaggerty's saloon, where over a glass he proposed, "I'd like to rent a corner of your bar to set up some gaming tables."

At first surprised, Mike said, "I thought it was gold you wanted."

"I do" said Darcy. "I'll pay you three hundred dollars a month for that corner over there."

"Sounds reasonable," said Mike. "You've got a deal."

Though for different reasons, Sam, like Darcy, had no urge to leave San Francisco. A member of a large family, he liked the sense of belonging he felt at the rooming house and spent many hours talking with Ma Brown in her kitchen. He learned that Pa Brown, who was off at the mines, had promised to build her a hotel of wood. As a carpenter, Sam sadly disapproved of the flimsy structures all around him, and the idea of building something way out here at land's end appealed to him. Besides, he reasoned, to work again in his familiar trade would help link his past life with the present. And so he set about seeing if he could bring Ma's dream to fruition. But though he searched everywhere, there wasn't enough lumber in town to build a small house, much less a hotel.

Then one day down on the waterfront he saw an enterprising merchant converting a derelict schooner into a warehouse, and out in the harbor he saw many more ships riding at anchor than had been there just a week ago. Suddenly he got an idea and leaped into an empty boat. Quickly he rowed to one of the nearest ships, where he shouted up, "Ahoy, anybody aboard?" Receiving no answer, he climbed a rope ladder flung over the side, and as he had suspected, found the ship deserted. Things were flung about on the deck and below in the saloon and cabins, indicating the occupants had left in great haste. But this wasn't what interested him. He began looking at the wood in the decking and bulkheads and the paneling in the cabins. It was all of good quality and finely fitted, and many of the furnishings were good too. With a quiet smile he returned to the deck where he began counting the abandoned ships desolately riding their anchor chains. There must be at least forty ships out there right now, he thought. And with more coming every day, I can build the finest hotel in San Francisco. Highly elated, he returned to the rooming house and disclosed his plan.

"If you'll help me," he said to Darcy and Rip, "we can build the hotel in a few weeks."

"I don't know," said Darcy. "I've just agreed to pay Mike three hundred dollars a month rent to set up my games in his saloon."

Just then Ma came in. "What're you boys up to?" she asked.

"Sam wants to build you a hotel," said Darcy.

"I could do it with some help, Ma," said Sam. "There's plenty of wood in that graveyard of ships."

"How many do you think we'd need to dismantle to get enough wood for the hotel?" asked Darcy.

"No more than ten, I'm sure."

"And ships will continue arriving until the gold gives out," mused Darcy. "We'd have a constant supply of new material. Sam, you've given me an idea. We'll build Ma's hotel, then we can build some other buildings—maybe even a gambling palace for me. We'll make a fortune!"

"You'd better see Pa's plans before you go flying off," said Ma.

"It's elaborate all right," said Sam as he looked at the drawings. "But I still think we can do it."

"Well, if you men are going to build my hotel for me, I'm going to pay you," smiled Ma. "Does room and board plus five dollars a week wages sound fair, Sam?"

"More than fair," he answered.

"At least I'll have somethin' jinglin' in my pockets again," said Rip. "Darcy won't let me have any of my winnings from the *American*."

"You can have your money if you want it," said Darcy. "I'm tired of your complaining."

"No, you know best."

"How would you like to run the wheel over at Flaggerty's place for me in the evenings?"

"No cards?"

"No cards."

"All right, if that's the best you've got to offer," Rip agreed reluctantly.

Sam began to study Pa Brown's drawings more closely. The plans called for a two-story structure to be built in two parts with twenty-five sleeping rooms in each wing, a commodious lobby, opulent dining saloon, and large kitchen.

"I don't expect you to do more than the first half," said Ma. "Pa should be home in winter to do the rest. The first wing's to go on the lot next door. Then we'll move over there, tear this down, and build the second wing where we are now."

As the days rushed by into August and the new hotel took shape, Sam, Darcy, and Rip made floating shells of five of the ships rotting in the harbor. They not only scavenged the lumber to build the structure itself, but they also salvaged inlaid wood paneling, carved pillars, stairways, and deck railing. Then they carried off the desks, chairs, bunks, glasses, dishes, and silverware; and they even rescued a piano from one of the vessels. Ma Brown's place was becoming one of the most elegantly, if a trifle bizarrely, furnished hostelries in San Francisco.

Then one afternoon when Darcy and Rip returned from a foraging trip, Ma greeted them, "I was hoping you'd be home for dinner. I'm having a little celebration. . .Pa's home."

"Pa?" queried Darcy.

"Yes, he came in from the mines to get some more supplies. It was quite a surprise."

"Where is he?" asked Rip.

228

"Over helping Sam put the finishing touches on the new dining room. I'm serving our first meal there tonight."

Darcy and Rip ran across to the new hotel. There, standing on a ladder in the center of the dining room, they saw a small man with a shining pate wreathed by a halo of gray hair. He was mounting on the ceiling a dazzling crystal chandelier which had once graced the dining saloon of the *Queen of the Seas*. As they approached he looked down, and his pink moon-shaped face broke into a cherubic smile.

"Be with you in a minute," he said. He finished securing the fixture and climbed down. "You must be Darcy and Rip." He extended his hands to them. "I want to tell you I sure do appreciate what you and Sam here have done for Ma. A hotel like this has always been her dream. She couldn't have pictured it any grander."

Though there were few women in San Francisco in August, 1849, Ma and November managed to locate nine besides themselves to invite to the ball to celebrate the opening of their Brown Palace Hotel. Since there were not nearly enough women for dancing partners, the men good-naturedly danced with each other as they had on the ships coming out.

In her apple-green silk dress, her cheeks rosy, and her eyes bright with excitement, November radiated a beauty Darcy had missed before. Escorting her out to the spacious porch after a fast reel, he said, "I think this is the first time I've seen you happy."

"I am. . .very happy," she looked up at him, her lips half-parted and her eyes shining.

He took a step toward her, then stopped. Suddenly it was Suzanne smiling up at him. He shook his head and said, "No, I'm not the one for you!" Tenderly he lifted her hand and kissed it. "Good night, November." He smiled at her a moment. "Sweet November." Then he quickly stepped off the portico and disappeared up the street.

Though she already sensed that he was far more sophisticated than she was, November looked after him with regret. While she was still standing on the porch in reflection, Ma came out. "Do you love him, child?" she asked.

"I don't think any woman could help loving him a little. He's attractive and charming." She gave a sad little smile. "But he's an adventurer, isn't he? He could hurt someone who deeply cared."

"You're wise, my dear. He'll never be one of the satisfied ones," said Ma and patted her hand.

Darcy headed for Flaggerty's. Since all of the regulars were attending the ball at the Brown Palace, the place was quiet. "Why didn't you go?" he asked Mike.

"Why did you leave?" retorted Mike.

"Because I——. None of your business!" he snapped.

"Exactly."

"What I need is a woman."

"Don't we all."

"You know what I mean."

"How would you like to be seven years without one?"

"Sounds like being in prison."

"It was."

At this moment two strange men entered the empty saloon. "Now oih tell you this is the plaice," said one.

"Naw," retorted the other. "It's too far out."

Their peculiar accents immediately identified them as a couple of Sydney Ducks, men who had sailed from the Australian penal colonies after hearing of the rich gold strike. Though some were escapees, others had served out their sentences; nevertheless, a Spanish law was still standing prohibiting anyone convicted of a felony from migrating to California, and for all of them entry into the country was illegal. Since there was no one around to enforce the law, they had come anyway, and at least a half-dozen ship-loads of them had arrived by this time. Gold had been the magnet, but few had gone seeking it. Instead, they had claimed an area surrounding Clark's Point as their own. This unsavory place, bearing the appellation of Sydney Town, was the center of vice, crime, and corruption in San Francisco, and cautious citizens gave the area a wide berth, particularly at night.

Darcy instinctively felt for his derringer and glanced at Mike to see if he realized the men were Sydney Ducks. Mike's face was a mask. The two newcomers swaggered up to the bar.

"Why it's auld Flaggerty," said one, breaking into a broad grin. "Wait'll Big Tom hears about this."

"This your plaice?" asked the other.

"Yeah," said Mike noncommittally, and in a tone of voice Darcy had never heard him use before. Mike's mouth was drawn down in a frown, severely emphasized by the droop of his long,

230

sandy walrus mustache. Never once taking his glacial blue eyes off the pair of criminals, he remained frozen in position.

"I tauld you it was the wrong plaice," the first man reiterated.

"Who's he?" queried the other, glancing at Darcy. "One of your boys?"

"Yeah," answered Mike in the same flat tone.

"Look, Flaggerty, we wasn't tryin' to move in," said the first one. "Big Tom sent us out to find some new gambling joint that opened up."

"That's my business," said Mike firmly.

"Come on, Beevy," said the other. "He's gettin' nervous. We was just askin'. We'll tell Big Tom you got this end of town."

"You do that," said Mike.

At the hasty exit of the Sydney Ducks, Darcy looked strangely at Mike. It was plain that he knew these two and a lot more besides. Deliberately getting down a bottle from the shelf behind him, Mike shoved a glass toward Darcy and poured himself a drink. He took a long, slow pull at his glass.

"Good Irish whisky," he commented. "I was a long time without that too." Then he peered into Darcy's eyes. "I suppose you'll be wantin' to know what that was all about?"

"I've been trying to piece it together, but it doesn't seem to fit."

"I may as well tell you, for you'll find out sometime anyway," said Mike. "I came over on one of the Australian ships."

"You were a convict?"

"Yes, I killed a man. . .years ago in England. It was a fair fight, but he was English and I was Irish. I was found guilty and deported to that godforsaken land. But I served my time out— seven years—and now I'm here. . .and I aim to stay."

"I'm an exile, too—disinherited."

"I thought I detected a bit of the bitter in you."

"No matter," said Darcy, shrugging. "I'd like to ask you one question, though, if you don't mind."

"Go ahead," said Mike, and took another long swig.

"Those two—they seemed afraid of you. I can't help wondering why."

Before Darcy had finished speaking, Mike drew a knife from a scabbard hanging down his back inside his shirt and neatly pinned an upturned ace of hearts to one of the gambling tables halfway

231

across the room. "Does that answer your question?" he asked, leisurely walking over and pulling the well-honed blade out of the table. "In Australia you lived by your wits or because you were quicker and stronger than anybody else. Yes. . .they were afraid of me. God, how I wish I could forget it!"

Darcy knew the discussion was closed and remained silent. But he wondered what the Sydney Ducks had meant by *territory*. Finally he asked Mike, "Is there some place you can get a woman in Sydney Town?"

"Not if you value your life. Better try Little Chile. I'll tell you what, I'll close up and we'll go over there together. Margarita should have a friend to suit you." He downed his drink and began to smile in the way of the old Mike.

Soon after the night of the ball Ma began detecting signs of restlessness in Pa, and one evening as they were preparing for bed he finally said, "Guess I'd better be getting back to the diggings if I'm going to make that strike before winter sets in."

"I guess so," said Ma a little sadly. "When you planning on going?"

"Tomorrow," said Pa.

It was the answer she had expected, but Ma went on playing the game they always played before Pa went off on one of his journeys. "You got everything you need?" she asked.

"Yes, I guess so. I'll miss you, girl. You know that, don't you?" he said, taking her in his arms.

Ma smiled at the word *girl* and gave him a hug and kiss. "I'll miss you, too, but I'll keep thinking of the day you'll be back with all that gold."

"You know," said Pa, his eyes lighting up, "I just got a feeling that this time—that just maybe—"

"Yes, Pa. What time do you want breakfast?"

"Early. We'll be taking the first steamer up to Sacramento. I guess I forgot to tell you—I'm taking Sam and Rip with me. Guess we'll have to wait to build the rest of your hotel till winter."

"That's all right. What about Darcy?"

"Says he's not ready yet. Don't know what's the matter with that boy—doesn't seem to have gold fever at all!"

"I wouldn't be too sure about that," laughed Ma. "He'll probably be able to buy and sell all of us someday. He's lucky, too. With him along, you'd be sure and make that strike."

As they alighted with their belongings at the noisy and bustling San Francisco waterfront, Kevin, Holt, and Mirina looked in bewilderment at the strangest sight they had ever seen. All along the shore were stacked boxes and barrels; on the skeletal frames of wharves workmen swarmed, madly pounding boards together, while other partially constructed piers looked totally abandoned; stretching several hundred feet out into the bay was a long wharf which stood out both for its look of solidity and because the work on it seemed to be progressing in an orderly manner. Picking their way through warehouses made of canvas and piles of goods covered by nothing but muslin awnings, they finally came out on an equally curious street faced by canvas stores with no fronts, sporting signs in languages they couldn't recognise.

Holt looked around in dismay, then braved, "I wonder if there's a hotel nearby?"

Seeking something familiar and substantial, the three newcomers walked up the street not stopping once to inquire about lodging in any of the tents labeled HOTEL they passed. As they progressed toward the outskirts of town, Mirina despaired they would ever find a place to stay, for it was painfully obvious no provision for women had been made in this tent city. Then they rounded a corner, and she stopped in relief before a brand new solid white painted building with a large gingerbread-trimmed portico, adorned with a row of alternating red and green ship's lights, jutting out in front of it. Standing on the porch was an older woman giving directions to two men who were mounting a sign reading, BROWN PALACE HOTEL—ROOM AND BOARD.

Noting Mirina's stare, Ma Brown asked, "Well, how do you like it? I had a dickens of a time getting it I can tell you."

"Do you have any rooms?" blurted out Mirina.

"It just happens I do," answered Ma. "and you're lucky. I usually have a waiting list. But there's been a mad rush to the mines the last week. Want to get in their last licks before winter sets in. Do you have any money?"

"Yes, ma'am," interjected Holt "We can pay."

"That's fine," beamed Ma. "I'm Mrs. Brown, but most folks call me Ma. Come on in and sign the register."

Darcy noted Mirina with particular interest as he entered the dining room that evening. "Who is she, Ma?" he asked.

"She's Mrs. Holt Compton, so keep that roving eye under control," said Ma. "The dark one's her husband."

"All right, but I still want to meet them."

"There's room at their table—providing they'll have you," said Ma, and led him across the room.

Mirina nodded politely when Ma introduced him, but made no effort to be charming. Then Kevin said, "Glad to have you join us."

"Sure," said Holt and resumed stuffing himself with stew, fresh white bread, butter, and milk. "I haven't tasted anything so good since I left home," he apologized.

Though Mirina had attracted him to the newcomers' table, Darcy soon recognized it was Kevin who shared with him his craving for power and dedication to achieve it. And instead of going to Mike's after dinner, he accompanied him to the parlor to become better acquainted.

While they talked, Darcy noticed Kevin kept casting furtive glances toward Mirina. Looking from one to the other, he wondered what existed between these two. There was something, he was sure.

Within a day Holt noticed that Darcy's name was included whenever Kevin talked about going to the mines. He blamed Mirina for this unwelcome addition to their partnership and vented his jealousy by quarreling with her and refusing to consider taking her to Sacramento with him.

"You'll not tie me down any more!" he exploded.

"But what am I to do?" she complained.

"I don't give a damn what you do!"

"Don't leave me, Holt."

"I wish I could. I wish to God I'd never laid eyes on you!"

"Holt!" she started to cry.

"You're staying here and that's final!" he bellowed and slammed out of the room.

November was cleaning the room next door and heard the entire quarrel. Full of pity for the sobbing girl, she rushed in to comfort her. At the first sympathetic words she had heard in many a day, Mirina spilled out all of her now real fright, lone-liness, and longing. "I'm going to have a baby, and he's leaving me all alone. He never did love me—and I don't love him either."

"But a baby," sighed November, "That will make everything all right. . .you'll see."

"No it won't," wept Mirina. "It may not even be his!"

November was shocked by the implication behind this ad-mission. If the baby wasn't Holt's, whose was it? The tall, blonde Kevin perhaps? She too had observed the stolen looks the two gave each other.

"It doesn't matter," said Mirina bleakly. "I'll die anyway, and he'll never know." Methodically she began to dry her eyes.

November was not sure what Mirina was talking about. "Doesn't Mr. Compton know you're going to have a baby?" she ventured.

"No, and it wouldn't make any difference if he did. You heard him. . ."

"No matter what you think, you should tell him."

"Oh, spare me those old sayings about a baby making all of the difference. Yes, it makes a difference all right. . .you're just that more firmly tied down."

"Then I take it you aren't planning on dying," said November slyly.

Mirina began to laugh. "No, I guess not," she finally said. "But I am scared."

"Then you should stay here in San Francisco. Doctors may be scarce here, but they're even scarcer at the mines."

"I know. But I have the feeling that if I don't go with him, I may never see him again."

Again November wasn't sure if Mirina meant Holt or Kevin. "I wouldn't worry. They nearly all come back," she said.

Holt stormed down to Flaggerty's to find that Darcy had finally allowed himself to be persuaded to join their party in the quest of the golden fleece and was eager to be off.

"How soon can we start?" he asked.

"Right away, I hope," said Kevin. "I don't have any money to waste like you and Holt do."

"You can leave me out of that," said Holt. "I have a wife to support." He poured himself a drink from the untouched bottle on the table, tossed it off, and quickly poured himself another. By the dark color in his cheeks and his heavy frown, Kevin knew he had had another fight with Mirina.

"How about leaving for Sacramento the day after tomorrow?" Kevin asked him. "That should give us at least a couple of months at the digs. They say the weather doesn't get really nasty till about mid-November."

"The sooner, the better," said Holt.

Holt remained at Flaggerty's drinking into the evening, so at dinner Kevin felt he should tell Mirina they were starting for the mines within a day. To his surprise she replied, "It's about time."

"He says you're to stay here," said Kevin.

"He's flattering himself if he thinks I have any intention of doing anything else," sniffed Mirina. "And you can tell him that he'd better find a lot of gold because I intend to be very rich."

"You can tell him yourself," said Kevin.

"I will," she said, and smiled her tantalizing smile, leaving him to wonder why she suddenly had given up her idea of accompanying them.

During his sojourn at the hotel, Darcy had discovered Ma was an expert on mining and the equipment needed for it. So that evening he took Kevin into the kitchen and asked her if she would help them.

"Glad to," she replied. "I'll make you each a shopping list. That way you'll save time and won't be duplicating each other. And mind you, shop in the stores I list. They're where you'll get the best bargains."

Though the barest of essentials, the supplies they purchased the next day cost nearly seven hundred and fifty dollars, and Kevin dolefully wondered if he ever would be out of Holt's debt.

Mirina said nothing further about accompanying Holt to Sacramento, and in gratitude he gave her a thousand dollars. "That should take care of everything you'll need until I get back in November," he said. "And by that time we should have a lot more."

"I hope so," said Mirina.

"I really do think that it's best for you to stay here."

"Of course. I didn't want to go anyway."

She even accompanied Ma and November down to the landing to see the prospectors off on the steamer. While the others talked animatedly, she and Holt stood awkwardly aside finding they had nothing to say. Finally she gave him a perfunctory farewell kiss, and they parted—almost total strangers—except for the still invisible child and a curtain of misunderstanding that lay between them.

Two short blasts of the whistle announced that the steamer was ready to churn out onto the bay and head for the Sacramento River.

CHAPTER **22** THE DIGGINGS★★★★★★★★★★★★★★★★★★★★★★★★★★★★

Early on the morning after celebrating Gray's birthday Gray, Tim, and Henry left the sycamore grove in search of mining equipment and information. Goldie remained in camp to give the wagon a long overdue cleaning. An hour after the men had gone Dora came over with some gossip. "I been talkin' to the folks in the Pittsburgh over there," she said, pointing. "They know the Milfords. . .seems our train was parked in this very same grove last week."

"Are the Milfords here?" asked Goldie eagerly.

"Sara and Mary are. They're workin' in one of them roomin' tents we saw yesterday. . .the Liberty Hotel, I think they said."

"Oh, come on, Dora, let's go see them and find out about the train."

"You go on. I still have a lot to do," Dora said. "Tim wants to sell the wagon and mules and get us settled on a little piece of ground before he goes off explorin'. Then when he gets back, gold or no gold, we'll have a start on our farm."

"I'm going to go see Mr. Ogilvy. He kept saying how hard help was to get last night, and I've had plenty of experience as a waitress."

"Workin' in a public place. I don't know. . .could be dangerous."

"But I have to have a job while Gray's gone," said Goldie. "And I don't know how to do much else."

In town Goldie soon found the Liberty Hotel. Inside Mary

Milford was vigorously sweeping the plank floor. She dropped her broom and shrieked, "Ma. . .Ma!" The two girls threw their arms around each other.

Sara Milford came running in from the back of the building, then stopped short, her eyes glistening with sudden tears. "Goldie Baxter, you're a sight for sore eyes," she gasped. Then wiping her eyes with a corner of her apron, she ventured hesitantly, "And Gray. . .?"

"Oh, he's fine," said Goldie. "Dr. Marshall cured him back at Fort Bridger. He and Tim Cunningham and Henry Bowles are out getting equipped for the mines right now."

"Henry?" questioned Mrs. Milford. "I thought he was with Rachel and Chuck Colby."

"They left him when he was sick," Goldie explained. She told them of the journey across the desert and how they had rescued Henry.

"That Rachel's a Jezebel," said Mrs. Milford. "Mark you, she'll come to no good end."

"Where are Dan and Mr. Milford?"

"We heard men were getting real pay dirt up along the Mokelumne River," said Mary. "So they went up that way."

"Now tell me about everybody else."

"I'm surprised at you, Goldie," said Mary. "You haven't asked about Zack. . .and he bein' sweet on you too."

Goldie felt the color rise in her face. "Oh, Mary," she said, "he was just being kind to me. But now that you've brought it up, where is he?"

"Somewhere up above Auburn," said Mrs. Milford. "He's got a big Mexican land grant up there."

"Yes, I remember," said Goldie.

"Anyway, he's got to register it with the United States Government now that California's going to become a state. So he's pretty busy."

"Is it really?" asked Goldie eagerly. "Is California really going to become a state?"

"Yes," said Mary. "They're holding a constitutional convention in Monterey right now."

"Oh, how exciting! Just imagine being citizens in a brand new state."

"Yes," said Mary. "We're aiming to stay. If Pa and Dan do well, we're going to buy a farm near here. This is rich bottom land. Zack says there'll be a lot of people to feed out here in a few years. In fact, they're already here. He's going to run cattle on his ranch, and I think he's apt to get rich."

Goldie looked at her keenly. Was she stuck on the famous guide? This thought disturbed her, but before she could figure out why, Darcy walked into the hotel. In his blue broadcloth suit, white ruffled shirt, and tall hat, he looked to her like the archetypical gambler. All he needs is a gold-headed cane, she thought. But as she sized up his features she concluded that, without question, he was the handsomest man she had ever seen.

"This is Goldie Baxter...Darcy Dupres," said Mary. "Goldie got in yesterday."

Goldie smiled at Darcy then turned back to the Milfords. "I've got to run, but I'll drop by again as soon as I get settled."

Excited by Goldie's copper-colored hair and deep blue eyes, Darcy decided he would like to further the acquaintance. "May I see you to wherever you're going, Miss Goldie?" he asked. Goldie glanced inquiringly at Mrs. Milford.

"He's all right," said Sara. "Just another young'un with gold fever. Come upriver from San Francisco with a couple of others day before yesterday."

"Oh, you've been *there,*" said Goldie.

"Yes, do you know San Francisco?"

"No...but it has such a beautiful name."

"Maybe someday it will have the beauty to match its name. But for now, it's no different from this."

On the way to Horace Ogilvy's Darcy told her of his home in Louisiana and what he had been doing since his arrival in California. Goldie, a little overawed, told him about herself and Gray.

She stopped in front of the La Portal Restaurant. "Thanks for escorting me," she said demurely. "I hope we'll meet again."

"Is this where you live?" he asked in surprise.

"Gracious no," she answered. "Right now my home's a covered wagon in a grove of sycamore trees near the river. I'm hoping Mr. Ogilvy will hire me so I can earn some money while Gray's off prospecting."

"I'm leaving for the diggings tomorrow," said Darcy. "But I'll find you again."

"I hope so. And good luck to you."

Horace Ogilvy was overjoyed to have an experienced waitress. She arranged to start the next day, then she hurried back to camp to tell Dora.

Later in the day Gray bounced in. "Tim's buying a farm east of here!" he said. "We met a man who wants to be rid of it. It's even got a house for Dora and the kids." Suddenly he stopped in his recital. "What're you going to do, Goldie?" he asked.

"I've got a job with Mr. Ogilvy," she beamed.

"But that's no different from home. Waiting on people all of the time. . .you might as well be back in Indiana." The smile slid from her face, and he quickly amended, "I mean, if we sold the wagon and mules you wouldn't have to work."

"I don't want to sit around. Aunt Opal would never approve. Besides, I think the wagon and mules are going to come in handy."

"How?"

"Well, in the first place, you've got to have transportation and something to pack your gear on when you go to the mines."

"You mean mounts and pack mules. But what good's the wagon?"

"Maybe we could run freight to the mines like the traders do."

"I don't want to be a freighter. . .I want to find gold."

"I don't mean right away. But if people are so anxious to buy the wagon, maybe we could hire it out."

"All right, we'll try it. . .at least until I get back in November. They say it rains something fierce in the hills then, and you can't do a thing."

It seemed no time before Gray, Tim, and Henry were outfitted for prospecting and it was time to say goodbye. Goldie stood in her tent in back of the La Portal Restaurant holding Gray's hand and winking back the tears.

"You will be careful?" she said.

"Sure," he answered. "And you, too." He gave her a long hug, mounted his mule, and started down the alley. At the corner he looked back. Goldie's arm was raised in a farewell salute.

Henry, Tim and Gray rode forth across the broad California central valley toward the mountains rising in the distance. They were headed for Jackson, where they had heard men were taking

240

out thousands along the Mokelumne and Calaveras rivers. From there they followed a stream dotted with the canvas tents of the prospectors up into the hills.

Riding along, Gray became curious about the wooden troughs several feet long that some of the men were using and drew up by one to get a better look. A man leaped out of the hole below his elongated sluice box and pulled a dirty bandana from his pocket to wipe the sweat from his face.

"This work's hotter 'n hellfire," he said good-naturedly.

"Would you mind telling me what that thing is?" asked Gray.

"You must be new," said the man. "This your first try?"

"Yeah," mumbled Gray. He hated to admit that he was a greenhorn.

"Well, this here's called a Long Tom. Come on over and Pete and me'll show you how it works. I'm Matt Farley." An equally grimy miner looked up and nodded. Tim and Henry joined Gray to watch the sluicing operation.

"First we pick and shovel the dirt outa this hole," said Matt. "And now that we've got the 'Tom' full, Pete's gonna open that little gate and let the water run through." Gray saw that a small stream that had been diverted away from the trough was now flowing through it.

"If we had more men we could keep the water runnin' through all the time," Matt continued. "But since there's just the two of us, we gotta do it this way." He picked up a hoe. "Now we move the dirt and gravel about, and the gold'll sink and catch in these riffles." He pointed to cleats fastened to the bottom of the Long Tom at various intervals. "Then finally what's left falls into the riffle box below, and the water and dirt go out as tailings." Soon the load was washed and Matt closed the gate to the Long Tom, diverting the water once more. "Then at night we pan wash what's left in the riffle box and dig out what's caught in the cleats in the 'Tom'."

"You mean you don't see what you've got till the end of the day?" asked Gray.

"That's right," said Pete. "But since you look like you ain't seen any gold yet, I'll just dig around in here and see what I can find." Moving the sand around in the riffle box, Pete picked up some faintly gleaming grains and put them in his palm. "There," he said. "That's gold."

"Gee!" said Gray, his eyes shining. Here at last, lying in the palm of Pete's hand, was the gold he had come thousands of miles to find. The stories were all true. There was gold enough for everyone.

As Gray, Tim, and Henry continued up the mountain, they kept a sharp eye for any sign of gold. That evening in camp they wandered up and down the stream with their picks and gold pans. Every now and then one of them would wash a panful of dirt and gravel in the water in an unpracticed way. They found nothing.

From then on, climbing ever higher in their quest, they methodically covered the stream, searching for the elusive gold. There wasn't a trace anywhere. Though they became discouraged at night, at the first streak of light in the morning they would be up and away.

Then one day Gray tethered his mule and turned up a small dry ravine cut into the side of the hills by the rushing waters of the winter rains. A few yards in he looked up and above his head saw something palely gleaming in a crevice. He quickly shinnied up the steep side of the acclivity, whipped out his knife, and began scraping at the rock. Within moments the prize was in his hand. It was unmistakably a nugget about the size of the end of his thumb. He let out a loud, "Whoo-ee!" and tore pell-mell back to the main stream. Tim and Henry dropped their picks. Gray was dancing up and down, shouting, "I've found it! I've found it! It's here. It's here!"

"God! That looks like gold all right!" cried Henry. "Where? Where?"

Gray led them back into the cut in the hill, and they began combing the ravine for further signs of the precious metal. Again Gray was the lucky one. Within a few feet of the place where he had discovered the nugget, he found an outcropping of gold.

Tim looked at the flecks of yellow on the surface of the ground where Gray had scraped the dirt away and choked, "Glory be. . . you've made a strike!"

"The gold must've washed down and caught in these rocks here," pointed out Gray.

"Yep, it must be a placer all right," said Henry, trying to sound experienced.

"And there's got to be more down there in the ravine bed," said Tim.

242

"And maybe a vein up there someplace," added Gray. He looked up the side of the mountain.

"Well, boys," said Tim, "it looks like we've got our claim. We'd better stake it." They drove some stakes into the ground around the strike and put their mark on them.

For the next five days they worked feverishly to construct a Long Tom and some boxes to haul the ore from the ravine down to the stream. At last they commenced mining but found the earth did not give up its riches easily. They dug, they hauled, they riffled the dirt, clumsily at first, but finally with the skill of veteran miners.

When Tim hefted their sack of gold at the end of their first full week of mining, he pronounced, "It's several pounds, boys. I can't believe it. If this claim keeps yielding like this, we really are going to be rich."

"I think we've earned a reward," said Gray. "Why don't we go down to Little Flats for the evening."

"All right," said Tim. "I've been longing for a good smoke. Maybe now I can afford some tobacco for my pipe."

In the little settlement five miles down the mountain, the Saturday night celebrating was well under way. A rough mining camp, Little Flats consisted of a few shaky board buildings and dozens of the now familiar tents. There were two stores and two restaurants, but all of the other structures housed saloons and fandango halls. Several thousand men were jammed into the few acres of space, all armed with guns and knives, and all starved for women, entertainment, and the comforts of their now sentimentally remembered homes. The saloon keepers, gamblers, and harlots were eager to fill the lonely miners' needs—for a price.

Engulfed in the tide of men, his ears unaccustomed to the sounds of the loud laughter and strident shouts jangling from the saloons, Gray felt ill at ease, and his first impulse was to retreat to the quiet and peace of their claim. But Henry's eyes began to shine, and he darted eager looks into the open tents where everybody seemed to be having such a good time.

"Let's go in one of these places," he said.

Surprised, Gray answered, "I thought you didn't drink."

"Well, tonight we're supposed to be celebrating, aren't we?" countered Henry

"You go ahead," said Tim. "I want to price tobacco in that store down there."

Gray said, "I think I'll go with Tim. We'll join you later."

Though the majority of men in the town were Americans, Gray reflected he had never seen so many foreign people in one place. The few Spanish señoritas looked exciting dressed in their bright frocks with swirling skirts and multicolored shawls, and he gaped at two Orientals wearing round black hats, their hair braided in queues hanging down over their high-collared blue coats. The cadence of their language sounded quite musical to him, and he wondered what they were talking about to each other. They passed some swarthy-looking men who, though dressed like the Yankees, were speaking another unknown tongue. Fascinated by these foreigners, Gray was reluctant to leave the street. Nonetheless, he followed Tim into the store.

Inside, by the light of the oil lamps, he saw a remarkable assortment of merchandise, considering the remoteness of the town and the difficulty of transport. On a shelf of tinned goods, he read on a label, "Pears." His mouth watered for a taste of the fruit, and he slowly reached for the can. Then suddenly he withdrew his hand as if it had been slapped. Further down the label he had read the price. "Four dollars!" he yelled. "Why, that can't be!"

In consternation he ran to the back of the store and interrupted Tim and the storekeeper. "Is that can of pears really four dollars?" he asked.

"That's right, mister," said the genial proprietor. "And it's a darn reasonable price, too. . .seeing how hard they are to get."

"But if we had to pay those prices, we wouldn't make anything but a bare living from our claims," protested Gray.

"Then you'd better live plainer, sonny, or find yourself a richer claim," chuckled the merchant.

At this moment Henry burst into the store. "Gray!" he shouted. "You'll never believe it!"

"Believe what?" asked Gray.

"Come on over to The Golden Bon Bon. Just wait till you see."

Gray blinked in amazement when he entered the saloon. Rachel Colby stood on a platform clad in a short skirt and cerise tights, revealing more leg than he had ever seen before on a woman. She was singing, but the wild cheers of the men from the mines were not for her voice but for the beautiful face, the figure, and the fine show of leg. At the completion of her number she blew a kiss to

244

her audience and retired to the rear of the saloon to the accompaniment of prolonged applause and foot stamping.

Before Gray had recovered his equanimity, she reappeared and headed straight for the table. "Well, if it isn't Gray Baxter," she said. "And Mr. Cunningham. And you, too, Henry. . .I'm glad to see you made it."

"No thanks to you," muttered Henry.

"What are you doing here?" asked Tim. "Did something happen to your husband?"

"Oh, no, Chuck's prospecting around here. But I've found out how you really get the gold." She gestured to the roomful of men. "They'll give me anything for a fond look."

"Oh?" said Tim, "and what does Chuck think of all this?"

"Whatever I want him to think," she replied.

"You haven't changed a bit," said Gray.

"For you I might," she said, reaching over and patting his cheek.

"Might do what?" asked a husky voice. They all turned to see Chuck Colby.

"Nothing," said Rachel. "Why don't you say hello to our old friends?"

"*You* again," said Chuck to Gray. "Still trying to fool around with my wife."

"I don't want anything to do with your wife," said Gray. He stood up. "Come on, Tim. . .Henry."

"Oh, no you don't," said Chuck. He swung at Gray and connected with his chin.

"Will you stop making an ass of yourself," hissed Rachel.

"Get out of the way," yelled Chuck. "This flea's been hopping around my bed too long."

"All right. . .all right. . .all right," barked the saloon keeper as he ran up with a gun. "If you wanna fight. . .outside!" He herded the group to the door. Chuck flailed at Gray with his fists all the way out. But when they reached the street, he produced a knife.

"Been a killin' here every Saturday night for five weeks," commented a passerby.

"What?" questioned Tim. "A killin'?"

"That's right, stranger," said the man matter-of-factly. "Looks like there's gonna be another one."

Gray had no desire to fight Chuck, and he had never used a

weapon against another man. He didn't even think to draw the knife he wore in his belt. But a voice penetrated his consciousness from the crowd. "Draw your knife! Get your own knife, man!" Grasping the handle and slowly drawing out his weapon, he faced Chuck. Gray took a cut across the back of the hand and, in turn, sliced Chuck's left arm. Enraged, Chuck dived, his knife upraised for the kill. But Gray jumped aside and Chuck fell in the dirt. Without thinking, Gray grabbed a board from a pile of construction material at hand and brought it down hard on Chuck's head.

When Chuck did not rise, Tim said, "Come on, lad, we'd best be going."

"Drop by the next time you're in town," said Rachel, who was languidly leaning in the doorway of the saloon.

A tall dark man stepped up to Gray and handed him a handkerchief. "Here, you'd better take this for your hand," he said.

"Thanks," said Gray. Tim began binding up the wound.

"Say, don't I know you from somewhere?" The stranger peered intently at Gray.

"No, I don't believe so. My name's Gray Baxter."

"But of course. Baxter. . .no wonder you look familiar. I met your sister in Sacramento. I'm Darcy Dupres."

"Oh, yes," said Gray. "Goldie told me about you. You working near here?"

"Yes, my partners and I have a claim a few miles upriver."

"By golly, so do we. We must be neighbors." He held up his bandaged hand. "I'll return this as soon as I wash it, and if you ever need anything, come and look us up."

"Thanks, I'll remember that," said Darcy and went back into The Golden Bon Bon to continue gambling.

The claim Darcy had staked with Holt and Kevin was paying poorly, and at present only his skill with cards was keeping the partnership solvent. The day after Gray's fight they assessed their claim as played out, and Kevin suggested they break camp and move farther upstream. Holt and Darcy quickly agreed. On the way up the mountain they passed the claim now named The Little Goldie, where Tim, Henry, and Gray were hard at work building a cabin.

"Looks like you're preparing to stay awhile," observed Darcy.

"The nights are gettin' a mite chilly," said Tim. "And we decided we might as well be comfortable."

"Our claim played out," said Holt. "We're looking for a new one."

"There should be pay dirt higher up, judging from what we've found here," said Gray.

"That's what we're hoping," said Kevin.

"Good luck," called Gray as the three headed on up the mountain.

During the next week construction of the cabin proceeded at such a pace that on the following Sunday night they slept under a roof for the first time since March.

"I'd almost forgotten what it was like," said Gray.

"What?" asked Tim.

"To have a home."

"Me too," said Henry. "God, that fire feels good."

From then until mid-November they worked The Little Goldie, never ceasing to marvel at the amount of gold they extracted from the sluice box every night. Their take now filled several bags, and not one of them could lift the entire amount anymore. They had a tunnel leading into the deposit and had washed away a small mountain of tailings. Still the claim was yielding richly. Gray's discovery had turned out to be a real glory hole.

One day in the middle of November the weather changed the even tenor of their routine. A chilling wind began to blow, biting through their flannel shirts and woolen jackets, and dark ominous clouds gathered above them. That night the rain began pouring down so fast and heavy that it seemed as if the sky had turned into a mighty river. In the morning in order to preserve their tools and keep the claim from being washed away, they were forced to go out into the flood. While Henry was shoring up the sides of the mine, Gray and Tim were carrying the Long Tom to a shed they had built near the cabin. Suddenly Tim slipped on the puddled rocks and fell down several feet into the ravine. Gray could not hold the Long Tom by himself and fell with it on top of Tim. Quickly he scrambled to his feet and frantically began pulling at the battered wooden trough.

"Are you all right?" he asked.

"I think I did something to my leg," said Tim, wincing in pain. Henry came sliding down the bank to help, and together they carried Tim back to the cabin.

247

"It feels like it's broke," said Tim as he felt his leg.

"Then we better put a splint on it," said Gray.

They bound Tim's leg between two boards, then Gray and Henry once more went out into the storm. Tim was quiet when they returned to the cabin two hours later. Gray looked at him apprehensively.

"It hurts bad, doesn't it?" he asked.

"This?" said Tim, rousing out of his reverie. "No, not too much. No, I've been thinking maybe this was a blessing in disguise. I really ought to be gettin' back to Dora and the young'uns. They need a man down there to run the farm."

"But the claim's still paying good," protested Gray. "You don't want to give up your share now, do you?"

"I'm not going to be much use for quite a while with this, and I'm satisfied. All I ever wanted was a chance at a decent living. I think my family and I'll have that chance now."

"How much do you reckon we have?" asked Henry.

"Could be between sixty-five and seventy pounds there."

"God!" said Henry. "That's several thousand dollars apiece."

"It isn't payin' as much as it was at first " said Tim. "But there's still plenty more there for the two of you."

Henry stared down at the floor. "I've been thinking too," he said. "You know that store I was telling you about back home? Well. . .with this money, I could buy it. And I've sort of missed my folks. And you remember me telling you about Beth? I've missed her, too. I guess I'm ready to go home."

Gray looked from one to the other. Suddenly he felt very much alone, and his longing to see Goldie nearly overwhelmed him. "When. . .when do you want to leave?" he gulped.

"As soon as this blasted rain stops and I can straddle a mule," said Tim.

"I'd like to leave right away too," said Henry. "I've seen enough of the elephant."

But the rain continued, and on the second evening after Tim's accident, they were sitting before the fire wondering if it was ever going to stop when they were aroused by a knock on the door. Gray opened it and peered out into the dripping darkness. Draped between Holt and Kevin was the unconscious form of Darcy Dupres.

"The whole damn side of the mountain caved in on us," said Kevin.

"What's the matter with him?" asked Henry.

"He's got a fever," answered Holt. "Been out of his head for two days."

"Were you able to save your dust?" asked Tim.

"What little there was of it," answered the embittered Kevin.

"But we've lost everything else—our tent, our supplies, our equipment. . .everything—except the mules," said Holt.

The next day dawned cold but clear. During the night Darcy's fever had broken, and though weak, he was rational.

"Since you're back with us," said Kevin, "Holt and I'd better see if we can salvage anything from our camp."

"What happened?" asked Darcy.

"We got caught in a slide."

"Oh, yes. . .the rain. . .I vaguely remember. Can I help?"

"No, you'd better stay here. We'll bring back what's left. That is, if there *is* anything left. Come on, Holt."

They went out, and Gray said, "I'll check the damage to The Little Goldie."

Tim looked after him a moment, then he swung his stiff leg off his cot.

"Here, you shouldn't do that," said Henry.

"Got to see if I can manage," said Tim. " 'Cause if it's still clear tomorrow, I think I'd better try and get down to Sacramento."

"I'll come with you."

"Do you think the mining's finished until spring?" asked Darcy.

"Don't know about that," said Henry. "I'm giving up mining for good."

"You're leaving your claim?"

"Yep," said Tim. "That is, me and Henry are. Gray's staying, though."

Darcy nodded, an idea taking form in his head.

When Gray returned, Darcy asked tentatively, "I don't suppose you've given much thought to taking on some new partners, have you?"

Surprised and hesitant, Gray said, "I really don't know how much more there is here. And actually the claim belongs to all three of us."

"I meant we'd buy in," said Darcy.

"What do you think?" Gray asked his partners.

"If you're willin' to take them on, I'm willin' to sell," said Tim.

"Me too," said Henry.

Gray had liked Darcy from the moment he had met him in Little Flats, but he knew nothing about Holt and Kevin. "Are they good workers?" he asked.

"They sure are, even if we do have little to show for it."

"I don't much relish working alone. So if you can settle with Tim and Henry, I'll agree."

"There's one other thing," said Tim. "Gray's the one who discovered this claim, and he's only had to split the take three ways. If you all come in, it would be a four-way split and I don't think that's quite fair. Gray's got a sister, and I propose she be made a full-share partner. That way, if anything happens to him, she'll be taken care of."

"That sounds reasonable," said Darcy. "Now how much do you want for your share of the partnership?"

"I think about two hundred and fifty dollars apiece for Henry and me would be fair," said Tim. Henry nodded.

"All right," said Darcy, "we'll buy you out for five hundred dollars."

"Now I'll just draw up the terms," said Tim. "And if Holt and Kevin agree, we'll all sign it."

When Holt and Kevin returned they agreed to the terms of the new partnership and everybody signed the paper Tim had drawn up. Holt and Kevin went along with Henry and Tim to Sacramento the next morning, for Gray had persuaded his new partners to stay on and work through the bad weather, and they needed supplies.

In Sacramento the La Portal had become a favorite gathering place of the businessmen, and from their talk and speculations, Goldie had learned that there was a great deal of money being made in catering to the needs of the burgeoning California population. "Trade and commerce. . .that's the ticket to wealth in this gold rush," she heard reiterated again and again. And the prosperous look of these merchants gave credence to their point of view. Why not join in the lucrative business of supplying the miners, she thought and began drawing up plans for opening a store in one of the gold towns.

Anxious to sell her idea to Gray, she hoped he soon would return for the winter. But more than this, she longed to see him. She had never been so lonely. The protracted rain of the last few days that had wreaked such havoc in the mountains had inundated

Sacramento as well, turning the streets into rivers of mud. Goldie's tent behind the restaurant leaked incessantly, and she wondered if she would ever get rid of the dampness and chill that penetrated her body. Mr. Ogilvy, already building his permanent restaurant of wood, planned a second story with rooms and had promised her one of them. But the thought of this future dry haven did little to alleviate her present misery. Dissatisfied with her work and everything else, she longed for some of the excitement she had come to California to find. Just when she thought she couldn't stand it any longer, Tim and Henry rode in with Holt and Kevin. They all talked at once, but Goldie finally made out that a new partnership had been formed.

"I was about to go up to the mines anyway," she announced. "And now that I'm a partner I guess I'd better."

"Gray didn't say anything about that," said Kevin hesitantly.

"I can pull my weight," she insisted.

"Well, if you say so," said Holt. "Since you're a partner I guess you've got the right."

"We've got a list of supplies to bring back," said Kevin. "Where can we buy them?"

"I know the best places," snapped Goldie. "Let's see the list." Kevin meekly handed it over.

"We're to bring them back in the wagon," recited Holt, overwhelmed by the crisp, businesslike manner of this new partner.

"We'll do more than that. We'll take two wagons," she announced.

"Two!" yelped Kevin. "What are you going to take up?"

"Don't worry," said Goldie. "I don't have much in household goods. How big a town is Little Flats?"

"I'd say four or five thousand."

"Has it got a store?"

"Yes, two of them. But they're so high on everything we decided we'd do better to buy here."

"That's my point," triumphed Goldie. "We're going to open a store. I've been making a list and I know exactly what to stock it with. The money in this gold rush is in commerce. We've got a good beginning. . .some capital, some mules, and a wagon. And I know where we can get another wagon cheap."

Carried away by Goldie's enthusiasm, Holt exclaimed, "I believe she's right! Look at the price of everything. We haven't made expenses yet."

"It's a cinch I haven't done anything but get deeper in debt since I got here," said Kevin. "So if you're for it, I'll go along too."

Within a few days the two wagons were loaded with Goldie's household goods, including a precious cast-iron stove, and the supplies for the new store they would open in Little Flats. The trio plus Happy and the two cats made ready to depart on a damp, cloudy morning.

Horace Ogilvy said, "I hate to lose you, Goldie. And I hope you'll consider the La Portal your home whenever you're in Sacramento. I should have my building up before long, and there'll always be a room for you."

"Thank you, Horace. You may be seeing me more often than you think if this store sells things the way I think it's going to."

"It will be my pleasure," said the small, upright man. "Good luck."

Kevin and Holt jogged the reins of their mules, and the two wagons churned out into the slippery, muddy street.

CHAPTER **23** CHRISTMAS, 1849✶✶✶✶✶✶✶✶✶✶✶✶✶✶✶✶✶✶✶✶✶✶✶✶

When they reached Little Flats, Kevin volunteered to stay with the wagons and the goods while Holt took Goldie and some of the houshold supplies packed on mules up to the cabin.

As they rounded a bend Holt pointed high above them. "There it is," he said. "You can see it from here."

Goldie looked up and said, "Come on. . .let's hurry." With Happy bounding ahead of her, she prodded her mule up the slipper trail until she finally reached the clearing where the cabin stood.

"Gray—Gray—where are you, Gray?" she shouted.

Happy barked joyously and dashed up the ravine to where Gray and Darcy were working at the mine. Throwing down his shovel,

252

Gray hugged the quivering dog. Then he rushed into the clearing and swooped up Goldie in a giant bear hug.

"Well, golly, Sis," he said, setting her down and drawing the back of his hand across his eyes. "Well, golly. . .I sure have missed you!"

"Nice to see you again, Miss Baxter," said Darcy, who had followed Gray down. "Where's Kevin?"

"Oh, he's down at Little Flats with the rest of the stuff," said Holt.

"Stuff?" asked Darcy and Gray in unison.

"Yes," said Holt. "We've decided to become merchants. It was Goldie's idea, but Kevin and I thought it sounded good."

"We're going to open a store in Little Flats," said Goldie.

"A store?" exclaimed Gray.

"Yes," she continued. "We're going to be *Baxter, Compton, Adams,* and *Dupres.* Doesn't that sound impressive? The B.C.A. and D."

Gray, never more aware than now of the sharpness of his sister's mind, was staggered by this announcement. "But we've been doing great," he protested. "Didn't Tim and Henry tell you how much gold we've taken out so far?"

"Of course," said Goldie. "But money soon goes if you don't put it to work to make more money."

Gray wondered where his sister had picked up such terms. Though he needed time to adjust to this new Goldie and the shift in emphasis of the partnership, there was no time. The goods were down in Little Flats. Resentful that she had moved in and changed the direction of his enterprise without consulting him, he said, "Well, I suppose if you've brought up a lot of stuff, we'd better try and sell it."

"It's a smart idea," said Darcy. "Business is booming in Little Flats. Why shouldn't we have a piece of it?"

For the next few weeks Goldie tended store in a tent set up on the main street of town, while her partners began building a three-room addition to the cabin and constructing a permanent store out of native stone. Since working the mines had become impossible with the constant deluge of rain, many miners, deprived of their source of income, were glad to earn supplies by cutting and fitting stones for the new store.

Seeking a fortune had not been the only concern of the argonauts who had come to make their home in the rich land of California. The convention composed of twenty-three Northerners and fifteen Southerners that met in Monterey on September 1, 1849, had drawn up a constitution and proposal for statehood that was approved by an overwhelming majority of the migrants on November thirteenth.

One of the main provisions of the new constitution was that the state would permit no slavery of any kind within its boundaries. Even the Southern delegates to the convention had approved this measure, for competition in the gold fields was keen, and there was strong feeling that each man should work his own claim either alone or in the company of partners. They considered that anyone who kept slaves would have an unfair advantage, and those who had used Indians or even hired help found themselves outcasts.

In casting their ballots in favor of the constitution, the men had also elected their first state governor, a legislature, and representatives to Congress. The new legislature had immediately convened and elected the first two California senators and sent them to Washington.

From this time on those who resided in California considered it equal with all the other states in the union. But there was a long fight ahead before the new state would be accepted by Congress, for the United States was already embroiled in the bitter controversy between the North and the South over whether the new territory acquired at the close of the Mexican War in 1848 should be free or slave. Zachary Taylor, the victorious general of that war who was now President of the United States, recommended that the new states should be admitted as free or slave according to their constitutions. But this solution was not satisfactory to either side, and during his brief Administration the first threats of secession were voiced by the Southern states over the North's insistence that all of the new territory must be free. In its bid for statehood California was caught in this controversy, and its admission would be held up until the Compromise of 1850 was voted by Congress. To the young men so far away in California longing for statehood, the debate appeared equivocal. Since they had voted that their state be admitted as free, they felt the Congress of the United States had no right to interfere.

As a result of the strong feeling of the men backing the law forbidding slavery in the mines, Little Flats was in an uproar early in December. Sam Wolff, a miner who had a claim near the town, had brought in ten Chinese laborers. That Sam loafed in his cabin all day while the Celestials were out working the claim was rumored up and down the streams and ravines that centered around Little Flats. By Saturday night of the week Sam had brought in his laborers, the miners were in an ugly mood and called a meeting in The Golden Bon Bon. Gray was there with the others, no longer avoiding the saloon since Rachel and Chuck had long ago left Little Flats to search elsewhere for gold.

One man opened the meeting by saying, "Sam Wolff's using slave labor in the diggings, and it ain't lawful."

"Maybe they're not slaves," observed Darcy. "He could be paying them."

"Well, I been to San Francisco," said another man, "and a whole boatload of these 'coolies' come in. That's what they called 'em, 'coolies.' And there was dealers there sellin' them to anybody who had the price. If that ain't slave labor, I don't know what is."

"Well, we've got to be legal about this anyway," said Kevin. "I move we bring Sam Wolff down here and see what he's got to say."

"Agreed," said the man who had called the meeting. "And since Adams is so anxious to protect Sam's rights, I suggest he head a committee to bring him in."

"We'll do it first thing in the morning," said Kevin.

"But that's Sunday," protested one of the men.

"Good day for a trial," said another. "It won't interfere with business."

At the hastily convened citizens' court held in the saloon on Sunday morning, the man who had first brought the charges against Sam set himself up as judge and prosecutor. But this presumption did not bother the miners since most of them had already made up their minds Sam was guilty, and the trial was merely a formality.

Then Sam Wolff, nervously pulling his mustache, stood before the bench—a faro table—looking at the jury, which had been chosen by lot, seated to his right. The judge, now acting as prosecutor, said, "We hear you been usin' slaves to work your placer."

"I don't own them," protested Sam. "They're just goin' to work for me for two years to pay for their passage. I got papers back in my cabin to prove it."

"We ain't interested in that. You didn't hire 'em, so they're slaves." He turned to the jury. "You all heard what he said. Now you can consult and decide what to do about it."

The jurors retired to the rear of the saloon, and after several minutes of discussion during which they all agreed Sam was guilty, one man proposed that they run Sam off his claim as punishment.

"We gotta run him off," he said, "so's nobody else'll dare try a trick like that around here again." The others nodded their heads in agreement.

"What about his claim?" asked another juror.

"If we run him off, he forfeits it, naturally."

"I mean what happens to it?"

"The only fair way to dispose of it is by lot," said the self-appointed foreman. "We'll all draw lots for it."

A furious Sam listened to the judgment of the jury. He burst out, "It ain't fair. I paid good money for them coolies. All any of you want is to steal my claim!"

"You been given a chance to speak your piece," said the judge of the kangaroo court. "The jury's decided you broke the law, and as punishment you gotta forfeit your claim and go."

Sam knew he was outnumbered. "All right, I'll go. But you don't need to think you're the law. There ain't no law here. It's only because you're all against me that you can do this. A real court wouldn't a let you."

"If you ain't gone by this afternoon, we may think of somethin' else," said the judge menacingly.

Holt was troubled by the decision of the jury. He complained to Kevin as they were leaving, "This couldn't have happened back home. We took away his property. I don't like being part of it."

"Sam knew the law as well as the rest of us," said Kevin.

"Maybe so. But they could gang up on anybody like that. I'll be glad when there are real courts to appeal to."

"We'll be left hanging like this until we become a state," sighed Kevin.

On Monday the miners of Little Flats were presented with a new problem. The Chinese, not one of whom could speak a word of English, were placidly working the claim as Sam had taught them to do. Sam had simply left them behind.

At a hurriedly assembled gathering in The Golden Bon Bon, the man who had won the claim asked, "What'll we do?"

256

"Run 'em off like we did Sam," said yesterday's judge.

"But we can't do that," said Gray. "They're strangers here. They'd starve."

"They're not our responsibility," said one of the miners.

"Oh, yes they are," retorted Gray. "We ran off Sam."

"All right," said the judge. "Since you don't want us to run 'em off, we'll give 'em to you and your partners. *You* take care of 'em. But mind you, we don't want to see any of 'em working on your claim."

"Hell, Gray!" said Holt as the partners returned to the store. "I feel as responsible as you do about this. But I don't know if we *can* take care of them. How'll we feed them?"

"The same as we feed ourselves," said Gray.

"Admirable stand," said Darcy. "But there are ten of them. How are they going to earn their keep since we can't use them on the claim?"

"Earn their keep?" exclaimed Goldie. "Why right here in this store! I can use at least half of them right now."

"Say, that's an idea," said Kevin. "We can use them for lots of other things besides mining—maybe building the new store or helping on the addition to the cabin—lots of things."

"That's all dandy," said Darcy. "But you're forgetting one little thing. They don't speak any English."

"Never you mind about that," said Goldie. "I'll teach them. Just go and fetch them."

"Maybe you'd better come too," said Gray.

"All right," said Goldie, methodically taking off her apron. "But somebody's got to mind the store."

"Not me," said Darcy. "I'm going with you. I wouldn't miss this for the world."

"Kevin and I'll take care of the store," volunteered Holt.

The ten Chinese became quite excited when Goldie, Darcy, and Gray dismounted and approached them. First they pointed to Goldie and chattered to each other in their peculiar language. Then they pointed to Gray, smiling and nodding their heads.

"It's your hair," said Darcy. "They've probably never seen hair that color before."

One of the coolies stepped forward and bowed low. Automatically Goldie bowed back, followed somewhat hesitantly by Darcy and Gray.

Through various hand movements, violent shakes of their heads, and even on occasion foot movement, the three messengers finally conveyed the idea that Sam Wolff had gone and was not coming back. At first the Chinese were stunned. Then they began chattering violently, their voices rising in alarm. Goldie and Gray were puzzled and tried to calm them.

"I know what's the matter," said Darcy. "It's those papers Sam said he had showing he was entitled to work them. It'll be hard to make them leave here without those papers since that's the only thing they can identify themselves with."

While the dispossessed Orientals squatted down on their heels outside, Darcy, Gray, and Goldie searched the cabin for more than an hour. "He must have taken the papers with him," said Gray finally. "We've been over every inch of this place."

Goldie desperately looked around the one room once more and found her eye drawn to the fireplace. "We haven't tried there," she said.

Pouncing upon the fireplace, they skinned their fingers and broke their nails in an effort to find a loose stone, but all to no avail.

"There's only one place left," said Gray as he began scraping the cold ashes out onto the floor. Then he took out his knife and pried at the hearthstones. Finally he found a loose one and lifted it out, revealing a little tin box.

In it they found ten pieces of paper written in Chinese and English. There was nothing else in the box, but they placed it back in its hiding place. Clutching the papers, and dragging a hundred-pound bag of rice, which they correctly surmised was food for the Chinese, they emerged from the cabin. When Gray showed them the papers and gestured that they should follow him, the Chinese nodded their heads and gathered their few belongings.

"I want something understood about these men," said Gray, as they rode down the mountain. "We're going to pay them regular wages above their room and board."

"Isn't housing, feeding, and taking care of them enough? That's going to cost money, you know," said Darcy.

"No," said Gray. "If a man works, he deserves wages."

"You're going to find out it'll be a big responsibility just taking care of them. They can't have much ability to do anything or they

258

wouldn't have come over here as slaves," said Darcy.

"A man's not a slave just because he's poor," said Gray hotly.

"Well, I can see it's no use talking to you," said Darcy. "You'll have to find out for yourselves. But just remember. . .if you give them too much license, you may find them telling you what to do. I've seen it happen with planters back home who were too indulgent."

"I don't know much about what you had back home," said Gray. "But I believe that paying a man a decent wage is the best way to get him to work well."

As soon as they got to town Goldie had the new employees put their bundles down in the canvas store. Then she identified herself and the others to the Celestials by pointing and saying the names. Imitating her as best they could, the Chinese chorused, "Holt, Kevin, Dahcy, Glay, and Goldie."

"That's fine," beamed Goldie. Then from the English translation papers she called the Chinese names and asked them to identify themselves.

"Hop Sing," said Goldie. He stepped forward. She nodded and continued down the list: "Pi Ling, Sun Luck, Mao Tai, Ky Sung, Che Lai, Tao Peh, Mu Fung, Chung Sun, and Kwang Soo." After each in turn had identified himself, Goldie posted their names so everybody could learn them.

She began showing them around the temporary quarters, but Hop Sing was more interested in what was going on outside, and Goldie was becoming irritated by his lack of attention. He stood for quite a while watching the men cutting and fitting the stones for the new store. Then he gestured to himself and his compatriots and pointed outside.

"Do you know how to do that?" asked Goldie. Although he didn't understand a word she said, Hop Sing nodded his head positively up and down.

"Well, then, come on," said Goldie and led the way out of the tent.

Within a few days the Chinese had almost completely taken over the building of the store, which was now expanded to include a large back room for their living quarters.

The town of Little Flats had experienced a reverse migration during the two weeks before Christmas, a time when homesickness and discouragement weighed the heaviest on the young men. But for the young partners of the B.C.A. and D. the dream was still there. As Christmas approached they accounted 1849 a momentous year. Although all of them except Kevin occasionally suffered pangs of homesickness as they recalled pleasant Christmases they had spent with their families in the past, this only made them more determined to make their first Christmas in California a memorable one, and they laid their plans for a traditional holiday with a tree surrounded by gifts.

During the week before Christmas, Darcy and Holt worked on the addition to the cabin, while Gray and Kevin took the two wagons to Sacramento to purchase more goods and some iron shutters for the doors and windows of the new stone store. With the roads on the lower elevations nearly impassable from the heavy rains, Kevin and Gray made poor time, and once they reached Sacramento, they found it crowded with men from the mines. They would have had no place to sleep except for Horace Ogilvy, who put them up in his nearly completed wooden building.

With his assistance they were able to locate the iron shutters and the stock for the store. And they bought a few Christmas gifts.

"Well, that should take care of everything," said Kevin. "Now we can start back."

"Not yet. I've got one more thing to do," said Gray.

"What in the name of God's that?" exploded Kevin, to whom the whole business of gift buying had seemed silly and a waste of time in the first place. In his entire life he had never given or received a Christmas gift. He had not been able to pay Holt any of the money he owed him, and he chafed at buying presents when he was so badly in debt. Anxious to get out of Sacramento before he was forced to waste more money, he continued, "We'll be lucky if we don't bog down somewhere now. Those shutters weigh a ton, and the wagons are crammed full. We haven't got room for anything else."

"These won't take up much room if I can only find them," said Gray.

"All right. What is it?"

"Some slates."

"Slates? What the hell do you want slates for?"

"The Chinese. . .to make it easier for them to learn to read and write. Besides," he added, "we don't have any Christmas gifts for them yet."

"Christmas gifts! They don't even know what Christmas is."

"It's time they learned if they're going to be Americans."

"Americans? Them. . .Americans? Gray, you have the strangest ideas I ever heard."

"I don't care. I'm going to get them some slates. Goldie's been having an awful time trying to teach them with those boards and charcoal."

"All right, I'll help look. Just to get you out of here, if nothing else. But this is positively the last thing I'm going to do. You're the one who's so keen on celebrating Christmas. I'd think you'd be a little worried about getting back."

Once more Horace Ogilvy's knowledge of Sacramento saved them hours of trudging, and soon they had bought the slates from a man who had been conducting a day school for some of the children in the town.

"Now can we leave?" asked Kevin impatiently.

"Sure," said Gray. "Won't the Chinese be surprised? I can hardly wait to see their faces Christmas morning."

Not far along the soggy road home they encountered more rain. Weighted down as they were, the wagons frequently became stuck, and Kevin and Gray were forced to get down in the quagmire and lead the mule teams. They proceeded in this laborious fashion back to Little Flats. Chilled, wet, and exhausted, they finally arrived on Christmas Eve. Holt and six of the Chinese were minding the store, for Goldie was spending the day working at the cabin with Darcy and the other four Celestials.

"Boy, am I glad to see you!" exclaimed Holt. "We'd about given you up."

"Can you unload this stuff?" said Gray. "We're nearly frozen."

"Sure. You two go on in by the stove. We'll get the things inside."

Two hours later Holt, Kevin, and Gray mounted mules packed with the presents and the ingredients for the Christmas dinner and headed for the cabin. "Tomorrow. . .no work," said Gray to Sun Luck, who was in charge of the group remaining at the store. "We come for you early. Understand?"

"Yes, yes, Blothuh Glay," said Sun Luck. "Tomollow." (Having learned that Gray was Goldie's brother, the Chinese had assumed this was a title to be appended to all of the names of their male employers. Thus they had become Blothuh Glay, Blothuh Holt, Blothuh Kevin, and Blothuh Dahcy.)

At the newly completed four-room cabin they viewed the decorations in delight. Darcy and Goldie, with the help of Hop Sing, Che Lai, Pi Ling, and Mu Fung, had transformed the rude dwelling into a bower. A pine tree festooned with bits of colored paper and cloth graced one end of the main room, garlands of evergreens swooped down from the rafters and draped the walls, and lanterns, many with red glass mantles, swung from the ceiling, creating a twinkling fairyland. After feasting their eyes, their noses began to wrinkle in appreciation; mixed with the fresh scent of pine was a tantalizing aroma of venison filtering from the oven of the cast-iron cookstove, reminding them all how hungry they were.

After supper the five Christians tried to explain to the Chinese with sign language and simple English the meaning of Christmas. The Orientals indicated they understood the exchanging of gifts and even managed to convey to their white friends that presents were often tied up in cloth in China.

"I wish I'd thought of that," said Goldie. "We have some calico down at the store."

But the meaning behind the giving of the gifts, the birth of Christ and the Christmas story, was something the partners found they did not have enough words or signs to tell. Like so many of the young migrants who had severed the ties of home and traveled so far for so long, they had not thought much about religion for many months. But now with the advent of Christmas and the attempt to explain its meaning to men from a completely alien culture, they realized that together with the belief in their own destiny, there was also a faith that God would permit them to fulfill it.

Although they retired late on Christmas Eve, they were all up before dawn the next morning. Darcy was dispatched down the hill to bring the other six Chinese up to participate in the day's festivities, for nobody would work in Little Flats that day. While he was gone the others set about helping Goldie prepare breakfast and the food for the dinner they would all enjoy that evening.

When Darcy and the Chinese returned, the Americans fascinated the Orientals with a carol sing around the Christmas tree. Then they all opened their gifts. The Chinese were so excited with their gifts that the others forgot themselves in the pleasure of watching them. At Goldie's suggestion, the partners had given each of them a glass jar with some gold dust in it. She explained to them that each week more gold would be added to the jars until they were finally full.

"Then you'll be able to do anything you want," she said.

"Ours to keep?" questioned Pi Ling.

"Yes. . .to keep," said Goldie.

The Chinese had demonstrated an affinity for mathematics and knew the value of the gold. Holding their jars as if they were precious jewels, they bowed in stately unison as a gesture of thanks. Then Gray and Kevin handed them the slates and pencils they had purchased in Sacramento and showed them how they were used. Soon the Celestials began drawing objects around the room for Goldie or one of the others to identify and print in English.

Finally Hop Sing made a gesture with his arm encompassing the group of young Americans, then bowed and looked quizzically at Goldie.

"Thank you," said Goldie and printed the words on his slate.

"Thank you," said Hop Sing, bowing.

"Thank you," chorused the other nine, each clutching his slate and bowing deeply. There was no doubt they knew the meaning of the words.

Thus the day of feasting continued, and as it passed pleasantly into evening, the emigrants felt closer to one another and to this new land they would soon call home.

CHAPTER **24** GROWTH AND TESTING OF THE
B.C.A. AND D.★★★★★★★★★★★★★★★★★★★★★★★★★★★★

At Little Flats the months of January and February, 1850, were as full as the previous months had been. The stone store with its iron-shuttered front was completed. A bunkhouse for the Chinese had been built by the cabin at The Little Goldie mine, freeing the back room of the store for stock. The acquisition of a milk cow and some laying hens furnished a surplus of fresh food, which sold for a high price to the miners.

With their many abilities the Chinese relieved the young partners of innumerable tasks both at the cabin and the store. But Kwang Soo and Chung Sun had the strangest talent of all. Their enthusiasm for washing and ironing not only furnished their employers with the cleanest clothes in Little Flats but also enabled the industrious Orientals to conduct a thriving laundry business on the side.

Operating the expanding B.C.A. and D. gave the partners sparse time for personal pleasure. They took turns working The Little Goldie, keeping the store, and going to Sacramento for supplies. In the towns they passed through en route, many merchants began requesting them to deliver packages and letters to Sacramento and also bring back goods. An express business was growing out of this enterprise, giving them a network of customers in all the towns between Sacramento and Little Flats. The sign out in front of their store read BAXTER, COMPTON, ADAMS, AND DUPRES, EXPRESS, HARDWARE, DRY GOODS, AND GENERAL MERCHANDISE, but B.C.A. and D. was becoming a familiar abbreviation in the thriving gold settlements.

March had barely blustered into the little mining community. It was Friday, and though Gray was absent in Sacramento on an express run, the partners held their weekly business meeting. The initial excitement of exploring new business possibilities had dissipated in the harsh reality of holding to schedules, meeting obligations, and planning for tomorrow. The easy camaraderie of youth working together in a common effort had been blunted by things happening too fast, and all, particularly Goldie, were showing signs of the strain. A zest for making the most of every opportunity possessed her. Charging ahead full tilt at all obstacles, she had developed a snap in her voice and a brusque manner neither admired nor understood by her partners.

After reading the financial statement from her account book, Goldie said abruptly, "Since we have ten thousand dollars above our emergency fund, I propose we look into the possibility of doing our own wholesaling."

"I think we ought to look into increasing the express business before we try anything else," said Holt. "That's what's made the real jump in profits."

"I've got another idea that would give us even more money to work with in a hell of a hurry," said Darcy.

"What's that?" asked Goldie suspiciously.

Though Goldie was strongly attracted to Darcy, he had shown no interest in her as a woman since she had come to Little Flats. In an attempt to show that she didn't care any more for him then he did for her, she had adopted a particularly crisp manner whenever she spoke to him. The friction between the two dominant personalities with such different ideas was only thinly veiled, and most of the partners' meetings were conducted in an armed truce with the two openly opposing each other.

"I know you may not approve," said Darcy, eying her coolly. "But there's a lot of money being made in the saloons and gambling halls around here, and I propose we open one."

"I could never be a part of anything like that," said Goldie primly. "Besides, it's too risky."

"I wish you'd come down off that cloud just once. I say we ought to move in where there's money to be made."

"The accounts prove we're making money with what we're already doing, so if we're going to do any expanding, it should be in the business we already have."

"Don't just sit there," said Darcy to the other two. "What do you think?"

Holt said uncomfortably, "I agree with Goldie. We should build on what we've got before starting something new."

"And what about you?" Darcy turned to Kevin.

Pleased with the progress of the company, in spite of his feeling that Goldie pushed too hard, Kevin said, "I think I'd have to go along with Goldie and Holt."

Piqued, Darcy stalked out of the cabin, effectively cutting off both of the other proposals for expansion.

The next day was Saturday, the store's busiest day, and the B.C.A. and D. remained open late in order to give the miners the opportunity to bank their gold dust, post money or letters to loved ones, or do their weekly shopping.

Goldie hated to be in town on Saturday nights, although she never mentioned it to the others. The violent character of the gold camp and the men in it as they tried to forget their week's disappointments in gambling, drinking, and whoring frightened her. She shuddered at the frequent screams, gunshots, curses, and raucous laughter that filtered in from the street and was always glad she was never left alone in the store.

Tonight was Darcy's turn to work, but he was still angry over the defeat of his proposal to open a saloon. About eight o'clock he said abruptly, "I'm going out for a while."

"But you're supposed to work tonight," she protested.

"I don't feel like working. So please, Missy Goldie, I like to go now if you no mind," he said in a mocking voice, aping the manner of the Chinese.

After Darcy left, Goldie jumped every time the door opened.

"All alone tonight?" commented one man amiably as he did his shopping.

"No," lied Goldie. "Darcy's out back checking stock."

She felt best when there were several men shopping at once and she was busy. But every time she looked at the clock, the time didn't seem to have advanced at all. About nine-thirty she was so tense that she nearly screamed when Darcy came back. He had been drinking, his dark curly hair was tousled, and he had spotted his white ruffled shirt.

"Oh, there you are," he chortled. "The girl with an account book for a heart. Yassuh, Boss Lady!" He bent low in a bow, draping his hand across the floor in front of him.

"I'm glad you're back," said Goldie, "even if you are drunk."

"No, no dear lady," said Darcy airily. "I am not drunk—I am intoxicated. And I'm not back. I simply need some more money."

"You shouldn't gamble when you're drunk."

"Do you know, Miss Goldie Baxter, what I dislike the most about you?" Taken back, she could only shake her head. "Well, I'll tell you," Darcy continued, swaying slightly as he spoke. "It's your self-righteous way of telling everybody else exactly how wrong they are about everything, without ever thinking that there might be something wrong with sweet li'l old you. What do you know about living? What do you know about anything, you conceited little prig?"

Goldie's eyes began to fill with tears. She turned away so he wouldn't see, but he only took this as a sign of disgust and dismissal. "Where's the box?" he asked harshly.

"Right there," said Goldie, trying to keep the quaver out of her voice.

266

"My God, woman," cried Darcy. "Haven't you got any sensitivity at all?" He grabbed her roughly by the shoulders, spinning her around to face him. Then suddenly he was kissing her. But as he felt her respond, he thrust her from him. "You drive me mad," he said, drawing his fingers through the strands of her copper hair. Then he quickly grabbed a handful of money from the cash box and left.

Goldie's nerves were completely gone. Misery, fear, and frustration engulfed her and she began to cry. Then the door opened admitting another customer, and she gulped back her tears. He finally left, and she wondered if eleven o'clock would ever come so she could go home. Two more men whom she had never seen before entered. They must be new in the district, she thought.

"May I help you," she asked.

"You sure can, miss," said one. "Don, check the back."

"We don't allow anybody back there," said Goldie in alarm. But the men paid no attention to her.

"She's all alone," said Don, returning from his survey of the storeroom.

The man facing her came right to the point. "We understand you've got a safe. Open it up!" He drew out a pistol. At the sight of the gun she let out an earsplitting shriek.

"Shut her up!" said the man with the gun. His partner grabbed her and clapped his hand over her mouth. Goldie, close to hysteria, began to shake all over.

Chung Sun and Kwang Soo, who were working late in their laundry next door, heard her scream. They quickly grabbed their knives, unlocked the back door to the store, and ran in. As they entered, the man with the gun fired but missed. Before he could fire again, Kwang Soo, with a cat leap and a lightning thrust, was upon the gunman. His eyes wide, the man stood there just a moment, the knife protruding from his chest. Then he crumpled slowly to the floor. In fright the other man dropped his hand from Goldie's mouth and ran out into the street shouting, "My partner—they've killed my partner!"

Men began pouring into the store, but Goldie, now in uncontrollable hysterics, was unable to tell anyone what had happened.

"Let's string 'em up," said one man, grabbing Chung Sun.

"Missy Goldie!" screamed Kwang Soo as two miners roughly

pinioned his arms behind him. The surly mob was hustling the two Chinese toward the door, each with a new coil of rope from the shelves around his neck, when Holt and Kevin rushed in.

"Hold everything right there!" shouted Kevin, drawing his gun and firing it in the air.

"Goldie, are you all right?" Holt called, unable to locate her in the mob.

"She's over there," said one man grudgingly. "We can't get anything out of her."

As Holt approached he saw that Goldie was wide-eyed, staring, and her body was trembling violently. "Goldie!" he shouted, turning her toward him. But she didn't see him. He shook her and slapped her across the face. "What happened?" he asked sharply.

The blow brought her out of shock. "The money!" she said. "They wanted our money. That man!" she screamed, pointing. "He tried to rob us!"

The thief tried to bolt through the crowd, but he was collared by one of the miners. "Looks like we're having the necktie party for the wrong men," he said.

"You're not hanging anybody," said Kevin, still leveling his gun at the crowd. "Now let Chung Sun and Kwang Soo go." The men hastily removed the ropes from around the Celestials' necks. "We'll confine this thief in the jail and try him tomorrow," continued Kevin.

"Yeah," said a grizzled miner. "Sunday's a good day for a hangin'."

After the mob left with the prisoner, Holt asked, "But where's Darcy?"

"It's my fault," said Goldie. "I quarreled with him. He left."

Darcy had passed out in the room of one of the girls at The Golden Bon Bon. He knew nothing of the robbery until the next day when the thief was flogged and run out of Little Flats. Though neither Holt nor Kevin said anything about the incident, he felt their hostility toward him for leaving Goldie alone.

Gray returned early in the week into this charged atmosphere with the proposal and the merchandise to open up a new store in a gold town up the road known as Hyattsville. "When I picked up the express, there were some letters and packages to be delivered up there," he said. "A big strike's been made close by, and lots of men have come in."

"We ought to survey the town before moving in to see if a store and express office would pay off," said Goldie.

"You didn't do much advance surveying here," retorted Gray.

"We've got more at stake now," said Kevin.

"Oh, to hell with it!" shouted Gray in disgust "Nobody wants to do anything if it isn't his idea."

"Well, as long as you've bought the goods you may as well go to Hyattsville and see if you can make a go of it," said Goldie pessimistically.

"Thanks for the enthusiastic support," said Gray. "I'll bet the rest of you will be quick enough to hop on if I do make it go."

"I'll support you even if the others won't," said Darcy.

"I like the idea," said Holt. "And another thing—it seems to me we'd better start pulling together or we're soon not going to have anything left to fight about."

"I agree," said Kevin. "For God's sake let's do something. Maybe some good will come out of this damn business yet!"

They stood looking at each other malevolently after Kevin's outburst. All five seemed to sense that if any more was said, the whole partnership would be dissolved right then and there. Something restrained them from saying the irrevocable words.

All the way to Hyattsville Gray seethed inwardly. So far he had been unable to fit himself and Goldie into appropriate complementary roles in either their family or business life. Goldie seemed to dominate to such an extent that he didn't feel himself to be his own man. He seldom had a night out on the town; he never had a drink; he never sat down to while away an hour at the gaming tables; and worst of all, he never even got to talk to a girl, let alone dance with one. Again he found himself wishing the thought that had plagued him all of the way from Indiana to California: that Goldie had never come. And again he found himself feeling guilty for harboring such a thought. But how can I ever prove myself with her always around and taking charge? he wondered. Everything was her idea. She doesn't want to be a partner, he thought stormily. She wants to boss. No wonder Darcy can't stand her.

After they had delivered the express in Hyattsville, Gray left Tao Peh and Hop Sing in charge of the wagon and started to check into a feasible place to set up a store. On the way he passed by a saloon. On an impulse he entered, walked up to the bar, and ordered a drink. Then carrying his bottle he went to one of the faro tables and watched the men play

After a while one of them said, "You want my place? I'm cleaned."

Gray sat down

The next hour passed pleasantly as he sipped his rotgut whisky and gambled, neither winning nor losing very much. He had learned his lesson on the Missouri, and whereas he found it a pleasant way of whiling away the time, he felt no drive to be a gambler. But for the first time in many months he was doing something because he wanted to, and this gave him a great deal of satisfaction.

By late afternoon, however, he had had a lot of liquor. He had ceased to gamble and was sitting at a table smoking a long black cigar, which he now knew better than to inhale. His ego repaired by the salubrious effect of the drinks, he imagined himself as appearing quite debonair.

He wasn't even surprised when Rachel came walking down the stairs from the sleeping rooms above the saloon clad in a vivid dance hall dress. In her harsh, sexy voice she belted out a song for the miners then came over to where Gray was sitting.

"Mind if I join you?" she asked.

"It's your territory," said Gray.

"Mattie, bring another glass, will you?" called Rachel to the bartender. "Chuck and I have parted company."

"It doesn't matter. I have no intention of renewing our acquaintance."

"Ooh, aren't we formal! Well, I didn't pack him off because of you. He ruined everything for me in Little Flats."

"You use everybody, don't you? How much have you taken off the miners up here by now?"

"Enough. I'll be moving on pretty soon."

"What do you want anyway?"

"To be rich. . .and to live. What's the matter with that?"

Gray laughed. "All I do is work. Where's the living?"

"I've always liked you, Gray," said Rachel. She leaned close to him so he could smell her perfume and see the empty space between her breasts in her low-cut gown. From habit, he started to turn away. "I mean it," said Rachel, grabbing him under the chin and kissing him. "How about having supper with me in my room where we can talk in private?" Gray hesitated. "It won't cost you a cent," she laughed. "Come on." She grabbed him by the hand. Gray knew he should return to Hop Sing and Tao Peh, but he also knew he wouldn't. And suddenly he knew something about her he must have always instinctively known: she wanted him just as much as he wanted her. And so he let himself be drawn up the stairs to her room.

With supper Rachel had champagne served, for luxuries were always available in the gold towns for a price. But dining elegantly only stirred Gray's impatience for the intoxicating girl he had so long coveted. It seemed the most natural thing in the world to be unhooking her dress, and then to be making love to her in her big four-poster bed. Rachel proved an expert teacher and ardent partner for his first sexual encounter. Fully gratified and highly pleased with himself, he fell back on his pillow and was soon fast asleep.

When he awoke the next morning, he felt a blissful inner contentment. He looked at the dark beauty of the girl beside him and felt not a twinge of regret for what he had done. His head was a little unsteady, but he was scarcely aware of it. Manhood surged within him. He was splashing himself with water in the washbowl when Rachel awoke.

"My, you're cheerful," she remarked testily.

"It's my good disposition."

"Don't I even get a good morning kiss?"

"Why of course," said Gray as he donned his coat and picked up his hat.

"But where are you going?"

"To open a store. I have to get Tao Peh and Hop Sing started on the day's business."

"But I thought we'd have breakfast together."

"I'll be back this evening," said Gray, kissing her. "We'll have supper."

As he emerged into the brisk March morning, he felt like a giant. The town looked good to him. At the end of the street he spotted an empty lot and had Hop Sing and Tao Peh move the wagon to the new location and open for business. Then he went about recruiting hard-luck miners to start quarrying stone for a permanent structure. All day he worked on the new store. Around six he returned to the saloon.

271

"Supper?" Rachel asked, drawing her fingers lightly over the back of his hand.

"Why not?" said Gray, debonairly tossing off the invitation and fully savoring his new role as roué.

Four days this idyllic situation continued. But on the evening of the fifth, when Gray returned to the saloon, Rachel wasn't there. Approaching the bar he asked, "Is Rachel still up in her room?"

"No," said Mattie. "She's gone. But she left you this." He handed him a note.

Gray felt a sudden sinking feeling in his stomach. Quickly taking his drink to a table, he sat down and opened the letter.

Dear Gray,

All good things must come to an end, and so it must be with us. I told you I was about ready to move on when you came. I've decided that now is the right time. I can't make any money with you around. You're a damn expensive package, you know. But it's been great. And I'll be seeing you around, sweetie.

Love,

Rachel

Dumbfounded, he stared at the letter. It must be a joke. . . surely it was just one of her tricks. But as he read the note again, the finality of the words jumped out at him. He was just something for her to play with. . .on a whim. . .to be discarded for a new partner and a new game when she became bored. The old doubts, handily dismissed a few days ago, flooded back, possessing his mind, and he was plunged into a gloom more intense than he had ever experienced. He went to the bar, morosely ordered a bottle, and returned to his table, where he drank himself into a sodden lump. Mattie finally sent for Hop Sing, who took him stumbling home. But the next morning, and the next, he was back at the saloon.

Alarmed, Hop Sing decided that something had to be done. Leaving Tao Peh to watch both Gray and the store, he mounted a mule and raced back to Little Flats. Galloping through the town, his wide pants legs ballooning in the breeze, his heavy blue coat flopping, and his pigtail bouncing, he did not pause until he reached the B.C.A. and D. store. He leaped down and ran inside, out of breath and out of English, to tell the news.

"What's happened, Hop Sing?" asked Goldie.

"Velly sick. . .Blothuh Glay," said Hop Sing.

"Sick!" shrieked Goldie.

"Heuh," said Hop Sing, tapping his forehead with his finger. "Blothuh Glay meet gull. . .all velly happy. Then gull go away. . .Blothuh Glay velly unhappy. . .go saloon." Hop Sing vigorously pantomimed taking a bottle and drinking from it. "Blothuh Glay velly sick." He shook his head sadly.

"Pi Ling," called Darcy. "Ride up to the cabin and fetch Brother Holt and Kevin. I'm going to Hyattsville with Hop Sing."

"I'm coming too," said Goldie.

"You won't like it."

"He's my brother."

"All right, come along. It might do you some good. Pi Ling, you'd better pack some things for Missy Goldie too."

"I do," said Pi Ling.

The practical Hop Sing insisted upon filling a wagon with goods needed in the new store and taking four more of the Chinese to expedite the building. "Minuhs no help," he said. "All time leave to look foh gold. We build in hully." He beamed at his countrymen.

"Well, little sister to the rescue," Gray greeted them when they entered the saloon in Hyattsville. "Pardon me if I don't stand up," he giggled. "But I might fall down. Pull up a chair."

"Can't we go someplace else?" asked Goldie uncomfortably.

"Oh, I forgot. . .this's not a nice refined place for a lady. Well, then go to hell! I'm sick of your ladyship. 'S'at clear enough for you?"

Goldie's face blanched. She stood dumbfounded, staring at him.

"Hey, Darcy," said Gray. "Pull up a chair. Let Miss Priss stand or leave or do whatever she damn pleases. Say, did you see the store? What'd ya think of it?"

"What was her name?" asked Darcy.

"Rachel." Then he looked defiantly at his sister. "Yes. . . Rachel!" His eyes misted. "We had it good, Darce. For five days we had it good. You know what I mean? Then she just left. Can you beat that? She just left. I been sitting here ever since trying to figure out why."

"Don't ever try to understand a woman," said Darcy, pointedly

273

looking at Goldie. "Not ever. Hey, mister," he called to the bartender. "You got any rooms in this place?"

"Yeah."

"Give me two, one for the lady and one for us."

"That'll be five dollars in advance," said Mattie, handing Darcy the keys. "Numbers two and three at the top of the stairs."

Upstairs, Gray stopped outside number three. "We had it so sweet," he said. "Right in there." Goldie's face went scarlet as she realized the full portent of what her brother was saying.

"Goldie never approved of Rachel," said Gray confidentially. "I think she was jealous." He turned on her. "You must be real happy now. Gotta be right about everything. . .the big boss. Yassuh, Boss!"

Goldie's head reeled. Gray was taunting her with practically the same words Darcy had used that awful night in the store.

"Why'd you ever have to come out here anyway, little sister?" said Gray. Then he began to cry. "There. . .at last I've said it!"

"Come on, Gray. . .in here," said Darcy.

Shocked and distraught at this second attack in less than two weeks by the two men she wanted most to please, Goldie retreated into her room. In bewilderment she sank into a chair to try and fathom how things had got so askew. Everything I've done has been for the good of the company, she reflected moodily. Then those hot words, "Boss Lady," flashed through her mind. What did they mean? She felt herself growing close to tears. But I mustn't do that, she thought. I can't think if I cry. And she had to think. The B.C.A. and D. could so easily fail. If they could only see. . .they must work hard now, because someday—and maybe soon—the gold would all be gone. "Strike while the iron's hot," Aunt Opal always said. Then when the business was stable. . .why, they'd have lots of time to play. . .all the time in the world. She had to make them see why she was always planning and looking ahead, and why it was important to devote every minute to the business now. Then they'd understand. Yes, it was surely because they didn't understand.

A tap at the door interrupted her thoughts. "Come in," she called. "It's not locked."

Darcy entered and lighted a lamp. She had not noticed until now how dark it had become.

Bringing the lamp over to the little round-backed chair into which she had sunk, he said, "Gray's asleep, and I think we should talk."

Though he sounded ominous, Goldie answered eagerly, "Yes, I want to talk to you too."

"I know what Gray said was rough on you," Darcy began. "But I hope you realize he was speaking the truth."

"Truth?" Goldie's eyes began to glisten.

Darcy spoke softly, but there was a deliberateness she did not miss. "Maybe you don't mean to, but you've been trying to control all of us. This is supposed to be a partnership, but you act as if it were yours alone. And now you're even beginning to interfere in our personal lives."

"I've never said a word——"

"You don't have to. That tight-lipped look is enough. The firm's not going to last if you don't stop it. You've got to let go. You're not our mother, you know."

"Mother?" Goldie quavered. What was he talking about? What did he mean? No, he wasn't talking to her at all; he was patronizing her. Bewildered and demoralized, she felt her spirit crumbling away. All she had planned to say flew out of her mind. Now not even pride could keep back the tears. She rushed over to the bed and flung herself upon it, sobbing pitiably.

Darcy followed her to the bed and said, "How can I talk to you if you act like this?"

"You all hate me!" she sobbed.

"If I hated you I wouldn't have bothered to come in here and try to straighten this out. We want to protect you. . .well, as if you were our sister."

"Sister!" First she was accused of acting like his mother, and now he was saying he thought of her as a sister. "I don't want to be your sister! I want——" She broke off.

Darcy looked at her searchingly for a moment. Maybe under that prim, remote manner there were feelings he hadn't detected. He started in a new direction. "What I'm trying to say is, we all need time to think of things besides the B.C.A. and D. We need to relax and enjoy ourselves occasionally."

"And you can't with me?"

"It doesn't have anything to do with you! That's the whole point!" cried Darcy in exasperation. "Let Gray live his own life. . .and me too, for that matter. And you live yours. Because if

275

you don't leave us alone—all of us—you're going to blow this partnership sky-high!"

Goldie just looked at him, tears streaming down her cheeks, her deep and painful sobs punctuating the silence. She still didn't understand. God, he thought, this was no way. He wanted to take her in his arms and kiss her and blot out her grief with the passion he felt surging within him. But something restrained him, and he said limply, "I hope you'll think over what I've said."

"Go away," she sobbed. "Go away and leave me alone!"

"All right. But I'm coming back in an hour to take you down to dinner. Be ready."

"I don't want you to take me to dinner, and I won't be ready."

In the doorway he turned and looked at her. "Yes you will," he said. He closed the door gently.

That evening Darcy was curious but delighted with Goldie's quick recovery from their afternoon encounter. He did not know that he had stung her beyond prudence, and a reckless spirit now possessed her. Wearing a new emerald green silk that Hop Sing had helped her fashion she was a sensation in the saloon, and neither she nor Darcy missed the daggered glances of the two bar girls who were not doing well with the customers because of her presence.

"Would you like to dance?" Darcy asked.

"It's been a long time," said Goldie, but her eyes began to shine.

"Do you know a waltz?" She nodded, and Darcy spoke to a man playing an accordion in a corner and gave him a little gold dust.

The musician inclined his head, and soon the romantic strains of a popular song in three-quarter time filled the rude wooden saloon. Darcy held out his arms and Goldie floated into them. Once again she felt the excitement of the closeness of this dark man.

Darcy was surprised at her grace. He had thought only Southern ladies could dance beautifully and display coquettish charm. Glancing down at her, he said, "Do you realize how exciting you are?"

Goldie's heart beat furiously. "You're just saying that because I'm the only girl around." She glanced up at him, then dropped her eyes.

Darcy's pulse quickened. He drew her closer, his lips brushing her shining hair. "I want to set you straight about something," he said suddenly. "I have never thought of you as a sister."

"Why, what are you trying to say, Mr. Dupres?" she dimpled at him.

Ah, she can flirt too, he thought. This was not the girl, simple and direct, he had met in Sacramento or who kept store in Little Flats. "Oh, I think you know" he said, his cheeks darkening and giving him an even more swarthy appearance.

Goldie thought him more attractive than ever. "It's divine to be dancing again," she said to hide her feelings.

But Darcy was not to be put off. Sensuously he caressed the palm of her hand. Goldie was electrified. But just then the music stopped. All of the men in the saloon broke into spontaneous applause, and then as if a signal have been given, they rushed over begging Darcy to introduce them and let them dance with his pretty partner. Goldie looked at Darcy covertly. Was he jealous? She smiled a dazzling smile and said she would dance with each of the men in turn.

As the music started again and Goldie whirled off, Darcy watched her for a while, the excitement and spirit she exuded possessing him also. His temples pulsed as he thought of sleeping with her. Desire and passion seized him anew, and he was powerless to suppress his need. He glanced around the room, his eye alighting on the two girls at the bar. They were tossing off man-size drinks and slamming down their glasses in rapid succession, constantly glaring at Goldie and the fickle men who surrounded her. Casually Darcy approached the bar. Both of the girls were young, but one was Spanish and seemed to have more fire than the other.

"Would you like another?" he asked the Spanish girl.

"No thanks, Mister," she said. "I'm leaving. There isn't likely to be anything going on here tonight. Your lady sure has those jackasses standing on their hind legs, don't she?"

"She's not my lady," Darcy laughed. "But you're right about the other. You can call me Darcy." He drew his finger invitingly down her arm.

"Oh, I get it—she won't sleep with you," taunted the Spanish girl. "What makes you think I will?"

"Because I'll make it worth your while." He suddenly stepped behind her and lightly brushed his lips along the back of her neck.

"How much?"

"This," said Darcy, holding out a bag of dust.

"Ha! Ha!" snorted the girl. "Come on, mister, you got it bad."

Later when Darcy returned to the saloon he looked around in alarm. Goldie was gone. "Where is she?" he asked the bartender.

"The young lady?" asked Mattie. "She went up to her room, must be a half hour ago now."

Taking two steps at a time, Darcy ran up the front stairs and rapped on Goldie's door, but he received no answer. Finally he turned away, his shoulders sagging. "I suppose she thinks I ran out on her again, damn it!" he thought. "I've got to get away from her."

Inside, Goldie was stifling her sobs. She had noticed the instant Darcy had gone off with the Spanish girl. She couldn't bear to think of his kissing and making love to that prostitute. But Darcy had informed her that these actions were none of her business. So rather than open the door and heap a tirade of abuse on him, which she knew she would do, she decided it was better to pretend she was asleep.

Before any of them had a chance to resolve their differences the next day, Kevin came flying up the road on another of the company mules. "Got a letter for you from San Francisco," he yelled at Darcy as he dismounted. "It's marked *Urgent* and came up by special messenger. So we thought you ought to have it right away. God, I'm thirsty!"

"Saloon's right over there," said Darcy.

When they had settled down with their drinks, Darcy opened his letter. "Hey, it's from November," he said. "Well, I'll be. Say, listen to this: 'Mirina's going to have a baby, probably the middle of April. She's never told Holt, but the doctor thinks he ought to be here. I'm writing to you, Darcy, because I don't know Holt very well, and I thought you might be able to tell him better. Ma thinks you ought to come down too. Those waterfront lots you bought are worth a fortune now, and she thinks you'd better do something with them because there's been threats of squatters moving in on them. You won't know the city, things are happening so fast. Ma says to tell you hello, and she'd like to meet Goldie and Gray.' This certainly changes things," said Darcy, looking up. "We'd better tell Goldie and Gray and make some plans."

"Yes, I suppose so," said Kevin, dragging himself back to the present. With the startling announcement about Mirina, his mind had snapped back to the night he had spent making love to her,

278

and desire mingled with guilt swept over him again.

They decided that Goldie would go back to Little Flats to keep the store while Kevin worked the claim; Gray, with the help of the Chinese, would continue to build the new store in Hyattsville, leaving Holt and Darcy free to return to San Francisco.

In a peacemaking gesture to Goldie, Darcy said, "We can check into your plan for doing our own wholesaling. We could build some warehouses and an express office on my lots. It looks like the time has come to put them to use."

Holt had seldom thought about Mirina these last few months and now at Little Flats when he heard he was about to become a father, he was stunned. His initial astonishment was soon replaced by delight, however. "Just wait till my father hears," he said. "We'll name him John after him. He'll like that. I must write him right away."

"He *may* be a girl," said Goldie sagely.

"He wouldn't dare," said Holt. Then he remembered the cool parting between himself and Mirina. She had as much as said she didn't care if she ever saw him again. But surely now that they were to have a child Mirina would change, he thought. But why hadn't she told him about the baby? He knew she must have known. And all through the busy days of preparing for the trip, this thought nagged him.

CHAPTER **25** SAN FRANCISCO, SPRING, 1850★★★★★★★★★★★★★★★★★★★★★★★★★★★★★

The torrential rains of the winter and spring of 1849-50 had inundated the valley where Sacramento stood. The rivers overflowed onto the wide flood plain and made canals of the streets. San Francisco had its share too. The thoroughfares—uneven, ungraded, unpaved—were quagmires. A sign posted at the corner of Clay and Kearney by an exasperated citizen who still had managed to retain his sense of humor read:

This street is impassable,
Not even Jackassable.

The precipitous hills rising directly above the bay had been practically denuded of brushwood as the desperate citizens cut and laboriously dragged the shrubbery down to the streets and dumped it in an attempt to fill the bottomless mudholes. When this didn't work, the streets became a dump for anything they couldn't use. Boxes, barrels, refuse, unwanted and unsaleable goods sent out from the East by shippers who still had no idea of what was really needed in California—all were thrown into the streets, only to sink desolately out of sight. The situation was so bad that horses, mules, and even some carts were lost forever in the sucking mud.

The sidewalks, equally treacherous, in some areas were constructed of shipments of surplus iron cookstoves, on top of which were placed barrels of bad Chilean flour and spoiled beef. In other places bales of tobacco, gold-washing machines, wire sieves, and rolls of sheet lead were laid out in an attempt to make walking possible at all. These same materials furnished precarious stepping-stones at street crossings. Many an entrapped citizen had to be pulled out of the holes by ropes; for once in, the mud acted like quicksand.

Despite the hardships caused by the weather, the population of the city had grown to twenty-five thousand during the winter, and buildings in ragged array staggered up the sides of the hills. The earth from these sandhills, already being transported down as fill, extended the level ground for building out into the bay. Thus lots previously on the waterfront were now several blocks back from it. Still standing in the harbor were the hundreds of ships that had brought the forty-niners, but now most of them had been put to use. Some had been converted into lodging houses, and over a thousand people resided in them; others were used as floating stores or warehouses. But many, anchored close-in, now were landlocked, confounding the eyes of those unaware that the bay had been partially filled in. Long Wharf extended several hundred feet out into the bay, and many other piers and wharves surrounded it.

Since Darcy and Holt had left in September, all of this was new to them. It was as if they were coming into a strange city for the

280

first time, with no familiar landmarks to guide them. Hop Sing and Mu Fung, who had accompanied them, were equally disoriented, and all four looked around in wide-eyed surprise. Darcy's pulse quickened as he felt himself responding to the call of this bizarre city to join in the pursuit of fortune in evidence all about. Heedless of the quagmire in front of him that passed for a street, he eagerly stepped out in search of a carriage. Dismayed as he sank down to his shins, he started to retreat. But before he could extricate himself, a horse, urged on by its rider, foundered through the mud, splashing him from head to foot with black slime.

Holt, who had long been annoyed by Darcy's excessive preening, burst into laughter and nearly fell off into the sucking mud himself. "Oh, oh, oh. . .what a sight you are!" he gasped.

"Don't stand there braying like a jackass," Darcy scowled. "Get us a cab!"

At the Brown Palace, Ma Brown looked at Darcy and chuckled. "My, my, I never thought I'd see the day you'd look like this. What in the world happened?"

"He fell in a hole in one of your streets," said Holt.

"You'd better get out of those wet things," said Ma. "I'll bring you up some hot water directly so you can wash some of that stuff off. I'd like to see if you've changed any. Can't tell a thing the way you're decked out."

"The hell with my personal appearance!" barked Darcy. "I'm sick of the topic."

"Then off you go. It's the room at the top of the stairs."

Darcy picked up his bag and left.

"I see he hasn't changed much," observed Ma. She peered at Mu Fung and Hop Sing. "So these are your Chinamen. Some of my roomers may have some funny ideas about them. But if anybody complains, out he'll go."

"Velly nice, Missy Blown," said Hop Sing. "But Mu Fung and Hop Sing have place to go. Make no tlouble heuh. . .have fliends on Saclamento Stleet."

Holt instructed them to report to the hotel later, then sent the two Orientals off.

"I've been noticing how your eyes have been darting about every time the door opens," said Ma. "Mirina's in her room. I'll take you up." She started to climb the stairs.

Holt was suddenly panic-stricken. He had not thought about

framing an overture to this reunion and was seized with the fear that he might start off on the wrong foot again.

"Guess who's here?" Ma said brightly as she entered Mirina's room.

Mirina was lying back on a small petit point chair, her feet resting on a footstool. As she saw Holt she flushed, and her hands instinctively flew to cover her figure, but neither they nor the petticoats she was wearing could hide her thickened form.

"How are you?" asked Holt stiffly.

"As well as can be expected considering my condition."

"But why didn't you tell me?" Holt blurted out the question. At this point Ma slipped quietly out of the room.

"Because I—I was afraid," said Mirina. Her hands fluttered nervously.

"I don't understand," said Holt.

"Because I didn't think you'd want it—or me." She decided for once that the truth was the best answer.

The sincerity of Mirina's confession struck Holt, and he realized that this girl whom he had married was just as afraid of life's responsibilities as he was. He knelt down and put his arms around her. "Of course I want you. I want you both," he said.

He kissed her tenderly. Mirina was overwhelmed. Even though she didn't love him, he made her feel wanted and secure. She responded to his embrace. Maybe the baby would serve to bind him to her, she thought. Her face brightened.

"We'll call him John after my father," Holt said. Then he paused. "That is, if it's all right with you." He was determined to name the baby after his father, and looked at her anxiously for any sign of disagreement.

Mirina laughed. "You can call *him* anything you like. But if it's a girl, I intend to name her."

"Oh, it will be a boy," said Holt confidently. "My family always has boys."

Mirina looked at him in alarm. He seemed so positive it would be a boy. What if it was a girl? Would he start to suspect something?

Holt never noticed her agitation. He was pleased that the reconciliation was working out so well and asked her to go for a drive. "The doctor won't let me do that, but a walk would be refreshing."

She got her shawl and the two sallied forth on the miscellaneous

282

goods that made up the sidewalks of the city. This was not the best form of exercise for a pregnant woman, but with Holt's steady arm to guide her, Mirina felt unusually safe this brisk, sunny day.

After cleaning himself up, Darcy found Pa Brown working on the new wing of the hotel. Pa was glad for a smoke and a chat. They had just settled down on a pile of boards when Sam Wackem came in with some more lumber.

Darcy beamed. "I didn't know you were back."

"I came back with Pa last November. Mining's not my trade. We didn't find a thing."

"What about Rip?" Darcy looked around as if he expected him to appear too.

"He decided to stay," chuckled Pa. "Said he was going to open a gambling hall and saloon up on the North Yuba soon as he got a stake."

"What about all the money he took with him?" Darcy's question dangled a moment.

"Parted company with it before he even had a chance to count it," said Pa.

"He'll be back one of these days, I'll bet," said Darcy. "Dead broke as usual."

With the assurance that Rip was all right, at least when Pa and Sam had left him, Darcy sought out November in the kitchen.

"What's all this bad news about my lots?" he asked.

"There are several squatters on them," said November. "I'll take you there."

"Oh, I think I can find my way."

"You don't understand. They've been filling in the bay to make more room for business. Your property's not on the waterfront anymore."

When they arrived in front of a group of flimsy sheds, housing a varied assortment of fly-by-night businesses, Darcy alighted from the wagon and approached a man standing in front of a small store. "I believe you're conducting business on my property," he began politely.

The man gave a guffaw and said, "You got any proof?"

"Why yes, yes I have," Darcy continued in measured tones. He brought out his deed title and showed the man where it stated that he owned this particular lot.

283

The man dismissed the deed. "It ain't worth the paper it's writ on. I'm claimin' squatter's rights."

"We'll just see about that," said Darcy. His eyes began to glitter. "We'll just see."

At the three other shops built on the vacant land he was treated similarly, and when he returned to the wagon he was cold with fury.

November glanced at him apprehensively. "I was afraid it would turn out like this. But I thought you might be able to do something about them."

"I intend to. I'm going to court. Who's the best lawyer?"

"It won't do any good."

Darcy let the reins go slack in his hand. "What do you mean?"

"The judges, the officials—everybody just bribes them. Nobody gets any satisfaction in the courts."

"I'll get some satisfaction. . .one way or another." He looked at the shacks grimly.

"Be careful, Darcy," said November. She laid her delicate but workworn hand lightly on his arm. "You have a wild streak that makes me fear for you."

Darcy turned to her with his engaging and disarming smile. "Don't you worry, sweet November," he said. "Everything's going to be all right."

That evening Darcy went to Mike Flaggerty's saloon to question the Irishman about his land, for Mike knew just about everything that went on in San Francisco, though he generally kept his knowledge to himself.

Over a glass of his best Irish whisky, Darcy asked, "Who's squatting on my land?"

"Nobodies," said Mike.

"How do I get them off? I understand it costs." Both men looked around the saloon rather than at each other, and their conversation to the casual observer would have appeared no more consequential than a comment on the weather.

"Probably need a court decision."

"Do I need a lawyer?"

"That usually figures in the expenses."

"What court and what lawyer?"

"Well, since it's a land case, I think it'd better be in *Honest* Judge Percy's court. And Tom Fellows is the lawyer you'll need.

He'll handle the judge's share. It'll be one flat fee."

"How much?"

"A hundred. Maybe a hundred and fifty."

"That's justice, huh?" Darcy slammed down his glass.

"Easy," said Mike. He looked guardedly around the saloon. "There's ears everywhere. You can't beat the system. Better get some buildings up on that land soon as you get it back."

Darcy's next frustration came when he learned that the tightness of the court schedule would delay the hearing of his case for two weeks. Deliberately going by the court several times during this period, he found it usually closed. *Honest* Judge Percy only sat for a couple of hours in the mornings, devoting approximately ten minutes to a case and spending the remaining hours of the day at the task of putting his ample income to use. He either strolled about town, his sharp eyes alert to investment possibilities, or drove out the road to the Dolores Mission, where he was supervising the building of a mansion for himself. Darcy even suspected that he hired the squatters to live on vacant land so he could keep his court docket filled with the cases that were contributing so handsomely to his pocketbook as well as to his notoriety as a judge.

On the appointed day in April, Darcy appeared with his lawyer, Tom Fellows, at Judge Percy's court.

"Ol' Percy's been in a cantankerous mood lately," said Tom. "Difficult to do business with. I sure hope this isn't going to be one of those days, or it might cost you more money than we figured on."

Darcy looked at Tom to see if he was joking, but decided he was not. Almost certain that Fellows and Percy were working in cahoots to fleece him, he covertly felt for his derringer. If this was the kind of game they wanted to play, he would be ready to call them.

Tom presented to the court the legal documents showing Darcy's title to the land in question.

But instead of finding in favor of Darcy immediately as he did with most cases, Judge Percy peered at the papers and said, "I don't see that these show a clear-cut title to the land for Mr. Dupres."

As if on a prearranged signal, Tom said, "I'm sure I can convince you of the rightfulness of my client's claim if we might just step into your chambers for consultation."

There were snickers and elbow nudging among the spectators as Judge Percy said, "We'll just do that. There'll be a fifteen-minute court recess."

Darcy sucked in his breath slowly. What he had suspected was about to happen.

In Percy's office Tom said, "Well, now, Paul, just what would you consider a fair amount so that Mr. Dupres doesn't have any more trouble over this petty legal matter?"

"I dunno," said the judge. "What do you think your client would be willing to pay?"

"I'll tell you what this client would be willing to pay," said Darcy with deceptive softness. "Just one-half of the amount I originally agreed to." Slowly he drew out his pistol and held it on the judge. "Sign this paper rendering the decision in my favor *now*, mister, or I will put a bullet through your brain, thereby saving the good people of this city untold future misery at your hands. Do I make myself clear?"

The voice that commanded was low but sharp, the hand on the gun was steady, and the eyes looking out from the face were frozen and impersonal. There was no doubt in Judge Percy's mind that if he did not comply with the order, Darcy fully intended to carry out his threat. The judge moistened his lips which had suddenly gone dry. "Quite clear," he rasped.

"Then sign and be quick about it!"

Tom Fellows, who had frozen at the sight of the gun, began to move. "I wouldn't, Fellows," said Darcy. He gave the lawyer a perfunctory look. "It would give me almost as much pleasure to shoot you as the judge here. Besides, I have something for you to do. Write out a receipt and sign it saying you have been paid in full for legal services rendered in this matter."

Scowling, the lawyer obeyed. "But you're making a mistake."

"I've had too much counsel from you already, Fellows—just write."

Judge Percy shoved the documents he had signed across his desk. "Here," he said, "but don't think this is the end of this, Dupres. You've started something I promise you're going to regret."

Ignoring these remarks, Darcy glanced at the papers, put them in his pocket, and dropped fifty dollars on the desk. "There, gentlemen, I think I'm being more than generous. By rights you

286

ought to be paying me for the trouble you've caused me. Through, Fellows?" He glanced at the lawyer. Fellows nodded.

Picking up the receipt, Darcy waved his pistol airily between the two men. "Then, gentlemen, shall we proceed back to the courtroom? I know everyone out there is anxious to hear your decision. And just one more thing, *Judge*. I'm a crack shot—so don't change your mind when you get out there."

Back in court Judge Percy said, "I find in favor of Mr. Dupres. The other gentlemen are ordered to vacate the premises."

Darcy went to Mike's saloon that evening expecting congratulations for his expertise in dispatching Percy and Fellows in their own game, but Mike was far from handing out any compliments. "You weren't very smart this morning," he said stiffly.

Surprised and taken aback, Darcy flared, "I suppose I should have paid them."

"There are ways of skinning a cat, but that's not one of them. Every crook in San Francisco will be looking for you."

"Let 'em look," said Darcy darkly, his good mood shattered.

"Can you really use that thing?" asked Mike, gesturing to the hidden derringer.

"If the occasion warrants it."

"It may," said Mike, moving off to serve another customer.

The next day Mirina's labor began. While waiting for Dr. Murphy, Holt sat beside her bed holding her hand, though he was frightened by the sight of her distorted body contracting in agony.

"Christ!" she cried as the pain gripped her. "Oh Christ—I'm dying!" Her nails dug deep into the palm of his hand.

Holt's face was drenched with sweat. Women did die giving birth. His own mother was dead because of him. His father's words came back: "She was so small and frail. . .but she wanted you so much." But did Mirina want this baby? Pangs of guilt shot through him. Was this to be his punishment for taking her for his pleasure. . .without love. To lose them both—Mirina and the baby? Then Mirina shrieked and squeezed his hand so hard, he gasped in pain. Now she was moaning like some trapped animal. He couldn't look at her. He wanted out. Why. . .oh, why didn't the doctor come? He couldn't bear any more of this.

As if in answer to his wish, November hurried into the room followed by Dr. Murphy, who took one look at Holt and said, "Outside, young man, you can't do any good here."

Feeling as if a great weight were being lifted from him, Holt released Mirina's hand to November and left.

"There," soothed November. "I'm here. . .don't be afraid." But Mirina tensed again. She was fighting against the birth with all of her being.

Dr. Murphy spoke insistently in her ear. "The pains are still several minutes apart, Mirina. Now I want you to listen to me. You must bear down. Don't fight the contractions. Work with them. Do you understand?"

Mirina's eyes came unglazed and flashed resentfully. "I'm going to die," she wailed. "And for something I don't even want."

"Nonsense," said Dr. Murphy. "You must work as I tell you, and everything will be all right."

But Mirina was too gripped with terror to obey him.

As the day dragged on toward evening, November was forced to substitute a knotted towel for her red and swollen hand for Mirina to grip. But she continued to bathe the tortured girl's face with cool water and to murmur soothing words to her.

Intermittently Dr. Murphy would lean down and say, "Bear down, girl! I say, bear down!"

But Mirina no longer seemed to hear or see those who were ministering to her. Her shrieks had become low, agonized moans, and frequently she was back on the ship, murmuring the names of Kevin and Holt or the fears of her pregnancy. Dr. Murphy became grave by evening. The baby must come soon if he was to save her. But still there was no sign.

Outside, Holt, full of recrimination toward himself, sat through the endless day, his head in his hands and his body shaking with dry sobs. God, how long it was! Did it always take this long, he wondered? Was she dying? He couldn't bring himself to go to the door and ask. And no one thought to come and give him a reassuring word.

Finally after sixteen hours of hard labor, John Kevin Compton was pulled kicking and screaming into the world.

"Ooh, he's a fighter," smiled Dr. Murphy in relief. "Nothing wrong with this lad." Quickly he handed the newborn baby to November to swaddle while he staunched the flow of blood from the weakened Mirina.

"It's a fine boy," he leaned down and whispered in her ear.

"Thank God!" said Mirina.

288

As soon as he had made her comfortable, he called Holt into the dimly lighted room.

Holt reached down and felt for Mirina's hand. "He's beautiful," he said. "And the doctor says you're going to be all right too."

"I'll never go through that again," she said. Her eyes seemed to blaze in her white face. "I'm warning you, Holt."

Taken back by her vehemence, he protested, "But you have a son—our son. Aren't you happy?"

"I'm happy that I'm alive...that's all."

Holt got up heavily and left the room. Nothing had changed. The wall they had built was still there between them. With a leaden heart he went into the parlor and sat down to write the news to his father.

As April gave way to May, Darcy's plans for his lots took precedence over everything else, and Holt had no time to mope about his personal life.

"We'll build the company offices and warehouse on the four adjacent lots," said Darcy. "But on the one on Washington off Portsmouth Square I'm going to build the biggest saloon and gambling palace in town."

"Goldie won't like that," said Holt.

"It has nothing to do with the B.C.A. and D.," snapped Darcy. He still smarted from his defeat over the gambling hall in Little Flats, and for a moment Holt's reference to that unhappy meeting dampened his enthusiasm. But he brushed the feeling aside and continued. "We could build a store too."

"Now *that* Goldie will like."

"I wish you'd quit referring to her," said Darcy in irritation. "There are four other partners, you know."

"Not for you there aren't. You've been trying to get the upper hand with her ever since we formed the B.C.A. and D."

"Look, Holt, do you want the company offices on this property or don't you?"

"Sure—sure I do, Darcy. But what about rent? You could collect several thousand dollars a month from anybody else."

"We'll build them three stories high, and I'll collect rent from the other tenants."

"Say, that's a great idea."

That night Darcy was down at Mike's urging him and Sam to come in with him on his planned gambling hall on Washington

Street when Mike interrupted. "That's in Sydney Town," he said.

"I don't care," said Darcy, "That's where the money is!"

"The Ducks are cackling," warned Mike, using the familiar term that described mischief afoot among the criminals.

Just then a faint cry of "Fire" penetrated the noisy cheerfulness of the saloon. Darcy's head went up. "Did you hear that?" he asked.

Again, unmistakably and much louder came the cry, "Fire!"

Men galvanized into action. Most of them belonged to the fire companies that had been formed after a major holocaust last December. The fire that had broken out on Christmas Eve had shown the San Franciscans how ill-prepared and vulnerable they were to this form of devastation. Since then they had organized themselves into volunteer fire departments and had begun acquiring the equipment necessary to fight a conflagration. They also had dug wells and cisterns at all of the intersections and had filled them with water from the bay, for in December they had been defeated by a lack of water. Although men privately said they knew the fire had been set by incendiaries, and the criminals of Sydney Town were blamed, there had been no trial, for nobody would publicly accuse them. And now on May fourth another fire was blazing. As Darcy ran outside with the others he heard a man who was running up the street scream, "It was set! It was done on purpose—just like the last one!"

"Now I know what the Ducks were cackling about," Mike muttered.

He ripped the cover off the huge cistern on the corner of the street, and with the help of Darcy, Sam, and the other patrons of the saloon he began wetting down the buildings in the block. The fire was still three blocks away, but a strong wind was fanning the flames right toward Mike's place. Ahead of them the gray shadows of Sydney Ducks darted in and out of the deserted buildings looting in methodical order. The firefighters now numbered several hundred citizens, but the blaze moved too fast for them, inexorably licking its way toward the saloon and finally engulfing it.

Though Mike worked like a madman, darting inside and beating at the flames with a rug and even with his hands, the fire gained on him. And the buckets of water the other men were throwing on the burning building were like droplets against the searing heat.

Coughing from steam and smoke, Mike finally emerged to stand helplessly by and watch while the saloon he had worked so hard to build was consumed and there was nothing left but a smoking, blackened ruin. The volunteers were able to stop the fire in the next block, but this was small comfort to the burly Irishman who had just lost everything.

The ache inside him too great for tears, he shrugged his shoulders, looked at the spot where his saloon had stood, and said, "I guess it's my fate."

"Come on up to the hotel," said Pa. "We'll have a bite and see what we can do about rebuilding it." Mike mutely shook his head, but he followed Pa and the others to the Brown Palace.

"If you ask me, it was deliberately set again," said Ma as she passed out steaming mugs of coffee, sandwiches, and wedges of pie to the smoke-blackened firefighters.

"No doubt about it," said Pa angrily.

"They were looting the stores just ahead of it just like there was no law here at all," said Holt.

"Why do you let them get away with it?" asked Darcy. He looked down the long table of men.

"People are afraid," said Pa.

"Well, this just can't go on," said Ma. "You men are going to have to do something about Sydney Town and that band of thieves that calls themselves 'Hounds.' "She walked over to Mike. "I've got a nice back room," she said. "You can stay there till we rebuild your place. It won't be the same, but we'll make it as fine as any saloon in town."

"I'm not going to rebuild," said Mike. He turned to Darcy. "You still want me to help you with that saloon down on Washington?"

"You mean you'd come in with me?" asked Darcy.

"There's nothing to stop me now."

"Hey, Holt," cried Darcy. "I told you things were coming my way."

Holt stared at his partner dumbfounded. How could he be so callous about Mike's loss, he wondered.

For one of the rare times in his life, Darcy blushed. He hadn't meant it the way it had sounded, but there it hung in the air, stopping all conversation at the table. Turning back to Mike, he muttered, "I'm sorry." He got up and left the room.

Mike motioned to Sam and followed him out. "No grudge," he said, holding out his hand, "partner."

"Darcy, you won't need me with Mike to run your place," said Sam. "I think I'll just go on back to Philadelphia."

"I'd still like you to come in with us," said Darcy. "We do need you." He turned to Mike for corroboration.

"Sure do," said Mike. "Somebody in this group ought to have a head for business, and since Darcy and I don't, it looks like you're elected."

"I don't have much money."

"That doesn't matter," said Darcy. "You can work out your third. Mike and I don't know much about building. You're chief architect and contractor."

From that night on Darcy was completely engrossed in building his saloon, and whenever Holt approached him about the business of the B.C.A. and D., he dismissed him quickly. "Whatever you decide is all right with me."

Holt awakened to the realization that if they were to expand the business to San Francisco at this time he was going to have to be the one to do it. As Mirina hadn't welcomed him back to her bed since the baby's birth, he directed all of his energy to the B.C.A. and D., spending long hours making out lists of supplies and planning how to proceed. When he had finished, he wrote to Goldie and Kevin giving them a complete account. An unaccustomed satisfaction and a sense of growing importance filled him as he posted the letter to Little Flats.

CHAPTER **26** A PILGRIMAGE TO
RANCHO RIO ORO★★★★★★★★★★★★★★★★★★★★★★★★★★★

The big freight wagon driven by Pi Ling and Mao Tai rolled down from the hills bearing Goldie toward Sacramento. Her mission was to find suitable office and store space for the B.C.A. and D. in town and to visit the Cunninghams and Milfords and other farming friends and ask them to sell their produce to the firm.

She noted with pleasure the cultivated fields that now lined the approach to the city. People have come to stay, she observed. Eagerly looking for changes in Sacramento itself since she had last seen it six months ago, she was gratified to see the number of fresh new wooden buildings that had been built. By the time she arrived at Horace Ogilvy's impressive La Portal, she had caught the fever of the humming city beside the rushing river. It was good to be back in the heart of things. Scarcely noticing the neat room above the restaurant which Horace showed her, she launched into an account of the central office and store the B.C.A. and D. wanted to build in Sacramento.

"And we've got to have enough space for warehouses," she finished breathlessly.

"Now, that's a real stumper," said Horace. He scratched the bald spot on the top of his head. "You thought about renting?"

"Kevin and Gray told me to buy if I could."

"Come to think of it, there is a spot. Not too far from the river. . .just a few blocks over. Was a feed store. You'd have a building to start with. Owner died. . .understand the heirs want cash. You want to go see it?"

"You just bet I do."

When she looked at the old, weathered, barnlike building, the split rail fence around the corral, and the generally dilapidated appearance of the place, she was disappointed. But it stood on an acre and a half of ground, and the land was included in the deal.

"It'll be worth a lot someday," said Horace.

"Yes, I suppose you're right," said Goldie unenthusiastically. "Ugh! The place is swarming with mosquitoes, and the ground's absolutely soggy. I don't know if we could do anything with it. But I'll show it to Pi Ling and Mao Tai."

"Why?" asked Horace in surprise.

"Because they're shrewd and I respect their judgment," she answered.

When Goldie brought Pi Ling and Mao Tai to view the property, they were ecstatic.

"We get it foh you, Missy Goldie," said Pi Ling.

Still doubtful, Goldie said, "But what about the mosquitoes? We'll never get rid of them. The place is nothing but a marsh."

"Get lid," said Mao Tai. "Get oil. . .lots oil."

"Whale oil?"

"Yes, lots oil. No mouh flying things."

"Well, if you're sure."

"Suuh," said Mao Tai with great confidence

"We talk to lawyuh," said Pi Ling. "Not want you be cheated."

"All right." She agreed, primarily because she was intrigued by the suggestion that the Chinese act as negotiators and wanted to see what they would do.

Horace Ogilvy took Goldie and her entourage to the office of Jack Lawson, the lawyer handling the property, and introduced them. Then he stepped discreetly back to allow them to conduct their business.

"We were wondering how much you were asking for the Meadows' feed store and property?" Goldie began.

"A fine piece of property," said Mr. Lawson. "Very fine." At this approach Pi Ling and Mao Tai began to frown. Mr. Lawson glanced at them uneasily but continued with an unctuous smile. "It's bound to increase in value." Pi Ling and Mao Tai began to shake their heads negatively and stuck their hands in their loose flowing blue sleeves.

"The heirs were thinking in the neighborhood of five thousand dollars," Mr. Lawson rushed on, rattled by the antics of the two Celestials.

Pi Ling looked pained, and Mao Tai closed his eyes in horror.

"Five thousand dollars?" questioned Goldie.

"Well, yes, that is the figure we had worked out." Mr. Lawson anxiously eyed the now inscrutable Chinese. He was thoroughly sick of this particular piece of property, which he must unload if he ever expected to collect his fee for handling the late Mr. Meadows' affairs.

"Well, I don't know," said Goldie hesitantly. "What do you think, Pi Ling?" She turned to the Chinese.

"Missy Goldie—no," said Pi Ling.

"Tellible plice," added Mao Tai. "Land no good." He shook his head negatively.

"I guess that's it then," said Goldie.

"Are these your associates, Miss Baxter?" asked the mystified lawyer.

"Oh, yes." Goldie smiled at him vacuously.

"What price do you think you would consider?" Mr. Lawson asked the Celestials.

"Two thousand dollah," said Mao Tai blandly without flicking an eyelash or changing his expression

It was Mr. Lawson's turn to be startled. "Two thousand?" he repeated faintly.

"Land bad," said Mao Tai.

"Low," added Pi Ling. "Damp. . .bad foh building."

"Flying things," said Mao Tai. He slapped at imaginary insects. "Unhealthy!" He nodded his head sagely at Goldie.

"Come, Missy Goldie," said Pi Ling. "We find bettah place."

"Now, wait a minute," said Mr. Lawson. "I mean, you'll have to admit that your offer is a bit low."

"Low!" exclaimed Pi Ling in mock indignation. "No want Missy Goldie be cheated. Blothuh Glay no like."

"No, and Blothuh Kevin, Holt, and Dahcy. No like at all," said Mao Tai. "We go."

"If you make it twenty-five hundred, you've got yourselves a deal," said Mr. Lawson. Nervously he pulled out a handkerchief and began mopping his red, perspiring face.

"No know," said Mao Tai. He turned to Pi Ling, and the two began rapidly chattering in Chinese. They flailed their arms about and vigorously shook their heads at each other as if to punctuate what they were saying.

Mr. Lawson, now completely demoralized by this unorthodox approach to business, darted his eyes back and forth anxiously from one Oriental face to the other. As the interchange between the two mounted in intensity, he finally threw up his hands and shouted, "All right. . .all right. . .you win. Two thousand dollars. And I'm well rid of it and you."

"We accept," said Pi Ling. His face shaped into a beatific smile.

"Velly good," said Mao Tai. "You dlaw up papahs now?"

"Yes, yes, of course," said Mr. Lawson. "Right away."

Buoyed up by the coup of gaining the Meadows' property for so reasonable a price, Goldie contemplated the second part of her assignment with even greater zest. She left Mao Tai to rid the place of mosquitoes and prepare the former feed store to house its new business and, accompanied by Pi Ling, began her tour of the farms with a visit to the Cunninghams.

Dora rushed into the yard and swept Goldie close to her thin, gaunt frame. Her calico dress was clean but faded and worn, and Goldie suddenly felt uncomfortable in her new gingham traveling dress and matching sunbonnet. But under Dora's hug all self-consciousness engendered by old friends meeting after long absence evaporated.

"Now let me look at you." Dora stepped back and surveyed Goldie from head to foot. "My, you do look prosperous," she commented without envy. "It looks as if that store of yours is doing well."

"Oh, Dora, it is." Goldie was radiant. "It really is. But what about you? The crops look good. Are you happy?"

"Can't complain," said Dora. "Tim's leg mended fine. And we just finished the barn. Guess you can tell—still smells of new wood. Children are all fine." She looked behind her. "Ruth, Adam, say hello to Goldie."

Nine-year-old Adam, who had been standing back and boring his fists into his pockets, said, "Goldie, you gonna make us some biscuits? She makes the bestest biscuits," he confided matter-of-factly to Pi Ling.

"It ain't nice to ask Goldie to work, Adam," said Dora. "She's company."

"No I'm not," said Goldie. "And I'd love to make you some biscuits." She picked Adam up by the elbows and started to twirl him around. "I can't do that as well as I used to," she gasped as she set him back down. "You're getting heavy."

"I'm as high as Isaiah's shoulder now," said Adam with pride.

Goldie made the promised biscuits and she and Pi Ling sat down to supper with the Cunninghams. Goldie told Tim that the B.C.A. and D. would like to buy chickens, eggs, wheat, and vegetables from him and some of the other families she and Gray knew.

"I'll be glad to sell to you," said Tim. "I'm already selling milk to several places in Sacramento."

"I plan to visit the Scotts and Hales and the Milfords, too," said Goldie. "I suppose they have much the same things you're growing."

"That's right," said Tim. "They're all farming just like me. What you really ought to have is a place to get meat. I hear the miners are really yelling for fresh meat."

"It would be a real feather in our caps if we could get any," agreed Goldie. "None of the other stores sells meat."

"Then you ought to see Zack," said Tim. "He's going into the cattle business in a big way, I hear. It ain't really too far to his place. It's near Auburn."

A tinge of pink came into Goldie's cheeks. She had been hoping she would be able to find out about Zack without having to ask, for she didn't want her friends to guess that his neglect of her since her arrival in California troubled her.

"Has he been here?" she inquired in what she hoped was a casual manner.

"No, he hasn't been down to Sacramento so far as I know," said Tim. "But he's been to Marysville and the Milfords have seen him. You can find out more about how to get to his place from them."

So he had been to see the Milfords, thought Goldie with resentment, and I'll bet Mary's got her hooks into him. She was surprised at how much it stung to think that Zack had taken the trouble to visit Mary Milford but hadn't even sent her a note. Not even a "where's my fifty dollars" note, she inwardly fumed. She looked at Tim to see if he would say more, but he volunteered nothing further.

Goldie found that her mind was not on business as she drove toward the Milfords, stopping at the Scotts and Hales along the way. She successfully negotiated with both families for their produce, but her thoughts were of Zack and how she could get Mary to talk about him without seeming obvious.

"Land sakes," exclaimed Sara, coming out of the house as Goldie and Pi Ling drove up in the buggy. "You do have the habit of turning up like the proverbial penny, Goldie Baxter."

"Not a bad one I hope," said Goldie. Pi Ling helped her down, and she said, "This is my friend and associate, Pi Ling."

"Oh, now, you must be one of them Celestials I been hearing about," said Sara. "You're welcome, I'm sure." She extended her hand to Pi Ling, who took it and gave it three solemn shakes up and down.

"Mary," called Sara. "Mary, look who's here."

Mary ran out of the house and screamed, "I know someone who's going to be mighty glad to see you!"

"Who's that?" asked Goldie. Sure that the answer would be "Zack," she felt the heat rush into her face and turned her head away.

"Why Dan, of course."

"Oh," said Goldie, and firmly hoped Mary hadn't seen her disappointment.

"I'll show you to your room while Ma's settling your Chinaman," said Mary. She led Goldie up the stairs to the second story of the farmhouse. "Saw Zack last week," she continued.

"Oh, did you?" said Goldie. Her heart began to pound, but she deliberately kept an offhand tone in her voice. "Does he live near here?"

"More nearer Grass Valley. But he was down to Marysville on business and stopped by. He asked about you."

So I should go to Grass Valley first, thought Goldie. Aloud she said, "That's nice. Is he doing well?"

"He's running beef on his place," said Mary. "Says he's going to build up a herd and sell meat all over the state."

"I wonder if he'd sell to us?" Goldie ventured as if the thought of contacting Zack had just occurred to her. Even Pi Ling would now see the logic of visiting Zack's ranch, she thought.

Her mind racing ahead in this manner, she scarcely listened until she heard Mary say, "He's asked me up to visit this summer."

"What?" said Goldie, startled back to the present.

"Oh, of course, he's asked Dan too," Mary went on. "But won't that be exciting? His land goes way up into the Sierras, you know. He's going to be terribly rich."

So Zack had not only come to see Mary but also had asked her up for a visit. What could he possibly see in her, Goldie wondered. She isn't even pretty, she thought uncharitably. Suddenly the whole plan to visit him seemed silly. It was so transparent he'd see right through it. She wouldn't be fooling him or anybody else. She was beginning to get a headache from Mary's going on about him, or from the long drive, or from both. At any rate, she wished Mary would go away.

At this moment Sara called from downstairs, "Mary, do come down here this instant and leave Goldie in peace to freshen up. Dan and Pa will be home any minute, and there'll be plenty of time to talk then."

At dinner that night she stole glances from beneath her lashes at Dan Milford, whom she hadn't seen for nearly a year. The awkward, gawky look of unseasoned youth had been replaced by the lean, raw-boned, tight-skinned look of a man of the soil. The girl who marries him can expect a good, hard, honest life, Goldie thought grimly. She wondered if this was the way Zack would look to her too.

Sara suggested that Dan take Goldie for a walk around the farm after dinner. This was something Goldie had anticipated but dreaded. Dan waxed enthusiastic over the grain, the garden, and the fruit trees the Milfords had planted, and on this safe ground Goldie displayed real interest. But after they had discussed the farm and the future of the state they found they had nothing further to say to each other and in awkward silence returned to the house

Goldie got Mathew Milford to agree to sell the firm his garden produce, wheat, and fruit before she and Pi Ling moved on the next morning. At least this part of the trip had been profitable, she thought, pleased with the contacts she had made.

"Now who we see?" asked Pi Ling. The astute Chinese had deduced that there was more to the side trip they were taking than a sounding out of new territory for the B.C.A. and D.

"First we go to Grass Valley to see if we could open up some stores in the north," said Goldie.

"Pi Ling know that. But who we see?"

"We see another old friend."

"Yes?" said Pi Ling encouragingly.

"He was our scout on the wagon train," Goldie continued. And then searching desperately for something to make the trip sound necessary to Pi Ling, she added, "And I owe him fifty dollars."

"Missy Goldie not tell all."

Again Goldie found herself blushing. "I did too!" she protested hotly.

"Pi Ling see," said the persistent Chinese.

They stopped at a wayside inn near Brown's Valley that night and the next evening arrived in Grass Valley.

Out of a sense of duty Goldie took a cursory look at the town. She concluded that it was prosperous and would be a good place to open a store. But now that she was so near to Zack, she found she couldn't keep her mind on business and hurried back to the hotel to get directions to his ranch.

"You can't miss it," said the heavy-jowled proprietor. "There are two tall pines on either side of the turn. . .about ten, mebbe eleven miles down the road. It's on the American River."

"Oh, yes, I see," said Goldie.

"Guess that's why he called it Rancho Rio Oro," the man laughed at his little witticism. "It's where they discovered the gold, you know."

The next day was soft and warm, affirming that summer was close at hand. All about them the hills were clothed in the intense green garb of spring, accented by the blue of the lupin and the gold of the poppies. And in the sunlight the sky was so brilliant and deep that Goldie thought she could see to eternity. Her spirit soared to the top and beyond the tall ponderosa pines through which they passed, and she took in the heady fragrance of the trees in greedy gulps. With every mile her confidence mounted. Surely nothing could go wrong on a day like today.

"Oh, I could stay here forever," she announced in breathless excitement.

She spotted two tall pines framing a wagon path to the left of the road. "This must be it," she said. Her voice was breathy with excitement. Soon she would see Zack. But would he be glad to see her? Her stomach began to somersault and her hands tensed in her lap as the buggy jolted up the road that was little more than a horse trail.

They drove, twisting and turning, back through the hills. The trail seemed endless. But just as both of them were beginning to think they had made a mistake, they came out on a clearing. Pi Ling stopped the buggy, and he and Goldie admired the primitive beauty of the buildings nestled beneath the towering oaks and pines. The ranch house, long and low, was constructed of rough-hewn timbers and had a shingled roof. A covered porch ran its entire length. In front of the massive front door and to the left was a hitching post and two rain barrels, and the entire dwelling was shaded by three giant oaks. Behind the main house and to the right was a huge barn, likewise constructed of rough-hewn timber. Beside it was a fenced corral in which several horses placidly paced, and in back of that was another small building which Goldie thought might be a tool shed. To the left of the main house and slightly behind it was another long low wooden building, and behind that still another. Since this last structure would have easy access to the kitchen, Goldie decided it must be the quarters for the house help. As if confirming her thoughts, a tall Indian girl appeared from around the left of the ranch house.

"Welcome to Rancho Rio Oro," she said. "Your business, please?"

"We came to see Zack. . .I mean Mr. Peale," Goldie said. "Is he here?"

"You are a friend?" questioned the Indian.

"Yes, I'm Goldie Baxter. I came out from the East with him on the wagon train."

"Oh," said the Indian. "Peale's out putting a new herd to pasture. He may not be back for some time."

"Oh, dear," said Goldie. "I hadn't thought he might not be here. Could we drive out to where he is?"

"Peale have twenty-five thousand acres," said the girl. "You might get lost."

"I just don't know what to do," said Goldie. "It's too late to find a place to stay the night."

"Peale would want me to offer hospitality," said the Indian with a shrug of her shoulders. "You may stay here."

More by the way she spoke and acted than by what she actually said, Goldie gathered that this Indian maiden was not pleased to have her there, and she wondered what her relationship was with Zack.

"You can sleep in the bunkhouse," the girl told Pi Ling. "That's where the men sleep."

Pi Ling bowed, then the girl turned to Goldie. "You come with me," she said.

"I presume you work for Mr. Peale," said Goldie as she followed the Indian through the heavy oaken door intricately worked with wrought iron hinges and bolts. "How do they call you?"

"Black Feather," responded the girl with obvious reluctance.

She showed Goldie to a room off a hall leading from the living room. Besides being neat and clean, to Goldie's surprise the bedroom was furnished with massive hand-carved furniture, and the bed, plump with a huge feather tick, was covered with a heavy lace bedspread. In addition to the bed there was a carved étagère centered with a full-length mirror, and a huge clothes cupboard. Totally unprepared for such elegance, Goldie was overwhelmed. Even the windows, fitted with real glass and hung with heavy brocade draperies, and the stone fireplace with its black wrought iron grate and bulky andirons betokened great wealth.

After she had hung her dresses in the carved cupboard and had bathed and changed her clothes—Black Feather had produced a real copper bathtub, some buckets of hot water, and some scented soap—Goldie investigated the rest of the house. Black Feather had disappeared and there was nobody else about. In the living room, dominated by a huge stone hearth, tree-filtered sunlight shining through the glass windows dappled the smooth plank floor with soft images and patterns, and the deeply carved Spanish pieces and upholstered sofas and chairs scattered about gave the room a feeling of luxury. But what caught her fancy was a small lady rocker with deep ruby red velvet upholstery which sat in front of the fireplace facing a large masculine-looking chair with rolled arms and covered in a wine-colored leather.

She clasped her hands in delight and ran over to sit in it. As she rocked back and forth soaking up the unpretentious beauty of the spacious room, she slowly began to realize that Zack was preparing this house for a woman. Had he already found her, she wondered. Was that why he had never written? Was he about to be married? With a pang she realized she didn't like the idea of a strange woman living in this beautiful house. But maybe she wasn't strange. It might be this Black Feather, although she doubted it. Was it Mary Milford? She had to know.

Her pleasure gone, she got up from the chair and for want of anything else to do, continued her tour of the house. There was a dining room furnished with a large carved table, twelve chairs, and two huge sideboards. Beyond that was the kitchen. Goldie peeked in, fearing another encounter with the sullen Black Feather. But the kitchen was empty. The long work tables, sink with a hand pump, and cast-iron cookstove reminded her of the inn back home. Like every other room she had been in, the kitchen was large, airy, and spacious.

Although she had not explored the rest of the house, she was drawn outside toward a small building by the barn. When she peered in, she saw that it was a blacksmith shop. The forge was lighted, and a wiry Mexican with a huge walrus mustache was standing over it beating on a piece of iron with a heavy hammer.

"Hello," said Goldie. "Did you do all of the iron work in the house?"

"I deed," replied the old Mexican.

"It's very beautiful."

"Thank you."

"The whole place is lovely."

"The patrón ees very careful about everything."

"Do you mean Mr. Peale?"

"Sí. He does not like me to call heem that. But that ees what he ees. . .a patrón."

Goldie wondered what a patrón was. "I didn't realize the place was so big," she said. "It never occurred to me that Mr. Peale wouldn't be here or within call, or I wouldn't have stopped."

"He'll be here by sunset. . .do not concern yourself," said the Mexican.

"Oh, I'm so glad. You see, I've come such a long way." Then she wondered why Black Feather had told her Zack was far away and she didn't know when he would be back. But she didn't want to take the time now to puzzle over the Indian's hostility, for she was far more interested in finding out about Zack and his ranch, and the old Mexican smithy seemed inclined to talk.

"I don't mean to pry," she said. "But does Mr. Peale have a lot of people working for him?"

"Sí. . .many. Some Indian, some Spanish like me. He runs a large herd now."

"I see," said Goldie, but she had been confronted with another unfamiliar term. Now what does running a large herd mean, she wondered? Then she remembered that Black Feather had said Zack had twenty-five thousand acres of land. Why that's several miles, she thought almost in panic. Zack had owned all of this— from the very beginning—and yet on the long trip out he had never mentioned the extent of his holdings.

She excused herself from the blacksmith and wandered toward the barn. She noticed a large chicken yard, not visible from the front of the house, and a small fenced pasture with some milk cows and newly born calves in it. And beyond that she saw a large vegetable garden with three more Mexicans toiling in it.

As more and more she realized the vastness of Zack's operation, her heart sank. She felt foolish about dealing with him for beef, foolish about offering him back the fifty dollars he had given her at Fort Bridger when Gray was so ill, and most of all, foolish about stopping to see him at all. What could he possibly think but that she was some silly moonstruck girl chasing after him? She crimsoned at the thought of his amusement. If she could only take Pi Ling and fly away before Zack returned! But the lengthening shadows in the yard told her the sun would soon be out of sight beyond the hills, and she could not leave now, for neither she nor Pi Ling knew the road. She must stay and brazen it out. Well, if she had to meet him, she reasoned, at least she would do so with dignity—just an old friend dropping by to see how he was. She'd give him no reason to laugh. Then she glanced down at her frock. This won't do, she thought in dismay. She must wear something to make her look older and more sophisticated.

She rushed indoors and stood before the carved étagère with its full-length mirror. She was the picture of girlish simplicity in her white dimity that belled out entrancingly from her waist. The dress was cinched in with the blue taffeta sash that matched her eyes and slippers. But girlishness was the last thing she needed now, she thought grimly. Frantic to be changed by the time Zack arrived, she unfastened her dress, fumbling in her haste, and opened the wardrobe, taking out the green silk she had worn on the trip to Hyattsville with Darcy in March.

That's better, she thought as she viewed herself in the mirror once more. The low décolletage revealed the emergence of her budding young breasts, and the tiny puffed sleeves exposed the whiteness of her arms. Her copper hair, swept back and poufed above her forehead, fell in long curls on her neck. She swirled around, enjoying the sight of her yards of skirt. Now let him come, she thought. She was pinching her cheeks to bring out the color and touching her comb to her hair when she heard the ranch dogs begin to bark, followed by the sound of stomping horses, creaking saddles, and men's voices.

It must be Zack, she thought. Completely forgetting her intention of being aloof and sophisticated, she hoisted up her skirts and ran for the front door. Her heart racing, she catapulted herself off the porch, then stopped short in embarrassment. She shot a look toward the dismounting men, hoping none of them had seen her indecorous charge, then carefully dropped her skirts and approached at a more sedate pace. But she could not keep the color out of her cheeks or her hands from shaking with excitement and apprehension.

Zack, already dismounted, was standing with his back to her. She breathed a sigh of relief that he had not seen her running. In his left hand he lightly held the reins of a magnificent golden stallion. Then Goldie's eyes widened. Black Feather was standing in front of him, and with his free hand, he reached over and chucked her under the chin. But she had no time to speculate about this, for Black Feather said something to him. He whirled

304

around, dropped the reins of his horse, and with effortless speed and grace stood before Goldie looking down at her. Without speaking he folded her into his arms and kissed her. She felt the pressure of his hard body against hers, and she was engulfed by the same wild thrill she had experienced on the other two occasions when he had kissed her. When he released her, her head was whirling so that she swayed. He held her by both hands at arms' length.

"Goldie," he said, "I wasn't ready for you yet."

Completely disconcerted, she stammered, "I—I brought you back your fifty dollars." She blushed a deep scarlet. What a fool thing to say, she thought.

But Zack only laughed and put his arm around her shoulders in a familiar manner. "Come on in," he said. "I've got so much to tell you. But first I've got to get out of these." He looked down at his work-soiled clothes.

And now Goldie noticed he wasn't wearing his white buckskins. Instead, he had on dungarees, boots, and a flannel shirt just like Gray or one of the other boys would wear. In fact, he was dressed no differently than the hundreds of miners Goldie had seen in the past months. But it wasn't his clothing that made him look so different; it was his face. She scarcely recognized him. Gone was the flowing light brown beard and mustache he had worn on the wagon train. Now Zack was clean-shaven except for a day's stubble of beard. His mouth was well-formed and sensitive, and it turned up at the corners; and his chin was straight and firm. Goldie decided he was a very handsome man as she stole furtive glances at him while they walked into the house.

"How do you like the place?" Zack asked, looking searchingly into her eyes.

"It's beautiful," said Goldie shyly. "I didn't realize you were so rich."

"It's a good spread, and I'm comfortable now. But I nearly lost it last fall."

"Yes, I heard."

"I've kept tabs on you too. Know all about you and Gray and the B.C.A. and D. Are you satisfied now that you've proved you can make your way in a new land?"

"We're really only starting. We've got big plans for expansion."

"Oh? Well, I'll have to hear about that as soon as I've changed."

"And I'd better see about Pi Ling while you're cleaning up," said Goldie. "He's in the bunkhouse."

"So you brought one of the Chinese with you."

"Yes, we never go anywhere without at least one of them along."

"A good idea. But don't worry about him. My men are polite." He smiled at her, then disappeared down the hall into one of the rooms Goldie hadn't seen. Suddenly she was seized with an overpowering curiosity to see Zack's bedroom, but she managed to resist it, and instead went out to the bunkhouse.

The hands, most of whom were of Spanish descent, were gracious to her, and, unlike Black Feather, made her feel welcome. She also could tell that though curious about him, they were friendly to Pi Ling. And so, satisfied that the Chinese was all right, she returned to the house.

She found Zack supervising two older Mexican women who were setting the table in the dining room. Black Feather was nowhere to be seen. In the center of the long table tall white tapers cupped in two elaborate silver candelabra flanked a centerpiece of wild flowers and forest fern.

"I remember how you like flowers," Zack said, glancing up. Then he returned to his work. He was as exacting and meticulous about the placement of each glass and plate as he had always been about everything on the wagon train.

Goldie was overwhelmed by the array of fine silver, china, and crystal. She tried to picture Zack sitting in the cabin in Little Flats eating off the plain crockery, but couldn't. She even found it difficult to recall that she had seen him eating beans off a tin plate on the way West. How much further apart they were now, she thought with a sweep of regret.

She felt further dwarfed when she saw the formidable length of polished table that would separate her from Zack at dinner. She decided she couldn't bear it. Meekly she asked, "Would you mind if I sat next to you at the head of the table? I'd feel like I had to shout from way down there."

Zack seemed pleased with the suggestion and ordered one of the Mexican women to reset Goldie's place next to his. During dinner he asked her about the B.C.A. and D., and Goldie tried to answer his questions as factually as she could. But she found herself distracted by his white ruffled shirt, silk tie, and green brocade coat. This was certainly a Zack she had never seen before. He ate his meal with an elegance that bespoke of breeding she could only guess at. The rumors about him on the trail came back to her mind. Oh, if she had only known how worldly he really was, she would never have come here, calling like a neighbor in Indiana. She felt swallowed up way beyond her depth. With difficulty she tried to concentrate on what he was saying.

"How long do you think it will take the B.C.A. and D. to become a paying enterprise?" he asked

"Oh, soon—or I guess it's that now," she fumbled. "Only we keep putting our profits into expansion."

Zack rose. Taking her arm, he escorted her into the living room, where logs were burning in the fireplace. In front of it sat a small table with a top of inlaid wood in intricate design. It held a silver coffeepot, two fine china cups and saucers, and a crystal bottle of cordial with matching glasses. Zack indicated that Goldie should take the red velvet rocker. He gazed at her a moment and nodded in satisfaction at the picture she made.

Then he said, "Since you're in the black, you really don't need to shepherd the firm anymore, do you?"

Goldie wondered what he was driving at. "Oh, I'll never be satisfied till we're a real success." She lifted the pot and began pouring the coffee. "Sugar?"

"Please." He took the cup. "I'm a success," he said.

Why was he stating the obvious, she wondered. Maybe he was making fun of her. She gave him a piercing look, but his face told her nothing. "That's why you should understand why I want to be one, too," she said.

"Goldie," said Zack with great patience, "I'm trying to tell you that I'm rich."

"Oh, I know that." She was at a loss. He was neither bragging to her nor patronizing her, but he didn't seem to understand what she meant. "I think it's wonderful—what you've done. And I hope to be rich like this someday too. And—and have lovely things like you have."

"Damn it, girl!" Zack exploded. "Can't you see I'm asking you to marry me?"

Goldie stared at him in amazement. Her mind was incapable of switching so suddenly from the discussion of money. She blurted out, "But I—I haven't thought about getting married. I'm not a success yet."

"What the hell's that got to do with it? Don't you see you will be rich and a success if you marry me?"

"It's not the same," said Goldie stubbornly. "*I* have to do it."

"So that's all there is to it. You want to get rich so you won't marry me."

"Well, no. I'm awfully fond of you. But——"

"Fond of me!" Zack shouted. "Is that why you kiss me the way you do?"

"I can't explain that," said Goldie. She wished he hadn't brought that up. Even now she could feel her blood surge at the thought of his lips on hers.

"Well, I can." He stood up and crossed over to her chair. "We were made for each other, you silly girl." He lifted her up roughly by her elbows and once more kissed her passionately, and this time violently.

She felt his arms shake and his strong muscles ripple. A mad ecstatic thrill seized her, and she put her arms around his neck.

"Say you love me," Zack whispered fiercely.

"Oh I do—I do love you," Goldie whispered back and lifted her face to be kissed again.

Zack bent down once more. Then suddenly he was lifting her in his arms and carrying her down the hall to the room Goldie had wondered about. He tenderly laid her on the bed; all of the time her hungry mouth was seeking his. His hands began undoing the basque of her dress, and she didn't care. This was an ecstasy, a thrill she had never dreamed of. He pressed his lips to her breast, and she stroked his head. Then abruptly he raised up.

"No, not this way," he choked. "By God, I won't have you this way!" He sprang off the bed. "You'll come to me of your own free will or not at all," he said firmly and left the room.

Goldie's head throbbed, and her mind reeled in a bewildered jumble. Why had he left her? What had she done? In a daze she sat up and blankly looked down at the open bodice of her dress. She gasped and began to cry. Shame flooded over her. "What's the matter with me?" she sobbed. "Would I act this way with any man?" What did Zack think of her now, a girl who would have surrendered without a moment's thought? How could she ever face him after this? Fumbling with the hooks, she fastened up her dress and climbed ungracefully off the bed. She peeked out the door into the deserted hall, then rushed down to the safety of her room. Once inside she threw herself on the lace-covered bed and sobbed herself into a fitful sleep.

Zack paced the living room for hours before going wearily to bed. "You fool!" he upbraided himself. "You unmitigated fool!"

Goldie remained in her room until late the next morning; her hope was that Zack would be gone off to his cows or anywhere just so she wouldn't have to face him. But she did not hear the men leave and finally knew that she must come out.

One of the Mexican women was tidying up the living room. "Ah, you up," she said. "We have nice breakfast now."

"I'm not very hungry," said Goldie mournfully.

"Have nice biscuits—very light," said the Mexican. "Good with blackberry jam."

Aware that further protest was futile, Goldie murmured, "Thank you."

While she was eating her breakfast, surprised to find that the food tasted good instead of like ashes, she heard the front door open and knew Zack had come in.

"Pi Ling tells me you want to contract to buy some of my beef," he began, quite distantly.

"Yes," said Goldie, "we would." She found it difficult to look at him and engrossed herself in buttering a biscuit.

"It's agreeable to me," said Zack.

"That's really why I came," lied Goldie.

"I see," said Zack. He sat at the far end of the table and spoke softly. "Goldie, I want to apologize for last night. It was just that seeing you after so long a time—well, anyway, I promise you it won't happen again."

But I want it to happen again, thought Goldie wildly, and knew she was blushing.

Zack continued. "Just one thing though...don't come back unless you mean to stay. If there's any business dealings, send Gray or one of the others."

Goldie nodded mutely.

"Well, I guess that's about all we have to say to each other," he said and rose from the table. He crossed to her chair, and Goldie's heart beat expectantly. But he merely reached down and put his hand under her chin. "I guess I thought you were more grown up than you are," he said, tilting her face up and smiling sadly. Then he turned and walked out.

309

A few minutes later she heard the jangle of harnesses, the halloos of the vaqueros, and the barking of the dogs as Zack and his men rode out to his herd.

Silent and subdued, Goldie climbed into the buggy beside Pi Ling and left the ranch. In Sacramento she found Gray overseeing the renovation of the Meadows' property. She rushed into his arms and promptly burst into tears. Gray patted her and looked quizzically at Pi Ling, who pointed to his heart.

When Gray found out Goldie had visited Zack, he knew the source of her distress, for he had been aware for a long time of Zack's interest in his sister. But he also knew that she would have to find the answer to her feelings about Zack herself. He wanted to help her, though, and thought part of her quandary was rooted in the fear of being lonely. Maybe if she got a real taste of city living, he reasoned, she might be better able to know her own mind.

"Why don't you stay in Sacramento to handle the express runs and our business deals?" he said. "This is the real center of all our operations. And since you keep the records and books, this is the logical place for you to be."

"Oh, could I?" asked Goldie. "I'd like that. But what about the others?"

"They won't mind. Holt and Darcy have sent a fellow named Sam Wackem back to Philadelphia to bring out a shipload of goods and some bricks for the store and office in San Francisco. They're operating out of temporary quarters right now. And, oh yes, Holt's building a house for his wife and baby. I think they'll both be tied up there for quite a while."

Goldie would have liked Gray to stay in Sacramento. With him to talk to, the perplexing problems of love and marriage faded away. But Gray had to return to Little Flats and Hyattsville. And with a heavy heart she realized that instead of seeing more of each other, she and Gray would likely see each other less and less. She sighed as she thought how differently everything was working out from what she had envisioned when she had conceived the idea of the B.C.A. and D.

As the June fog swirled around the hills of San Francisco and Mirina never once came up the hill from the hotel to see the house Pa Brown and Hop Sing were helping him build for her and little John, Holt's disposition became as dour as the days. Often he wondered why he was even building the house. He and Mirina still slept in separate rooms at the hotel, and he never saw her except at dinner.

Full of glum thoughts about the mess he had made of his life, he was astounded one morning to see Hop Sing indiscriminately fitting together the expensive dining room woodwork and banging nails into it at random.

"What the hell's the matter with you today?" he roared.

Hop Sing jumped. "Solly, Bothuh Holt," he said, "have been thinking of something else."

"Well. . .go on."

"Do wonduh if could have some gold flom little glass jah."

"It's your money. You've earned it. How much do you want?"

"Don't know," said Hop Sing. "May need a lot, maybe not so much."

"Say, you're not thinking of setting up a business, are you?" teased Holt.

"Oh no," said Hop Sing. "Not foh business, foh pleasuh. Boat come in yestuhday flom China."

"Yes, I heard," said Holt, beginning to scowl again. "They're going to sell some more of your countrymen into slavery—only they don't call it that. They call it hired labor."

"Not intelested in that. Some on boat is gulls."

"Oh, now I see. You want to buy a wife."

"No wife," said Hop Sing. He shook his head in disdain. "Slave gull. . .to do bidding of mastuh."

"No, Hop Sing, that's wrong," Holt said firmly.

"Why long?"

"Because nobody should be a slave. Slavery's wrong." Hop Sing stared at him, and Holt knew he did not understand. For a moment he was at a loss to explain, then he said, "Look, you didn't like it when Sam Wolff owned you, did you?"

Hop Sing looked alarmed. "I offend Blothuh Holt? You sell me?"

"That's the whole point. I could never sell you—" Hop Sing's face showed relief—"Because I don't own you."

Hop Sing looked bewildered. "No own?" he questioned.

"No. No man has the right to own another man."

"Oh, Hop Sing see now," said the wily Oriental. "But this diflent. This not man. . .this woman."

"The same thing applies to women."

"But then," said Hop Sing in real distress, "how do I get woman? Blothuh Holt have woman," he sulked. "Why cannot Hop Sing have woman too?"

"You can. But you mustn't *own* her."

"But if do not buy, cannot have."

Holt pondered for a moment, then said, "I'll tell you what we'll do. I'll go with you. Then you can pick out the one you want, and I'll buy her and we'll set her free."

"How I be sure I get huh from that?" said Hop Sing darkly.

"Well—" Holt cleared his throat. "We'll just have to let matters take their natural course."

"All light," Hop Sing reluctantly agreed. "But what about othuhs?"

"What others?"

"Othuhs. . .Mao Tai, Che Lai, Sun Luck, Pi——"

"Stop, stop! You mean you all want wives?"

Hop Sing smiled at the word "wife" but nodded.

"I don't think we'd better get them all at once. I'll tell you what. We'll buy three. Since there are ten of you, surely three of you would like three of them."

"Sound leasonable," said Hop Sing.

"One thing though," Holt said. "If any of you and the girls decide you want to live together, you're going to have to get married. Do you understand that?"

Though Hop Sing showed he thought Holt's insistence on adhering to convention was ridiculous, he agreed.

Holt added forcefully, "You're an American now, Hop Sing."

For a moment Hop Sing looked at Holt in astonishment, then uncertainly he said, "Hop Sing is Amelican like Blothuh Holt."

"Yes," said Holt. He knew that legally this wasn't true, but it was the principle that Hop Sing would understand.

Later in the day Darcy dropped by the house, and Holt could tell he was excited about something.

"I heard a boatload of China boys arrived last night," he said.

"Yes, I know," said Holt evenly as he continued to apply the ceiling molding in the dining room.

"Can't you stop for a minute and come on down? Listen, if we could get some they'd make cheap labor for us."

"What do you mean?" asked Holt. He could feel his throat tighten, and he climbed down from his ladder.

"I mean, if we bought fifty or a hundred of them, we could build up our chain of stores in no time. Think of all the wages we'd save." He chuckled.

"You're talking about human beings," said Holt icily. "They're not animals just to buy and use."

"Well, if we don't buy them someone else will."

"But if we do buy them we'll have to set them free and pay them regular wages just like we do Hop Sing and the others."

"You know we can't afford to do that. Look, Holt, no matter how much you may dislike it, slave labor is a fact. It's used all over. I come from a whole way of life that's based on it, and it works. It's the only way to make money."

Holt was surprised at his own calmness. "I'm just going to say two things. First, California is going to be admitted as a free state."

"It hasn't been admitted yet, and that's the very issue that's holding it up."

"I know that. But it will be admitted, and on that basis. And second, besides myself, you have three other partners who have been raised to loathe slavery. We could never use that kind of labor to build anything, no matter how much we wanted it."

Darcy's face reddened. "Have it your way and be damned then! I'm trying to get us ahead. We could never afford to buy a hundred Chinese and set them free."

"No," said Holt. "But we might be able to do it with twenty or so."

"Well, then," said Darcy, smiling once more and clapping Holt on the back, "let's go to the auction tonight."

"I'm already going."

"You are?" Darcy's face showed his surprise.

"Yes, I promised Hop Sing I'd buy three of the girls for wives for our boys."

"Oh, you are the sly one."

"You're my second bout for the day," said Holt uneasily.

313

Almost unbidden his mind returned to Rio de Janeiro, and once more he felt the agony of the men he had seen chained together in long slave coffers plodding through the streets. He was unable to shake the feeling that by even participating in a slave auction he would be helping to perpetuate a system he believed to be wrong.

That evening when Holt followed Darcy and Hop Sing down the steps of the cellar on Du Pont Street where the auction was being held, he was revolted by the fetid smell of unwashed bodies and sour breath that rose up from the blackness below. He felt the blood drain from his face and for a moment was sure he was going to be sick. God, how did I ever get into this? he thought in dismay as he reached for his handkerchief to hold to his nose.

As if from a long distance away, he heard Darcy say, "They're selling the women down there. I'll be down at the other end where the men are if you want me." Then Hop Sing tugged insistently at his sleeve.

"Blothuh Holt, come. Must get closuh," he said.

He pulled Holt down toward a platform where a white man with a stubble of beard on his chin was chewing on the end of a black cigar and calling for bids on a frail-looking Chinese girl standing in front of him. Dissatisfied with the response he was receiving, the auctioneer finally tore her cheap cotton jacket down to her waist, revealing her barely formed breasts. The girl's expression did not change, but Holt thought he detected a glistening moistness in the corners of her eyes. Outraged, he stood staring at the girl, unaware that Hop Sing was once more tugging at his sleeve.

"Blothuh Holt, bid," hissed Hop Sing.

In a daze Holt heard a strangled cry of, "Five dollars—I bid five dollars." Then he was amazed to discover that he was the one who had cried out.

Someone else bid seven-fifty, and Holt said ten. He finally got the girl for fifteen and supposed it was because she was so young. The auctioneer pulled up her coat around her and indicated she was to go with Holt, which she meekly did.

"Now folks," said the man, "we can't have no more of this. It ain't hardly payin' for their passage. This is as fine a lot of girls as you'll ever want to see. All virgins—I swear it!" He winked at the assembled men, who guffawed and knowingly clapped each other on the back.

His eyes now having become more accustomed to the gloom, Holt noticed that besides white men there were many Chinese bidding on the girls. They were assembling their purchases as they acquired them in long lines along the wall. It dawned on him what the girls were for, but he asked Hop Sing.

"Oh, they foh the houses," replied the Chinese. "You know. . . wheah men—" he paused as he searched for the right word— "play," he finally said and smiled.

Holt felt unclean. He wanted to get out of this hole and away from the sense of shame it gave him, but he was wedged in so tight he couldn't move.

Sometime later the auctioneer put on the platform a soft, shy girl who kept her head down and was visibly trembling. "Now what'm I bid for this little beauty?" asked the trafficker.

Hop Sing signaled Holt, and again he started the bidding. At Hop Sing's insistence he continued to bid until the girl was theirs for twenty-five dollars. By this time some of the procurers had assembled their chains of human flesh and filed them out. But though the cellar was now half-empty, Holt still felt as if he were suffocating. He wished fervently that Hop Sing would hurry up and make his final choice so they could leave too.

At last a third girl whom the Oriental fancied was placed on the auction block. She looked more sophisticated than the other two but otherwise seemed much the same to Holt. He got her for twenty dollars, then told Hop Sing to wait outside with the three girls while he saw if Darcy was ready to leave.

"Are you finished?" he whispered in Darcy's ear when he found him. "I can't take much more of this."

"You do look bad," said Darcy. "Your first slave auction is kind of unnerving, I guess. Been so long I'd forgotten about that. You'll get used to it after a while."

"I don't want to get used to it," said Holt. "Ever."

"Did you get the girls?"

"Yes. What've you done?"

"Nothing yet. The bidding's been too high."

"Well, come on then, let's go. We don't need any laborers anyway."

"Not just yet, Holt. When most of them are gone, I'm going to offer him a flat sum for the remainder. My father used to do that in New Orleans. Got some pretty good buys that way. . .never lost."

"Do what you like. But remember, we can't go over five hundred dollars."

"I know," said Darcy. "I won't be long."

"I'll meet you back at the hotel."

When Holt got outside he took several deep breaths and mopped his brow with his handkerchief. He looked at the three pieces of paper he held in his hand. They said that he was entitled to the services of the three Chinese girls for five years. It was incredible. Whatever it was called—earning passage money, working for room and board, or simply bonded service for a given length of time—to him it was slavery and could not be disguised. These Chinese were not free to find work or live where they wished, and they were subject to the whims of a master, who might even have the power of life and death over them. He knew that if he lived to be a hundred years old, he would never forget that cellar or the degradation he had witnessed there. And he vowed he would never be a party to the crime of trafficking in human beings again. He turned to Hop Sing and said, "I'd better learn these girls' names. Supposing you introduce me."

Hop Sing spoke to the girls in a Chinese dialect which fortunately they all understood. "This is Lotus Yung," he said, pointing out the second girl they had bought. "And this is May Low." He pointed to the girl the auctioneer had stripped to the waist. "And this is Jasmine Sun." He indicated the one with more curves, and Holt thought he detected that this was Hop Sing's favorite. Then Hop Sing spoke rapidly in Chinese to the girls, ending up with, "Blothuh Holt."

Then he raised his arms as if leading a chorus, and the three girls bowed in unison chanting, "Blothuh Holt."

Holt couldn't help smiling. "Tell them," he said, "that they will be helping Ma Brown around the hotel for a while until they learn some English and some American ways."

Hop Sing again chattered in Chinese, and the girls responded. "They pleased," he said.

Unhampered by the feelings of guilt that bedeviled Holt, Darcy succeeded in procuring the services of twenty-three Chinese laborers for a flat fee of four hundred and fifty dollars. He immediately put them to work building the warehouse and store on the four lots on the Battery.

"That Jasmine's sort of cute," observed Darcy as she waited on the tables in the dining room the next night.

"Never mind," said Holt. He inclined his head toward Mirina.

"If you ask me, she's a whore," said Mirina matter-of-factly. She stood up and handed Holt her shawl. He looked at her in shock, then automatically took the shawl and placed it around her shoulders. "Good evening, gentlemen," she said and left the table.

Holt stood staring after her for a moment. Ladies shouldn't know about such things, he thought. Or, if they did, they should keep it to themselves. He turned to Darcy, his face reflecting his consternation.

"Don't ask me how," said Darcy. "But women do have a way of knowing."

The Fourth of July was marked by a spectacular display of fireworks by the Orientals, and during the following week Holt's house was nearly completed with the assistance of Hop Sing and some of the laborers. Now that the end of this long project was at hand, Holt's interest in the affairs of the B.C.A. and D. revived. It was late at night and he was sitting at the desk in the parlor of the hotel writing a letter to Goldie in Sacramento informing her that the San Francisco office was now ready to join the express chain, and that he and Darcy had purchased some goods which they wanted to send up to be sold in Sacramento and the mines. He was deeply engrossed in listing the merchandise standing in the new warehouse on the Battery when Hop Sing came in screeching.

"I give huh plesents and she play with othuhs. Blothuh Holt you must stop!"

"What must I stop?" asked Holt.

"Jasmine," said Hop Sing in despair.

"Now I told you it would be up to her which one of you she would marry," said Holt.

"No mally!" screamed Hop Sing. "Play! She got man up theah!" He pointed up toward the rooms at the rear of the hotel that had been assigned to the Chinese girls.

"What?" shouted Holt, leaping to his feet.

"Someone with huh now," wailed Hop Sing. "And I buy huh plesents."

"Never mind about that," said Holt. He ran back to the kitchen and up the back stairs. When he got to Jasmine's room, he hammered loudly on the door.

"All right, come on out—I know you're in there," he said.

"Don't be in such a hell of a hurry," drawled Darcy's voice.

Holt was stunned. Then he began to shake with anger. He should have guessed that this was what Darcy had intended all along, he thought. He heard the bed creak and the lock click. The door swung open revealing Jasmine lying in bed and Darcy standing there wearing only his pants.

"For God's sake, Holt," he exploded, "You've probably wakened the whole hotel."

Holt was aghast. He had expected to see Darcy sheepish and contrite. Instead he was belligerent. "How could you?" he choked.

"So you're still the naive one? I thought Mirina had wised you up. This girl's nothing but a prostitute."

"I don't care what she is," said Holt through taut lips. "You're not going to do anything here. Now get out."

"Just a minute, boy," said Darcy. His voice was harsh and contemptuous. "You're not telling me what to do. You've got too many problems of your own."

A sick wave of rage swept over Holt. He knew what Darcy meant and needed to hear no more. But for some unknown reason his mind prolonged the moment of calm before the inevitable battle, and he heard himself ask, "What do you mean?"

"I mean that a man who hasn't got his doesn't want anybody else to get any either."

Holt's face contorted in fury and his lips drew back across his teeth. Snarling, he sprang at Darcy, raining murderous blows on his face as if he wanted to smash it beyond recognition. With equal ferocity Darcy struck back. Again and again they knocked each other to the floor, only to rise and continue the fight. The hall was filled with staring people when November ran up, still fastening her dressing gown. Without thinking of her own safety, she stepped between Darcy and Holt screaming for them to stop. Holt knocked her down with a blow intended for Darcy. He didn't even see her until that moment. Suddenly his anger was spent.

"My God," he exclaimed. He sank to his knees beside her and lifted her in his arms. "November, oh, November, what have I done?" He clasped her to him and began rocking her back and forth, moaning.

"It's all right, Holt," said November. "It's all right. You didn't hurt me."

Holt looked at her as if seeing her for the first time. Mirina, who was standing directly in front of him, caught the full impact of the care in his eyes. She shivered as if in a chill wind and looked down at her own thickened body, which had not regained its shape since bearing the baby.

Darcy, although badly battered, had not missed the look on Holt's face, and was the first to recover his presence of mind. He reached down and helped November to her feet, steadying her as she shakily rose. Then with his other hand he reached down to Holt.

"I apologize," he said. "I had no call to say what I said."

Holt grasped his hand and stood up. He looked at Darcy in wonder. "I wanted to kill you. I was blind—I didn't see anything." He shuddered and reached over to touch a faint blue spot that was beginning to appear on November's cheekbone. Then he turned and walked quickly to his room. He never even noticed Mirina standing there.

As Holt was putting the finishing touches of white paint on the woodwork in the nursery the next day, he was astounded to see Mirina standing in the doorway holding Jay (Pa Brown had said the baby was "saucy as a jaybird" one day, and the name had stuck).

"I thought it was time to see the house," she volunteered.

"It's almost ready," said Holt.

"Yes, I see it is. It looks nice."

"I've only bought a few pieces of furniture. I thought you might like to furnish it."

"Oh, we can manage on what you've bought. I'm sure it's very nice."

"No, we'll need a lot more. There are a couple of furniture stores downtown now. You can get most anything from them. And then we'll need curtains and draperies, unless you don't want to——" he trailed off.

"Oh, but I do. It'll be fun to furnish it."

"Well then, that's settled. This is Jay's room."

"I'm sure he'll like it."

"You've got your own room too. Would you like to see it?"

"Yes, but I thought——" she stopped in dismay. She hadn't thought of this. Separate bedrooms. That could only mean that Holt had given up the idea of living with her as a husband. This was going to be difficult to surmount, but she had to try.

319

"Wouldn't it be nicer if we shared a room?" she ventured. "I mean. . .well after all, we are married."

"I'd disturb you," said Holt evasively. "I keep such odd hours now. Since I've been working on the house, I've had to do most of the company business at night." He didn't know exactly what had happened, but he no longer desired Mirina. Whatever they had had even in the way of physical attraction was burned out and dead. He had determined to go on with the charade of their marriage only for the sake of Jay.

That night in her room Mirina carefully examined her nude body in the mirror. "Revolting!" she shuddered. "Fat, bulgy, flabby. . .utterly revolting. You disgust him!" She resolved to stop eating. But no one at first noticed the change in Mirina's eating habits because they were so surprised at the change in her daily routine. She threw herself wholeheartedly into decorating and furnishing the house and was out most of the day. She scoured the city for the right pieces of furniture and then supervised their proper placement in her home. Her taste was excellent, and under her watchful eye the bare rooms gradually began to acquire personality.

Holt was pleased with the way Mirina had taken hold of furnishing the house and with the look of comfort she was achieving, but no desire for her as a wife returned. He was pleasant and impersonal in his relationship with her, but he seethed within. He was not yet twenty, and when he thought of the long, loveless years ahead and the hard bargain he had made, it was almost more than he could bear. But by God, I'll stick with it! he thought.

CHAPTER **28**   A RIFT IN THE PARTNERSHIP★★★★★★★★★★★★

The steamer was late arriving in San Francisco, but Kevin didn't mind. All day he had alternated between elation and dread at the prospect of seeing Mirina again. He would have preferred it if Gray had made this trip. But when the summons came to start the express to San Francisco, Gray was deeply involved in negotiating the expansion of the B.C.A. and D. into the northern mining area above Grass Valley, so Goldie had asked Kevin to make the initial run.

The steamer inched up to its berth, and Kevin looked down from the deck to see Holt jauntily waving his flat hat at him.

"You look wonderful," said Holt. Kevin came down the gangway to the dock and the men shook hands. "How's the mine?" Holt asked.

"Not paying too much now," said Kevin. "But Gray and I still work it once a week to keep the claim. And we're opening up a whole new string of stores along the Yuba. We've already tripled the express business and we aren't even in full operation yet. But we're stretched pretty thin. If we only had some more Chinese, we could cover all of the towns."

"Why don't you take some of the new workers back with you then?"

"How many could you spare?"

"At least ten. . .maybe fifteen. Most of the heavy construction work is done on the buildings now, and the house is finished. You got here just in time for the housewarming party. It's tonight."

"Then Gray will be all the more sorry he couldn't come. By the way, how are Mirina and that godson of mine? I'm anxious to see him."

"Oh, fine. They're both fine. I'd take you by, but everybody's kind of busy now—getting ready for the party, you know."

Kevin sensed that this wasn't the reason for Holt's reluctance to go by his house, but dared not ask anything more. It was as if Mirina stood bodily between them, and he would never be able to talk freely with Holt again. He was filled with a feeling of helplessness and regretted that he had come. But he was here and must stay at least until morning, and he must hide his emotions until then. With a false heartiness he said, "I'd like to see the office and warehouse."

"That's where we're heading," said Holt.

Soon they pulled up in front of an impressive frame building three stories high. "Well, here we are," said Holt and jumped off the wagon.

Kevin's mouth flew open in surprise. "This?" he asked.

"Yes," said Holt. "The office and store are on the first floor of this building. That's the warehouse over there on the next lot. And

321

that scaffolding beyond is for another warehouse and office building. We rent out the space we don't need for the B.C.A. and D."

"Whew!" exclaimed Kevin. "I had no idea we had anything so extensive."

Darcy ran out to the street. "I've been waiting for you," he said as he grasped Kevin's hand. Then he turned toward the buildings, his eyes shining with pride. "What do you think of them?" he asked.

"I'm flabbergasted," said Kevin in honest admiration. "I'm really flabbergasted!"

"I couldn't leave till I saw your face," said Darcy happily. "But now I've got to go to the saloon. I promised Mirina I'd bring by some champagne for the party tonight, and I'm late."

"Saloon?" asked Kevin. "What saloon?"

"It's on my lot on Washington Street."

"You mean you own a saloon?"

"Yes, in partnership with Mike Flaggerty and Sam Wackem."

"I'm beginning to see why your letters have been so dull," said Kevin with mock severity. "You left out all of the interesting details. Please tell me more about the saloon."

"I tried to give it the look of some of the better places back home."

"He means it's plush," cut in Holt.

"I'll take you down to see it after the party tonight," said Darcy. "But right now I really have to get that champagne."

"Before you leave," said Holt, becoming serious, "I promised Kev he could take at least half of the Chinese back with him. They're shorthanded with the new stores and all."

"It's all right with me," said Darcy. "We don't need the other buildings in such a hell of a hurry."

"Good," said Kevin. "I've chartered a sloop to carry that Chilean grain you bought up to Sacramento tomorrow, and I could send some of those Chinese workmen up on it."

"Take as many as you need. Now I really must go. See you tonight."

That night at the housewarming Kevin's eyes darted enviously about, and he couldn't help begrudging what he saw. The house was not large, but it exuded an air of elegance. The furniture, mostly of mahogany, but with some pieces of rosewood and wal-

322

nut, was well-made and handsomely carved. Many of the tables had marble tops, the upholstered pieces were done in rich satins, velvets, and brocades, and Brussels lace curtains hung at the windows. With his knowledge of shipping prices, Kevin figured that the furnishings alone must have cost several thousand dollars. But in addition to this he noted that the floors were of lustrous hardwood, the walls were covered with expensive paneling, and there were elaborately carved moldings and pillars throughout the house. It wasn't fair for the company to provide Holt and Mirina with such luxury—and with servants too, he thought as he spied a Chinese man and woman weaving in and out among the guests bearing trays of refreshments—when the rest of the partners were practically camping out.

Then as the evening progressed, he noticed something peculiar. Holt and Mirina were never together. In fact the whole party appeared to him to be a mere show for the guests. Darcy would know the truth, he thought, and was about to suggest that he make good his promise of showing him his posh saloon when Mirina breezed brightly up and took his hand.

"You haven't seen Jay yet," she said and drew him up the stairs. At the top, well out of sight of the guests, she turned to him and pressed her body close. "Have you missed me?" she asked. Then slowly she drew his lips down on hers. Unbidden his arms went around her and crushed her to him. His lips traveled from her mouth to her throat and finally to her breasts.

"Stop. . .not here. . .Holt—"

Like a douse of ice water the name penetrated his passion and Kevin dropped his arms to his sides. For a long moment he stood looking at her, still breathing heavily. Then he said, "Now you know. Yes, I've missed you, and wanted you, and hated myself and you for it. Don't tantalize me again. I'll not be drawn off into dark corners for furtive kisses." He turned to go.

"Holt and I haven't been living as man and wife for months. So you can rest your mind about that."

"Is that your doing too?"

"At first it was. . .but I had a reason. I nearly died bearing Jay. You couldn't know what that was like—ever. But then it was Holt. He doesn't want me anymore. And that's the truth."

"I'm sorry for you, Mirina. And sorry for what you've done. But you're not going to use me."

"But I tell you Holt doesn't care."

"Well, I do." He started down the steps.

"Don't you want to see Jay? He is your——"

"I know, I'm his godfather. All right, I'll see him." He followed Mirina into the nursery where Jay lay asleep, his blonde curls reflecting the light from the night lamp by his bed.

"Well, what do you think of him?" asked Mirina.

"Why, he looks fine to me," said Kevin.

"Do you like him?"

He was at a loss for a response and couldn't understand why Mirina had asked such a question, but decided it must be motherly pride because she was looking at him expectantly. And so to indulge her he said, "Yes, I like him."

"I'm glad," said Mirina. "I didn't know if you would."

"What difference would it make?" asked Kevin, more puzzled than ever.

"Someday maybe I'll tell you." And before he could answer, she smiled mysteriously and glided from the room.

Jay began to stir and whimpered slightly. Kevin patted him absently and said, "There, there, fellow...it's all right." Jay seemed reassured and slept on. As he stood there looking at the child, Mirina's meaning hit him like a lightning stroke. He counted the months. Yes, yes, it could be.

He picked up the lamp and peered at Jay more closely. Except for the blonde hair, he could see no identifying mark that would make the baby his. He shrugged his shoulders and set the lamp back down. But if this wasn't it, what was Mirina driving at?

His evening spoiled, he returned downstairs in search of Darcy. But as he was looking through the parlor, his eyes passed over and then returned to a sight which made him wonder about the future of them all. November was standing in front of a column which adorned the archway separating the parlor from the sitting room, and Holt was standing in front of her. He wasn't touching her, but the way he was looking at her was unmistakable. "He's in love with her," he gasped. "My God, he's in love with her!" His mind in a flurry, he couldn't stick anything together; so completely absorbed was he that he didn't see Darcy approach.

"It's true," said Darcy. "I had no way of warning you. Come on. Let's go down to my place where we can talk."

Kevin was unprepared for the elegance of Darcy and Mike's El

Dorado. Although the main saloon with its bar and wooden tables differed little from any of the other places in the area, in back there was a large public gaming room done with a dazzling gold and white flamboyance, and there were several private rooms. In one of these, richly furnished and decorated in a deep wine color, Darcy poured them each a glass of Irish whisky. He outlined everything he and Holt had done since leaving Little Flats, and finished off with a discussion of the deteriorating relationship between Holt and Mirina.

"However, I don't believe he's really in love with November," he said. "I think he's still reacting to Mirina's rejection. He honestly tried to make a go of it with her, you know. But lately she's been trying to make up to him, and he'll have nothing of it. I guess it's too late for them now. But it's none of our business."

There was a veiled warning in his voice, and Kevin wondered how much he knew. But there was no way of finding out without revealing his own guilty part in the whole affair, and he decided this was no time to do that. Pleading a long day, he excused himself. He wanted to be alone so he could think. But when he reached his room at the hotel, he was so tired he immediately fell asleep.

There was little time for reflection the next morning, for the chartered sloop had to be loaded with the wheat for the Sacramento mill. By the time the boat with ten of the Chinese aboard had weighed anchor, it was late afternoon; and the next morning, accompanied by five more of the Chinese and carrying the express packages, Kevin took the early steamer upstream.

In Sacramento Goldie noticed immediately that the fifteen new Chinese men knew little English and remarked, "I guess I'll have to open up school again."

"Yes," said Kevin. "But you may have a problem. There are eight more of them still in San Francisco. . .and three girls."

"Girls? Why girls?"

"Oh, they help Ma Brown and November in the hotel. And one of them's a nursemaid for Jay, I guess."

"I'll bet Jay's darling now. Who does he look like?"

"Look like?" said Kevin, startled. "How the hell should I know? He looks like a baby."

"I guess it's been a long day for all of us," said Goldie quietly. I'll see you in the morning." She rose to go.

325

Kevin stood up and put his hand lightly over hers. He wanted to tell her his fears, but all he could do was look at her.

"What is it, Kev?" she asked.

"Nothing," he sighed and released her hand.

A week later when Kevin returned to San Francisco with the express, Holt overheard him and Darcy planning an evening on the town with a couple of girls from Little Chile. He was querulous the rest of the day and slammed out of the office at six without a word to either of them.

Throughout dinner Mirina made several attempts at conversation, but he answered her in monosyllables.

"Don't you think Chop Suk is turning out very well as a cook?" she asked.

"Yes, very well," he answered

"I'm so glad we got away from that hotel. The food was ruining my figure. And Jay's so much better off here. May's an excellent nurse."

"That's good."

"Is there anything you'd like to have me do? I mean. . .around the house, or just anything."

"No, everything's fine." If she didn't stop talking, he thought, he'd explode. How could she pretend like this when their world was lying in pieces around them, he wondered. Suddenly he couldn't stand sitting there another minute and abruptly rose and threw his napkin on the table. He flung out of the room.

Alone in the parlor he hid his face behind the newspaper, and his thoughts wandered to November. But he didn't want a chaste and distant love. He wanted a woman beside him, warm and willing, her blood racing with his as their bodies became one. And this could never be, not as long as he was married to Mirina. If only something would happen. . . but that was wishful thinking. What could possibly happen? He laughed derisively at himself. I might as well go to bed, he thought. Mirina must be asleep by now, and I won't have to say anything to her. And tomorrow? Well, tomorrow there was work, and he could forget again. Just then Mirina called to him.

"Holt, come here."

So he was going to have to see her again tonight, he thought. Well, he might as well get it over with. "All right, I'm coming," he called back.

When he reached the open door of her room, there was no question of her intent. She was clad in a sheer, pale green night-dress, which was tucked and ruffled around her bosom. Her fine long dark hair, held back by a matching ribbon, was draped around her shoulders, and the room was scented with perfume.

"Come in here closer," she said. She held out her arms to him "Holt, it's been so long."

At first he simply stared at her. Her eyes were lustrous and inviting. He shook his head in disbelief. How could she be making such a proposal now, he wondered. Then he said, "Mirina, I'm sorry—I just can't."

"Why not?" demanded Mirina, but still in a soothing voice.

"For so many reasons. . .Can't we just let it go at that?"

"No, we can't," she snapped. "I want to know why you won't treat me as your wife."

He couldn't understand why she wanted to hear words that could only be painful to them both, but she was demanding an answer, and he finally said, "Because I don't love you."

"That didn't stop you before," she said, her tone ugly now.

"I know. . .and I'm sorry for that." He shook his head. "That's just it. We've done too much to each other—I'm sorry."

"There's someone else," screamed Mirina. "Don't try to deny it. I've seen you with that hotel maid."

"Don't call November that," he said coldly. "She's the only friend you've got."

"Yes, a real friend," shouted Mirina. "Stealing my husband while I was helpless."

"She couldn't steal what you didn't have or want."

"Don't give yourself such superior male airs. Do you think you're the only man I've known? I've had ten times the man you are!"

"I don't want to hear about it. Your past doesn't interest me."

"How about Kevin and Jay? Do they interest you?"

"I'm warning you, Mirina, don't say another word. It's only for Jay's sake that I'm here at all."

"How noble of you," she hissed. "Particularly when he isn't even yours!"

Holt reeled in shock. He hadn't expected her vindictiveness to go this far. Even little Jay, he shuddered. "What do you mean?" he said. "Of course he's mine. He couldn't be anybody else's."

"Couldn't he?" Mirina's lips turned up in a malicious smile.

Then he knew she wasn't dissembling. She had cuckolded him. His face contorted with anger and he sprang toward the bed shouting, "When? When did you and Kevin?"

"I thought that might interest you," she said. "And I don't mind telling you it was the night we were married."

"So you've made a mockery of our marriage from the very beginning!" He clenched his fists tightly and held them to his sides in order to keep from hitting her. How he wanted to knock that smirk off her face. What a fool—what an utter fool he had been!

"You needn't act pious with me, Deacon Compton," she snapped. "Your fidelity hasn't been exactly above reproach, you know."

"You never loved me," he said more as a statement of fact than as an accusation.

"No, no more than you loved me. But you were so taken with yourself—rescuing the poor little trampled flower from the streets of Rio—that you never even noticed I didn't care a fig for you. And now go on and tell November how shabbily you've been treated. But I'll tell you something else. You don't love her either. You're too in love with yourself to care about anybody else."

But Holt wasn't listening. He was only interested in one thing. "Was that the only time you and Kevin——?" he asked.

"Yes," she answered in a hollow voice.

"Then what makes you so sure Jay's his?" he persisted.

"Oh, I don't know. His hair. . .his eyes. . .I don't know."

"I could divorce you for what you've done."

"But you won't. . .unless you want your dear November's name dragged through the mud."

"I believe you would do that."

"You bet I would. You're not going to get rid of me."

"What about Kevin?"

"What about him?"

"Does he know?"

"No, now get out and leave me alone!"

For a moment Holt stood hesitantly in the hall. Then he walked purposefully into Jay's room and looked intently at the sleeping baby. Yes, you could be Kevin's, he thought. But what if it was just some fantastic lie? Mirina was capable of such a cruel trick, he knew. Yet her words had had the ring of truth. But *why* had she told him? Then in a flash of insight he knew. He reached down and touched Jay's small round hand, and unchecked tears wet his cheeks. "You were mine," he cried. "And she's taken you away from me!" He would never be able to look at Jay again without a gnawing doubt. In one fell swoop she had taken away his son and his friendship with Kevin. If she wanted revenge, she had it now. His shoulders sagged, and suddenly he felt old. His dragging feet took him out of the room and down the stairs. Like a sleepwalker, he put on his hat and coat and went out of this house of hate he had built. He never wanted to return.

Hours later he somehow had arrived at the door of the office. Slowly his mind groped back through the numbing fog of shock and pain trying to think why he had come here. He needed time— time for reflection. If he could only get away so he wouldn't have to see Kevin. Ah, that was it, he thought. That was why he had come. . .to take the express. He could be gone by daylight, and wouldn't have to see anyone . . . not until he had decided what to do.

When Holt entered the office of the B.C.A. and D. in Sacramento the next afternoon, Goldie dropped her pen. "Oh dear, I've made a blot," she said. Then she ran around the desk to embrace him. "But it was worth it—it's so good to see you."

"It's good to see you too," said Holt.

"But my, this is a surprise. I thought Kevin——Is Kevin all right?"

"Oh, yes, he's fine."

"Well, you don't look so fine." She scrutinized his face more carefully. "Is something wrong?"

"No——" he began. Then he stopped. "Yes, Goldie, something's wrong. But I can't talk about it. . .not yet anyway."

"All right," she said. "I'll put the express in the safe and lock up. Then we'll go up to Horace's and get you a hot meal, a bath, and a comfortable bed."

Holt almost smiled. It was nice to have Goldie temporarily taking charge and mothering him again as had been her habit at Little Flats. "But shouldn't I be taking the express on?" he asked.

"You can do that in the morning. There's a stage out bright and early."

"A stage?"

"Oh, yes, we've really become quite civilized. We have several stages a day in Sacramento now—to almost anywhere."

At dinner Holt asked, "Where's Gray?"

"Why, he's up in Downieville right now."

"I think I'll go up that way first then. I want to see old Gray."

The first part of the journey in the coach to Marysville the next day was reasonably smooth on the dust-clogged road. But later as they followed the winding Yuba up and down over the hills, the road became rough and the men were bounced around like loose beans in a bag. Despite the discomfort, Holt found the trip to his liking. The parched, brown look of the land through which they passed suited his mood, for he felt dry and burned out too.

They stopped for the night in Brown's Valley. The next day they were either constantly climbing up or skidding down steep hills, where the driver's uninterrupted pressure on the brake created a friction so great that Holt thought the wheel would catch fire from the flying sparks. Frequent stops for fresh horses were necessary on this grueling trip. This consumed a great deal of time, but Holt was grateful for the chance to get out of the confining coach and stretch his legs.

In the late afternoon after they had reached the summit of a particularly tortuous hill, the driver paused to rest the winded and blowing horses before making the hectic descent.

"Be in Camptonville for supper in a couple more hours," he called back cheerily.

"You may be, but your money won't," came a voice from behind the rocks. "Now, mister, you just climb down from that box slow and easy so's I don't have to use this." Two men appeared brandishing guns and slowly walked toward the coach.

"We ain't carryin' anythin'," said the driver, but he did as he was told.

"We'll see about that," said the first bandit. "Bert, climb up there and see what he's got."

"Ain't nothin' up here but some bags and boxes," said Bert in a disappointed voice.

"Well now, that's too bad," said the leader. "Because now I'm going to have to rob all of you nice folks." He poked his gun through the stage window. "Climb out of there one at a time. And keep your hands above your heads."

Holt got out, but left the carpetbag of express in the coach on

330

the chance the robbers wouldn't look inside.

From the first passenger the leader lifted a watch and a small purse which he opened. Then he snorted, "Ten dollars! My God, mister, you oughta be robbin' me!" He laughed mirthlessly and approached Holt.

"What've you got?" he demanded.

"This," said Holt, and drew out the pistol in his belt and fired. The bullet caught the bandit in the stomach and he fell to the ground. But his partner wheeled and fired, hitting Holt in the right knee.

"I'm hurt," the first bandit called. "For God's sake, Bert, get me out of here!"

Instead, Bert ran for the rocks. One of the other passengers quickly picked up the wounded bandit's gun and fired at the back of the retreating robber just as he reached the top of the rocks. He fell screaming into the gorge below.

"Good riddance," said one of the other men.

The driver leaned down over Holt. "You all right, boy?" he asked.

"It's my knee," gasped Holt in pain. "I think it broke my knee."

"Here, let me see," said the driver. He tore Holt's pants leg back. "Hmm...we'd better get you to Camptonville in a hurry."

"What about him?" asked a passenger. He pointed to the wounded robber, who was groaning.

"Like to leave 'im right here for the vultures," said the driver as he spit out a long stream of tobacco juice. "But s'pose we can't do that...ain't supposed to be Christian. Put 'im inside, but try to stop that bleedin' first. Don't want 'im dirtyin' up my coach. Use some o' them rags." He indicated the debris the now dead Bert had made of the contents of the luggage. "The rest of you help me put this stuff back some way. We gotta get movin'."

As soon as everything was back on the coach, the bandy-legged driver climbed back on his box, gave a "Haw" to the nervous horses, and they careened down the hill at breakneck speed.

Inside, a silver-haired man with a mustache, immaculately dressed in a pearl gray suit and top hat, said to Holt, "That was a brave but very foolish thing you did, young man. Were the contents of your carpetbag so important that you had to risk your life?"

331

"I don't know," said Holt. "I guess I made a botch of it—I usually do."

"On the contrary," said the man. "I owe you more than you'll ever know. I'm carrying some very valuable mining stocks on my person. I hope I may have the opportunity to repay you some day. The name's Rawlings—Henry Rawlings. And if you ever need anything, look me up. My home's in Sacramento."

At Camptonville Mao Tai had the men place Holt on a comfortable bunk in the back of the tent that was still serving as the B.C.A. and D. store. Then he looked at Holt's leg.

"Tsh, tsh, velly bad," he fussed. "But we fix. Che Lai is velly good doctuh. He up load with Blothuh Glay. I get."

"No, not tonight," said Holt. "It's too dark...you'll break your neck."

"Mao Tai know way."

But Holt was not reassured. He had seen the Chinese ride too many times and was sure that one of them was going to end up at the bottom of a canyon someday because of the mad speed they always maintained. "Can't you wait till morning?"

"Che Lai and Blothuh Glay be back in mohning," said Mao Tai cheerfully. "You sleep if can. Do not wolly. I take expless." He mounted a mule and rode off into the night.

Holt was feverish when Che Lai and Gray arrived the next morning. "You idiot," Gray said. "Why didn't you just let them take the money? We could have made it up."

"I don't know," answered Holt dully. "Can you fix it?" he asked Che Lai, who was examining his knee.

"Velly bad," said Che Lai.

"What's very bad mean?" asked Holt anxiously.

"Bullet in bone," said Che Lai. "I think is splintuhed."

"Can't you get it out?" asked Gray apprehensively.

"Yes, I take out," said Che Lai. "Must take out. But velly bad." Then he brought out some strange instruments that Gray and Holt had never seen before.

"Why, you're a real doctor, aren't you?" said Gray in surprise.

"Yes, I am doctuh," said Che Lai.

"But that's what you should do," said Gray, "instead of working for us."

"Would have few patients in youh country," said Che Lai wryly. "Maybe someday. Now must get to wuhk. Will huht velly

332

much, so must use this fuhst." He brought out a small vial.

"What is it?" asked Holt tensely.

"Will not huht," said Che Lai. "But will make sleepy and stop pain. In my countly we have flowuh that help much if used plopuh."

After ministering the bitter substance to Holt, Che Lai laid out his instruments. When he was ready, he asked, "How Blothuh Holt feel?"

"Light and airy," Holt smiled. "And my leg doesn't hurt anymore."

"Good. We staht," said Che Lai. "Blothuh Glay, you talk to Blothuh Holt."

"Well, first off," said Gray. "How come you brought up the express? Where's Kevin?"

"I wanted to see you," said Holt thickly.

"Why?"

"Oh, everything was such a mess." The morphine was not quite strong enough to keep him from yelling at this point as Che Lai probed for the bullet. Holt's face was perspiring heavily, and Gray was wiping it with a cloth wrung out in cool water.

"Blothuh Glay," said Che Lai. "Must hold leg tight." Gray leaned over and held Holt down.

"He's not mine, you know," called Holt.

Gray looked at Che Lai, who shook his head and went into the wound again with a long pincerlike apparatus.

"Aah!" cried Holt. "Want to die...No way out. November... where are you, November?"

Gray looked at Che Lai, who now had small beads of perspiration on his upper lip but still kept probing for the elusive bullet.

"Aah!" cried Holt again and went limp.

"I think he's passed out," said Gray.

"Is good," said Che Lai. "Ah...is theah." He grasped the pincers securely and began drawing them out of Holt's knee. And as the surgical instrument emerged, Gray saw the ball between its ends.

Che Lai quickly discarded the instrument and brought out a salve which he applied to the wound. "Must splint leg stlaight," he said. "But cannot be shuh if it will heal."

"You mean he might lose his leg?" asked Gray in horror, failing to note that Holt was conscious once more.

"No!" screamed Holt. "Gray, don't let him take off my leg."

"It's all right, Holt," Gray soothed. "It's all right. He's taken out the bullet, and it's going to be all right." But over Holt's head he exchanged a grim look with Che Lai and wished he could be as sure of the outcome as he sounded.

CHAPTER 29 BITTERNESS, LOSS, AND DEFEAT********

After reading the letter from Goldie telling about the attempted robbery and Holt's wound, Darcy said to Kevin, "You go tell Mirina. I'll take the express up to Sacramento and find out how serious this is."

Kevin rapped at the door of the little frame house for a long time before he was admitted by a harried May holding a screaming Jay in her arms. The house looked as if a battle had been fought there. Broken china and lamps littered the floor, and most of the furniture had been turned over. Good God, he thought, had Holt done this?

"Where's Missy?" he asked in alarm.

May gestured up the stairs.

Kevin ran up the stairs. Mirina's door was wide open; she was lying on the bed, her dressing gown awry and her hair uncombed. Bottles of perfume were smashed on the floor, and the vanity mirror which had come all the way around the Horn was broken. There were empty liquor bottles rolling round the bed, and from a glass hanging in Mirina's limp hand, more of the amber stuff was pouring out on the Brussels carpet. She roused herself as Kevin entered.

"Oh, it's you," she said in a disinterested voice. "Scuse the mess . . . Chop Suk left."

"What's all this about?" he asked.

"I've just been having a little party. A very private party. . .just for me." She tried to focus on him. "But you're welcome to help me celebrate." She sat up too abruptly and fell on her side hanging over the edge of the bed. Kevin put out an arm to steady her, but she slipped from his grasp and half fell to the floor. "Now, where's that damn bottle?" she complained as she crawled around in her stained dressing gown rattling the bottles together.

Kevin helped her to her feet and settled her back on the bed. "There's some right here," he said, holding up an almost empty bottle.

"Good." She tried to smile but was unable to control the muscles around her mouth so it looked more like a leer. "Pour yourself a drink. I'd do it. . .but might spill. There's a damn glass around here somewhere." She brushed her hand over the night table and knocked off the remaining bottles and glasses. "Oops, sorry," she giggled.

"First tell me why we're drinking."

"Oh, didn't I tell you? Very rude of me. Why, it's a farewell toast to my departed husband. He's been gone ever so long now." She began to sniffle. "Doesn't care about me. . .and after I fixed everything up so pretty." Chameleonlike her mood changed and her eyes began to glint maliciously. "So I smashed everything. What the hell do I care? He said he didn't want me. . .and I had on my prettiest nightdress." She clawed at her dressing gown. "See." She looked down, then scowled. "Oh, it's spotted. My pretty gown's all spotted. Well, I'll take care of that." She poured some of the whisky on the front of her gown, and rubbed the material between her hands.

"I don't think that will work," said Kevin. Gently he took the bottle from beneath her arm and set it back on the table.

"Doesn't matter," shrugged Mirina. "Who wants to be pretty for him? The bastard!" She sprang off the bed, picked up the bottle, and hurled it against the already spattered wall. She began to laugh and slumped down to the floor. "But I got even. Ha, ha, ha, I got even! Even with you both." She threw a defiant look at him.

"How did you get even?" he asked quietly.

"I told him the little bastard was yours!" she shrieked. "Ha, ha, ha, you should have seen his face." She paused a moment. "Now you can get the hell out of here too. I don't need you either!"

A welcome feeling of relief poured over Kevin, blotting out the guilt he had carried for so long. Holt knew at last, and he was glad. But a hollow ache soon replaced his elation. How Holt must hate him now. Well, there would be plenty of time to ponder that later,

335

he reflected. Right now he had to get Mirina sober so they could decide what to do. He reached down and pulled her to her feet. "Come on," he said. "We're going downstairs."

"Don't want to," pouted Mirina.

"Sure you do." Then he called, "Make some coffee, May. And make it strong."

He manipulated Mirina, reeling, pitching, and giggling, down to the kitchen, where he propped her up in a chair.

"Your kindness is touching," she said in something of her old mocking tone.

"I want you sober so you can see what a hell of a mess you've made of everything."

"You don't sound very much like a lover."

"I am not your lover. Just because once——"

"Oh, but once was quite enough." She roguishly wagged her finger at him.

Kevin looked at May, who was busily setting out the cups and saucers. "Never mind about that," he said. "Go see what you can do about cleaning up the mess in Missy's room."

"Yes, Blothuh Kevin," said May and left the room.

"She doesn't know what's going on," laughed Mirina. "Thinks I'm sick."

"She knows damn well you're drunk!" He set the coffee off the range and brought the cups over.

"Oh, you're angry. Is it because you're afraid you might get stuck with me?" She began to giggle again.

"No," he said. "Now shut up and drink this."

After three cups of the thick black brew, she said, "I don't feel so well."

"Good," he said cheerfully and reached for a basin.

"In fact, I think I'm going to be very sick." She visibly paled.

"Here," he said handing her the basin.

"Hold my head!" she cried.

As he obliged, he wondered about the strange attraction this hard, selfish girl had for him. Instead of being repulsed by her drunkenness, coarse manner, and dirty, disheveled appearance, he accepted them all as simply being Mirina. He could think of no other girl in the world who would have brazened out the showdown scene with Holt as he imagined Mirina had done. He held back her tousled hair while she heaved up her insides, and found that he was neither appalled nor surprised at anything about her.

Finally she sat up, her eyes enormous in her bloodless face. "I think I'll go to bed," she said shakily.

While Mirina slept, Kevin helped May put the house back in order. As he worked he pondered how to tell Mirina about Holt's accident. But most of all he wished he knew how to face Holt. He must go to Sacramento, he told himself. Oh, God, he thought. What good would that do? How could he be so naive as to think he could clear himself by simply saying he was sorry. Since every approach seemed ridiculous to him, he rejected them all and was still in a quandary several hours later when Mirina reappeared. She was pale but obviously sober.

He decided there was no point in delaying any longer telling her about Holt. "Do you think you can take some bad news now?" he asked.

She looked startled, but nodded.

"Holt was shot up along the Yuba somewhere. He was carrying the express on the stage. He might lose his leg."

For once guilt sprang up in her eyes, but she did not flinch. "Should I go to him? After what I've done?"

"I can't tell you what to do."

"I think he'll be better off without me. I really did make a mess of things, didn't I? It looked so simple back in Rio—just marry some nice young man and leave. Somehow things never seem to work out the way you think they will." Jay wailed above them, and she went to tend him.

Kevin knew he should leave, but he didn't want to. For a long while he paced the parlor waiting for Mirina to return. But she didn't come, and finally his desire drove him to climb the stairs and seek her.

She was sitting in front of her cracked vanity mirror, brushing her long dark hair. Her rose-colored dressing gown heightened the paleness in her cheeks, and reflected licks of fire from the lamp flamed in her dark eyes. "I thought you'd gone," she said in her throaty voice.

"You knew damn well I hadn't."

"All right. Let's say I'm glad you didn't go."

He walked over to where she was sitting and clasped his hands tightly on her shoulders. Then slowly and deliberately he turned her around and drew her up from the bench. She put her arms around him.

337

"I could just use you again and go."

"I don't care. I don't care. It's been so long."

They kissed in the same surging passion of that dark night a year ago on the ship in the harbor of Rio. Kevin picked her up and carried her to the bed and made love to her passionately, fiercely, and sometimes tenderly

Goldie wondered what was the matter with her. She had been longing for Darcy to come to Sacramento. And now here he was standing before her and she didn't feel the least twinge of excitement.

"Well, where's the invalid?" he asked

"Over at Horace's," she replied.

"I guess I'd better run over and see him before reporting back here for assignment." He clicked his heels together and brought his hand up in a mock salute.

She wanted to tell him that if this was the way he was going to act, he could go on back to San Francisco. But she decided to put a curb on her tongue at least until they knew what was going to happen to Holt. "Before you go——" she said.

"Yes?" he turned back to her, his eyes alert.

"There's something you ought to know. The leg's infected. The doctor wants to amputate. But Holt won't hear of it. We don't know what to do. You see—" her eyes filled with tears—"Gray promised him he wouldn't let them take it off unless Holt said so."

Darcy sank into a chair, the mask of jocundity completely wiped from his face. "What a clod I was to come here the way I did. The truth is, I was so wrapped up in myself and how you'd react to me that I hadn't even given poor Holt a thought."

Goldie looked at him in puzzlement. "I don't understand," she said.

"There's no point in hiding it any longer. I have a saloon and gambling hall in San Francisco. But it isn't a part of the B.C.A. and D. I have two other partners."

So that was why both Kevin and Holt had been evasive about discussing what Darcy was doing, she thought. "You know I don't like it," she said. "But I'm glad you told me."

338

"Hey, Darcy," Gray cried as he came into the office. "Lord, am I glad to see you. Goldie and I have been about to tear each other to pieces over this. Has she told you?"

"Yes."

"Then come on, I'll take you over."

"Mirina should be up soon," said Darcy as they left the office.

"I don't think so," Gray replied. "Mirina told Holt he wasn't the baby's father. She said it was Kevin."

"That doesn't surprise me one bit," said Darcy. "I used to watch Mirina and Kevin look at each other when they first came to San Francisco, and I always suspected there was something between them."

A sickening sweet stench permeated Holt's room, and Darcy knew without looking that the leg was infected. But he deliberately assumed a light air. "You gave us a hell of a turn," he said. "Everybody's worried sick about you in Frisco."

Holt's bright and feverish eyes searched Darcy's face. "I see you know why I left."

"What do the doctors say about that?" Darcy gestured to the leg.

"It's *a* doctor, and we don't talk about what he says. . do we, Gray?" He reached for Gray's hand.

"Holt, you've got to be realistic," said Darcy.

"To hell with that! I'd rather be dead!" He held tightly to Gray's hand and looked imploringly into his eyes. "Gray, you promised."

"Yes, I promised," said Gray huskily and turned his head away.

Downstairs once more Gray voiced the fear that had been haunting him. "If he won't let them take his leg, I'm afraid he'll die."

"I take it Che Lai hasn't seen him since he took the bullet out."

"No, he had to stay up at the store. We were pretty short-handed at the time. But we've sent ten of the new Chinese up since then."

"Well, it wouldn't do any harm to have Che Lai come down and take a look before we decide to do anything else."

"But the doctor said the salve Che Lai had put on the leg wasn't any good and took it off."

"How the hell would he know! I'd trust my old Mammy back home more'n any doctor I ever met. She knew how to heal."

339

"Che Lai is hardly like your Mammy. He's a Chinese doctor."

"So? I'll bet he still knows more than that barber you've got."

"You're right. It won't do any harm to get his opinion."

"I'll go get him," said Darcy.

It took a day for Kevin to fix his courage to the point of taking the steamer to Sacramento. But he knew he had to face Holt now or he would not be able to remain in the partnership.

When he came into the office, he read in Goldie's confusion her knowledge of the whole affair. "I'm glad you know," he said in relief. "It's too painful to have to discuss. I've come to see Holt. Do you think he'll see me?"

"He's not very well off," said Goldie. "I don't mean just his leg—though that's bad enough, heaven knows." She gulped.

"Goldie, I've got to see him." His voice was impassioned and urgent.

She hesitated a moment, then said, "All right. But, Kev, don't expect too much. He's not like he used to be. . .well, you'll see what I mean."

Kevin tapped on the door of Holt's room; then without waiting for a response, he opened it and stepped in. The stench staggered him. He stood staring, unable to speak.

But as soon as Holt saw who it was, he roared, "Get the hell out of here!"

"I've got to talk to you," said Kevin, recovering his voice.

"What do you want? My blessing? Well, I'll tell you what you've got—my curse!" His eyes blazed.

Kevin spoke quietly. "I know there's no excuse for what I did, but I had to tell you I'm sorry."

"God, you've got brass to come here!"

"I don't ask your forgiveness. . .or your friendship. But if we could just get along for the sake of the partnership."

"The partnership! Is that why you're here? Well, you can have your damn partnership. I'm getting out. . .just as soon as I'm able. I'm going home."

"But you can't do that. It's just beginning to amount to something."

"I don't care about it anymore. And I don't want to discuss

340

anything with you. Now, get the hell out of here and leave me alone!" For a moment he glowered at him, then turned his face to the wall.

Kevin felt drained and defeated. He had gambled on a vestige of old friendship remaining and had lost. It wasn't Holt who would leave but himself. Once more he would have to start from scratch. Only this time, he sighed, he would be leaving behind the friends and the life he had always wanted. Well, there was no help for it. He shrugged his shoulders and pulled out his watch. Just time enough to make the steamer for Frisco, he thought. He didn't want to see Goldie and Gray again. Nobody could help him now.

When Darcy got to the little town of Moon's Rest where the company had opened a new store, he found no workers and Sun Luck distraught. He grabbed Darcy by the lapels and sobbed brokenly in Chinese.

"Now calm down, Sun Luck," said Darcy. "You know I can't understand Chinese."

"All gone," groaned Sun Luck in English. He clasped his hands to his head. "Blothuh Dahcy send bad men."

"I presume you mean the new workers. What did they do?"

"Steal." Sun Luck brought out the broken cash box and gestured to the nearly empty shelves in the tent.

"How many did you have working for you?"

"Five." Sun Luck held out the fingers of one hand. "Wuh to build new stoah" He pointed to the half-finished store next door.

"Yes, I know. Now tell me exactly what happened."

"Last night while I sleep, ally lun way with money and goods. Bad men!"

"You're right about that," Darcy sighed. "They were convicts. I got them cheap because of that."

"Knew they come flom plison."

"You did? How? Did they tell you?"

"No, just knew."

"We'll tell all of the towns around here to be on the lookout for them. They're too conspicuous to get very far."

"I alleady do that. Have told all stage dlivuhs. . .and othuhs too."

"Good. Then 1 guess I'd better get on. Brother Holt's leg is very bad. We'd like Che Lai to look at it."

"He in Downieville. Blothuh Dahcy like to lest? Sun Luck take up express and bling back Che Lai."

"No. . .no, I'll go. There are some more of the new men up there, aren't there?"

"Yes, five. Some in Camptonville. . .and some in Downieville . . .if have not lun away."

"Or done something worse. They were convicts too."

As Darcy rode along the narrow trail, he had plenty of time to regret the purchase of the twenty-three convicts as laborers. He had not told Holt why he had been able to get the Chinese so cheaply at the auction, so no one in the B.C.A. and D. except himself knew the men had been taken from the jails in China. Most of the other bidders in the cellar did not want to deal with convict labor. At the time he had scoffed at their timidity because he thought of the Chinese as he did of the Negro slaves who might sometimes lie, cheat, or pilfer, and occasionally even kill each other, but seldom ran away or harmed their masters. Now for the first time he realized that the men he had bought were individual human beings capable of individual acts of violence.

At Camptonville he was relieved to see the two Chinese working for Mao Tai cutting and fitting stones for the new store which was adjacent to the B.C.A. and D. tent.

"Have you had any trouble with these new men?" he asked Mao Tai.

"No, they good," he answered. "No tlouble."

"I'm glad to hear that. But I want you to be careful around them just the same. They were convicts. The five that were at Moon's Rest robbed the store and ran off."

"No have to wolly about that with these," said Mao Tai. "They in plison because had no money and could not pay debts."

"I'm glad you know their background. But I should have told everybody about them. In fact, I never should have bought their services when I knew it was illegal for them to be in the country."

"Will all come out all light," said Mao Tai philosophically. "How Blothuh Holt?"

"Not good at all. I came up this way first to get Che Lai. How much further is it to Downieville?"

"Maybe twenty mile. Will be late when you allive."

"In that case I'd better be on my way."

In Downieville he found that Che Lai still had two of his three workmen, and the one who had decamped hadn't taken anything with him.

"Just because in plison doesn't make bad," said Che Lai. "I know. I was in plison myself."

"Yes, I remember now...your politics, wasn't it?" Che Lai nodded. "I guess most of these fellows are going to work out. Do you think you could trust the two you've still got alone with the store for a week or two?"

"I think so. Why? What mattuh?"

"It's Holt. His leg is worse. There's a peculiar odor in his room. I've smelled it before at home when one of our men got his arm caught in a winch. I think it's mortified."

Che Lai shook his head in concern. "Did he not use the ointment I gave him?"

"No! They got some damn fool doctor in Sacramento to look at the leg and he took the ointment off."

"No know if I can do anything now."

"If you can't, I'm afraid he'll lose his leg."

"I will go. Will take wagon down fuhst thing in mohning."

For two days after returning to San Francisco, Kevin fought against the conclusion he had come to after talking to Holt, but there was no other way out. He couldn't remain with the company because if he did, Holt would go. And he couldn't do this final thing to him. So the only thing left to do was to take Jay and Mirina, if she'd come, and leave. Now that he was certain what he must do, he hurried to tell Mirina.

"Where the hell have you been?" she greeted him sourly.

"I had to think," said Kevin. "And I've made a decision."

Without enthusiasm, she asked, "And what's that?"

"We'll go down south—maybe to San Diego. There's talk of money to be made there as well as here. It's a rich land."

"You mean run away and leave everything to him? Why should you be so generous?"

Kevin glared at her. "I've been up to Sacramento to talk to Holt. And I know now we'll never be able to work together again.

343

I've decided to take the steamer for Monterey next Monday, and I'm willing to take you and Jay with me and provide for you."

"But how? You haven't got anything."

He smiled ruefully. Those were practically the same words she had repelled him with in Rio. "I know that," he said. "I'll have to start over."

"But what if you don't make it?"

"That's a risk. And whether you want to gamble what you have against that is up to you. If you decide to come, send May to the hotel with the message."

"Won't you be back?"

"No, Mirina, I won't be back. You'll have to make this decision yourself. And frankly, I don't know any better than you if we should go on together."

The oppressive heat of this August afternoon in Sacramento had reduced Goldie and Gray to lounging in the office and weakly fanning themselves with rolled-up pieces of newspaper when Che Lai brought the big freight wagon into the yard, sending the dust up in choking clouds and arousing the somnolent flies.

Although Che Lai was alarmed with the report on Holt's condition, he said, "Tonight when it is cooluh, I will see what can be done. Now will take time to bathe and lest so will be leady."

That evening the heat struck them in waves as Goldie and Gray followed Che Lai up the stairs of the La Portal to Holt's room on the second floor. Goldie gasped as the hot air burned into her lungs, and she thought of Holt lying helpless, bathed in sweat. No matter how many times she changed his linen, she could not keep him comfortable. His room was stifling, and it was impossible to keep the flies from swarming around the festering wound. Day by day she had seen him growing weaker, and now that aid at last was here she feared it was too late.

Suddenly she grasped Gray's arm. "I'm scared," she said.

Gray's upper lip was beaded with perspiration, and he looked grim, but he patted her hand and said, "Sis, we've got to have hope."

Holt's dark eyes glittered in his moist face, but he managed a faint smile at the sight of Che Lai. "Glad you came," he said.

344

"What this?" asked Che Lai as he began removing the dirty bandage from around Holt's knee. "When last change?"

"The doctor said to leave it as it was," volunteered Gray. "So we haven't touched it."

"Man not doctuh but fool!" exploded Che Lai.

When he finally had unwound the filthy linen, and Goldie saw the contaminated flesh beneath, she thought she would faint. But she fought back her nausea as Che Lai disdainfully handed her the foul-smelling bandage with the tips of his fingers.

"Buhn," he commanded.

"Yes," she gulped and fled down to the kitchen, where she threw the filth in the stove.

On the way back she met Gray. "He wants hot water—boiling hot, he says."

"All right, I'll get it."

"And he wants these to boil, too." He handed her some sharp knives and instruments.

She shuddered as she grasped the surgeon's tools. "What's he going to do?" she asked in a hoarse whisper.

"I don't know. But he said he'd try to save the leg."

Goldie clung to this thought while she watched Che Lai dose Holt with morphine and direct Gray to pour several glasses of whisky into him.

"But still must tie down ahms and legs," said Che Lai. "Cannot have him move." When this was done, he said, "Now hold him steady." Then he leaned down over Holt. "This will huht bad," he said. "I have not enough to give you to take away the pain."

"I don't care as long as I keep my leg," said Holt in a relaxed voice. "Hey, that would make a good song, wouldn't it? *I don't care as long as I keep my leg. . . .* How about whipping us up a tune for it, Goldie?"

"Sure, Holt," she said.

"Bite down on this," said Che Lai. He slipped a soft piece of wood into Holt's mouth.

Gray felt himself grow weak as he watched Che Lai lift out bits of shattered bone and cut away the rotten flesh. He glanced over at Goldie to see how she was withstanding the ordeal. Her lips were pressed together in a white line as she automatically bathed Holt's face. He had lost consciousness long ago. When Che Lai asked for something, she handed it to him like an automaton.

345

Gray looked away and wondered if any of them would ever be the same again

Then Che Lai suddenly stopped working and laid his head down on Holt's chest. Frantically he began untying the ropes that held Holt down. Goldie and Gray fumbled to assist him as he lifted Holt by the waist and then let him back down again. After repeating this movement several times, Holt began to breathe normally again, and Che Lai laid him gently back on the board they had placed across the bed. Then he rapidly finished the operation and cauterized the opening with a white-hot bar that had been lying in the coals in the downstairs stove.

"If I got it all, the leg will be saved," he said. "If not—" He shrugged his shoulders.

"Oh, dear God, I hope you got it all." Goldie's voice was barely audible.

"His haht missed," said Che Lai. "We must keep close watch on him next twenty-fouh houhs. You both go out. Look at flowuhs, tlees, bleathe flesh aiuh. I take fuhst watch."

"But you need rest," protested Gray.

"Maybe aftuh bit Pi Ling will come and sit, and then I lest."

"I'll ask him now," said Goldie.

She found Pi Ling waiting in the hall. "How Blothuh Holt?" he asked.

"We don't know. But would you watch him for a while so Che Lai can rest?" She was having difficulty focusing on Pi Ling and felt queer. "He had to cut out so. . .so much of his flesh." Her voice trailed off and she suddenly went very white.

Pi Ling stepped to her side to steady her. "Blothuh Glay," he called. Gray came out of the room and Pi Ling said, "Bettuh take Missy Goldie away. I go in to help."

On the way downstairs Goldie said, "Gray, I admire people most tremendously who take care of sick people, but I. . .I don't think that is something I was meant to do."

"You were stout as a man in there," said Gray. He gave her shoulder a squeeze. "I was proud of you." He walked her out on the back porch. "God, it's hot. Let's take a walk. There may be a breeze down by the river."

"And thousands of insects."

"No more than in Indiana. Or had you forgotten?"

"No, I guess not. Remember how mad Aunt Opal used to get

346

when one of them would light in the buttermilk?"

Gray chuckled at the memory. Then a tinge of sadness crept into his voice as he said, "But how long ago it seems."

Goldie looked down at her spotted and sweat-stained gingham. "Oh, Gray, I don't think I'll ever feel young again after tonight," she mourned.

Kevin didn't know whether to be elated or downcast when May told him that Mirina had decided to go with him. He sent the Chinese girl back with the message that he would be by to pick up Mirina and Jay early Monday morning. Then he sought out November. He found her in the dining room setting the tables for dinner.

"May I talk to you for a moment?" he asked.

"Why, yes, I think I'm all finished here," she said.

"I don't know how to begin," said Kevin after they sat down by a window that looked out on the wide veranda of the hotel. "It's about the reason Holt went away so suddenly. You see. . .Mirina told him that he wasn't the father of Jay."

"I don't think you have to explain anything," November interrupted him.

"You knew about Mirina and me?"

"I suspected there was something between you."

"Ever since Holt's accident I've been doing a lot of thinking. And after seeing him, I've decided that it will be better for everyone if I just disappear. I've asked Mirina to come with me, and she's accepted. It'll make it easier for you and Holt too."

"For me and Holt?" Her soft brown eyes widened in surprise.

"Why yes, aren't you in love with each other?"

"My stars, no! I hope that isn't what's behind your sacrifice. I feel sorry for him, he's so unhappy. But love? No, Kevin, I'm not in love with him."

Kevin took a moment to digest this revelation. Then he said, "I think you'd better inform him because I'm certain he thinks he's in love with you."

"Oh dear, I hope that isn't what made Mirina——" She stopped and looked at Kevin in horror.

"No, I'm sure it wasn't."

347

"Then why must you leave and give up everything you've worked so hard for?"

"I can't see any other way. Holt told me he never wants to see me again."

"But your share of the business. . .you should get something for that."

"I wanted to ask you about that. I know I didn't put anything into it but my sweat, but it's worth quite a good deal now. Do you think it would be fair if I took a couple of thousand to get started someplace else and called my debt to the company even?"

"I think it would be more than fair. But I wish you'd talk to the others before taking such a drastic step. Holt hasn't cared for Mirina for a long time. . .if he ever did. I'm sure if you'd stay, in time this would all be forgotten."

"If he hadn't got shot. . .but as it is, whether he loses his leg or not—I mean, the wound will always remind him of what I did."

November sighed. It was true. Everything was linked in one long unhappy chain. She put her hand on his arm. "I wish it was different," she said. "When do you plan to leave?"

"We'll take the steamer for Monterey on Monday."

"I'll miss you, Kevin."

He turned his head away and his voice became tight. "I don't want to say goodbye to the others. I've written them a letter explaining everything. Will you deliver it?"

"Yes. But it's all wrong." She looked up at him and her eyes filled with tears. "Everything's all wrong."

"Don't. . .don't pity me, November," Kevin said. "I'll start again. . .I'll just have to start all over again."

CHAPTER **30** A TIME FOR CHANGE★★★★★★★★★★★★★★★★★★★★★

Monday dawned cool and foggy in San Francisco, already portending the advent of fall, when Kevin brought a dray up to the little white house and helped the driver load in Mirina's many boxes and bundles. Beside her pile of belongings, Kevin's two

348

large valises looked small and lonely. When the van was loaded, Mirina came out carrying Jay, and silently they set out for the docks.

At the waterfront they boarded the small steamer and looked out at the misty city for the last time, each lost in his own reflections. Mirina soon turned her back on what now represented the past and walked to the other side of the ship. For Kevin it was not so easy to sever his ties, and long after the steamship had dropped the ropes that leashed it to the land, he was still looking back eagerly searching for familiar landmarks, until at last they were well out in the bay heading for the Golden Gate and he could see no more.

As the stern-wheeler from Sacramento left the river and paddled out into the bay that same afternoon, Gray thrilled to his first sight of San Francisco. But he was no longer a stranger to strange places, and as soon as the boat had docked he hailed a carriage and gave the driver the address of the B.C.A. and D. offices on the Battery. As he rode along with his colorful carpetbag full of express packages, his senses responded to the smells, sights, and sounds of the building city and the beckoning sea. He felt a longing and a fulfillment at the same time. Why, it's like falling in love, he thought and wanted to wave and shout to those he passed in the streets.

So surprised was Hop Sing to see Gray that for a moment he forgot his Oriental decorum and threw his arms around him. Then, regaining his composure, he backed off, placed his arms in his sleeves, and solemnly bowed. "Solly, but Hop Sing velly glad to see Blothuh Glay," he said. "Have news of Blothuh Holt?"

"He's getting better every day. Che Lai saved his leg, thank God!" He looked around the office. "But where's Kevin?"

"Blothuh Kevin take steamah away this mohning."

"What do you mean *away*?"

"Ally gone. Him and Missy Milina."

"But where did they go?"

"Say go to San Diego maybe. But befoah go, Blothuh Kevin give lettuh to Missy Novembuh to give to you."

At the hotel November said, "I guess you'd better read the letter first. Then I'll be glad to tell you anything I know."

As Gray read, he realized the difficulty Kevin had had in reaching the decision to leave. When he came to the part about

349

taking two thousand dollars of the company funds, he said aloud, "He was entitled to much more."

At the end Kevin wrote: "I'm going to try to make a new life for myself, Mirina, and Jay in the southern part of the state. I don't believe that any of us really have anything more to say to each other, so I hope none of you will try to contact me. My remaining regret is that I wronged you, Holt. I hope that by the removal of my presence you will be able to think of what has happened less painfully. Ever your friend, Kevin."

Gray looked up at November as he folded the letter. "It's strange," he said. "I came down here to tell him that Holt was going to divorce Mirina and make a scandal. I was worried about how to tell him. Now I find I don't have to tell him anything, and I'm sorry and relieved at the same time. Do you know what I mean?"

"Yes," said November.

He gave her a searching look and knew she did understand. Never before had he felt so comfortable with someone he had just met, and he wondered if she felt the same. "Since this is my first trip to San Francisco," he ventured, "would you be my guide and show me around?"

"I'd love to," said November. Her soft eyes glowed and her cheeks flushed as she smiled at him.

"What would you like to see first?" she asked. "The El Dorado? It's a real showplace. I frequently go there." Gray's eyes widened in surprise and she hastened to explain. "I take Mike his dinner on the evenings he's busy. He's one of Darcy's partners, and he'll certainly want to meet you."

At the El Dorado Mike poured himself a glass of his favored Irish whisky and joined Gray and November at a table. Although Gray instantly like the rugged Irishman, he became uneasy as they talked. Mike tried to be casual, but he failed to camouflage his concern.

"When will Darcy be back?" he inquired.

"He'll be bringing down the express next week," said Gray. "We'll be taking turns until Holt gets well."

"Tell him things are quiet—too quiet. There's something brewing with the Ducks, but I haven't been able to find out what."

"I hope there isn't going to be another fire," November said anxiously.

"Hard to tell. But I'm sure they're up to something. Everybody's too close-mouthed."

"Do they come in here?" asked Gray. He surveyed the men in the room with new interest.

"You'll find them in all of the bars in this part of town," said Mike. "They regard it as their territory."

"What do they do?" asked Gray, his voice husky with suppressed excitement.

"Drink their drinks and keep their peace if they know what's good for them," glared Mike.

Back in his room at the Brown Palace late that night, Gray pondered what Mike had said, but the warmth of November's good-night kiss still lingered, and his mind refused to deal with Mike's ominous warning. He wanted to laugh and sing, but most of all he wanted to be with her once more—right now. Never had he had a better time with anyone. And yet they had done nothing extraordinary. After watching the acts of entertainment at the El Dorado, they had simply walked the fog-shrouded streets of the city. But he could still feel the light pressure of her hand in his, and her gentle voice still pulsed in his ears.

He had never felt this way about a girl before—not even Rachel. He tried to assess the difference between November and Rachel and decided that with November, he felt as if she was interested in him and with him, but with Rachel he was always aware she was only pleasing herself. But he wondered if November was in love with Holt, for he remembered how Holt had called her name when he was delirious. He didn't like to think of her kissing Holt the way she had kissed him. "She just couldn't be in love with him and kiss me like that!" he exclaimed aloud. "She would have said something. Surely she knows I want to marry her." He sat up in bed startled. Marry her? The words had come to mind unbidden. But of course, he thought, pleased with himself. That was what this was all about. He wanted to marry November.

On Monday, the second of September, Goldie was sulking in the office in Sacramento. She was hot and miserable, and she jumped every time she heard a noise in the corral or freight yard. Zack was due to arrive with fifty head of beef today, and she was sure every sound she heard signaled he was here. Darcy was up in Little Flats, and Gray had returned to San Francisco on Friday. She had hinted in every way she knew how that she would like to make this trip with him. But during the past two weeks he had been remote and preoccupied, and she couldn't get through the barrier. Though she wondered why he was acting this way, she was much too concerned with her own problems to give it much serious thought.

She wasn't ready to see Zack again. The memory of their last meeting was still too painful. And what he had said that awful May morning gnawed at her mind and filled her with dread. "Don't come back unless you've come to stay," he had said. And now he was coming here—this very afternoon. Would he expect an answer? An answer she didn't have? She glanced at the clock—only three? Oh, why didn't he come? She could face anything better than this awful waiting.

An hour later she heard a wagon pull into the yard and rushed to the open window. Then her shoulders drooped and she felt the hot perspiration trickling down her arms and legs from her moment of exertion as she saw Pi Ling climbing down from the high seat above the wheels. She toyed briefly with the idea of sneaking off to the La Portal and leaving Pi Ling to receive the shipment of beef. But that would only postpone the eventual meeting and prolong her misery, she decided.

"How was everything up North?" she asked listlessly as Pi Ling came into the office.

"Evlything fine," said Pi Ling. "Stone stoahs all finished at Moon's Lest, Camptonville, and Downieville. Velly nice."

"That's good," said Goldie without enthusiasm.

"Have expless."

"Then put it in the safe."

"Blothuh Zack allive yet?" asked Pi Ling.

"No, he has not, and I don't care if he never comes."

"Take long time to dlive cattle. . .velly slow. If no come today, will come tomollow."

Another whole day of waiting, thought Goldie. I simply can't bear it. Aloud she said, "If only I knew the answer."

"Best not delay decision too long," said Pi Ling. "Who no make up mind may soon find have nothing to make up mind about."

As he left the office, Goldie pondered what he had said. What if Zack grew tired of waiting and married someone else? She felt a chill at the thought of his looking at another woman the way he had looked at her that night on the ranch. And yet she couldn't give up the B.C.A. and D.—she looked around the room with pride—even if it meant losing him.

She was still unhappy and out of sorts when she carried Holt's supper up to him that night. But what she saw as she opened the door drove all thought of her own problems clear out of her mind. Holt was standing upright in the middle of the room.

"Christ!" he yelled. "I thought you'd never get here. I was about to fall flat on my face."

"Here, I'll get you a chair!" she exclaimed. Hastily she set down the tray and started to pick up a chair.

"No, don't do that. Stay right there. I'm coming over to you."

"Do you think you ought to?" she started to ask, but Holt was already moving toward her. He was swinging his stiff leg awkwardly, but definitely putting his weight on it.

When he finally stood in front of her, he put his hands on her shoulders and smiled jubilantly. "There, I did it." Then he bent down and gave her a boyish kiss. "That's for being the best nurse in the world," he said.

Embarrassed, she began fussing with the tray. "Come and eat—you must be starved. Do you want to sit in a chair?"

"Tonight and every night from now on." He sat down stiffly.

She set the tray in front of him. "I'm so glad you're better because I've got something to tell you. I didn't want to say anything about it before because I didn't want you to feel left out. But now I'm sure you'll be able to come too."

"Come to what?" asked Holt in bewilderment.

"The party I'm giving, of course. You know Horace is redecorating the restaurant?"

"I've been hearing about nothing else these past weeks."

"Well, he's promised to have it done by the eleventh. And we're going to celebrate Gray's birthday and its opening at the same time. I surely do hope you'll be well enough to help me because I've invited just scads of people—all our old friends from the trail and all of the new friends we've made out here—just everybody."

"Well, you have been busy. All right, I promise I'll be fully recovered by Gray's birthday so I can help you."

"You're a dear. But mind, I don't want you straining yourself."

The next day she began the long vigil of waiting for Zack once

353

more. Finally at two o'clock she heard the trampling of many hooves and the hallooing of the vaqueros. He's here, she thought. Her heart began to pound, her palms became moist, and suddenly her throat felt very dry. She stood transfixed in the middle of the office, unable to think or move.

Zack found her standing there a few minutes later. He wanted to rush over and crush her in his arms, but instead he just stood in the doorway and slowly smiled. "How are you surviving the heat?" he asked in his soft accent.

"It makes me almost long for winter," she gasped. Her heart was pounding so that she was sure he could hear it way over there in the door, and she felt his presence so acutely that she could scarcely breathe. Would he kiss her now? But he made no move. She felt a faint disappointment as she recalled the warmth of their last meeting. "It must have been awful for you eating the dust of those cows all the way."

"It wasn't too bad, but I could do with a bath."

"Would you like Pi Ling to show you over to Horace Ogilvy's? I—I've got to stay here till six unless the boys come in today."

"You minding the office all alone?"

"Yes, Gray's in San Francisco and Darcy's up at Little Flats and Holt—"

"I heard about what happened to him. How's he doing?"

"Oh, he's coming along fine," she answered, relieved at finding an impersonal topic to discuss. "He walked a little yesterday."

"Glad to hear it. You can introduce me to him later."

"Yes. Have you had a good summer?" she asked.

"I think you could call it that. I believe I'll be able to supply your stores with a continuous string of beef from now on. My herd is growing fast, and will get bigger if I don't get hit by rustlers. Some of my neighbors have had a few head stolen."

"Oh, I hope they don't bother you."

"I'm not too worried. My men are prepared to deal with rustlers."

"I'm glad. Have you been on the ranch all summer?"

"Yes, but I had some company in July. . .friends of yours, Mary and Dan Milford." He mentioned her name first, thought Goldie jealously. "Mary's quite a horsewoman. I taught her how to rope and tie while they were there. You'd think she'd been born on a ranch."

"I can ride too," said Goldie. Then she could have bitten her tongue off.

"I know you can," said Zack. He seemed amused at her outburst, and she sought for something to say that would divert him from thinking about what she meant.

"How's Dan?" she asked sweetly.

"Fine," said Zack. "He's going to make a fine farmer. I understand you're buying produce and wheat from the Milfords."

"That's right. We're the only stores in the whole mining region that stock fresh fruit and vegetables. And now we'll have beef too." She glanced out the window at the full corral with satisfaction.

"I guess I'd better try to get rid of some of this dust." He looked down at his clothes. "Where is this Ogilvy's place?" Goldie instructed him how to get to the La Portal. "Say, what do we do for dinner around this town?" he asked casually. "I brought my best suit, and I'd like to escort you to the finest."

"We usually eat at Horace's. But there is a new place, and I haven't been out in ever so long." Her eyes began to sparkle with anticipation.

"Neither have I. Shall we make it a date?"

"Yes, if you don't mind making it late. I have so many things to do first."

"How about eight?"

"Oh, that would be lovely."

Goldie contemplated the evening with pleasure. The new restaurant, called La Belle Magnifique, was reported to have thick red carpets on the floor and golden chairs with red velvet seats. She knew that Horace's décor in the La Portal would probably equal if not surpass this latest rival's when his new furnishings arrived next week, but going out tonight would give her an excuse to dress up. Several weeks ago she had fashioned herself a new dress of white dotted swiss with a pink taffeta sash, but had had no occasion to wear it.

Gray was bursting with news when he arrived on the afternoon steamer. He had decided to ask November to marry him. On this second trip he had spent five blissful days with her and now was certain he wanted to make it a lifetime. Eager to tell Goldie about his discovery, he rushed to the office.

But as soon as Goldie saw him she said, "Oh, I'm so glad you got in early. Zack's here and he's asked me to dinner at La Belle Magnifique. I know you've been on the river all day, but would you mind watching the office? I want to wash my hair."

"Sure, Sis," he said. He was disappointed, but he realized that this would not be the best time to tell her his news.

Goldie took care with her preparations for the evening. She washed and brushed her copper hair until it gleamed. As she bathed she was pleased to note that her skin had recovered fully from the weathered look of a year ago. Her hands were once more soft and smooth, and her face and neck were no longer burned raw and red by the sun and wind. Just at eight she tied a pink ribbon in her curls to match her sash and whirled once around before the small mirror on her dresser. The white dress billowed out like a cloud. Highly pleased, she went downstairs to meet Zack.

When she stepped into the kitchen, Gray stood up and crossed over to her. He took her by the hand and leaned down and lightly kissed her cheek. "You look beautiful, Sis," he said. "Have a good time."

"Dazzling," said Darcy, who had also risen. "Absolutely dazzling."

Then she turned to Zack. But instead of complimenting her, he just stood there smiling. Suddenly she was unsure of herself once more. Had she overdone it? she wondered. Was she too schoolgirlish? She wished she hadn't put the ribbon in her hair.

Zack didn't say anything because he was once more seized with doubts about his pursual of her. With the pink ribbon tying back her riotous curls, she looked terribly young to him. Maybe ten years difference in age was too great a span after all.

As soon as they left, Gray said to Darcy, "I've got to talk to somebody or bust. I'm in love with November, and I want to marry her. But I'm worried about Holt."

"You needn't," said Darcy. "He may have thought he was in love with her for a while. But that's all over. I really don't think he's ever been in love with anyone. That's part of his problem."

"Have you?"

"What?"

"Have you ever been in love?"

"No, thank God!"

Gray began to laugh. "Then what makes you such an authority?"

"I guess I did sound like an ass," said Darcy wryly. "But let's get back to you and November. Have you asked her yet?"

"No, I haven't. And listen—don't say anything to Goldie about this, will you? I want to tell her myself. . .but at the right time. At the moment she's so engrossed with Zack I don't want to upset her."

"You're right, it will upset her. Sometimes she acts like she thinks you're her personal property. But maybe there won't be any problem after all. It looked to me tonight as if Zack was about ready to propose."

"He already has."

"You mean she—— Why? Is there somebody else?"

"Not that I know of."

"You're as close-mouthed as Mike Flaggerty."

"Since you brought the subject up, I thought you were smitten with Goldie yourself."

"I am, but I've no intention of being tied down again."

Gray's eyebrows shot up in surprise. "I didn't know you'd been married."

"I wasn't. But back home I had what was called an arrangement with a mulatto girl. She gave me a son."

Sensing he had struck a painful note, Gray said, "I guess you'd rather not talk about it."

"No, you may as well know the whole thing." He poured out the story of Marie and the duel and of his father's subsequent disinheritance. "And that's why I don't ever want to get involved seriously with a woman again. Goldie's a wonderful girl, but she's possessive just like Marie was. It may be a characteristic of all women."

"Not November."

"Maybe not. And if so, you're lucky. But for myself, I'm not willing to run the risk with one of them again."

At La Belle Magnifique the dinner was long, expensive, and elaborate. Goldie chattered away to Zack about Horace Ogilvy's planned refurbishing of the La Portal. "I think it'll be even more elegant than this," she said as she surveyed the room. "And he's promised to have it done by Gray's birthday."

"When will that be?" asked Zack.

"The eleventh, and I'm planning a marvelous party. Everybody's coming. You'll come, won't you?"

"That's just a little over a week," said Zack doubtfully.

"But you can come, can't you? All of our old friends from the train are coming."

"Then I surely must be there too."

Something about the way he answered suddenly made the whole idea of the party seem childish. She looked at him closely but could detect nothing in his bland face. She decided she was being overly sensitive. "I have another favor to ask," she said. "I know it's awfully big, and if you refuse I'll understand."

"What is it?"

She took a deep breath. "You know how crazy Gray is about horses. Well, I want to give him one for his birthday. . .and I was wondering if you'd sell me one of those beautiful golden ones I saw at your ranch. I've never seen any like them before, and I know Gray would just love to have one."

"Yes, I think I've got one he'd like. I'll see that it's delivered on time."

"How much will it be?"

"How much do you think it's worth?"

"Now you're teasing, but I know they must be valuable. I've got a hundred dollars saved. But I think I might be able to get Holt and Darcy to come in with me and make it two hundred."

"One hundred will be enough."

"Are you sure?"

"Yes, a hundred dollars will be sufficient."

"That's awfully nice of you, Zack. I was so afraid you wouldn't want to sell one." Since even old nags were still bringing a high price in Sacramento, she knew he was practically giving her the horse. He was generous and understanding. She wished she could see him more often. Then maybe she wouldn't feel so strange around him. Suddenly an idea occurred to her. "Have you ever thought of living in town?" she asked.

"As a matter of fact, if I'm elected I may be spending quite a bit of time in San Jose this winter."

"But you didn't tell me you were running for office," said Goldie in surprise.

"I haven't had the chance," he said with obvious amusement.

Goldie blushed. It was true. She had entirely monopolized the conversation with her talk of Gray's birthday. How self-centered he must think she was. "Tell me now," she said.

"Some of the ranchers have asked me to stand for the legislature. For some reason they seem to think I might win."

"Oh, you will—I know you will!" she exclaimed.

"It's too bad you can't vote," he said sardonically. "I could use the support. But seriously, we do need some laws to protect our property from land grabbers and our herds from the rustlers."

"You *are* worried about the rustlers, aren't you? Do you have any idea who they are?"

"One of them's an old acquaintance."

"Who?"

"Chuck Colby. And I predict he's going to end up with a noose around his neck."

"I'll bet that won't displease Rachel much. We've seen her, you know. Or rather, Gray has," she amended.

"It's probably partly her fault he's like he is, although he wore no halo on the trail, either."

"I always thought they were well matched," sniffed Goldie.

As they drove down by the river later, a light breeze was blowing off the water, giving the air a freshness that had been lacking in the dry and dusty streets of town. Goldie was grateful for the air, for she had eaten too much of the lavish dinner and her new dress was tight about the waist. She langorously leaned back in the carriage and let the soft wind blow over her. They passed several spots where she thought it would be nice if Zack would pull off so they could watch the river in the moonlight, but he kept the horses walking at a steady pace. At first she was puzzled, then she became exasperated. What was the point of putting on a new dress and wearing scent if a man didn't try to kiss you or at least flirt with you and pay you compliments, she wondered? She sat up and stole a surreptitious glance at him. Good grief, was she boring him? He hadn't said anything for the last five minutes. He wasn't even looking at her. Suddenly the memory of his lips on hers that evening on the ranch swept over her and she shivered.

"It's beginning to get cool," he said. "I'll take you back."

This was the last thing she wanted, but she didn't dare protest for fear he'd ask her why she had shivered.

When they reached the back porch of the La Portal she thought, Maybe he thinks I don't want him to kiss me. Happy that she had hit upon the reason for his aloofness, she lifted up her face and pertly said, "You may kiss me good night, if you like." Then she wondered what she had done wrong. Zack's face began to redden, and a scowl erased the pleasant lines about his eyes.

"When I want to kiss someone, I'll initiate the action," he said in a scathing tone. "Don't ever try a simpering school-girl flirtation with me again!" He turned his back on her and lunged up the stairs.

Hot tears stung her eyes at the shame of being scolded like a child. "I'll never understand him," she whispered fiercely. "Never, not if I know him a hundred years!" Sobbing in frustration and bewilderment, she blindly stumbled up to her room.

In the morning Gray could plainly see that once more things had not gone well between Zack and Goldie. Neither of them had anything to say at breakfast, and soon afterwards Zack left for his ranch. Under the circumstances Gray decided it wouldn't be wise to tell Goldie about November.

Darcy had brought Chung Sun and Mao Tai back with him from Little Flats, and this morning he took them on to San Francisco. They had been the winners in a lottery the Chinese had devised as the fairest means to decide which of them would have the first opportunity to view and perhaps marry the Chinese girls now working for Ma Brown. When they arrived at the Brown Palace, Darcy arranged for Ma to introduce the suitors to the girls, then took the express down to the office.

"Velly glad you come," said Hop Sing. "Two ships allive today with fine cahgo. I think should buy. One have tobacco nobody heuh want, and othuh have boots and shuhts. Stoahs have too many heuh. . .I check. But we could use up at mines."

"You're right," said Darcy. "Our stock is low. I'll see to it right away. How about the mail? Was there any word from Sam?"

"Solly, no lettuh flom Blothuh Sam. Maybe no fina blicks."

"No, I don't think that's it. He may have had trouble getting a fast ship. Now, where are the ships with those cargos located?"

"One at numbuh five and the othuh at piuh eleven."

"All right, I'll go see what I can do."

With only slight dickering Darcy managed to secure the goods the firm needed from both ships at a good price and arranged to have them picked up the next day. Then he went back to the Brown Palace.

"Come have dinner with me," he said, catching November's hand.

"I've already eaten," she replied.

"Then have a cup of coffee."

"All right." She sat down at the table with him.

After Lotus had served them, he leaned over and said, "Wednesday is Gray's birthday, and Goldie's giving a big party for him. She's invited everyone, but she doesn't know about you. And I want you to come."

A faint pink crept into November's cheeks. "Oh, but I couldn't intrude," she said softly.

"Intrude! Why Gray would rather have you there than all the rest of us put together."

"I don't know if I could get away," she hesitated.

"Yes, you can. I've already talked to Ma."

"Well, if you think it's all right."

"I know it will be. Now, I want you to take the steamer up on Wednesday, and I'll meet you."

November looked deeply into his eyes for a moment. "It was dear of you to think of me, Darcy," she said.

He released her hand and shrugged. "I had to have a present, didn't I?" He stood up. "I thought Mike would be here by now."

"I've been taking him his dinner the past week. He won't leave the El Dorado. Says he's got to keep his eyes on things. I've never seen him like this before. It worries me."

"I'll go down and see if he's found out anything."

After they closed the saloon that night, he and Mike sat down for a talk. "Anything new?" Darcy asked.

"Nothing," said Mike glumly.

"Any of the girls in Little Chile know anything?"

"If they do, they're not saying. That's one of the reasons I think this concerns us."

"I sure wish Sam would get here with that load. I'd feel a lot better if our buildings were made of bricks."

"So would I."

On Saturday morning Darcy was down at Long Wharf when the Pacific Mail steamer came in. "Anything from Philadelphia?" he asked one of the stevedores hoisting the mail sacks.

"Can't say," answered the man. "You'll have to wait till they sort it at the post office."

After standing in the mail line for nearly an hour, he was rewarded with the long-awaited letter from Sam Wackem. Eagerly he scanned it.

—The Panama crossing was fast and I got back to Philadelphia in record time. No trouble with the cargo, but had a devil of a time getting a ship. But I finally got one, and she's a fast beauty. Got to go around the Horn though. We're leaving in the morning. With God's blessing, I trust I'll see you in a few months.

Sam

The letter was dated June 17. If it's a clipper, he could be here within the week, he calculated to himself. He tucked the letter in his pocket and went down to communicate the news to Hop Sing.

Instead of being elated at the news about Sam and the cargo, Hop Sing looked dour. Darcy decided he must have had another rejection from Jasmine and attempted to tease him into a better humor. "She'll have to give in one of these days with your persistence," he said.

"That not what mattuh, Blothuh Dahcy. It express business. Lost thlee customuhs today!"

"Did they say why?"

"They say going to tly new company, name of Stah Express. New company plomise delivuh twice a week. Customuhs say we too slow."

"Twice a week—why, that's impossible!"

"But Stah Express plomise. And that not all. I heah othuh express company going to open in a week or two, and thlee new banks have opened in last month."

"In that case, we'll have to think of a way to meet the competition."

"Yes, leceipts down this week. Missy Goldie won't like."

"You're right about that. But don't worry, Hop Sing, we'll have a general meeting when I get back to Sacramento. We'll find a way to beat these new companies." But he wasn't as confident as he appeared. Maybe they had grown too fast, he thought. Their cash reserves had been seriously reduced by the new buildings and enterprises, and their assets were thinly spread. A setback of any kind at this time would do serious damage. More than ever he hoped Mike was wrong about the plans of the Sydney Ducks, for a fire could wipe them out.

On Tuesday Darcy had risen before dawn and was hurriedly dressing when he was interrupted by the appearance of all three Chinese.

"I'll have to shave while you talk," he said as he pulled on his boots. "We've barely got time to pick up the express and make the seven o'clock steamer." Chung Sun and Mao Tai looked uncomfortable. "You do recall I said we'd leave early?" he questioned them.

"Yes, Blothuh Dahcy," said Chung Sun. "But——"

Hop Sing's face waggled for a moment between expressions of happiness and sobriety. Then he blurted out, "Blothuh Dahcy, I wish to mally Jasmine."

"I know," said Darcy patiently as he peered at himself in the tiny mirror. "But Jasmine has to agree to marry you."

"But Blothuh Dahcy," Chung Sun interjected. "That is what's new. Jasmine has agleed."

Darcy thought he saw him wink. But when he turned around he wasn't sure, for Chung Sun's face was as bland as ever.

Unable to contain himself any longer, Mao Tai burst out, "May and I also wish to mally."

"This is unbelievable," said Darcy in amazement. "Both of you?" He looked from one to the other, and Hop Sing and Mao Tai nodded. "Then my heartiest congratulations." He extended both his hands to them. "But what about you?" he asked Chung Sun.

"I have met a young lady whom I wish to know bettuh and would like leave to lemain in San Flancisco the lest of the week."

"Aren't you forgetting Gray's birthday party tomorrow?" reminded Darcy.

"If it all light with you, Mao Tai and I will come up with Missy Novembuh," said Hop Sing.

"But come back next day to plepauh foh weddings," said Mao Tai.

Darcy found himself having difficulty keeping up with them. "And when are the weddings?" he asked.

"Sunday," said Hop Sing. "Will be double celemony, and want evlybody come."

"That's pretty close," frowned Darcy. "I don't know if we can take another holiday so soon. We've lost four express customers already and can't risk losing any more."

"But evlybody must come," protested Mao Tai. "Especially Missy Goldie."

"Well, I guess we could come down on Saturday," said Darcy, "if Gray and I divide the route and both collect the express from the mines. Yes, I think we could do it that way."

"Knew Blothuh Dahcy would allange," said Hop Sing. "Now we go and let you continue plepalation foh juhney."

"Would you stay a minute, Chung Sun?" said Darcy. And after the others had left he asked, "Now tell me, how did you ever get Jasmine to agree to it?"

"Oh, velly simple. I just talk to huh a little. Tell huh how she have lifetime slave...no have to wuhk. She like velly much. Decide Hop Sing make fine husband."

Darcy began to laugh. "That was slick. I think we're going to see a change in old Hop Sing. Now, about these weddings. Do we have to make any arrangements?"

"Is all done. You will be guests. Don't fohget though—want Missy Goldie to come special.

"I'll see to it personally."

That afternoon in Sacramento Holt's leg was sending sword-stabbing pains up to his brain. Despite the aid of his gold-headed cane, he could find no comfort as long as he had to stand on his feet, and a continuous stream of customers in the store had given him no opportunity to rest.

Now, for the first time all day, the store was empty. With a sigh he started to hobble toward the haven of the chair behind the desk in the office. But he had scarcely taken two steps when a hired rig whirled into the yard. Through the settling dust he saw Darcy lightly hop off the seat.

"Damn it! Why didn't you send a wagon to meet me?" he stormed. "I had to leave a load of goods on the dock."

"There isn't a wagon," said Holt wearily. "They're using all of them at the La Portal."

"Well, I can't just leave the stuff there."

"You'll have to wait till Gray comes." He stumped slowly toward the door. "I've got to sit down."

"You shouldn't be here all alone."

"Well, I am." He reached the chair and sank heavily into it. Then he swung his leg up and propped it on the desk. "Ah, that's better," he sighed. "You know, this is the first time I've sat down all day."

"Where are Goldie and Pi Ling?"

"At the La Portal. Everybody's at the La Portal getting it fixed up for that damn party tomorrow night. The place is in an uproar . . .and for what? A birthday—God, we all have birthdays—What's so special about a birthday anyway?"

Darcy shrugged. "You know how attached Goldie is to Gray."

"It seems like an awful waste of time and money to me."

"You're right about the money. This party isn't coming at a very opportune time."

"Why? Something wrong in San Francisco?"

"The express is way down and it may get a lot worse."

"Why?"

"Competition. A new outfit opened this week and another's opening soon."

A wagon creaked into the freight yard. "That must be Gray. Help me get this stuff into the safe. He doesn't need to know anything's wrong till after tomorrow."

"All right." Holt hobbled over to the safe and opened it. "And don't let him in the barn. One of Zack's stallions is in there. Goldie bought it for a present, but I said you and I'd go in on it, too."

Though Horace insisted his permanent guests eat in the kitchen that evening, Gray remained unsuspicious. He was bursting with news and could hardly wait for everyone to sit down.

"We won't have to worry about those five Chinese who ran away from Moon's Rest anymore," he said.

"And why not?" asked Goldie absently. She was thinking about what still had to be done before tomorrow night.

"Because they're all dead," said Gray.

Goldie suddenly became alert, and the others looked at Gray expectantly. "What happened?" asked Darcy.

"They tried to rob Bart Wood's store in Hangtown yesterday," said Gray. "Two of them got shot, and the other three were tried and hung by a miners' court today."

"Poor souls," said Goldie. "It's a sad end for them." She was remembering the hot summer nights when the La Portal had become a schoolroom, and the Chinese had sat at the tables beneath the flickering yellow lights of the lamps, their heads with their long black queues bent over the tiny slates as they tried to master an alien tongue.

"Don't waste your pity on them," said Darcy. "They were a bad lot."

"Not entirely," replied Goldie.

"All right, I won't argue it because I've got some news, too... good news—Chinese weddings in San Francisco on Sunday!" He told them the whole story.

"Oh dear," said Goldie. "That means we'll all have to go to San Francisco on Saturday."

"That's right," answered Darcy. "But if we pick up the express from the mines before, we won't be behind."

"In that case we'd better get to bed," said Gray. "Sounds like the rest of the week is going to be busy."

On the morning of September eleventh the brilliant sun was high in the sky and was streaming in the windows of Gray's small, crowded second-floor bedroom when the heat-thickened air finally awakened him. He leaped out of bed, grabbed his father's watch from the washstand, and tried to read the time through sleep-confused eyes.

"Ten o'clock!" he yelped and began splashing water in the heavy ironstone bowl.

A few moments later Pi Ling tapped on the door and glided in with a well-laden breakfast tray.

"Why didn't somebody wake me?" complained Gray.

"Evlybody busy. But have wagon outside and will take to office when you leady."

Gray leaped into his clothes, bolted his breakfast, raced down the stairs, and jumped into the wagon beside Pi Ling before ten minutes had elapsed. Pi Ling shook the reins over the backs of the mules, and they jerked off toward the B.C.A. and D., arriving with a flourish directly in front of the corral gate a few minutes later. Gray would have had to be blind to miss the golden horse decked out in a heavily carved Spanish saddle staring at him across the corral fence.

"I didn't know Zack was here," he began. Then he whirled on

Pi Long suspiciously. "Is that what this is all about?"

At this moment Goldie, Darcy, and Holt trooped out of the office wearing broad grins on their faces. "Surprise!" they cried in unison. "Happy birthday, Gray!"

"You mean he's mine?" yelled Gray in excitement

"From all of us," said Goldie

"He's beautiful." He walked over to the horse and stroked his long golden nose. "I only wish I had time to ride him."

"You do. We don't have to collect the express until tomorrow," said Darcy.

"And Pi Ling needs you to help him in the store today," said Holt. "Yesterday was too much for me."

Gray lightly vaulted the fence and mounted the spirited horse. As Darcy opened the gate, he was off at full gallop for the river. For a moment Goldie watched the retreating figure of her brother, then she turned and said, "I guess the rest of us better get back to work. We've still got a million things to do before tonight."

All day friends from the entire mining region kept arriving, their wagons and saddlebags laden with food and gifts. To all of these migrants, Gray's birthday would not only be a reunion but also a Thanksgiving for their first bountiful year in California. Goldie spent a good deal of time directing the many arrivals to the hotels and boarding houses where she had reserved space for them. Most found their rooms quickly and returned to help with the transformation of Horace's restaurant. More than fifty pairs of willing hands laid out the soft green carpets, hung the matching green velvet draperies tied back with golden tasseled cords, and placed the heavy mahogany tables and rose upholstered chairs for the banquet that evening. As the room gradually came to order, Goldie believed it surpassed La Belle Magnifique in elegance, for in addition to the new furniture, the walls had been covered with heavy gold cloth, and six glittering crystal chandeliers that had come from France were hanging from the ceiling. Even though she had participated in the redecoration of the restaurant, she was dazzled by its opulence and could scarcely wait to see Gray's face when he saw it for the first time that evening.

The heat intensified as the afternoon waned, and Goldie, noting the lengthening shadows, became more harried. She ran to greet each new arrival hoping it would be Zack and could scarcely contain her disappointment when it wasn't.

Darcy slipped away to the waterfront just before four to meet the steamer from San Francisco. Every few minutes he took out his watch. Why did it have to be late today, he wondered? When the vessel finally arrived at four-thirty, November and her three Chinese escorts (for Chung Sun had decided to come after all) were the first ones down the gangplank. Scarcely taking time for greeting, Darcy quickly herded them and their luggage into the wagon and set off for the La Portal.

As they pulled up in the alley behind the restaurant, Darcy said to the Orientals, "Go on in and see if you can help Goldie. I'm going to take November down to see Gray."

Just before they reached the company yard Darcy had November hide in the back of the wagon. Then he wheeled up in front of the office shouting, "Delivery for Mr. Gray Baxter."

Gray ran out laughing. "Now what are you up to?"

"My birthday present," said Darcy, and November stood up in the back of the wagon.

Gray froze in position, his mouth hanging open. "November," he finally managed to say.

"Don't just stand there, help her down. I've got work to do," chided Darcy.

Gray obeyed and lifted November out of the wagon. Darcy turned the team. "See you later," he said as he drove off.

Gray still didn't speak, but his mind was whirling.

The longer the silence between them continued, the more uncomfortable November became. "I guess it wasn't such a good idea for me to come up after all," she said.

"No, no, it was a wonderful idea—it was just that it was so unexpected. I'm overwhelmed. Did you just get here? I mean, have you met Goldie yet?"

November laughed. "Yes, in answer to your first question, I just got here. And no, to your second. I haven't met Goldie yet."

"Then I'd better take you right up to the La Portal." He turned around and nearly stepped on Pi Ling, who had come up behind him.

"Blothuh Glay must stay till six."

November stepped between Gray and Pi Ling. "I don't believe I've met you yet," she said. "I'm November York."

Pi Ling shook her hand solemnly. "Velly happy to meet you. But cannot leave till six."

November laughed and turned to Gray. "Since Pi Ling says we stay until six, we stay until six. Now come on and show me around."

Gray reluctantly agreed. He was still wondering what Goldie would think when she met November that evening.

Goldie was alone in the now completely transformed dining room when Zack finally arrived.

"When you told me Horace was going to redecorate, I had no idea it would be as fancy as this," he said as he entered.

"Oh, so you're finally here," said Goldie in a stinging tone. "I was beginning to think you weren't coming at all."

The smile disappeared from Zack's face. "If I'd had any idea of the reception I would receive, I wouldn't have bothered," he said.

And now Goldie noticed his dirty, sweat-stained clothing and the tired look around his eyes, silent evidence of his long, hard ride. He must have left something very important in order to keep his promise and not disappoint her. "Is something wrong at the ranch?" she asked.

"Not anymore. We caught the rustlers. Chuck Colby was one of them. They're in Nevada City awaiting trial. I have to go back tomorrow."

"Oh. . .I was hoping maybe you could stay longer this time."

"Do I detect some tender feelings hiding behind those frowns?"

"Don't tease me now. . .I couldn't bear it. It's been such an awful day."

"It looks like everything's ready."

"But it's been so much work. . .and in this heat. And nobody would do anything the way I wanted it done. And now they've all disappeared."

"They're probably dressing. It's after six."

"Is it? Oh dear. . .then I guess I'd better get ready—and you, too."

"Do I have the same room?" asked Zack as they went into the kitchen.

"Yes, I saved it for you." Then Goldie stopped and stared. Pi Ling had just driven the wagon up in back of the restaurant, and Gray was helping November out. "Who's that?" she asked.

"I don't know," said Zack. "I never saw her before."

Still holding November by the hand, Gray walked into the kitchen. "Look at the surprise Darcy brought for my birthday," he said exuberantly. "This is November York from San Francisco."

Goldie stared at November. Why had Darcy invited this strange girl to Gray's birthday party, unless——? Was Gray? Her eyes narrowed and she gasped, refusing to accept the thought that had rushed into her mind.

Zack saw the fear in her eyes and moved to fill the gap before Gray or November noticed. "I'm delighted to meet you, Miss York," he said. "I'm Zack Peale."

"Zack's an old friend, and this is my sister, Goldie," Gray beamed.

"I would have known you anywhere," said November, taking both of Goldie's hands. "I've wanted to meet you for such a long time."

In the interval Zack had provided Goldie had regained her composure. She looked at November keenly. "Why, yes of course, you're the girl who works at the Brown Palace, aren't you?"

"That's right," said November.

"Since Darcy asked you up to celebrate Gray's birthday, you must join the rest of us at a dinner we're having in one of the local restaurants."

"How lovely," said November.

Then another unpleasant thought occurred to Goldie. "Did Darcy engage you a room?" she asked.

"He didn't say anything about it, I'm afraid."

"Then I guess you'll have to bunk with me. We haven't time to find other accommodations now. The dinner reservation's at seven."

During the next hour while her hands flew through the intricate maneuvers required for bathing, dressing, and taming her stubborn hair, Goldie's eyes continually turned on November, and with each look she became more frightened. Gray could not be engaged in a casual dalliance such as he had had with Rachel, for November had neither the beauty nor quicksilver nature that characterized the flirt. No, this girl represented a real threat, and Goldie felt powerless to cope with it. Oh, why couldn't things have stayed the way they were? she inwardly wailed.

But time would be the winner. She could neither hold onto the past nor hold back the future. Gray was replacing the uncertainties of boyhood with the more profound uncertainties of a man, and fight against it though she might, her own metamorphosis from girl to woman was no less surely taking place. Nothing she could do would make them children again or return them to the old, simple relationship.

The men were waiting by the carriage Goldie had ordered when she and November came down. Once more Gray grasped November's hand and leaned over and whispered something in her ear that made her eyes sparkle and her cheeks pink. Goldie caught her breath at the beauty hidden within the plain girl. She looked at Darcy, Zack, and Holt, and their eyes affirmed her own assessment. Gray and November were in love. Her misery was complete.

From the moment he walked into Horace's new dining room to receive the congratulations of the crowd of friends Goldie had assembled, Gray felt a strange oppressiveness. All through the lavish dinner climaxed by the presentation of Mary Milford's monumental birthday cake, he maintained a fixed and uneasy smile on his face, for this whole affair had forced him into a deep soul searching, and he didn't like the answers that were crowding his mind. His heart in his eyes, he turned his gaze on November. In response her smile assured him that she felt as he did. But this only intensified his uncertainty about adding the responsibility of a wife and family to the already too great burden of caring for Goldie.

"What is it?" asked November, earnestly searching his face.

"Nothing," he replied and got up to help the other men push the tables and chairs back against the brocade-covered walls and roll up the green carpet. The orchestra began to play, and in turn he danced with November, Goldie, and finally with Mary Milford. Though Mary made casual conversation, Gray soon noticed that her eyes were jealously following Zack as he waltzed with Goldie. So Mary wanted Zack, he thought. And Zack wanted Goldie. And Goldie? Who or what did she want, he wondered. And what about the others who were here? With new eyes he looked at his friends crowding the room: at the pioneers who had lived so close on the trail now straining at polite conversation; at the Chinese, ill at ease among the strange whites who guardedly stared at them as if they were freaks; at the miners suffering in their boiled shirts and embarrased by the elaborate pretentiousness of the affair; and at the businessmen of Sacramento who had nothing in common with the miners or the farmers and were bored. Not one person in the entire room looked happy or content. What was California to them all, he wondered? A new place had not changed their natures. The same things bothered them here that had bothered them back in the States. The same fears lay buried within them, and the same dreams still lay within them unfulfilled. In a deepening depression he excused himself from Mary and left his own party.

A little later Zack found him sitting on the bank of the river idly tossing stones into the black water. "I saw you leave," he said briefly.

"It was suddenly just too much."

"If you think it's bad to be nineteen," said Zack ruefully, "wait till you reach my age."

"It isn't the age. It's me. I'm not like you. I'm never sure of anything—I'm always afraid of making a mistake."

"Is it November?"

"Yes."

"Do you want to marry her?"

Gray felt his heart twist at Zack's words. Suddenly he blurted out, "I wish Goldie would marry *you*."

Zack gave a wry smile. "I've a feeling that would solve a problem for both of us. But whether she does or not, you mustn't let her keep you from following your own course."

For a long while Gray sat staring at the sluggish water. Now was the time—he must make the decision now. And he knew in his heart what he must do. He straightened his shoulders and turned to Zack, a new decisiveness in his voice. "November and I belong together, and I *will* ask her to marry me. Thanks, Zack."

Zack stood up and brushed the seat of his trousers. "I guess we'd better be getting back before they send out a search party."

Shortly before Gray and Zack returned, Darcy came up to Goldie and said, "As soon as this soiree of yours is over, I think we'd better have a business meeting."

Fright leaped out of her eyes. "Tonight? Why? What's happened?"

"Now don't start imagining things. Here. . .dance with me. You look like a ghost."

The feel of her soft, trembling body in his arms made him remember how long he had desired her, and forgetting where they were, he drew her close and rested his cheek on her bright head.

"It's all right, I tell you. Now don't worry."

She jerked her head away and flared. "Don't worry! When Gray's about to——" Abruptly she stopped.

Darcy lifted a black eyebrow. "To be married," he finished blandly.

"Yes," she said in relief that at last the words had been spoken. She laid her head on his chest.

"Your name should have been Antigone."

"Why? Who was she?"

"A Greek girl who ruined her life because of her brother." She started to protest, but he reached up and stroked her curls. "Give up, Goldie. You can't hold him forever."

At this moment Zack touched Darcy lightly on the shoulder. "May I?" he inquired. His tone was polite but his blue eyes were cold.

Darcy read the message clearly, and an odd thought suddenly struck him. What perversity in Goldie's nature could possibly make her fail to recognize the depth of Zachariah Peale's love for her? "Of course," he said to Zack and stepped aside.

Goldie was lost in confusion as she read accusation in Zack's eyes. "We were just—I mean he was—oh, what's the use, you wouldn't understand."

"Try me," said Zack.

"He was just trying to cheer me up." Zack didn't look convinced. "There...I knew it wouldn't be any use trying to explain to you! Besides, I don't see why I should." She glared at him.

"No reason at all," he said calmly. "Am I to take that for your answer?"

"My answer?" She was lost. What could he possibly mean?

"Yes—to my proposal. Or had you forgotten that, too?" His voice was like ice.

"Oh no, Zack, I didn't mean——" she began. Then the accumulated disappointments of the whole horrible day came crashing down upon her: the party, the company, Gray—and now Zack too. She began to tremble violently; she stumbled and would have fallen if Zack had not held her. She looked up at him helplessly.

Quick to recognize she was close to hysteria, he spirited her through the kitchen door and out to the back of the restaurant, where he sat her down on a wooden bench Horace kept beside the water cistern. His strong arms encircled her and he cradled her head on his chest. "There," he said softly. "It's all right."

She broke into muffled sobs. He didn't say anything, but his arms tightened around her, and she felt their warmth and security. She could tell him her fears, and he would understand. "I wanted it to be such a nice party. But everything's gone wrong."

"The best laid plans of mice and men," he said.

She knew he was making light of her but didn't mind. Now that she had started she wanted to tell him everything. Sure he would find a way to ease the pain in her heart, she rushed on, "And Gray. . .it was all for him. Everything was for him, and he didn't notice anything."

Zack's arms relaxed their grip around her, but his voice was soothing. "Of course he did."

"No, no, he didn't. It was as if he wasn't even there. He didn't see anything but November. I try so hard but nothing ever goes the way I want it to."

"You can't run the world, Goldie. Things have to take their own course."

She knew what he meant, but a part of her still fought against the truth. "But everything was going so well. I guess that's really why I set so much store by this party. It was proof of what we'd done and how far we'd come. And now——"

"And now you have to let go, Goldie. Gray's ready to make his own promises."

"I know you're right," she said and closed her eyes. She was too tired to think any more. And besides, it was so pleasant to rest in Zack's arms and feel the hardness of his cheek against her head. She put her arms around his waist and snuggled closer. He was saying something about having to be away because of a fight for the legislature, but she found it difficult to follow him and was soon fast asleep.

A moment later Zack's face tensed though he spoke quietly. "Now that Gray's taken care of, are you ready to marry me?" But his only answer was her even breathing. He looked down at her, then shrugged and smiled sardonically. "Sleep, my princess," he said. "I'd kiss you if I thought it would really waken you." Lightly he brushed his lips across her hair, then swung her limp body into his arms and stood up.

"Zack," she murmured.

"Sh," he whispered. "I'm here." She drifted off again, and he carried her into the kitchen.

He met Darcy coming from the dining room. "Good God, what happened?" he asked. "Did she faint?"

"No, she's asleep. I'm taking her up to her room. Get November to come and undress her, will you?"

"Gladly, but I don't know where she is. We were going to have a meeting, and I've been looking for Gray to tell him."

"To hell with your damn meeting! Can't you see she's exhausted?"

"All right. All right. I'll find November somehow. I guess we can postpone the meeting till morning."

Gray was walking along the river with November. He had brought her down here to ask her to become his wife. But now he found he was afraid—afraid she would refuse him. He gulped in a great quantity of air. Then he cleared his throat and stole a sidewise look at her. The breeze had playfully lifted a strand of her hair and laid it across the softness of her cheek. In wonder he let out all of the breath he had gathered. Then he was drawing her into his arms, his lips hungrily and passionately seeking hers.

When they parted, trembling and breathless, he took her hand and led her into a grove of trees. He took off his coat and spread it on the dry grass.

"Sit here," he said. "I have something to ask you." He sank to the ground beside her and took both of her hands in his.

"Oh, Gray..." she said. "Oh, Gray..." Then they were kissing each other again.

"I want you to marry me." For a moment he rested his cheek against hers. Then he raised his head and turned to her. "I love you, and I want you to marry me."

With her hands on his cheeks November drew his face down and kissed him. "I'm so happy," she whispered. "I love you. I've been waiting for you...I think all my life."

"You mean you will?"

"Of course I will." Tears came into her eyes. "I think I'm going to be silly and cry," she said.

His face broke into a boyish grin and he sprang to his feet. Raising his arms high above his head, he lifted his face to the starry sky. "Oh God, I'm so happy!" he shouted. Then he sank to his knees beside her again. "You're sure?"

"I'm sure."

He crushed her to his chest. "Let's make it soon. I don't want to wait."

"Neither do I."

He grasped her hand and drew her to her feet. "Come on, let's tell everybody."

Darcy came toward them out of the moonlight. "So here's where you've been hidden away," he said. "I've been looking for you."

"Oh, Darcy," said November shyly. "Gray has asked me to marry him."

"Well, this is a surprise." His black eyes glinted mischievously. "Then I guess there's nothing left for me to do but kiss the bride." He stepped toward November, then turned to Gray with mock deference. "With your permission, of course."

"If you'll try to restrain that passionate Louisiana nature of yours." But Darcy was already carrying out the action. "There, now, that's enough," said Gray.

"Be happy, sweet November," said Darcy. Then he turned to Gray. "Fortune has favored you, my friend. I'm not sure you deserve her."

"Oh, come on," said Gray. "Now what brought you down here anyway?"

"November's needed back at the La Portal to put Goldie to bed."

The corners of Gray's mouth turned down in dismay. He had completely forgotten Goldie. A dryness stuck the sides of his throat together, but he managed to ask, "She's all right, isn't she?"

"Of course she is. She just wore herself out working on this party for you and then was too tired to enjoy it. She fell asleep a while ago, and Zack and I thought it would be a bit indelicate for us to undress her and put her to bed." He winked at November. "What with all of those fasteners and secret underpinnings you women wear."

"Never mind," said November. "I can guess how dumb you are about such things. Come on, Gray." She grasped Gray's hand and drew him back the way they had come.

The party was over when they reached the restaurant. November hastened upstairs to Goldie, and the guests, their minds filled with the burdens they must reassume in the morning, bid their good nights and went to their beds.

"Come on out in the kitchen," said Darcy to Holt and Zack. "Gray has something to tell you."

"I hope it's good news," said Holt. Darcy didn't reply but went into the pantry. When he returned he had a bottle of brandy and four glasses. "What's this?" asked Holt.

Darcy poured them each a tumblerful, then looked at Gray. "Shall I tell them?" Gray nodded. Darcy raised his glass. "I propose a toast to Gray and November. May they have a long and happy life together."

Holt's face was a mask. Then he smiled wryly and grasped Gray's hand. "I'm glad for you . . . glad for you both," he said.

They drank the toast. Then Darcy proffered cigars around. He struck a light and leaned forward in his chair. "I think we'd better have that business meeting," he said.

"In that case, I'll turn in," said Zack. "I have to get back up North tomorrow. I'm having quite a battle for that assembly seat."

"Why, who would oppose you?" asked Gray.

"People who'd like to keep things unsettled out here for a long time to come, without any laws to restrict their operations."

Holt's mouth turned down in a forlorn scowl. Zack's talk of law accented his frustration over his own problem. In the present state of limbo, how could he possibly free himself from Mirina. "I know how you feel," he said. "For weeks I've been trying to find out where I can go to get a legal divorce."

"What about Henry Rawlings?" asked Gray. "Maybe he could help you."

Zack's eyes flickered interest. "He's no lawyer."

"I know, but he's got a lot of connections. . .and he owes Holt a favor. He would have lost a lot of money if Holt hadn't prevented that stage robbery."

"He's powerful all right," said Zack. "But he's ruthless and potentially dangerous. I'd stay clear of any dealings with him."

"But what can I do?" asked Holt.

Zack scratched his head. "Frankly, I think you'd better wait until we're a state. It's a cinch the Army won't handle a divorce case, and I doubt if anything else you'd get would be worth the paper it was written on, and would cost you plenty, besides."

"But the way things are going, it could be months or even years before we get statehood."

377

"I don't think so. People aren't going to put up with present conditions much longer. Something's going to happen—and soon."

"If we only had statehood now," sighed Gray.

None of them had any way of knowing that President Fillmore had signed the act making California the thirty-first state in the union only two days previously, for the news wouldn't reach the new state for more than a month. In the moody silence that followed, Zack retired upstairs

Then Darcy said, "I've got some other bad news. There are some new express outfits opening in San Francisco. One of them, called the Star Express, has already taken away four of our old customers by promising courier pickups and deliveries twice a week between San Francisco and Sacramento. They haven't branched out to the mines yet, but I suspect they will soon. We've got to meet the same time schedule if we expect to stay in the express business."

Gray was dismayed. "But how? We're spread so thin now, it's all we can do to make it once a week."

"How about using Hop Sing or some of the others to augment the express runs?" asked Holt.

"Except for the convicts, they're spread as thin as we are. If we put them out as couriers, who will run the stores? We certainly can't use the convicts," said Darcy.

"Then what can we do?" asked Gray.

"I don't know. But we'll have to come up with something—and soon." Then Darcy smiled. "But the picture isn't all black. I've got some good news too." He pulled out Sam Wackem's letter and read it to them, concluding, "He could be here any day now."

Gray's innate optimism returned. "That's great!" he exclaimed. "The profits from the load should help offset the express losses."

Holt nodded, and on this more encouraging note they went to bed.

The black of night had lightened to the gray of dawn when Goldie came awake. At first she felt a strangeness though she knew she was in her own bed in her own room. Slowly she became aware of November lying asleep beside her, with her brown hair gently cascading over her evenly rising and falling breasts. A sense of loss vaguely mixed with a sense of shame engulfed her. Her thoughts were topsy-turvy. She needed time by herself. . .to think. . .before she could talk to either Gray or this girl he had

378

chosen. Stealthily she slipped from the bed, dressed and stole down to the kitchen. She threw some wood on the banked fire in the stove and set some coffee water on to boil. While she was waiting she sat down to face herself and her actions of the day before. And as she recalled her behavior, shame became the dominant feeling. I was selfish and ugly, she thought. A child. . . I've been acting like a child. That's what Darcy and Zack were trying to tell me. But I don't know what to do—I don't know how to act. I feel so alone. . .so utterly alone. She buried her face in her hands, still unable to lay to final rest the jealousy and possessiveness so closely woven into her relationship with Gray. The water boiled up and fell sizzling on the hot stove. With the detachment of long practice she made the coffee and poured it. With her fingers tightly enclosing the hot cup as if seeking its warmth to thaw her inner chill, she once more sat down at the end of the long work table. Gray found her there a few moments later.

She couldn't help blurting the obvious. "My, you're up early."

"I know. I wanted to talk to you."

He poured himself a cup of coffee then drew up a stool and sat cornerwise from her at the table. "Goldie, I've got something to tell you. I wanted to tell you last night."

She knew what he was going to say, but found it impossible to help him in the telling. Instead, she parried, "I'm sorry I left the party so abruptly."

"It was a wonderful surprise, Sis—but you shouldn't have worked so hard on it. But that isn't what I wanted to talk to you about." She watched his brown eyes soften. "I'm in love, Sis. . . with November. And last night I asked her to marry me."

To keep from crying and making a fool of herself, she began to rattle, "I can't say it's much of a surprise. Well, my goodness, the way you two looked at each other, it was plain as anything." Gray began to smile, and she ran helplessly on. "And I know November must be a dear girl. She'd. . .she'd have to be to win your heart. Though I've scarcely had a chance to say two words to her. . . what with the party and everything."

"Goldie!" Gray said sharply.

She stopped as suddenly as she had begun and looked at him through misting eyes. I will not cry! she commanded herself in silent agony. I will not cry! Aloud she finished lamely, "And I hope you'll be very happy."

Gray put his hand over hers. "It won't change anything, Sis," he said.

"Of course it won't." She forced herself to smile. "I'll just have a larger family—a brother. . .and a sister."

"Wait till you get to know her. She's wonderful. And it makes me feel wonderful. . .just to be around her."

"Oh, Gray——" This time she didn't try to hide the tears. "I hope some man says that about me someday."

"I know somebody who *thinks* that way about you right now."

Yes, she knew Zack was standing in the wings like an actor waiting for his cue. But if she married him, she'd have to give up the B.C.A. and D. Wives could only do what their husbands did. She wasn't ready to do that. . .not yet. "I wish I knew my mind as well as you do," she said.

They had no time to talk further because the other guests began to assemble in the kitchen. Through a hurried breakfast, Darcy and Holt briefly outlined for Goldie the problems that had been discussed at the business meeting. Then as suddenly as they had gathered, everybody was gone. Zack had ridden off with Gray toward Little Flats, Darcy had accompanied the Milfords along the road to Marysville on his way to the northern mines, and all of the Chinese with the exception of Pi Ling had gone on to San Francisco with November and Holt.

Now that Goldie was alone the tears would not come. Her mind was too filled with new fears for the life of the firm. Why hadn't they listened to her? She had told them they were developing the business too fast, that their assets were spread too thin. And now they were losing the express. And the stores—how could they keep the Chinese in the stores with all of them marrying? Not that they didn't have every right to. But it just couldn't be happening at a worse time. Winter would soon be here, and the miners would be coming down from the hills. And though this might mean an increase in business in Sacramento and San Francisco, especially for the saloons and gambling halls, for the B.C.A. and D. it would be the slowest time of the year.

Though the steamer trip to San Francisco had been more tiring than he thought it would be, Holt was up early the next morning. After informing Hop Sing he would be down to the office later, he limped off to Army headquarters.

In a brief interview with the garrison adjutant he found, as Zack had warned him, that the temporary government had made no provisions for handling divorce cases. Next he sought out a lawyer Mike had recommended. But the lawyer told him he knew of no way of obtaining a divorce other than through the courts in Holt's native state of New York. Sure that it would be years before he would be free if he followed this advice, he determined to see Henry Rawlings as soon as he returned to Sacramento. A powerful banker like Rawlings might be able to accomplish things that lesser men could not.

Buoyed up by this thought he went to the office and found Hop Sing sadly examining the express.

"Expless no pick up. Blothuh Holt, what we do?" he asked.

Holt sighed and shook his head. "I don't know," he said. "I honestly don't know."

To Goldie nothing about the long dreamed of trip to San Francisco with Darcy and Gray seemed real until Gray kissed November after they arrived at the Brown Palace Hotel. But before she could start feeling sorry for herself, Ma enveloped her in a motherly hug, and Pa planted a kiss on her cheek. Then they introduced her to May and Lotus and Hop Sing's fatal attraction, Jasmine. And before she even realized that November and Gray had slipped away, Darcy had deposited her bags in her room and whisked her off to see the company offices on the Battery.

After supper at the hotel that evening she had hardly settled down with Darcy and Holt in the ship-furnished parlor when Chung Sun and Kwang Soo entered, their sober faces indicating that they had something important to discuss.

"Come join us," said Darcy, with an unconscious acknowledgment of equality that indicated how much his experience in this new land had broadened him.

"Thank you, Blothuh Dahcy," said Chung Sun without sitting down, "but Kwang Soo and I have ploblem. Have so much business in laundly that cannot handle it alone.

"Then why don't you hire some Chinese here in San Francisco to help you?" asked Darcy.

"We tly this aftuhnoon," said Chung Sun. "But evlybody alleady have jobs. Now that new stoahs all finished in Noath could maybe we have some of those men? Will pay same wages as B.C.A. and D."

"How many would you need?" asked Darcy.

"Maybe five light now," said Kwang Soo.

"What do you think?" Darcy turned to the others.

"I don't see why we couldn't spare five of them," said Holt. "I don't expect we'll be building anything for some time."

But the two Chinese still stood looking unhappily at their employers. "Is there something else?" asked Holt.

Chung Sun swallowed hard, then burst out, "Ky Sung have been keeping stoah ally lone in Little Flats foh many weeks. Kwang Soo and I feel we no longuh help company. We feel it only light we withdlaw."

"You mean you want to be entirely on your own?" asked Holt.

"And leave us?" interjected Goldie.

"Yes," said Kwang Soo.

Goldie's face fell. She didn't mind losing the men from Downieville and Moon's Rest, but Chung Sun and Kwang Soo had been with them from the beginning, and she would never forget their heroism the night of the robbery in Little Flats, when they had risked their lives for her. They stood looking at her anxiously with their warm, brown eyes. She knew if she asked they'd stay, but she couldn't bring herself to do it. "It won't seem the same without you," she said with difficulty.

After they had gone, Darcy said, "It was bound to happen. They'll all leave us eventually."

"We were doing so well," sighed Goldie. "And now everything's going wrong."

"We're just suffering growing pains," said Darcy.

"Growing pains!" she snorted. "Downtown this afternoon I counted at least six signs offering express services—to say nothing of the new stores and banks. Don't you realize we've put so much money into expansion that we haven't any cash for an emergency?"

Before Darcy or Holt could answer, November and Gray rushed in. "We've got something to announce," said Gray. "We've decided to be married next Sunday."

Goldie was dismayed; the express in trouble, the loss of Chung Sun and Kwang Soo, and now this. Almost a whole workweek frittered away, and more time off in prospect. We might as well close up, she thought bitterly. Similar thoughts were plaguing Darcy and Holt, but neither of them said anything, and Gray and November didn't seem to notice.

Hop Sing and Mao Tai were married to Jasmine and May the next morning in a Chinese temple on Du Pont Street. At the nuptial banquet that followed, Goldie willed a vivacity she hadn't felt in months. Recklessly she flirted with both Darcy and Holt, so that by the time she withdrew to dress for the evening, Darcy's desire for her was greater than it had ever been, and Holt was smiling and laughing once more.

Later when Goldie appeared at the head of the stairs in the sparkling emerald gown that turned her hair to flame, Holt's face became radiant, and with his cane tapping a staccato accompaniment, he crossed the polished floor of the lobby to offer her his arm. But Darcy was not to be denied. Swiftly he bounded up the stairs, taking Goldie's hand and tucking it beneath his arm.

"Where to, oh beauteous creature?" he whispered in her ear.

"Where do you want to take me?" she parried.

His eyes swept over her in bold appraisal. Instinctively her hands flew up to her breasts as though she had suddenly been disrobed. Her cheeks pinkened and she gasped. But he only laughed at her discomfiture and said, "Why, to the El Dorado, of course." His black eyes dancing, he swept her out the door to a waiting carriage. There was nothing for Holt to do but follow.

Most of the saloons and gambling halls of San Francisco were twenty-four-hour establishments, dirty and sordid by day but magically transformed with the evening lighting of the lamps and candles into places of romance and gaiety. The El Dorado was an exception, though even its splendor was beginning to dim under constant hard use. But to Goldie it was a forbidden fairyland made all the more glamorous by her lively imagination. Darcy was showing her about the saloon and enjoying her naive pleasure in its close excitement when Mike grasped his arm and drew him aside.

"Something's going to happen soon. The Ducks are cackling louder," he said. "We'd best keep sharp the next few days."

Darcy looked about and noticed there were more of the Sydney element patronizing the El Dorado than usual. "I'll keep my eyes open," he said tersely.

Though Goldie had never shown a romantic interest in him, Holt had become accustomed to her solicitous attention while he was hurt and now he didn't like sharing her with someone else. Jealously he observed the excitement dancing in her eyes as she followed Darcy's movements. When Darcy returned, Holt looked around restlessly and said, "Let's go someplace where they have some entertainment. This is pretty dull."

"All right," said Darcy. "The Nile Lily has a piano and man to play it. And I understand they've got a female dancer opening tonight."

"That's more like it," said Holt. Then he turned to Goldie. "You'll find it exciting. It's a real Sydney dive."

The Nile Lily was hazy with smoke, noisy with the shouts of the patrons, and dirty with the accumulated filth of spilled drinks, tobacco, and food, but expectant excitement charged the thick air. Then a dancer billing herself as "The Queen of the Nile" appeared in a filmy costume through which her bare breasts and legs could be plainly seen. She began to undulate slowly, gradually increasing the tempo of her gyrations until she was wildly flailing her arms, legs, and torso in a savage tribal exhibition of passion.

The performance would have aroused any man, but for men denied the normal companionship of women it had the effect of ignited powder. Their faces beaded with sweat, they began to pant, scream, cheer, and stomp, and at the close of the act in one mass movement laid siege to the stage. In the jostling and shoving that followed, tempers began to flare, and within seconds several fights had erupted in the crowded saloon. One burly man attempted to spirit Goldie off and probably would have succeeded if Holt hadn't dealt him a knockout blow on the crown with his cane.

"Let's get out of here!" yelled Darcy as he lifted Goldie up by her waist. Then with Holt beating a pathway before him with his cane, he charged for the door.

Once outside, Goldie and Darcy didn't stop running until they were two blocks away. Then panting, they leaned against a building and laughed until the tears came. Darcy was standing facing Goldie, his hand resting beside her head. Suddenly their eyes locked and they both stopped laughing. Raw emotion lay bare between them. Spellbound, Darcy bent down to kiss her.

Holt came up and snapped them out of their dream. "Do you want to see some more?" he asked. He was panting too. Goldie suddenly felt guilty that she had forgotten him. She tore her eyes away from Darcy's. "Why not?" she cried gaily. "We got out of that one all right, didn't we?"

"True, but I think we'd better pick a little milder place this time," said Darcy, slowly taking his arm from the wall and stepping away from her.

"How about Lefty's?" asked Holt. "They've got what they call a three-piece orchestra—all men."

Even without a female entertainer, Lefty's was crowded to capacity with men buying drinks at the long bar or gambling at the faro and roulette tables. Goldie was amazed at the number of men populating the saloons. And on Sunday too, she thought.

"Are these places like this every night?" she asked.

"Yes," answered Darcy. "And most often in the daytime too."

"But when do they work?"

"When they run out of money," said Darcy.

"I don't understand it," said Goldie.

"What else is there to do?" said Holt. "There's nobody waiting for them in their rooms. In places like this you can forget for a while."

Though still disapproving, Goldie glanced around with more sympathy. At a table in a far corner of the room a tiny man with a ginger beard, dressed in a ragged plaid suit and a battered beaver hat, attracted her attention. He looked so pathetic she was about to point him out to the others. Suddenly as if sensing she was staring at him, he looked up and directly at her; then darting his little, round eyes at Holt and Darcy he looked terrified, quickly rose, and disappeared through a tattered curtain behind the bar.

"That's strange," commented Goldie.

"What?" asked Darcy.

"A little man over there," Goldie pointed to the table. "As soon as he saw us, he ran behind that curtain like a frightened rabbit."

Just then the three-piece band started to play, but most of the men paid no attention, and the only notable effect of the music was to raise the noise level. After a couple of numbers Darcy leaned over to Goldie and shouted, "Let's find another place. This is driving me crazy."

"No, I think I've seen enough," she answered. "Besides, I'm taking the early steamer tomorrow, so I guess I'd better go back to the hotel." But she was only making excuses to get away from him because the passion he had aroused in her out on the street refused to subside. She needed to think, and she couldn't with him sitting so close beside her that her flesh tingled and her pulse raced. Or was it really not Darcy at all but only the champagne and music?

"As you like," said Darcy. His voice was calm and his face was bland. She was sure he couldn't possibly be feeling the agitation she was, for even these impersonal words made her heart flutter. He leaned toward Holt and said, "Goldie wants to go home. Are you ready?"

"No, I like it here," said Holt abruptly.

Out on the street Darcy said, "There's still something you haven't seen, and you ought to."

"What's that?" she asked, her curiosity aroused.

"It's a surprise. Do you want to come?"

"If you think I should."

He hailed a cab and gave the driver the address of Holt's house. They settled back in the carriage and he casually put his arm around her shoulders. Once more she felt her skin prickle and kept herself from shivering by sheer willpower. Soon the driver stopped in front of the house.

"But what's this?" she asked.

"The house Holt built," said Darcy. "And since the company owns it, I thought you'd like to see it."

"It looks very nice," she said in disappointment.

Darcy jumped out of the carriage. "But you have to see the inside," he said, offering her his hand. "It won't take long. Then we can walk back to the hotel. It's just down the hill." He pointed to where she could see the red and green ships' lights winking on the portico far below.

Inside, Darcy lit a lamp and holding it before them led her first to the kitchen, then up the stairs to the bedrooms. All the while he kept up a steady stream of chatter, pointing out various things to her like a guide in a museum. Then he brought her back downstairs.

"This is the living room," he said. "And back behind here is the parlor." He slid open a door. "Come on in."

"It's a lovely house," she said. "And a real asset. If we ever really got pinched for money, we could sell it."

He caught her hand and her pulse leaped. "I didn't bring you here to talk business," he said.

Involuntarily she drew back toward the door, but still holding her hand, he followed her; and when she could retreat no farther, he bent forward and kissed her. Instantly she was aflame. She raised her arms and put them around him, and at the same time she could feel his around her drawing her close. Her head was swimming. He must stop. . .No, he must never stop. Then he did. He lifted his face and she was lost in his burning eyes.

"God, how I've wanted you," he said. "I've never wanted any other woman the way I've wanted you!" He lifted her up and carried her to the sofa.

He loves me, she thought in wild ecstasy. He always has. He was kissing her again, and she was limp without strength or will of her own. His hands traveled down her arms and around her back, and she thrilled to his touch. Then he was kissing her throat and searing the area between her breasts.

"Stop, you mustn't," she protested weakly and sought to push his head away. But his hands were sliding her gown off her shoulders, and his hungry mouth was seeking her half-bared breast. She was sinking defenselessly when an outside noise penetrated her consciousness. With frightened strength she pushed him back.

"What was that?" she gasped.

"Nothing," he said in a soothing voice and tried to bend her back with a kiss.

Then she heard a cane tapping and recognized Holt's voice singing "Oh, Susannah" slightly off-key as he fumbled with the door lock.

"Hush!" Goldie said, though Darcy hadn't uttered a word. Then frantically tugging her shawl around her shoulders, she bounded off the sofa and put out the lamp. "I've got to get out of here!" she gasped in panic and blindly tore through the house and out the back door.

"Well, I'll be goddamned!" Darcy exclaimed in amazement. For a moment too stunned to move, he heard Holt lurch up the stairs to the bedroom above. Then he roused himself and left the house. But instead of following Goldie back to the hotel, he turned in the direction of Little Chile and assuagement in the arms of the Spanish girl, Rosita.

Spurred on by shame and fear, Goldie fled down the hill to the Brown Palace and did not stop until she had gained the safety of her room. There with trembling fingers she lit the lamp and sank down in a chair, her breath coming in wrenching gasps that soon turned to sobs.

"What is the matter with me?" she cried. "How could I do such a thing? Darcy will never have any respect for me again." Then she wondered at her choice of words. "Respect?" Why hadn't she said "love"? Abruptly she ceased crying and removed her hands from her wet face. What had there been of love in that mad confrontation? Darcy didn't love her. He had said *want*. . .That was what their relationship was—nothing more. It was Zack who loved her. "Oh, what a fool I've been not to see the difference," she moaned. Suddenly she ached to have Zack beside her, to feel his strong arms and his unwavering support.

On the trip upriver the next day, both Goldie and Holt were preoccupied and had little to say to each other. Goldie was still upset from her encounter with Darcy. Her cheeks flamed at the memory of their kiss, making a part of her long for another meeting. And if she felt this way, she wondered, how could she possibly love Zack? Unable to answer this question, her mind remained in turmoil.

Holt knew he never would feel master of himself again until he was free from his marriage, so he decided not to delay in seeking the help of Henry Rawlings. Just before they docked he decided to tell Goldie.

"Can you manage the express alone?" he asked. "I want to see Henry Rawlings before he leaves the bank."

"It's about the divorce, isn't it?"

"Yes. He's my last hope, and I may as well find out right now if he can help me."

At tne bank Henry Rawlings shook Holt's hand warmly and after exchanging a few pleasantries asked what he could do for him. Though not usually reticent about discussing his personal problems, Holt found it difficult to tell Mr. Rawlings just why he had come. Finally, however, feeling as schoolboyish as he had felt under the gaze of Captain Hewitt on the *Sea Skimmer,* he stammered out his marital difficulties.

Henry Rawlings began to frown. For though unmarried himself, he regarded a marriage as a legally binding contract and was loath to participate in the dissolution of one. But he also disliked feeling indebted to Holt. It occurred to him that this would be a rather simple means of discharging an unwanted obligation.

He thoughtfully scratched his chin. "Yes, I think I may be able to arrange an annulment for you," he said, "since the marriage ceremony was performed in South America and under rather peculiar circumstances to say the least. . .Yes, I think it could be arranged with no trouble at all, though it may take a few weeks. But a little money judiciously placed should speed things along."

"Oh, that's all right!" exclaimed Holt. "I'll pay whatever it costs."

"Indeed no, I'll not take a penny from you. It will be a relief to me to be able to pay a long overdue debt."

"You don't know what you've done for me. I'll be eternally grateful to you, sir."

"Let's just say we'll be even. Now, I'll let you know as soon as the papers come through."

CHAPTER **33** FIRE IN SAN FRANCISCO★★★★★★★★★★★★★★★★

Rip Packet drew his tattered jacket around his bony shoulders and slipped through the chill dawn along the gray shadows of buildings by a circuitous route to the Brown Palace, where he entered by way of the kitchen.

Ma Brown was firing up the stove in preparation for breakfast and did not hear or see Rip until she turned around. Then she jumped and shrieked. But upon closer inspection of her dirty and disheveled intruder, she exclaimed, "Why Rip Packet, is that you?"

"Yes, ma'am" answered Rip. Once more intimidated by the forceful Ma, he hastily snatched his battered hat from his head.

"Not another word," said Ma tartly. "What a sight you are! Get out to the pantry and get the tub down. I'll have hot water there in a jiffy. Thank heavens I just made some good soft soap."

"But Ma, I got——" Rip started to protest.

"And hand me those filthy rags," continued Ma, ignoring the interruption. "I'm going to burn them."

"But Mrs. Brown!" exclaimed Rip, trying to hang on to a shred of dignity.

"Not another word." Ma imperiously pointed her finger to the pantry. "In."

Rip's small shoulders sagged in defeat, but at the door he turned and made one last effort. "I gotta see Darcy."

"After you're clean," commanded Ma.

Half an hour later Rip emerged scrubbed and dressed in some of Pa's old clothes which were much too big for him and accentuated his hollow cheeks and skinny, clawlike hands.

Ma scrutinized him carefully. "Land sakes, you're all shriveled up! Why, a bird could lift you and carry you off! Now you sit right down here and eat. I got some nice wheat cakes, some fresh berry jam, and plenty of bacon and eggs."

"But when can I see Darcy?" wailed Rip, now almost in tears.

"When you've fueled your body," retorted Ma. "I'll bet you haven't had a decent meal since you left."

Dutifully Rip ate every bite of the mammoth breakfast. Ma beamed. "There now, don't you feel better?"

"I'll feel a lot better when I see Darcy."

"Very well, go on up to his room."

"No," screeched Rip. Fear leaped out of his eyes. "I dasn't be seen. Would you tell him to come down here?"

A moment later when Darcy entered the kitchen, Rip ran over and threw his arms around him. Startled at his un-Riplike behavior, Darcy looked down on the small ginger head. "It's high time you decided to come back," he said. "What's wrong? Ma says you're scared of something."

Rip's voice was hoarse and barely audible. "The Sydney Ducks—" he backed away from Darcy and looked warily around the room—"they want to kill you."

"Oh, come on now, Rip," Darcy scoffed.

"I'm serious, goddamnit!" Rip shrieked. "It's that Big Tom and his gang. They plan to murder that Judge Percy and Tom Fellows and make it look like you and Mike done it. And then murder you and set fire to the city to cover up their tracks."

"Where did you hear this?"

"Last night. I was sleepin' behind the bar at Lefty's. I been his swamper the last coupla months."

"Then it was you——"

"Yeah. I seen you Sunday night. I got some pride. . .I wouldn't a come now 'cept I had to warn you."

"You scrappy little devil. Scared as hell, but you came here anyway. Will you tell everything you can remember to Mike and Gray if I go get them?"

"I ain't goin' anywheres. Too damn glad to be here. . .alive."

While Rip was repeating his tale of Big Tom's plot for the benefit of Mike and Gray, there was a knock at the kitchen door.

"You expecting anyone?" Darcy asked Ma.

"No. You better all go into the pantry while I see who it is."

Ma cautiously opened the door. Outside stood a Spanish girl with a rebozo wrapped around her head and shoulders.

"Please, could I see Meester Dupres?" she asked.

"Just a minute," said Ma.

The men had left the pantry door open a crack. "There," whispered Rip. "I told you. That's the first step. . .to lure you to Little Chile so they can put you out of the way."

"Maybe," said Darcy. "We'll know for sure in a minute." He crossed to the back door.

The girl looked up. "You are Meester Dupres?"

"Yes. What do you want?

"Rosita sent me. She wants you to come tonight at eleven-thirty. She eez een trouble."

"What kind of trouble?"

"I don't know, señor."

Darcy nodded. "All right, tell her I'll be there."

Gray burst out of the pantry after the girl left. "Why did you do that?" he asked. "It's like Rip says, they're using this Rosita to set a trap for you."

"That's true," said Darcy. He pulled out his derringer. "But now that we know their plans, we can prepare a few surprises of our own."

391

"I've got a scatter gun at the El Dorado," said Mike. "I can hold off an army with that. Where you need men is at your buildings on the Battery."

"We'll post Hop Sing and Mao Tai there," said Darcy. "They're both good shots."

"And tell them to shoot anyone who even looks suspicious," said Mike. "With this wind, once a fire starts there won't be any way of stopping it."

"I'd better follow you to Rosita's," said Gray. "Somebody could be waiting in ambush for you."

"Rip can do that. We need you in reserve."

"Reserve for what?"

"The Ducks didn't mention you. So I figure they don't know about you. You'll be our surprise weapon."

Rip wrinkled his brow. "That's right. There was one I couldn't place—couldn't see 'em, you know, only hear—he wanted Darcy out of the way. And Big Tom wanted to get Mike. But nobody said anything about you."

"That doesn't mean I can't do anything."

"We need you outside the El Dorado when it closes at two o'clock, because that's when the Ducks'll make their move."

"But what if something happens before then?"

"Too many people around. They like to operate when the city's asleep," said Mike.

"There's only one thing I wish we knew," said Darcy, "and that's where they plan to start the fire."

"We could post a man in every block around there," said Gray.

Mike shook his head. "As soon as we did that, the jig'd be up, and Big Tom'd just choose another night."

"That's right," agreed Darcy. "Luck may decide our fortunes tonight."

Gray looked skeptically at Darcy's small weapon. "And our lives," he added.

At eleven-thirty that night a fight broke out in the El Dorado. Mike moved swiftly toward the embattled pair intending to throw them out before the single fight turned into a general brawl. But when he reached the belligerents he realized he had made an error in not arming himself with something more than his knife. They were both Sydney Ducks. Quickly he looked around. The other customers were hastily making their way toward the doors, except for two more of his former convict associates who were moving toward him. He drew his knife from the scabbard that hung down the back of his neck and waited.

Big Tom came in the open door and said softly, "You can only get one of us with that. And then we'll have you anyways. So you might as well give up peaceful, Mike."

Mike hesitated a moment. He was hopelessly outnumbered, but if he could stall them long enough, Gray might come. "Whaddaya want?" he asked.

"Nothing right now," said Big Tom smoothly. "Just the loan of your place for a while. Tie him up."

The two who had faked the fight pinioned Mike's arms behind his back and tied them securely.

"Now put him behind the bar and tie his feet. And for Christ's sake, put a gag on 'im," continued Big Tom. "Bar the door, Alf. And put out the lamps."

"Why don't we just finish 'im off now?" asked Georgie.

"Because we want it to look natural when he burns, yuh bloody fool!" bellowed Big Tom. "It's got to look like he was goin' to take Percy and Fellows out in the Bay and dump 'em, but he got caught in the fire."

Over in Little Chile Darcy had just arrived at Rosita's. She threw her arms around him and drew him into her shack. The place was more dimly lighted than usual, and Darcy felt the presence of someone else in the room.

"Take off your coat and get comfortable," said Rosita. She flashed a smile, but he noticed she was trembling.

He drew her into his arms, effectively placing her between himself and a dark corner of the room. "What is it?" he asked.

"Nothing. . .I'm just silly." She tossed her head and attempted to draw away.

He tightened his hold on her. "You didn't send for me because of something silly."

"No. Eet's my brother." Again she attempted to break his grasp, but Darcy held firm.

"Rosita!" A voice called from the corner.

"All right," she screamed and wrenched free.

At the same instant Darcy drew his derringer and fired into the gloomy corner. He heard a sigh, and something clattered to the floor.

"Miguel. . .oh, Miguel," sobbed Rosita. She ran over and knelt beside the slumped figure.

"I failed. Oh, my God, I failed," gasped Miguel and was still

"You've keeled heem," Rosita cried. She snatched up the knife lying near Miguel's outstretched palm and sprang at Darcy. "I hate you!"

Darcy twisted her arm and the knife dropped. "Now who was he?" he asked. "Your lover?"

"No!" she spat out, her eyes full of hate. "He was my brother."

"Why was he trying to kill me?"

"Because they told heem to. They would keel heem if he deedn't do as they say. They can make us do anything."

"In that case, I'll feel a lot safer with you in my custody for a while." He opened the door. "Rip, come on in here. We're going to take Miss Arguellos along to the hotel with us."

Ever since Darcy and Rip had left for Rosita's, Gray had been uneasy. "Something's not right here," he said to November. "Our time schedule's wrong. . .I know it."

"What makes you think that?"

"The eleven-thirty appointment for Darcy. It's been bothering me all day." He pulled out his watch and saw that it was almost twelve. "I'm not waiting until two o'clock. I'm going down to the El Dorado now."

"Let me come with you."

"No—you wait for Darcy and Rip and tell them where I am." He picked up his coat and started for the door.

"Gray—" he came back and kissed her—"be careful. . . ."

"Don't worry. I've got a hunch everything may turn out all right now."

But as he hurried toward the El Dorado, the sky began to redden in the direction of the company office and warehouses, and the fire bells began clanging furiously. Half-clothed men poured into the streets to hitch on to their fire brigades. His progress temporarily slowed in the press of people and carts, he

394

hesitated for a moment. Should he go over to the B.C.A. and D. and see what he could do to help there, he wondered. Then he remembered that Rip had said the Ducks intended to murder Mike. He began running toward the saloon. He rounded the corner of the El Dorado as Georgie and Alf were about to toss a lighted lamp into a pile of oil-soaked rags heaped against it.

"Halt or I'll shoot!" Gray shouted though he had no weapon.

But he had no time to ponder what foolishness had made him come out unarmed, for Georgie hurled the lamp at him and ran off with Alf down the alley. The lamp landed harmlessly in the street, guttered and went out, and Gray rushed over to pull the rags away from the side of the building. But once more he thought of Mike and tore around to the front door. He found it barred and couldn't force it. Frantic, he ran around to the back. The door was open and he rushed in calling, "Mike! Mike! Where are you, Mike?" There was a slight rustle behind the bar. He found a candle and lighted it and went over to investigate. He spotted Mike, trussed up and gagged. "You're alive, thank God!" he exclaimed.

Quickly he removed the gag and Mike gasped, "Hurry. . .we gotta get down to the B.C.A. and D. They're goin' to set fire to it."

Gray shook his head. "There's a fire going over that way already. Are you all right?"

"Yeah. Just mad at myself for bein' tricked. But I'm luckier than some. . .Judge Percy and that Fellows won't be makin' any more deals. They're both lyin' down there in a skiff. . .deader'n two fish." He pointed to the trapdoor in the floor of the saloon which led down to the water since the bar was in an area that had been built out over the bay.

"Will they be back?" asked Gray, jerking his head in the direction the firebugs had fled.

"Not Georgie and Alf."

"Then let's get going. Maybe we can still save the B.C.A. and D."

The front door rattled. "Take the scatter gun," whispered Mike as he lifted a pistol from behind the bar and put out the candle.

Then they heard footsteps going around to the back. "It's only one," hissed Gray.

As the man entered the saloon, he fell over a chair. "Christ!" he cursed. "Mike, are you here?"

"We're both here," said Gray, recognizing Darcy's voice.

"Well, for God's sake, why don't you have a light? I nearly broke my leg."

"We thought you might be one of the Ducks," explained Mike, this time lighting a lamp.

"I scared them off a few minutes ago. They were about to burn the place down," said Gray.

"They didn't get us here, but from the looks of the sky, they've done the job at the warehouses," said Darcy.

The fire had been set two blocks away from the B.C.A. and D., but the wind had carried it rapidly to their block, and by the time they got there, the firemen were battling to save their buildings. Gray and Darcy watched in despair as the roof of the office building caved in with a shuddering crash. They rushed along the fire lines looking for a familiar face. Finally they found Mao Tai.

"Where's Hop Sing?" Gray asked.

"No know. Last saw, said had to go get something from safe."

Just then Jasmine rushed up. Her face was blackened with soot, and her hair was flying. Weeping wildly, she began screaming in Chinese.

"Hold on, hold on," said Gray. "In English and not so fast."

"Hop Sing. . .Hop Sing!" she screeched and gestured toward the office building almost engulfed in flames.

"Is he in there?" Gray's eyes widened in horror. She nodded mutely, the tears streaming down her face. Without thinking, he started running toward the burning building.

"Stay back! Stay back!" voices shouted from the fire lines.

"You can't reach him now," yelled Darcy. "The whole building's about to go. . .oh, what the hell!" He leaped over the barricade and followed Gray into the burning building.

"Hop Sing," shouted Gray, then choked on a cloud of smoke.

"I caught. . .I caught!" screeched Hop Sing.

Gray picked his way through the debris into the back room. A rafter from the floor above had fallen down across Hop Sing's queue, effectively pinioning him. "We'll have to cut it off," gasped Darcy as he entered the room and sized up the situation.

"No . . . no!" screamed Hop Sing. "No cut off!" He folded his arms across his chest. "I die heuh."

"Look, we haven't got time to discuss it," said Gray. He took out his knife and began hacking away.

396

Hop Sing sobbed wildly. "I disglaced." When his head was at last free from the rafter, Darcy and Gray lifted him up bodily and carried him from the building.

As they crossed to safety behind the fire lines, Jasmine ran up and threw her arms around Hop Sing, crying endearments in Chinese. But Hop Sing turned away and would have run if Darcy hadn't restrained him.

Jasmine spoke to him again, but he simply bowed his head and said nothing. "I tell him it no mattuh about his hauh," said Jasmine. Suddenly Hop Sing looked up and rattled off something in Chinese, then cast his eyes down at the dirt again.

"I no cauh if we can nevuh go back to China," Jasmine said slowly in English. "I not wish to have glave in ancestral land." She jutted out her chin. "I now Amelican. What China give me or you but bowed head, pained back, and suhvant's queue? Be glad it gone. Now you can hold head up. . .can have hauh like Blothuh Glay and Dahcy." She smiled. "Jasmine like much bettuh. Want man, not slave."

For a moment Hop Sing stood silent as though thinking over what she had said. Then very slowly he raised his head and wordlessly reached out to take Jasmine's hand.

Helplessly Gray was watching the flames consume the company they had worked so hard to build, and a rage as hot as the blaze swept over him. Savagely he thrust himself into the long line of men swinging the leather buckets hand to hand from the cistern in the street to the burning buildings and back again. He hoisted the buckets rhythmically until his shoulders ached and his mind was numb. All through the night they worked, endlessly it seemed. Then at last, as the sky began to lighten to the gray of morning, the fourth major fire of the infant city was brought under control. Gray slumped heavily onto an overturned bucket, dumbly staring at the black smoke curling up into the leaden dawn. "It's gone," he muttered unbelievingly. "It's all gone."

San Franciscans responded to the holocaust with cries of outrage and demands that the guilty Sydney Ducks be ferreted out and brought to trial. But the city's anger had its only outlet in words; all of the accused had dropped from sight, and there were no law officers to find them and bring them to justice.

On Wednesday afternoon Darcy and Gray returned to the blackened and still smoking ruins to see if there was anything salvageable. All that remained standing was a half-charred warehouse. Gray shrugged his shoulders and sighed. "I guess we'd better put off the wedding," he said

Darcy looked up from where he was sifting and sorting through a pile of debris. "Postponing your wedding won't help us out of this."

"But we haven't any money for rebuilding. Goldie was right. We shouldn't have expanded so fast."

"I have some money...in the safe at the El Dorado. And we can borrow some more." He was lying, but he didn't see any harm in easing Gray's mind.

Gray grinned. "So you had some money stashed away all the time. No wonder you weren't worried when Goldie said we didn't have any in the bank."

"I'm worried all right. I wish Sam would get here with that ship. I'd like to rebuild in brick. These fires are coming along a little too frequently to suit me."

But Gray was no longer listening. They could rebuild...and he would be married to November on Sunday as planned.

News of the disaster in San Francisco didn't reach Sacramento until late Wednesday, and then the fragments of information were distorted and contradictory. As the evening progressed, it was being rumored that San Francisco had been leveled, and both Goldie and Holt became increasingly alarmed.

Che Lai was on the crowded steamer when it finally arrived on Thursday. He gave them a full account of the fire and the Sydney Ducks' plot. Then he handed Goldie a note from Darcy. Hastily she tore it open and read:

"We've been wiped out here—Everything! As you already know, we didn't have any cash. But Ma and Pa are lending us two thousand, and Mike has scraped up another thousand for us from his saloon profits. It isn't near enough though, and I had to sign two notes to pay for some lumber we ordered. It's gone sky-high, and everybody's demanding cash. As soon as Sam gets here with that cargo we'll be all right again. But in the meantime we've got to have more money, so if you can find *anything*, send it back with Che Lai. At least none of us got hurt...though it was pretty close for Mike and Hop Sing."

Darcy

She folded the paper and frowned.

"We haven't got a plugged nickel to send," sighed Holt.

"I'm going to San Francisco in the morning," Goldie announced

"Why?" asked Holt. "We're going on Saturday for the wedding. One more day can't make any difference."

"I thought maybe they'd postpone that now."

Holt gave her a keen look, but she busied herself at the desk. "The letter didn't say there was any change in plans," he said. "I think we'd better go when we're expected."

For Goldie Saturday was a day to endure. As soon as she and Holt got off the steamer in San Francisco, she went to the site of the B.C.A. and D. Gray, Darcy, and Sam were working on the framework of a new office building already rising on the blackened ground.

Gray answered her question. "Oh, the money," he said. "Everything worked out as soon as Sam arrived." She stared at him blankly. "He brought the bricks and some goods for the store." He patted her arm. "We'll be back on our feet in no time. You'll see."

"Come on, Gray!" shouted Darcy. "Sam and I need some help with this beam."

"I gotta go," said Gray. "See you at supper. Maybe you can help Ma and November with the wedding fixings. . .that's women's business."

In the end she spent the rest of the day helping Ma and November in the kitchen, the last place in the world she wanted to be, for listening to their happy chatter only reminded her that the next day she would lose Gray forever.

Then it was Sunday and the wedding was over. She was standing at the end of the pier holding the bouquet November had thrown to her from the steamer rail. She looked down at it with dull eyes. She could scarcely remember that November had carried this same nosegay, or that she had been a witness at the ceremony. All she knew was that now she was alone, and November wasn't. A tear slid down her cheeks; she hastily brushed it away. She had no time for tears. She must get Darcy to go over the accounts with her before she followed the honeymooners to Sacramento tomorrow. But by that time they'll be on their way to the cabin at Little Flats, she thought. Another tear slipped by her eyelid. Don't be a goose, she scolded herself, and averted her

399

face as Darcy helped her back into the wagon.

"I think we should have a business meeting and get our finances straightened out," she told him on the way back to the hotel.

"You'd get a false picture if I tried to explain things to you now," he answered carefully. "Wait till we sell Sam's cargo. Then I promise you I'll sit down and go over everything with you."

"But don't you see? I've got to enter all of these transactions in the books."

"And so you will—just as soon as there's something to enter."

He spoke with a finality that made her afraid to argue with him. Later that evening she questioned Holt but found he knew no more than she did. She was sure something dreadful had happened and the company was in deep trouble, but she was helpless against Darcy's unyielding wall of silence. Unspeakable fears clutched her mind throughout a sleepless night. Nevertheless, in the morning, wan and exhausted, she boarded the steamer for Sacramento.

Darcy's reluctance to discuss the financial status of the company disappeared as soon as Goldie's steamer pulled out into the bay. On the pier he turned to Holt. "Sam's cargo was boots, shirts, shovels, and hardware," he said. "If we want to make anything from it, we'll have to hold it till spring. So I'm afraid we're going to have to sell the bricks."

"But those are for our buildings," protested Holt.

"Don't you think I'm as sick about it as you are? But those notes I signed are five thousand dollars each, and the first one's due and payable on October fifteenth!"

Holt stared at Darcy a moment. Then he exploded, "Five thousand dollars in three weeks? Why, we haven't got a prayer of raising that!"

"Not unless we sell those bricks."

"You should have told Goldie and Gray." His eyes were dark and accusing. "They had a right to know."

"It wouldn't have changed anything. And it would have spoiled the wedding. Besides, I never know how to break bad news to Goldie. I'll write them. But first I want to see if I can find a buyer for those bricks. Want to come?"

"No, I'll work on the new buildings with Sam and Hop Sing."

"Then I'll see you this evening."

Darcy didn't return to the hotel until Holt was halfway through supper that night. By the look on his face as he crossed the dining room, Holt knew he had more bad news.

"What happened?" he asked as soon as Darcy sank into a chair.

"I couldn't sell them. . .not unless I wanted to give them away. The people who need them are as strapped as we are and have no cash."

"God! Now what'll we do?"

"I don't know. Break the news to Goldie and Gray. That's first, I guess. I'll write tonight."

CHAPTER **34** STATEHOOD AT LAST★★★★★★★★★★★★★★★★★★★★★

In the first two nightmarish weeks following receipt of Darcy's letter, Goldie explored and discarded plan after plan for raising the five thousand dollars by October fifteenth. Horace was unable to help, having mortgaged the La Portal in September to pay for its fancy refurbishing. Gray wrote from Little Flats that the stores were barely earning enough to pay the Chinese wages and suggested that they ask Zack if he could make them a loan.

"No," she wrote back. "I don't want to ask him for anything."

Then Henry Rawlings sent word that he had good news for Holt concerning his divorce. And at last an idea began to germinate in her mind. Rawlings owned the Statehood National Bank. She had heard he was a hard-nosed businessman, but if Holt made the request, he might lend them the money. With this in mind, she wrote to San Francisco and asked him to come up right away.

"It's a good idea," said Darcy. "Besides, the note's due in a week, and we haven't got any other doors open to us."

On the steamer to Sacramento the next day Holt was filled with misgivings about his ability to extract a loan from Henry Rawlings. He felt gauche and inadequate in the presence of this shrewd, sophisticated entrepreneur. But they were desperate. If the B.C.A. and D. was to be saved, he must find a way of persuading Rawlings they were a good risk. His mind was still searching for the right approach when he entered the Statehood Bank. Henry Rawlings

401

was standing behind a counter with a sheaf of bills in his hand. He looked up and smiled.

"Well, young man," he said jovially, "I certainly have got some good news for you."

Holt found it difficult to bridge the gap between the threatened loss of the company and a divorce, which now seemed trivial. He murmured, "Hello, sir."

If Rawlings noticed this lack of enthusiasm, he gave no sign. Immediately all brusque efficiency, he sent his clerk next door for his lawyer and ushered Holt into his private office, where he showed him an impressive hand-lettered document stating that his marriage to Mirina was annulled. "There now, what do you think of that?" he beamed.

"I hardly know what to say," stammered Holt. "I'm most awfully grateful." He gazed at the document, digesting the knowledge he was at last free. Then Mr. Jones hurried in, and, under his direction, Holt signed several copies of the annulment. Rawlings gave the lawyer instructions to find Mirina and send her a copy; and as Mr. Jones left, Holt offered to pay the banker for his trouble.

"Tut, tut, my boy." Rawlings held up his hand and shook his head. "Please, we won't discuss it—I consider I have just paid off a debt that has weighed heavily on my conscience."

Holt felt emboldened to tell him about the destruction of the B.C.A. and D. buildings in San Francisco and of the notes Darcy had signed in order to get money to rebuild. Henry Rawlings' smile changed to a frown as he listened to Holt's recital, and Holt felt he was gaining the financier's sympathy. Finally he said, "And so you see, sir, we don't have the money to meet the first note. And my partners and I were wondering if your bank would loan us the five thousand dollars." Rawlings simply stared at him. "At interest, of course," Holt hastily added. Rawlings began to laugh. Unable to see that anything he had said was funny, Holt was dumbfounded by this response.

"That you should come to me," choked Henry Rawlings. "Oh, the irony of it...it's really too bizarre." He became convulsed with mirth again.

"I don't understand," faltered Holt.

"I hold that note, young man," Rawlings boomed, his mirth suddenly gone. His gray eyes glinted metallically. "My agent bought it."

402

"Well, then surely sir, you could grant us an extension."

"I'll grant you nothing," Rawlings snapped.

"But——" Holt couldn't believe this was the same man who had just helped him.

"You amateurs," Rawlings shook his head in reproof. "That's what's the matter with doing business out here. Too many amateurs. Oh, I'll admit you made a nice start—good string of express offices. . .stores might even turn a profit eventually. In fact, what you've done fits in exactly with my own plans. That's what interested me in acquiring your firm in the first place."

Holt was staggered. "Acquiring our firm?"

"Yes. You would have lost it eventually anyway. You were riding on Lady Luck, and you rode her too far. That's what I meant by amateurs. . .faulty judgment. We professionals will own all of the businesses out here in the long run."

"I wouldn't be too sure." Holt's surprise had been replaced by anger.

"No need to get testy," said Rawlings evenly. "I'm not going to throw you out in the street. I want you and your partners to run the company for me. With a few changes in operation, of course."

"Work for you?" Holt exploded.

Rawlings took no notice of the interruption. "There's no point in discussing it right now," he continued. "Later, when you've had time to think about it rationally, you'll see I'm right. If it hadn't been me, it would have been somebody else. Now you'll have to excuse me." He began riffling through some papers on his desk. "Your note is due and payable on October fifteenth. I shall expect the cash or the forfeit of the company. Good afternoon."

Stunned, Holt made his way back to the freight office of the B.C.A. and D. Bitterly, he told Goldie what had happened.

"You mean he really wants to ruin us?" she asked for the second time.

"Yes, yes, yes!" answered Holt. "You wouldn't believe anyone could change so much in such a short time. You just wouldn't believe it."

Riding into Sacramento that evening, Gray felt elated but paradoxically apprehensive. Two days before, with November's approval, he had set out from Little Flats on his golden stallion to locate Zack and ask him to loan the company the money. His search had ended last night in Marysville, where he found Zack

403

meeting with some of the important men who were backing his campaign for the California Assembly.

As soon as he heard Gray's story, he asked, "Why didn't you come to me sooner? It's going to be a tight squeeze to get the money to you by the fifteenth."

"I know," said Gray. "But we were hoping up to the last that we wouldn't have to borrow at all. If Sam's cargo had sold. . .or the bricks. . . .But nothing worked out, and as things now stand, we're going to go under if we don't get a loan."

"I can't leave this campaign now. . . .A cancelled speech might spell my defeat. But I promise you I'll have the money to you by the fifteenth. Now tell me, how's Goldie?"

"Fine, I guess." He hesitated a moment, then burst out, "I may as well tell you, she didn't want to ask you. And she doesn't know I'm here."

Zack shrugged and laughed sardonically. "Tell her I'll see her as soon as this election is over."

Holt and Goldie were sitting at the end of one of the long wooden work tables when Gray entered the La Portal kitchen. As soon as she saw him, Goldie leaped to her feet. "What's happened?" she cried.

"Nothing," answered Gray. "In fact, for the first time in several weeks, I'd say everything's all right. I've just come from Zack."

Goldie felt as if she had lost something, something it had been very important that she keep. "You didn't!" she gasped, her voice low and accusing.

"Yes, I did. And he's going to loan us the money."

Now she remembered what it was she had lost. . .independence. Nothing would ever be the same again. "But I wanted us to do it ourselves," she wailed.

"What did you expect to nappen, Sis? Some fairy godmotner to appear or something? Well, Zack's our fairy godmother, and we ought to be damn glad he's so generous. Give me some food. I'm tired—I've been in the saddle all day." He slumped into a chair.

Gray's bluntness reduced Goldie to silence, and she hastily got up to fill his plate.

"I think it's simply great," said Holt. "This afternoon I thought we were finished for sure. Wait'll you hear who holds that note." Gray listened in disbelief as Holt told about the disastrous interview with Henry Rawlings.

404

Goldie didn't expect the five thousand dollars to arrive right away, but when no messenger had reached Sacramento by the morning of October fourteenth, she began to worry. She sent Pi Ling to meet every steamer that day, and she jumped up eagerly whenever a rig pulled into the yard; but each time she was disappointed. Now it was almost six. The last steamer had arrived over an hour ago, and the stagecoach was in. It was time to face the truth. No messenger was coming. Either Zack hadn't been able to raise the money on such short notice, or he had misunderstood where to send it. Whatever the reason, it was all her fault, for if it hadn't been for her false pride, Gray would have gone to Zack sooner. Yes, because of her silly vanity all they had worked for and all they had dreamed of doing would be gone tomorrow when Henry Rawlings claimed his forfeit. The B.C.A. and D. would vanish and leave no trace, brief-lived as a fairy ring on the morning grass.

Her stomach felt leaden and she ached with remorse, but she could not cry. Tears would only be a cheap refuge. She put her hands to her temples and pressed hard. If only she could find the money—but where? The sound of a horse coming into the yard faintly penetrated her consciousness. Involuntarily she leaped to her feet. It's probably only another customer for the store, she thought. But hope drew her outside once more. Then she stopped in the doorway. "Zack," she gasped. But how could it be? Gray had said he couldn't come himself. And yet here he was, dismounting from his horse. Relief made her knees weak, and she leaned against the door frame. They were saved!

Zack pushed his hat to the back of his head, undid his saddlebags, and came toward her smiling. Contrarily, this cheerful mien affronted her. How could he smile after making her wait till the very last minute? It was maddening. Irritation strengthening her legs, she stepped out into the yard.

"Where've you been?" she demanded pettishly.

He chucked her under the chin, then suddenly bent down and kissed her. Her strength ebbed away in a warm tide, and she tingled down to her very toes. She could cling to him forever. But abruptly he drew back and cocked a quizzical eyebrow at her. "It takes time to round up five thousand dollars," he said as if nothing had happened.

"I didn't mean. . ." she stammered in confusion. "I mean. . . we're most awfully grateful."

405

"There's no need to grovel. I was glad to help."

"I wasn't groveling," she snapped.

"That's my girl." His eyes danced in merriment as he nonchalantly draped an arm around her shoulders and gently drew her toward the office

Oh, fumed Goldie to herself, barely able to resist pulling away. Whatever he does is perfectly all right. But if I make any overtures, I'm groveling. I'll never understand him. . .never!

"Thought any more about my proposal?" he asked in an offhand manner.

"What proposal?" she inquired aloud, suddenly sweet.

She felt the muscles in his arm tighten across her shoulders, but his voice remained calm. "My proposal of marriage," he said.

"Well, yes," she coquetted, "I have."

"And?" His fingers were biting into the flesh of her arm.

She felt cornered and didn't dare look at him. "I haven't made up my mind yet," she said helplessly.

Deliberately he withdrew his arm from around her and handed her the saddlebags. "Here's the money," he said through tight lips and left.

Serves him right, she thought as she massaged her bruised arm. Groveling, indeed! Turning, she saw Pi Ling watching her, his black brows lowered in sad reproach. Immediately contrite she said, "I don't mean to be that way—it just comes out."

"Miss Goldie lucky to have love of patient man," said Pi Ling to the wall. "Have waited long time while she glasp at moonbeam. But patience have limit. . . .If she not stop soon, love and man will both be gone."

Grasp at a moonbeam, thought Goldie wildly. Was he referring to Darcy? But how could he possibly know about that? She looked sharply at him for a clue, but it was as if he had drawn a curtain and no light showed through. She blushed and lowered her eyes. "Why is everybody but me so sure I should marry Zack?" she asked quietly.

"Others see what Missy Goldie miss maybe," answered Pi Ling.

That night she decided to apologize to Zack, but he made no move to be alone with her, and she was too stubborn to initiate any action herself. "Oh well, I'll tell him tomorrow when he's in a better mood," she told herself before drifting off to sleep. And again she was wrong. The next morning Zack was gone. A whisper of fear constricted her heart. Was Pi Ling right? And to think it was only yesterday she had thought her only problem was to get the money to save the B.C.A. and D. Now she had it, but what had she lost?

When Goldie's note telling of the payment to Henry Rawlings arrived in San Francisco, Darcy paid little attention. Never an aficionado of manual labor, he now hated working on the new office building. By Friday his spirits were so low that everything he did was an effort. He had just made his tenth unsuccessful try at fitting a window into an opening on the third floor facing the bay. Deliberately he laid down his hammer and chisel and rubbed his sore hands together. He winced as the pressure revealed a new blister. He turned his hands palm-side up and bellicosely surveyed the scars and callouses. Hands like a nigger, he thought bitterly. How Jacques would gloat if he could see him now! Resentfully he picked up the hammer again and brought it down hard, striking his thumb instead of the chisel. He swore passionately and hurled the hammer across the room. Although this explosion did nothing to relieve the smart of his thumb, it drove away his gloom. He rested his hands on the windowsill and leaned far out into the fresh, salt wind. It blew his hair back in streams behind his ears and stung his eyes till the tears came.

He looked down at the town—his town, he thought with pride. Buildings were going up all around, bigger and finer than those that had been consumed by the fire. The streets were teeming with people, and they all appeared to be hurrying toward the waterfront. Idly he wondered why as his eye wandered toward Long Wharf. Just the *Oregon* coming in, he thought. But there was something different about her. Yes. . .it was that banner she was flying. Now a flotilla of boats was joining her, and men were scrambling up her sides. "Why, it's just like in forty-nine," he exclaimed aloud. While he stared in amazement, every whistle and bell in San Francisco seemed to go berserk, and he reeled back from the window, clapping his hands over his ears.

"What in hell's going on?" he called down the stairs.

"I don't know," called back Holt. "Can't you see anything up there?"

"Just the *Oregon* coming in. She's flying some kind of banner, but I can't make it out yet. Wait a minute. . .she's coming around

407

...'California...Is.. a...State!' 'California is a state!' Wowee! Did you hear?" He dashed down the stairs and collided with Holt on the first flight coming up. They threw their arms around each other and rolled to the bottom. Picking themselves up, they laughed hysterically and once more embraced, whirling round and round.

"We're a state! We're a state!" screeched Rip dancing up and down and tossing his battered beaver at the ceiling. Sam, his eyes glazed, danced with his arms outstretched in a wide circle, occasionally leaping up and clicking his heels together. Hop Sing, Che Lai, and Ky Sung, who were helping with the building, for once dropped their Oriental decorum and stared open-mouthed at their cavorting friends.

Pausing in his gyrations to catch his breath, Darcy noted their bewilderment and walked over to them.

"Blothuh Dahcy velly happy?" questioned Hop Sing politely.

"Yes, very happy," said Darcy. "We're not outsiders anymore. We're a full-fledged state in the United States of America."

"We not Amelican alleady?" asked Ky Sung.

"Yes. But well you see...it's like this...like we were orphans who've found our parents. And now are members of a family. We belong."

"Velly impohtant to belong to family," observed Che Lai.

"Come on everybody," called Holt. "Let's all go down to the pier and see if one of us can get a paper."

As they moved out to join the throng of jubilant citizens in the streets, the little Sacramento River steamer was already firing her' boilers in preparation for a record run to the city that would one day be capital of the new state. It bore the scraps of paper that told of President Fillmore's historic signing of the ratification measure on September ninth. Today was Friday, October 18, 1850.

As the revelry swept through the streets of Sacramento that night, Goldie felt very much alone despite the company of Pi Ling and Horace Ogilvy, for those she felt closest to were elsewhere. She missed Gray more than ever and wondered what he and November were doing this night. She sat down to write them the glorious news.

The tidings reached Little Flats long before Goldie's letter. Several riders had been dispatched directly from the dock to the mining towns bearing the story of statehood. Both Gray and

November were in the store when the rider galloped down the main street of Little Flats shouting, "Statehood at last! Statehood at last!"

"Whoopee!" yelled Gray, and in his exuberation picked November up by the waist, tossed her high in the air, caught her, and kissed her. "We ought to have a party," he cried.

"I've got just the thing," she said. Skipping lightly behind the counter, she reached behind the cash box and brought out a bottle of wine. "I found this when I was checking the stock. I was saving it for a special occasion and this looks like it."

Zack, in Nevada City when the report of statehood came, took time out for a hasty toast to California prosperity in the hotel bar. He was delivering another speech that night in what had turned into a bitter campaign. His opponent had made telling mileage by repeatedly coloring Zack as a member of a powerful ranching clique. While he honestly admitted the ranchers supported him, Zack also knew his antagonist's support came chiefly, though secretly, from a group of land promoters and mine monopolists interested in exploiting the new state solely for their personal benefit. He was determined to stop them if possible.

In his speech this evening, a key one in his strategy, he intended to ask his audience whether they wanted a state dominated by mine monopolists or one that would be truly democratic. Now that statehood was a reality instead of a distant dream, he was pretty sure what the answer would be. Tonight, he felt, was going to mark the turning point of this campaign.

After savoring the taste of statehood for a day, the citizens of San Francisco decided to throw a huge party for themselves to mark the glorious event and chose October 29th as the day. Ma Brown was planning a pre-ball dinner at the hotel, and at such a grand affair Darcy wanted to have no one on his arm except Goldie. Thus when Hop Sing arrived in Sacramento with the express the following Monday, he also carried a letter to Goldie from Darcy. The number of packages and parcels was larger than it had been for many weeks. When Goldie commented on this, Hop Sing informed her with solemn dignity that the B.C.A. and D. was gaining back many of its old customers.

409

"Most of new companies not to be tlusted," he said.

"And who's been spreading that tale about?" she teased.

"Have all been doing duty."

"I'm sure you have. But I'm still afraid we won't make enough to pay that second note in December."

"Missy Goldie not wolly. We have money by then."

"I'm glad you're confident," she laughed

Hop Sing told her that the new warehouse and office building were almost complete, and that most of the offices had already been rented. "We in new home too," he said. "Now ally live in house Blothuh Holt build. Che Lai luhning how to cook."

"But he's a doctor!"

"No mattuh—he like cooking."

"In that case I guess it's all right," she said absently. She had opened Darcy's letter. Normally she would be flattered by the invitation and excited at the prospect of attending an elegant ball; but since her quarrel with Zack a week ago, everything had lost its savor. She folded the letter and sighed. "I don't think I'd better go," she said.

Hop Sing looked startled and hurriedly stuck his arms in his sleeves. "Will be velly nice pahty. Missy Ma planning gleat banquet. . .evlybody coming. And Bothuh Dahcy say I to make shuh you say yes."

Pi Ling came in. "What long?" he asked.

"Missy Goldie no want to go to Statehood Ball in San Flancisco next week," said Hop Sing.

"We can't afford it, Pi Ling," protested Goldie. "Besides, I haven't got anything to wear."

But Pi Ling had known her too long and recognized she was only making excuses. He decided to give her some free advice. "Lettuh a fine thing," he said. "Can ease pain in haht in lettuh. Evlything look much bettuh when haht not heavy."

Goldie looked at him strangely for a moment. How did he always know what was troubling her, she wondered? And why hadn't she thought of the way out herself? All she needed to do was write Zack and apologize. How simple it was. But composing the letter was difficult. It took several hours of labor that evening before she was satisfied. And then she really wasn't. What she longed to do was tell him in person.

Observing at breakfast that his tonic had not had the desired

410

effect, Pi Ling urged her to attend the ball. More to please him than for any other reason, she agreed.

The next week passed quickly, but her spirits continued to droop. Then, just before she was to take the steamer for San Francisco, she received a reply to her apology from Zack. He was more frank than he had ever been with her before. He told her about the fight he was having and of what winning the legislative seat meant to him. He even apologized for his rudeness when he had brought the money for the B.C.A. and D. to Sacramento. Her face glowing, she pressed the letter to her breast when she finished reading it. Pi Ling smiled in satisfaction.

"Missy Goldie have good time in San Flancisco," he said.

"Oh, I will!" she cried. "I will!"

There would never be such a social occasion in San Francisco as the Statehood Ball held on October 29, 1850. Nearly everybody was invited and nearly everybody came; but though there was scarcely a female of any age or occupation in the entire region who was not present, the men still outnumbered them two to one.

Realizing that they would go unnoticed in the crowd, Big Tom and his gang chose this night to return to the city. At the weapons check at the door to the ball, they gave token guns and knives, then carried concealed weapons into the hall. The room was so thickly packed with bodies it was difficult to move. Nevertheless, Big Tom spread his boys out with orders to find Mike and Darcy and keep close watch on them until he gave the signal to do them in.

Rip, resplendent in a new plaid suit, was the first to spot a Sydney Duck in the crowd. Immediately alarmed, he set out to find Darcy, but his small size, which permitted him to escape the ex-convict's attention, proved a disadvantage in locating Darcy in the throng. Finally he bumped into Mike.

"I seen Beevy over there," he rasped in his coffee-grinder voice.

"If he's here, so are the rest," said Mike as his eyes began searching the faces passing by.

"I gotta warn Darcy. Where is he?"

"I don't know. But it's all right. . .I'll take care of it." He disappeared, and Rip began searching again. Suddenly the crowd parted for a moment, and he was staring straight at Wilcox Forbes, the gambler on the ship from Panama who had sworn to get even with Darcy. Rip gasped and frantically backpawed his way

411

through the sea of bodies until several waves of them separated him from the card shark. He now knew it was the voice of Forbes he had been unable to identify the night at Lefty's when he overheard the Sydney Ducks' plot. Darcy's life was in danger again.

Oblivious to everything but his own pleasure, Darcy was devoting the evening to the conquest of Goldie. Her attitude had been pleasant but impersonal since her arrival. His vanity challenged, he eagerly set about proving he could have her if he wanted her. The crowded conditions of the hall aided him in exercising his sexual magnetism, and he was unashamedly exploiting his opportunity. Since it was impossible to dance, he held her tightly as they swayed together, occasionally brushing his lips against her hair or for a moment resting his cheek against hers. Once more falling under the spell of his dark good looks and excited by his touch, Goldie found herself wishing the dance would go on forever. Then late in the evening she accidentally backed into someone and, turning to apologize, found herself facing Rachel.

"Well, it's a little world, isn't it?" commented Rachel. Her dark-fringed eyes swept over Darcy, then boldly issued him an invitation. "And who is this?" she asked.

"Darcy Dupres," said Goldie. "Darcy, this is Mrs. Colby."

"Nice try, honey," said Rachel, giving Goldie a patronizing smile before returning her attention to Darcy. "My friends call me Rachel," she said.

"How's Chuck?" asked Goldie, determined not to give up, for she realized that Rachel had decided to make Darcy her catch for the evening.

"I haven't the slightest idea—haven't seen him since your protector put him in prison. I always knew Zack was a spiteful man." She took Darcy's arm. "Poor Chuck couldn't even steal a purse. I ought to know. He tried to steal mine once." She gazed at Darcy with dancing violet eyes as if sharing a droll secret with him. "The poor boy made an awful bungle of it." The music started again, and she looked expectantly at Darcy.

Desire flamed in him. How exciting she was...experienced ...and as eager for him as he was for her. He had to have her. He held out his arms. "Shall we?" he asked in his soft pulsing voice. Her eyes gleaming her triumph, she swept him a curtsy, and he danced her off without a backward glance.

412

Too stunned to think at first, Goldie stood forlornly gazing after them. Then her lips began to quiver with humiliation and disappointment. Desperately she looked around for some private place to cry. Oh, blessed God, there was a row of columns behind the refreshment tables. If she could only reach them before. . .She stuck her fist in her mouth and fled across the room. Countless bodies buffeted her, and numerous partnerless men grabbed at her, but she shook them off and ran on, not stopping until she swept around the end of a table to the passage behind and leaned her forehead against a pillar. But she was not alone.

Ma Brown, standing only a few feet away, stepped over and inquired anxiously, "What is it, child?"

Goldie turned, choked, "Darcy——" then burst into tears, laying her head on Ma's bosom.

Ma put her arms around her and patted her. "Darcy's a will-o'-the-wisp. Saw a new face, I'll wager." Goldie nodded. "That's nothing to cry about," Ma continued. "He'll leave her for another." But Goldie found no comfort in this observation and cried all the harder. Ma decided on another approach. "A young girl like you should be out there dancing, not wailing in a corner. You wait here—I'll find somebody."

Moments later Ma returned with Sam in tow. "I'm out of practice, but I'd sure be mighty pleased if you'd favor me with a dance, Miss Goldie," he boomed in his deep, bass voice.

Goldie mutely placed her hand on his arm, which was easier to reach than his shoulder. Sam saw her bright blue eyes and warm red lips and thought Darcy must be out of his mind to leave her for another girl.

Despite his warning and his huge size, Sam was a surprisingly good dancer, and after they had danced several numbers, Goldie was beginning to enjoy herself once more. They were standing near the door at the end of a fast reel. As the final note died away, Goldie thought she heard a shot outside. She looked at Sam and saw that he had heard it too. Without thinking, she dashed through the door just in time to see Darcy bending over the scarlet-dressed Rachel, who was lying beside a carriage. Unconsciously her eyes looked around for an assailant, and in the shadow of an adjacent building, she saw Mike lean down and extract a knife from the prone figure of a man. She rushed over to the carriage and knelt down.

She put her hand to Rachel's mouth but felt nothing. Then she felt her wrist for a pulse. She looked at Darcy. "I think she's dead," she said quietly.

His face was very white. "My God," he said. "My God!"

A crowd gathered around the carriage. "Let me through," said Dr. Murphy. Briefly he examined Rachel. He shook his head. Rachel was dead.

Rip tore up, screaming, "Darcy, it's Wilcox Forbes who done it!" He pointed to the corner where Goldie had seen Mike, but Mike was no longer there—only the body of the gambler. "He's the one I heard in Lefty's that night. He was tryin' to kill you!"

Darcy got up from beside Rachel and went over to where Forbes lay. So Rachel had been killed by a ball intended for him. It was his fault she was dead. Or didn't that have anything to do with it? He couldn't think clearly.

Goldie couldn't take her eyes from Rachel. It could have been me, she thought. It could have been me. She was chilled. . .and suddenly aware of the transitory nature of life. Death could come to the young. She knew it. . .had seen it. And yet always before she had felt immune—untouched. But this time. . ."It could have been me," she whispered again and stood up. She wanted Zack. He always knew the right thing to do. . .was always there when she needed him. Zack wouldn't leave her alone as Darcy had done. And yet if Darcy hadn't deserted her—she shuddered and began to tremble—she might be lying there dead instead of Rachel.

Much later, after the undertaker had claimed the bodies and the others had returned to the hotel, Mike rejoined them. "Big Tom got away," he said simply, then moved off to get a cup of coffee. Darcy looked after him a moment, then wheeled slowly around and stared at Goldie. She was sitting quietly, her hands folded in her lap, not talking and not looking at anything. He hadn't said a word to her since the shooting; more accurately, he hadn't said a word to her since he had left her in the middle of the ball. And now he felt driven to apologize. He took two cups of coffee from the side table and went over to her.

"You look like you could use this," he said as he handed her a cup.

"Thank you." She looked at him and their eyes locked in one of those rare moments of complete understanding between two individuals. No words of explanation were necessary. Their relationship was changed. All passion was gone, and in its place was left only the warmth of two people who had shared something sweet and something terrible. Rachel's death had separated them permanently.

"I'm sorry, Goldie. . .for everything," he said.

A flicker of a smile crossed her face. "Don't be. It was a hard way to find out, but better that we did."

Darcy nodded. "Will you be going back in the morning?"

"Yes." And now she genuinely smiled. Within a week the election would be over, and Zack would be back for her answer. She knew what it would be.

CHAPTER **35** NEW HORIZONS★★★★★★★★★★★★★★★★★★★★★★★★★★

In the store in Little Flats, Gray crumpled Goldie's letter into a ball. With glazed eyes he looked across the street at The Golden Bon Bon. Was that a flash of scarlet at the door? Hope hastened his heartbeat. His eyes strained into the darkness of the saloon, half expecting to find Rachel standing there, a slow, mocking smile on her lips relishing the joke she had played on Fate. He could almost hear her low-keyed laugh. His Adam's apple suddenly felt too large for his throat.

"I have to go out for a while," he called to November and without waiting for a reply strode into the street.

Outside he ran, not stopping until he was high on a hill overlooking the town. In this lonely place he sank down and lifted his hands to his face. His fist still clenched the letter telling of Rachel's death. Slowly he opened his fingers, letting the paper drop. A capricious wind picked it up and danced it down the mountainside until it was gone—like Rachel. Never again would she suddenly appear to kindle the fires within him. He lowered his head to his chest. His sense of loss was overwhelming. But why? He loved November. . .was happy with her. Yet Rachel had drawn him like a magnet. The excitement she generated had pounded through his body, and he had found her irresistible. Could he ever have explained that to November? No need to worry about that anymore. Yes, with Rachel gone, life would be less complex, he sighed, but infinitely more dull.

He sat silent a long while, lost to time, and when at last he lifted his head, he saw the sky was an incredible blue. Had it ever been so blue? Breathing in deeply, he became aware of the pungent odor of decay that marked fall and the end of a life cycle. But on the trees nearby, stirred by a playful breeze, copper and gold leaves winked at him as if to remind him that spring would follow winter, and they would live again. Ah, that was it. A compassionate sadness replaced the empty feeling within him. Poor Rachel—so much wanting to live. And for her, there would be no spring.

He rose to leave and saw November standing at the crest of the hill. Outlined against the sun, her brown hair shot flashes of bronze. Never had she looked more beautiful. For a moment she stood there panting. Then she spoke. "I was worried. . .you were gone so long. Chung Sun said you came up here."

He moved swiftly toward her, his arms extended wide. "I'm all right now."

In a rush she came to him and buried her face in his chest. "Don't ever leave me!" she cried in muffled tones.

He clasped her tightly. "Leave you? Why, you're the best thing that's ever happened to me. Don't you know I love you?" He bent down and kissed her, tenderly at first, then with mounting passion, until the memory of Rachel followed her substance into the shadows.

During the ten days following the debacle of the ball in San Francisco, Goldie had waited impatiently for Zack to come to Sacramento. But now that he and his vaqueros were herding fifty head of beef into the B.C.A. and D. corral, panic seized her. The affectionate phrases carefully rehearsed for this moment flew out of her mind, and before she could compose new ones, he was standing in front of her, his eyes boring into hers. All she could manage was a weak smile, but there was no answering warmth in

416

his face. In fright, her heart began skipping wildly. Why didn't he speak? Had he found somebody else? Or was it only that he had lost the election? She must break this silence or her lungs would surely burst. "Did . .did you win? I mean, are congratulations in order?

"The election?" His voice was devoid of emotion, but his eyes were ablaze. "Yes, I squeaked through."

If he would only stop looking at her like that. She looked away in confusion. "Then I suppose I ought to kiss you." She laughed nervously.

"If you have to think about it, don't bother," he snapped.

The harshness of his voice filled her with dread. Pi Ling's warning tolled in her head like a dirge. Had she dallied too long? Her heart was pounding so that words tumbled out of her mouth in a cascade. "I'm ready to close. We must toast your success with a bottle of Horace's champagne. Would you like to eat there or someplace else?"

"It doesn't matter."

His shoulders drooped, but she was too immersed in her own misery to notice. Now she was sure he didn't want her anymore. She bit her lip and turned away. "Maybe you'd rather not eat with me at all."

The sight of her turning away from him snapped his restraint, and the passion he had held in check for so long came unleashed. Light as an Indian he vaulted the rail separating the desk from the rest of the office. "By God, I'll make you mine if I have to take you now!" he said, grabbing her and spinning her around.

For an instant she saw his blazing eyes, then he was kissing her, and every nerve tingled. As his insistent lips traveled to her throat, she threw her arms around him and cried, "I love you!"

Abruptly he stopped and stepped back. "What did you say?" he asked in disbelief.

"I love you."

He was silent, but his eyes searched her face until she had to look away. Her heart was still pounding, and her voice was barely audible. "I wanted to tell you when you first came in, but I didn't know how."

He lifted her chin with his hand, forcing her to look at him. "You're sure?" She nodded. Once more he drew her into his arms, but this time his embrace was almost casual. "How soon can you be ready to leave here?" he asked.

417

"I'm sure we'll be solvent again by the time the legislature opens in January. We could be married then and go on to San Jose."

His arms stiffened against her back, and his voice became harsh. "You'll have to do better than that. I've waited long enough."

"When then?" she asked uneasily.

"I've been intending to go to Monterey on business. We could be married before and make it our wedding trip." He glanced at the calendar on the desk. "How about November twenty-third? It's a Saturday and most of our friends could come then."

"But that's only two weeks away," she cried in panic.

He moved around the side of the desk, picked up her pen, and began punching holes in an express blank with it. "I thought you said you were sure," he said quietly.

She knew she had lost. They would marry on his terms or not at all. Still, she couldn't stop herself from making one last effort to keep what she had and get him too. "It's just that we've got that second note due in December, and it doesn't seem right to leave before then."

"Why not? Or don't you think Gray and the others are capable of handling it?"

She flushed. He made her sound conceited. "I didn't mean it that way," she protested.

"I'm sorry, but that's the way it sounded to me. Or maybe you've had some second thoughts about your hasty decision of a moment ago."

Hot words bubbled up within her. But if they quarreled now . . .and they were perilously close to it. She stole a look at him as he furiously drove the pen into the blank. Involuntarily she shivered. He was right. In a way she was afraid. . .afraid of him and of her own weakness. At his touch she became lost. . .no longer in control of herself or her destiny. And yet she couldn't let him go. . .not this time. She took a deep breath. "I've no regrets, Zack. We'll be married on the twenty-third."

As if reading her mind, he crossed swiftly to her and tenderly enfolded her in his arms. "Dearest," he whispered, "don't be afraid. I would never hurt you."

Her heart resumed its normal beat. Here in his arms she was safe, and for now that was enough. She would think about leaving Sacramento and the B.C.A. and D. later. Maybe she wouldn't have to give them up completely.

418

The next two weeks passed like a dream. Pi Ling unobtrusively bore the brunt of the operation of the B.C.A. and D. while she frantically sewed on her trousseau and made arrangements for sheltering and feeding the many guests expected to attend the wedding. Her days breathless, at night she tumbled into bed too tired to think.

Thus it was a shock when Gray and November drove into the yard on November twenty-first in a freight wagon containing their belongings and with a joyous Happy barking his greeting from the high seat. The sight of Gray's dog upset her, and the smile of welcome froze on her face. Suddenly the dream was over and the full significance of what she was about to do struck her. Gray was moving to Sacramento to take her place. And she—why, in two days she would be married and leave all of this forever. Tucked away on an isolated ranch, she would never play more than a passive role in the business again. A partner, yes. But in name only. She could scarcely hold back the tears during their brief exchange of greetings and was relieved when Gray drove November off to Horace's to settle in.

Listlessly she returned to the office. As she sat sewing on her white China silk wedding gown, she bit her lip and asked herself why her heart had suddenly turned cold. She *did* love Zack. But there was still so much she wanted to do. Why couldn't she give up her own ambitions? This was wrong. A bride shouldn't feel this way. But she did!

Her hands fell idle in her lap. From the desk Pi Ling watched her for a while then came over and gently touched her shoulder. "I finish hem," he said. "Missy Goldie come work on books."

She got up hastily and retreated to the desk lest he see the tears that were about to splash down her cheeks. But she soon became totally absorbed in the accounts and was unaware that Gray had returned until he put his hand over the column of figures she was entering and said, "You can work on this later. Right now I want to tell you about our plans. You're still a partner, you know"—he winked at her—"even if you are getting married."

Startled, she looked up. "What plans?"

"Well, you know Holt and Darcy's plan to open an express office and store in Monterey. Well, in addition——"

"Wait a minute. I never heard anything about expanding to Monterey."

"Where've you been? Don't you read the mail? Besides, what have you and Holt been talking about when he's brought up the express?"

Goldie blushed. "I guess I really haven't been paying much attention lately. Still, I don't think he's mentioned a store in Monterey."

"He must have. We've already bought the land, and Rip Packet's carrying express down there regularly on the steamer."

"But what about the money we owe Mr. Rawlings? How can we afford to buy land and put up another store now?"

Gray scowled. "Goldie, you've got to stop being so negative about everything. Darcy and Holt don't like it. And frankly, I don't either."

"Somebody's got to ask unpleasant questions. And you haven't told me where the five thousand dollars is coming from yet."

"Hell! Darcy makes enough in one week on his tables at the El Dorado to cover that."

"I see. . ." Her voice was hollow. Even before she was married, they were doing things as if she weren't there.

Gray attributed her lack of enthusiasm to anxiety. He put his arm around her. "There's nothing to worry about, Sis. Business will pick up in the spring, and we're making good money from the rentals in the San Francisco buildings right now." He paused. "Everything's growing, Goldie. If we don't, we'll die."

She lifted her eyes to his and saw he didn't understand. "I feel so left out," she said.

"Nobody wants to leave you out. But you've got to go along with the times. Different products and different methods of doing business are needed from those we used a year ago. Darcy and Holt recognize it and so do I. Even mining's different. The men are combining claims and forming companies. And it makes sense—the more workers, the more profit. I bought into one of them for us above Little Flats."

"You didn't give up our claim. . .and the cabin?" she trailed off.

"Of course not. This is a new strike higher up, and it already looks rich."

"How much did it cost?"

"Only a couple of thousand, and it wasn't all cash."

She sighed. "More notes?"

"No, we're buying the stock out of our share of the profits."

"I see. And what else? How else must we change?"

"We've got to expand into new areas. . .but ones that we know something about. For instance, Holt's bought a big tract of prime timberland above Hangtown."

"Timber?"

"Sure, the building industry's booming. You can see that right here in Sacramento. And I'll bet there isn't a man in California that knows more about lumbering than Holt does." His brown eyes glowed. "We've already started logging, and will be shipping to the valley in less than a month."

Things were worse than she had expected. All she could see was money going out and nothing coming in. She was so dispirited she could scarcely protest, "With winter coming on?"

"It's the best time. When else could we hire the men cheap? By spring they'll all be off chasing gold again."

She was stricken. How could all of this have happened in less than two weeks? They were spread too thin—just like before the fire. Hadn't they learned anything? Henry Rawlings would win after all. Everything she had worked so hard for would be gone. And she'd be stuck away on Zack's ranch unable to do anything about it. Oh, why couldn't he have waited a little longer?

Gray was impatient. "Don't you understand? There's no limit to what we can do now. California's going to be the greatest state in the union." She tried to smile, but instead her lip quivered. He took her hand. "What is it?"

She shook her head, unable to speak.

Gray thought he understood. "Is it getting married?"

Her eyes widened in surprise. Getting married? Yes, she was afraid of that too.

He began to smile. "You don't have to worry about that. Zack loves you. Everybody feels a little uncertain at first—I did too. But you'll find marriage is a great experience. There's nothing else like it. It's not just the sex"—he reddened slightly, for they had never said much about this subject to each other—"but the sharing. It's hard to explain. You see, you know you're still one person, and yet. . .you're not. . .because you're part of somebody else, and well, they're part of you."

She had a glimpse of what he was talking about, but it slid away into anxiety again. Ever since he married November he talked in riddles, which increased her sense of remoteness from him.

421

Her depression carried over into the next day and did not lift even with the arrival of Zack that evening. Frightened once more, she was diffident about being alone with him. Zack's buckskins were dusty, a two-days' stubble of beard covered his chin, and tired lines were finely etched around his eyes. Once again she was too wrapped up in her own doubts to take notice of his appearance or to see the joy fade from his eyes at her constrained response to his kiss.

He stepped back a pace, his eyes searching her face. "What's the matter, sweetheart?" he asked. "Is the firm in trouble again?"

"No, oh, I don't know. It's me, I guess. . ." She sighed. "I seem to be out of step lately.

"Nonsense, you'll never be out of step."

"Oh, but I *am* according to Gray. They're expanding again—mining stock, timber holdings, a store in Monterey, and heaven knows what else. And they never told me anything about it!" She began to cry, all of her tensions, fears, and uncertainties at last bubbling to the surface. "They say I—I'm negative. But they're spending money before we make it. And we still owe Henry Rawlings five thousand dollars. . .not to mention what we owe you." She turned a tear-stained face up to him.

Zack's face clouded. "Is that all that's bothering you?"

The significance of his question eluded her. Like Gray, he simply didn't understand. She sniffed. "Isn't that enough?"

If only he could shake some sense into her, he thought. He took a step toward her, his eyes sharp. "I'm relieved to know it wasn't anything so insignificant as our marriage tomorrow." His voice was rough and sarcastic.

In shock she abruptly stopped crying. For once she saw herself through his eyes. She stared into his face and remembered the first time she had ever seen him, when he had rescued her from the roustabouts on the *Missouri Belle*. How petty she must look to him now. "Oh, Zack," she cried, "I don't know why you'd want to marry me at all!"

"It's because I love you, you silly girl." God help me, he thought, as he took out his bandana and handed it to her. She was still so young. "Here, dry your eyes," he said. "It'll all work out. You'll find yourself." But the thought lingered that he might be wrong.

At precisely ten o'clock the next morning, clinging to Gray's

422

arm, she entered the church to be married to Zack. The structure was newly constructed, crude, and still smelling pungently of green unseasoned lumber; in all, ideally suited to the marriage of a couple out to tame a new land barely touched by the finger of civilization. But Goldie's immediate concern was not the suitability of the chapel. She was thinking how unseasonably warm the day was and how heavy the weight of her silk dress and multitudinous petticoats. November, standing to the left of the altar cool and serene in a summer-weight blue tarlatan, was an affront. She felt surrounded by hostility and half-expected Mary Milford to stick out her tongue as she passed by on Gray's arm. And though he walked beside her, it seemed that Gray had deserted her. She couldn't even talk to him anymore. She looked stonily ahead. But there was Darcy grinning at her from the front pew. How dare he gloat over her? A violent trembling surged over her. She wasn't going to make it. . .and in front of all these people. She shut her eyes tight to turn back the sickening wave of nausea. Then she felt Gray pat her hand and heard his voice close in her ear. "It's all right, Sis. Everything's going to be all right."

Magically, her trembling ceased, and she opened her eyes. She was standing before the altar, and though she hadn't seen him, she felt Zack's presence on her right side. She loved him. Everything would be all right.

Later at the reception, with each glass of champagne she drank, things became even brighter. Why, being married was no different than being single, she thought. It would be fun. It was a gay crowd that trooped to the San Francisco steamer at noon, and Goldie, sure of her charm in her bottle-green traveling dress and pert matching bonnet, was the gayest of them all. Since a number of the guests were returning on the same boat, the party continued throughout the trip. And even after they reached the city, there was no time to think and no time to be afraid, for Ma Brown had a wedding supper waiting for them with more champagne.

Finally, her head spinning, Goldie begged to be excused. She started up the stairs to Ma's best bed-sitting room. Halfway up, Jasmine stepped out of the shadows. Goldie leaped backwards, her hand clutching for the rail.

"Oh, please, I no mean to flighten," said Jasmine in her soft vocie.

"It's the champagne," said Goldie. She put her hand to her forehead. "I'm not seeing too well."

Jasmine held out a package wrapped in silk and tied with a gold cord. "Foh you," she said. "From Hop Sing and me. . .foh wedding night." She cast her dark velvet eyes downward so Goldie could only see the black fringe of her lashes on her cheeks. "Men like the feel of silk." It was almost a whisper. She thrust the nearly weightless package into Goldie's hands, and without waiting for thanks, gracefully bowed and silently disappeared down the stairs.

In her warm firelit room, Goldie opened the present. A shimmering jade green gossamer gown of silk cascaded through her fingers. She caught her breath. Gently she picked it up and holding it in front of her surveyed herself in the tall tilt mirror. It was just her color. Instinctively she knew it would have the effect it was designed to achieve. Her eyes sparkled wickedly. Nice girls weren't supposed to know these things. Guiltily she looked at the high poufed bed where her demure white long-sleeved nightdress was laid out. That was suitable for a bride. She sighed and looked down at the fragile vision in her hands. She wouldn't have much time—Zack would soon be here. But if she hurried, she could at least try it on. In a frenzy she divested herself of her clothing, scattering her dress and petticoats wildly about the room completely contrary to her orderly nature. Then at last she felt the smooth silk slip down her bare body. Flushed from her exertions, she turned once more to the mirror. She reached up and unfastened her hair. The copper curls came cascading over her shoulders and down her back as Zack entered. She stood frozen in confusion, the firelight shooting sparks from her hair and eyes.

Zack was dazzled. For a moment he stood motionless, not even breathing, remembering the sunlit day half a continent away on the Little Blue River when he had stood spellbound watching her wash her hair. He had desired her then, and he desired her even more now. Slowly he let out his breath and crossing to her enfolded her in his arms. "You're so lovely," he whispered, "I'm almost afraid to touch you."

He kissed her tenderly, then more and more insistently. She entwined her arms around him and her fingers rippled through his hair. She felt his hands stroking her body, and a wild thrill of ecstasy came over her in wave after wave. She scarcely knew he had lifted her up and placed her on the bed. Then for a moment he was gone. "Don't stop. . . don't stop. . ." she called. He slipped in beside her, and soon they were locked in the passion of first union, resolving forever some of her doubts about marriage.

But in the morning Zack said, "I didn't want to say anything yesterday, but would you mind terribly if we postponed our trip to Monterey? I should get back to the Rio Oro. There could be a heavy snow any time now and the ranch isn't ready for it."

Her heart felt cold. So soon to be isolated, and with people she barely knew. "Can we stop in Sacramento on the way back?" she asked.

"Only briefly, I'm afraid."

"Could we. . .could we come down for Christmas then?

"No. I'm sorry, but I can't leave the ranch so soon again." He was brusque, showing his irritation with her for dwelling on such a trivial matter when he had so many important things on his mind. "We'll have plenty of time to talk about Christmas later," he said.

On the way upriver on the steamer she thought of nothing but the forthcoming holiday, seeing it as a dismal day spent in a strange house surrounded by strangers. The more she brooded over it, the more she magnified the bleakness, and the more enchanting the Christmas of the previous year seemed. How happy they all had been in the cabin above Little Flats, believing in themselves and their future. She could hardly believe all that had happened in the short year since. She and Gray were both married, Holt was divorced, the firm deeply in debt, the Chinese scattered, and Kevin gone for good. If only she could make it like it was; if just for one day they could once more all be together. Then maybe everything would be all right again. Yes, that was it. . .everybody must come to Rancho Rio Oro for Christmas. Once again she forgot to think about Zack.

In Sacramento Gray agreed to bring as many of the company family as possible to the ranch for Christmas. But Goldie's happiness over this triumph lasted only the length of time it took Zack to drive them to his long, low house sheltered by its mammoth oaks. Scarcely had they removed their coats and been welcomed by Maria, the housekeeper, when Vallecito, Zack's foreman, burst in.

"Bad news, señor Peale," he said apologetically. "There ees a storm een the high mountains. The passes are already closed."

"Looks like I got back just in time," said Zack. "Tell the men we'll be going out early tomorrow. We won't have more than a couple of days to round up the strays and bring them down."

"Si, señor, I'll have the men ready," said Vallecito and left.

Goldie was aghast. "You don't mean you're going out in the morning?"

"I must. This is my living, Goldie. . .and yours too, now. It takes hard work to keep it going. And with the campaign I've had to be away too long."

"Yes, of course," she said, but how she dreaded to face her first day here alone.

Zack was already up and pulling on his boots in the cold, cheerless bedroom by the time she awakened the next morning. Before she could remember why he was up so early, he had left the room. Hastily she rose, groping for the washstand in the semidarkness. "I might as well be back in Indiana," she grumbled. She picked up his dirty washbowl, emptied it into the slop jar, and poured some icy water into the basin for herself. But she had no time for complaint. If she didn't hurry, Zack would be gone.

He glanced up and smiled as she entered the warm dining room. "Glad you're up. . ." Her heart skipped a beat, but his next words were like a dash of cold water on her spirit. "We'll be in the north high pasture if anything happens."

"The north high pasture," she repeated dully. He didn't really care whether he saw her or not. She sat down and poured herself a cup of Maria's strong coffee.

426

"Yes," he continued between mouthfuls. "I'm taking Vallecito and most of the men. Send Ramón if you need me. He knows where to go."

She took a swallow of the scalding liquid. "I will."

Abruptly he pushed back his chair and rose. "I'll be back for dinner—but late." He came around the table, absentmindedly kissed her and left.

Outside she heard him call to the men, the sounds of their mounting, then nothing as they rode beyond earshot. She toyed with her coffee cup and looked at the remains of his breakfast. A lump slowly rose in her throat.

The door to the kitchen swung open, and Maria entered. "Ah, you are up, señora, I will bring you some hot breakfast." She picked up the platter of congealing beef and eggs.

Goldie sucked in her breath sharply and fixed her gaze on her empty plate. She mustn't cry in front of the servants. "No, thank you," she said. "I'll just have coffee."

"Sí, señora," said Maria and went back into the kitchen.

Two weeks passed, with Zack and the men gone every day preparing the ranch for winter. With the house and the meals taken care of by the capable Maria and her staff, there was nothing for Goldie to do except work on her Christmas presents in lonely silence. Then suddenly it was December fifteenth. The five thousand dollars was due Henry Rawlings today. What if they hadn't been able to pay? The idea was agony, and Goldie wandered around the house more dispirited than ever.

By afternoon she was beside herself with worry and couldn't stand being alone another minute. Timidly she opened the door to Maria's domain, the kitchen. The women who were gaily chattering in Spanish as they prepared the evening meal stopped as they saw the slim young mistress standing hesitantly in the doorway.

Maria looked at her in surprise since this was the first time she had ventured near the kitchen. "Something for you, señora?" she asked.

"No. . .no. . .nothing," stammered Goldie. "I—I just wondered if there was something I could do."

With a flash of insight Maria understood. The strange Yankee girl was lonely. Not being an unkind person, she said, "Sí, I think I can find something." She looked around the littered kitchen. "Can you make bread?"

427

"Oh, yes—anything," Goldie answered in a rush.

At first she was happy just working alongside the other women, but as they continued speaking in Spanish, she soon felt more isolated than ever. Finally she asked Maria if they would teach her their language so that she might join them in conversation.

"Sí, señora," said Maria and communicated her request to the others. One of the women gestured to Goldie, speaking rapidly and earnestly. Maria nodded.

"They agree eef you weel teach them English," she said.

"Oh, yes—I mean, *sí* " said Goldie and they all laughed.

Under the tutelage of her five teachers she soon learned a number of Spanish words. But in the process she discovered that none of the women could read or write. "We'll soon fix that," she said. "I'll teach you to read and write in English and Spanish both." The afternoon passed so quickly, she was surprised when she heard Zack and the men returning.

During the next days, through the English lessons she became friends with the ranch families and gained their help in preparing for the approaching Christmas holiday. Her thoughts were happy because the skies were clear, and now nothing could keep Christmas from being the way she wanted it to be. At night she chattered to Zack about Gray and what they would do when he arrived, never noticing the shadowed look that came into his eyes or the tired sag of his shoulders. Yes, her world would be perfect if only—if only she knew the note had been paid.

Then, as if in answer to her wish, just one week before Christmas Eve she heard a wagon approaching the clearing. From the window she saw it was Pi Ling and Sam. She charged out into the yard shouting as she ran, "Did they pay? Are we out of debt?"

Pi Ling smiled and nodded, "Yes, evlything all light now."

She gripped the wheel as he jumped down. "I'm so glad! And I'm glad to see you."

"Sure is a long ways in here from the road," commented Sam as he swung easily to the ground. "If it hadn't a been for Pi Ling, I'd a thought we was lost for sure."

Goldie beamed at them. "But you got here, and that's all that counts. Now tell me all the news." Then suddenly she grasped Pi Ling's arm in fear. "Gray...all of you are coming for Christmas, aren't you?"

Pi Ling's eyes penetrated hers. "Would wuhld fall in if didn't?"

428

She looked away in confusion. She knew what he meant. But she couldn't help herself. They *had* to come!

At last he said, "Evlybody coming. Blother Holt and Dahcy, Hop Sing, Jasmine, Che Lai. . .evlybody. All allive day befouh."

"It'll be just perfect," she said. "Remember last year?"

"I lemembuh," said Pi Ling.

But he still had a peculiar look in his eyes that made her ask, "Is something wrong?"

"No, nothing," he said. "But have more news. Blothuh Glay and Missy Novembuh have bought house in Saclamento. Is velly nice house. They move in today—maybe tomollow."

For just a moment her good humor was dampened by the thought that Gray might prefer to spend his first Christmas with November in their new home. But she immediately rejected the idea by telling herself if that were true, he wouldn't have told her he would come to the ranch in the first place.

At supper Pi Ling and Sam told of the signs of a hard winter they had seen on the express run. Zack nodded in agreement. "Yes, even the animals seem to sense it," he said.

"Don't talk that way," said Goldie. "You scare me. I couldn't bear it if something happened to prevent us from having our Christmas together."

The men looked at each other, and for a moment an embarrassing silence filled the room. Then Pi Ling spoke. "Meat velly scahce now. Need beef foh stoahs. Blothuh Glay send us to see if you have any.

"I might be able to cut out twenty-five head," said Zack. "But I'm afraid that will be all until next spring."

"Good," said Pi Ling. "Will bling velly good plice now."

Zack stood up and stretched. "I guess I'd better turn in. I've been working my men pretty hard the last few days. And tomorrow will be no exception if I'm to start twenty-five head of beef to Sacramento for you. Most of the vaqueros have families, and I want them to be back here for Christmas. It's a pretty important holiday for them."

"We must leave uhly too," said Pi Ling. "Is velly long ways to Little Flats."

In Sacramento Gray and November were moving into their new house though they only had piecemeal furnishings. But they were too excited over their first home to wait for the furniture November had ordered to come up from San Francisco. The house, a two-story clapboard decorated with fine gingerbread cutouts on the porch and upstairs balcony, had been built by a young miner who had struck it rich early in forty-nine. But by the time it was finished, he had received a letter from his sweetheart back East telling of her marriage to a man who had stayed home. Bitter with disappointment, the miner marketed it cheap and then left Sacramento.

"Weren't we lucky?" asked November as they stood on the porch.

"I'm lucky," said Gray, "since I met you." Then he picked her up and carried her into the house.

"What was that for?" she asked in surprise.

"To make sure our good fortune continues," he answered, kissing her.

"You're not superstitious, Gray Baxter."

"No. Just practical."

She looked happily around the living room. "Can you believe it? It's ours. If only——"

"If only what?"

"Oh, nothing." She smiled. "I was just thinking about Christmas."

"Never fear, madam," he made a sweeping bow. "Our house shall not be bare for Christmas. Pi Ling and Sam are bringing down a tree from Little Flats."

"You knew."

"I felt the same way. If only Goldie hadn't made such a big fuss over our coming to the ranch. . . ." He shrugged.

She reached over and took his hand. "I understand."

At Rancho Rio Oro by midmorning of December twenty-second the wind had shifted and was blowing raw and cold from the northeast. But Goldie was engrossed in wrapping her presents and didn't notice; in the kitchen the women, busy preparing pheasant, quail, beef, and venison for the big feast, didn't notice either. But Zack was aware and began to worry about the return of the men he had sent to Sacramento a few days earlier. Then when he and Goldie awakened the next morning the snow was

430

already heavily drifted in the hollows, and the silhouettes of the trees could scarcely be seen through the thick flakes as they swirled about in the roaring wind.

"What does it mean?" asked Goldie in dismay.

Zack replied frankly, thinking it best not to delude her. "I'm afraid it means we'll have no outside guests for Christmas."

"Oh, no!" she cried. "It can't mean that. Maybe it will stop."

"It's a blizzard, Goldie. Nobody will be able to come up here, not even if it stops by tomorrow."

"Then let's go down. I can't bear the thought of spending Christmas alone."

"Alone?" The word was strangled. But she didn't hear. Her mind and heart were set on only one thing.

She turned eagerly to him. "Yes, if we left right away we could make it. . .I know we could."

He looked at her as if she had lost her mind. "We can't get out anymore than anybody else can get in," he said shortly. "I'm going to see how the animals are weathering it."

She followed him out with sightless eyes, then turned back to the window. The snow was piling against the panes in soft half-moons. "They'll come," she whispered. "Gray will do anything to be with me for Christmas. Why, we've never been apart."

In Sacramento that morning the streets were moving rivers of mud and the rain was still falling. "I wonder how bad it is in the mountains?" Gray mused aloud at breakfast.

"No telling," answered Holt. He and Darcy and the rest of the party from San Francisco had arrived the evening before. "But I think we'd better find out before we go anywhere."

"Yes," Gray agreed. "It would be foolhardy to start out if we can't make it."

"I hope Vallecito and the men from the ranch are safe," said November. The vaqueros had delivered the beef the previous day and immediately left to return to the Rio Oro.

"No need to worry about them," said Gray. "They're Zack's best men. They won't do anything foolish."

"And I trust we won't either," said Darcy. "Shall we go and see what we can find out?"

They were drenched before they had gone two blocks, but many people were out, and in the business district they heard rumors of a blizzard in the mountains. They decided to go to the stage office to wait for the stage. When it finally arrived more than two hours late, the driver made his report to the office then tacked a sign on the bulletin board which said: "No more stages today....Roads impassable."

Darcy fought his way to the driver through the crowd of Christmas travelers and asked, "Is there snow?"

"Yes, a blizzard," the driver answered.

"Well, that settles it...at least for today," said Gray as they made their way back to the warm clapboard house.

"I think that settles it for good as far as I'm concerned," said Darcy.

When they told the others the news, November exclaimed, "Goodness, I'd better make some plans and lay in some provisions for Christmas."

"Yes, it looks like we'll be spending the day in our own home after all," said Gray.

"Poor Goldie," said November, "she was so counting on us."

"It isn't as if she were alone," said Holt. "Zack must have fifty or more people working for him."

"That's right," said Gray. "She won't even miss us."

At the ranch Goldie continued her Christmas preparations as if nothing unusual was going on outside. Zack came in at noon and stood in front of the living room fire sipping a whisky to warm himself.

"I'm having the men move the tables from the barn to the bunkhouse," he said. "We'll have to have the fiesta there tonight, as well as the Christmas dinner tomorrow."

"But why?" asked Goldie.

"Because I've got to get as many animals into the barn as possible...and into the sheds, too. The temperature's falling. They can't stand the cold."

"But that means it will stop snowing soon, doesn't it?"

"Not necessarily. But even if it does stop, the drifts have made the roads impassable."

She scowled. Why did he have to be so pessimistic, she thought? It was almost as if he didn't want the others to come.

All day Zack had hoped she would remember they had been married just one month ago today, but she never gave him or their marriage a thought. That night he was too disappointed to make any overtures toward her.

It continued to rain in Sacramento the next day, but the gay crowd in the clapboard house was no longer paying any attention to the weather. They were too busy decorating their Christmas tree, wrapping their presents, and preparing their Christmas dinner. It *was* almost like last year...only Goldie wasn't there.

About noon the snow stopped falling in the mountains. But the skies remained leaden, the wind increased in velocity, and, as Zack had predicted, the temperature dropped sharply.

"It's stopped...it's stopped," Goldie fairly sang. "Now they'll be here soon. You'll see."

Tired of arguing with her, Zack went out to the bunkhouse to be with his employees, some of whom would have husbands and fathers missing for Christmas since Vallecito and the men could not return now. He found their good-humored and realistic attitude toward the situation far more appealing than Goldie's childishness, and he resented more and more her selfish concern with her own disappointment.

Though she knew better, all through the afternoon Goldie clung to the stubborn hope she would see Gray ride up through the heavy drifts. Periodically she would wander into the big kitchen where Maria and the girls were preparing the evening feast.

"They should be here soon," she would say.

"Sí, señora," Maria would reply and shake her head sadly as Goldie wandered out again.

That evening the Mexicans enacted *Las Posadas*, a pageant portraying the Holy Family's search for a place to stay in Bethlehem. But Goldie remained impassive to its message and took no pleasure in the gay fiesta that followed. She refused to eat or dance or participate in the festivities in any way, plainly showing she regarded the whole evening as an ordeal.

It was still early when she said to Zack, "I'm tired. I'm going to bed."

He was furious. "The least you could do is show some appreciation for all the work my people have gone to to make it a pleasant evening for you," he said icily.

"I don't feel happy," she scowled. "And I'm certainly not going to put on a show of it just for the sake of your ranch hands!"

"No, you couldn't do a damned thing that might put you out a speck for somebody else, could you?"

"Why should I when the people I care about aren't going to be with me for Christmas?"

He grabbed her by the shoulders and shook her. "It's your brother!" he shouted. "You're sulking because of your brother!"

"Well, what if it is? We've never been apart at Christmas before." Tears clouded her eyes

Abruptly he released her and said almost to himself, "What a damn fool I've been not to see you'll never let go of Gray *or* your precious B.C.A. and D."

"What's wrong with wanting to be a part of something I've helped build?"

"God! Will you ever grow up?" he asked savagely. "I'm sick of watching you juggle the two lives you'd like to live. This ranch has to be built up and managed, and I want a wife and partner to help me do it! If this isn't what you want, then you don't want me either—and you can go to hell for all I care!" His voice was cold and his eyes glacial.

"What?" she gasped. "Oh, oh, oh!" She lifted her skirts and ran out of the bunkhouse, through the snow, and into the house. When she reached the bedroom, she threw herself on the bed and sobbed out her misery.

Nobody loved her. Gray hadn't made the slightest effort to get to the ranch. And Zack didn't care about her feelings at all. . .he just ignored her and didn't try to understand.

But as time passed and she realized Zack was not going to come either to apologize or comfort her, her mind turned on the events that had led up to this unhappy Christmas Eve. She had insisted that Gray and the others come up to the ranch. But why? To recapture what they had had last year? But that was impossible. You couldn't go back. . .shouldn't even want to. And then when she knew they couldn't come—how selfishly she had behaved—completely ignoring the needs of the ranch families who would also have loved ones missing. And Zack—why, she'd been so wrapped up in herself she hadn't paid any attention to him at all. How could she have treated him like that?

She remembered how he had tried to keep the wagon train from leaving her when Gray was so sick at Fort Bridger. And even the year she hadn't seen him he had been thinking of her. . .building this beautiful house. And when they were about to lose the B.C.A. and D., when there was no one else to help, he had left his campaign for the legislature and brought her the money so they wouldn't go under. Yes, from the very beginning he had always been there to help her. And what had she offered him in return? Shame flooded over her. How could she give so little to the man she loved? Heartsick and searching for the answer, she drifted into a troubled sleep.

When she awoke the sun was shining for the first time all week. She climbed awkwardly from the bed. Her limbs were stiff with cold, her eyes felt swollen, and her green dress was badly mussed. With distaste she looked at her image in the mirror and wondered, who could love that?

Despite the cold of the room, she bathed and put on fresh clothes. Her mind turned on last night's thoughts. Perhaps she and Gray should have stayed home in Indiana where they belonged. But no. . .even had they remained there, the carefree days of girlhood would have passed. Gray would have married and she would have too, severing forever the ties of childhood. Her troubles were not caused by leaving home. She had chosen her path because she had believed in a future in California. And Zack had hovered in that future, suspended in time, to be brought forth at her convenience. She sighed as she remembered Zack's eyes last night. . .the way he had looked at her as he said "you'll never let go." What had everybody been trying to tell her that she had missed or stubbornly refused to see?

Slowly her mind toiled toward the painful truth. She was rejecting her marriage not because she doubted her love for Zack but because she was trying to hold on to a time of life that was past and should exist only as a cherished memory. She had been wrong—terribly wrong. How could Zack ever believe she loved him now? Maybe he didn't care anymore. How could he after the way she had behaved. . .so blind. . .so unfeeling? She must try to make it up to him. But first she must ask his forgiveness. But where was he? The house was so silent. Had he left her alone for Christmas as she had deserted him on Christmas Eve? She had to find him.

She opened the heavy door and ran from the bedroom. When she reached the end of the hall, she stopped. She could see him across the living room sitting at the head of the long dining table, a cup of coffee before him, his head in his hands. A sob rose in her throat. Oh, I've ruined Christmas and maybe his whole life for him, she thought. Will he ever have me again?

He looked up as she approached. His face was puffy and unshaven. He looked so fierce she faltered a moment, her resolve

435

nearly deserting her. Then she squared her shoulders and walked up to his chair.

"I want to ask you to forgive me," she said in a barely audible voice. Her mouth felt so scorched and dry she wondered that she could speak at all. Frantically she searched his face for some sign that he cared.

Zack simply stared at her. During the night he had drowned his marriage in strong Mexican whisky and was not prepared for so sudden a change.

Interpreting his stare as disbelief in her sincerity, she rushed on. "I—I've been wrong about a lot of things. It was wrong of me to insist upon having Gray and the others here for Christmas in the first place. And then once I knew they couldn't come. . .to behave the way I did was selfish. . .childish. . .and stupid."

Zack still said nothing.

She felt her courage ebbing away. If only he would speak. Didn't he have any feeling left for her at all? She looked at him imploringly. "I—I hope you will forgive me because. . ." Oh, why didn't he help her? Was he even listening? He must listen. She rushed on. "Because I—I've got an awfully nice present for you. And. . .oh, Zack—" Unable to restrain herself any longer, she hurled herself at him. "I do love you. . .and I've missed you so." Tears were streaming down her face.

He pulled her down on his lap and rocked her, patting her curls. This was the Goldie he had fallen in love with, the high-spirited and courageous girl of the trail. "There," he said, lifting her tear-stained face in his hands. "We'll say no more about it."

Then he kissed her. Without reservation she knew at last she belonged to him.

"Merry Christmas, sweetheart," he said. "Come. . .I've got a present for you too." He took her by the hand and led her over to the pine tree he had brought in from the woods, and they sat down on the floor before it.

In Sacramento, Gray, November, Holt, and Darcy were sitting down to breakfast. And throughout the new state, the glad shouts of "Merry Christmas!" were heard from gold camp to town, from the mountains to the sea. Those who had come for gold had found something far better than their dreams—a rich, unspoiled land. It was the beginning.

THE OVERLAND ROUT